D1592571

*Jumping the Broom*

TYLER D. PARRY

# *Jumping the Broom*
## The Surprising Multicultural Origins of a Black Wedding Ritual

The University of North Carolina Press  *Chapel Hill*

© 2020 Tyler D. Parry
All rights reserved
Set in Arno Pro by Westchester Publishing Services
Manufactured in the United States of America

The University of North Carolina Press has been a member of the
Green Press Initiative since 2003.

Library of Congress Cataloging-in-Publication Data
Names: Parry, Tyler D., author.
Title: Jumping the broom : the surprising multicultural origins
    of a black wedding ritual / Tyler D. Parry.
Description: Chapel Hill : The University of North Carolina Press, 2020. |
    Includes bibliographical references and index.
Identifiers: LCCN 2020016907 | ISBN 9781469660851 (cloth : alk. paper) |
    ISBN 9781469660868 (pbk. : alk. paper) | ISBN 9781469660875 (ebook)
Subjects: LCSH: Marriage customs and rites—History. | African Americans—
    Marriage customs and rites—History. | Weddings. | Marginality, Social.
Classification: LCC GT2690 .P37 2020 | DDC 392.509—dc23
LC record available at https://lccn.loc.gov/2020016907

Cover illustration by Jeannette M. Bradley.

Portions of chapters 1, 2, and 3 were previously published in a different form as
"Married in Slavery Time: Jumping the Broom in Atlantic Perspective," *Journal
of Southern History* 81, no. 2 (2015): 273–312. Portions of chapter 6 and the conclusion
were previously published in a different form as "The Holy Land of Matrimony:
The Complex Legacy of the Broomstick Wedding in American History," *American
Studies* 55, no. 1 (2016): 81–106. Used here with permission.

*For Shanelle, with all my love and devotion*

# Contents

# Graphs and Figures

## Acknowledgments

This book began with a wedding. As my fiancé, Shanelle, and I discussed the various cultural rituals to include in our nuptials, she felt that "jumping the broom," a tradition about which we both knew only basic information, must be the capstone of the ceremony. Our minister, Richard Holley, requested that I write a brief synopsis of the tradition to share with attendees unfamiliar with the practice. As I was completing a B.A. in History at the University of Nevada, Las Vegas, and had access to a university library, I excavated the available primary and secondary source material and gave him a large, multi-page report that examined the ritual's connections to the British Isles and its transatlantic influences among various groups in North America. A bit overwhelmed by the document, Brother Holley courteously suggested that "five or six sentences" was probably sufficient for his brief explanation. Though I drastically reduced that original report and resubmitted it to him, I remained fascinated by what I found, specifically the broomstick wedding's transatlantic appeal. I wondered why such an influential custom had not received sustained scholarly analysis. After I acquired my B.A. in History, applied to graduate school, and jumped the broom with Shanelle, the ritual continued to pique my intellectual curiosity and followed me into the Ph.D. program at the University of South Carolina.

While this book explores my specific interests in slave marriage and diasporic wedding rituals, I owe significant intellectual debts to those who influenced me both before and after my wedding. One of my first advocates in the public school system was my eighth-grade English teacher, Ms. Bailey. Though I was not doing particularly well in her class, she sensed that I was capable of much more and recommended me for Honors English as I entered high school. I was surprised by her recommendation, but she refused to allow me to believe that she made a mistake. A similar experience occurred in my tenth-grade World History class, when Ms. Shepherd, despite my own protestations, recommended me for the honors course in American history for my junior year. Both of those moments exemplify the abilities of educators to influence students to believe in their own abilities, even if the immediate returns appear inconsequential. I have never forgotten those moments, and it is now evident to me that both changed my intellectual trajectory.

As I entered the University of Nevada, Las Vegas (UNLV) and eventually declared a major in history, I benefited from the attention of faculty who embodied the best of scholarship and teaching at a public university. Elspeth Whitney, a distinguished medievalist, taught excellent courses on medieval women and introduced me to the ways in which new generations of scholars can find the stories of marginalized people, even when the records appear scant. She also advocated for my entry into UNLV's Honors College, which provided intellectual challenges that prepared me for the rigors of graduate education. David Holland not only offered fascinating courses on American religion, but provided crucial mentorship as I entered the Honors College and prepared my letters for PhD programs. The courses taught by Elizabeth Fraterrigo, David Wrobel, Maria Raquel Casas, Gregory Brown, Russell Gollard, Heather Lusty, and David Schwartz were crucial in advancing my intellectual curiosity and scholarly pursuits at UNLV. I also met a number of friends in the history program who remain influential in my intellectual journey, and I extend a specific thanks to Claire White, Debbie Rainer, Adla Earl, and Megan Lee Morey for our conversations both during and after my experience at UNLV.

My interest in the African Diaspora and the Atlantic world was born through enrollment in a class called "Comparative Slavery" at UNLV taught by Dr. Kevin Dawson. The stories of diasporic Africans fascinated me and the way Kevin presented the material was infectious. I soon found myself frequenting his office to discuss graduate school and the somewhat ridiculous idea (at least at the time) of my becoming a doctor of philosophy. But he always reassured me, wrote multiple letters of recommendation, and believed in my capability to succeed in graduate school. He also encouraged my enrollment in the Ph.D. program in history at the University of South Carolina, the department that has fostered my intellectual development and professionalization beyond my wildest expectations. I genuinely believe that if I had not enrolled in that pivotal class during my junior year at UNLV, I would not be at this point. Perhaps I can never fully repay Kevin, but I hope that this public acknowledgment suggests my deep appreciation for everything he has done and continues to do.

At the University of South Carolina I benefited from the careful attention and camaraderie of many scholars and peers. First and foremost I would like to thank Daniel C. Littlefield for accepting me as his student, reading the first draft of this current project in 2009, directing my dissertation on another subject, and investing significant amounts of time to developing me into a scholar and intellectual. Dan always allowed my mind to roam and encouraged me to investigate new questions. I could not ask for a better adviser. A hearty thanks to Matt D. Childs, who quickly became a personal friend and stellar mentor. When others told me to slow down, Matt always motivated me to keep my momentum and to believe my scholarship is an important contribution to historiography. I also extend a special thanks to Mark M. Smith for encouraging me to think more imaginatively about cultural history and not forget the Marxist scholars who asked similar questions decades before me. A genuine thanks to Thavolia Glymph of Duke University, who read my early publications on jumping the broom and provided excellent comments for the new directions I could take my research. Additionally, I would be remiss if I did not thank Kay Edwards, Tom Lekan, Joshua Grace, Bobby Donaldson, and Adam Schor, all of whom were exemplary models of effective teaching and public engagement. Each of them encouraged me to think more broadly about my subject and its relationship to a wider audience.

Graduate school is a strenuous exercise in patience and sanity, and I am grateful for my friendships and affiliations with a number of individuals and groups during my five years in Columbia, South Carolina. Caroline Peyton and David Dangerfield served as constant sources of support and encouragement. I would also like to recognize the "breakfast club" comprising Caroline, David, Tim Minella, and Allen Driggers for some great Thursday mornings: thanks to all of you, and I look forward to seeing your books get published! I also extend heartfelt thanks to the members of the Atlantic History Reading and Writing Group: Robert J. Greene II, Andrew Kettler, Jacob Mach, Matt Childs, Neal Polhemus, and Chaz Yingling: many chapters in this book benefited from your careful and thought-provoking critiques. I also send many thanks to Candace Cunningham, Jennifer Taylor, Brian Robinson, Ramon Jackson, and Evan Kutzler of the American History Reading and Writing Group for helping me contextualize my secondary projects in twentieth-century African American history. I would also like to recognize the help and guidance I received from David Prior and Michael Woods, two exemplary scholars who carefully critiqued my writing and offered crucial advice in preparing for the job market.

Institutions and entities within the University of South Carolina proved valuable for providing funding, work experience, and establishing valuable friendships. I had the pleasure of working with the African American Studies Program on multiple occasions, and I extend special thanks to the Valinda Littlefield, Valerie Ashford, Makeira Simmons, Todd Shaw, and Kimberly Simmons for creating a wonderful work environment. Entities within the University of South Carolina, including the Walker Institute, the Institute for

African American Research, the History Department, the Graduate School, and the Vice President of Research, all provided critical funding during my graduate school years. Additionally, special thanks is owed to various other institutions that provided generous funding: the John Hope Franklin Research Center at Duke University; Harvard University's International Seminar on the History of the Atlantic World; the Social Science History Association; Florida International University's African and African Diaspora Studies Department; the Bilinski Educational Foundation; the National Endowment for the Humanities; and the American Historical Association.

The transatlantic framing for this work has allowed me to travel throughout the Atlantic and meet numerous scholars who have both directly and indirectly influenced this project. While only listing their names does not do justice to their valuable contributions, I believe they should, at the very least, be acknowledged: John K. Thornton, Joseph C. Miller, James H. Sweet, Juan Jose Ponce-Vasquez, and James Sidbury. I also met many colleagues and friends in these travels, including Dueane Dill, Kristin White, Mariama Jaiteh, Randy Browne, Mamyrah Prosper, Synatra Smith, Candia Mitchell Hall, O'Neill Hall, Ibrahima Thiaw, Boubacar Barry, and Jean Muteba Rahier. I would also like to thank the incredibly helpful employees of the various archives I visited while researching this project, including the special collections departments of the University of Tennessee, Howard University, University of California, Berkeley, University of Kentucky, Tulane University, and the College of William and Mary. A number of you went above and beyond my expectations, and my bibliography would be much slimmer if not for your helpful contributions and interest in my project. I also appreciate the archives of Jackson State University, Southern University, and the University of Southern Mississippi for granting public access to their valuable digital collections.

Throughout my academic career I have enjoyed the camaraderie and support of so many friends and colleagues. At California State University, Fullerton (CSUF), I send a special thanks to Siobhan Brooks, Natalie Graham, Brady Heiner, V. J. Kuan-Roberts, Cindy Rouze, Alexandro Gradilla, Patricia Perez, Gabriela Nunez, Ben Cawthra, Gregory "Chris" Brown, Sheryl Fontaine, Natalie Fousekis, Anthony Sparks, Gwendolyn Alexis, the late Charlene Riggins, Terri Snyder, Stan Breckenridge, and Joy Hoffman for their support, friendship, and encouragement as I began my first academic job. I owe specific gratitude to Edward Robinson, who I had the pleasure of working with at CSUF. He graciously assigned my articles to his class, had his students jot down their questions, and invited me to give a guest lecture. I still have their questions in my research folder, and they were very helpful in framing this project and improving its content.

Through their research and friendship, my colleagues throughout the wide sphere of academia continue to influence my approach to historical writing and the experiences of African-descended people in the diaspora, and I'd like to specifically recognize Deirdre Cooper Owens, Hilary Green, Shawn Leigh Alexander, Rana Hogarth, Lyra D. Monteiro, Tera Hunter, Javon Johnson, Randal Jelks, Kelly Kennington, Kendra Gage, Clayton Finn, Emily West, Christian Pinnen, Kellie Carter Jackson, Liz Pryor, Daryl Scott, Adam X. McNeil, Emily West, Randal Hall, and John Boles for their positive roles in my professional development.

I send a heartfelt thanks to the organizations that foster such connections, including the Association for the Study of African American Life and History, the Southern Historical Association, the American Studies Association, and perhaps most of all, the African American Intellectual History Society (AAIHS). Through AAIHS I've worked with many wonderful scholars, including Chris Cameron, J. T. Roane, Sasha Turner, Melissa Shaw, Grace Gibson, and Phil Sinitiere. I send a specific thanks to Keisha Blain, who first invited me to contribute to AAIHS's blog, *Black Perspectives*, on a regular basis, asked me to serve as its book review editor, and then encouraged me to run as a candidate for AAIHS's vice president position. Keisha's tireless work in advancing the mission of AAIHS is nothing short of exceptional, and it is an honor to work with her and serve the organization in these various capacities. I'm looking forward to the future!

A few people offered tremendous assistance in structuring and confirming this project's historical and contemporary relevance, reading large sections of this manuscript before I submitted it for peer review. A special thanks to the members of my Southern California writing group, Justin Gomer, Sharla Fett, and Erica Ball. Without their suggestions and critiques on multiple chapters, this book would be a far inferior product. A special thanks to Imani Strong and Michael Woods, both of whom agreed to read the entire manuscript before I sent it to the press. They are both remarkable scholars and true examples of professional selflessness. I am grateful both of them affirmed this project's importance by generously reading it in its early stage and providing feedback.

I am remiss if I forget the wonderful editorial team at the University of North Carolina Press, each of whom made this process of publishing very comfortable. A specific thanks to my editor, Brandon Proia, who believed in this project from the beginning and whose efforts made this a far superior book. Thanks to Dylan White, Elizabeth Orange, Dino Battiste, Lara Gribbin, Anna Faison, Kate Gibson, and many others who have worked to make this book a reality. This book certainly benefitted from your attentive reviews.

To my brothers John, Mathis, and Joe Parry, and my sister, Heidi Stern, I express my love and appreciation for all of your support and for reminding me that I am still just your little brother. I cherish all of you, especially in your ability to still make fun of me. For my parents, Stanley and Carol Parry, words cannot adequately express the sincere appreciation and love that I hold for you both. Everything you taught me about public speaking, self-confidence, and a love for knowledge resonates in each word of this book. For now, all I can do is say thank you for everything. To my late grandparents, Mary Wright and Ray and Marjory Dubois. I express my deepest love. To my in-laws, Ariel, Karen, and Mandy, I am deeply grateful that my siblings found such wonderful people with whom to share their lives. To my in-laws through marriage, Ardella Roberts, the late Lewis Roberts Sr., Elizabeth Roberts, Vincent Roberts, and Lewis Roberts Jr., I thank each of you for making my initiation into your family so comfortable. Since all of you have heard of this phantom manuscript for nearly a decade, I truly hope you enjoy the final product.

Finally, I must recognize the three people who remain the most positive forces in my life. To my two daughters, Nazanin Zipporah and Yara Tsehai, you both provide so much joy in an unstable world. I look forward to watching you both grow and hope you know that I will travel to the ends of the earth to support your dreams. To my wife, companion, and most ardent supporter, Shanelle Lynn Parry, to whom this book is dedicated, words cannot adequately express my appreciation for the sacrifices you made in supporting my dreams. I love you more as the days pass and seasons change. Perhaps you can only be summarized by the concluding section of Nikki Giovanni's poem "Ego-Tripping" that describes your majesty: "I am so perfect so divine so ethereal so surreal / I cannot be comprehended except by my permission / I mean . . . I . . . can fly / like a bird in the sky." You remind me every day why I feel this way about you. Each page of this book is a reflection of your commitment and support toward me. If not for you, and our jump over that broom so many years ago, this book would simply not exist. Ride or die, with love eternal.

*Jumping the Broom*

# A Multicultural Tradition

In the early twentieth century, an anonymous woman told an interviewer her story of a broomstick wedding that took place on an antebellum southern plantation. It was her mother's recollection, one she returned to often, that "when the colored folks got married, the man would lay the broom down on the floor with the bushy end to the north, then he would take the girl by the hand, then they step over the broom, then backward again. Then the girl picked up the broom, laying it down again with the bushy end facing the south, then the girl took the man by the hand and they step over it and backward again, to keep evil away and bad spirits through their life." It was an exciting ritual to witness, for "mother said many a night she would steal down and watch when she heard some of the colored folks were going to get married."[1]

The enslaved couple's actions were rich in unspoken symbolism. The ritual process undertaken in this wedding likely reflected generations of cultural adaptation and reinvention that characterized many enslaved communities throughout the Americas. Given how receptive people of African descent were to adopting and innovating different cultural expressions while simultaneously creating their own, one can surmise that the ritual blended a variety of beliefs into a single ceremony.[2]

By clasping one another's hands, the couple exhibited a symbolic bond that denoted partnership and the ability to complete tasks as one. The man initiated the ceremony by providing the broom, laying it down, and taking the woman's hand before the jump, and his bride repeated the same actions after she reversed the broom's position. One could interpret these maneuvers as a sign of completion, reflecting the journey from engaged to wedded. Just as the man initiated the courtship, the woman confirmed it by accepting his proposal and initiating the ritual's conclusion. In this sequence, the groom completed his tasks to begin the process, but it only concluded when the bride fulfilled her obligations. In other areas of the South, the bride's refusal to step over the broom sometimes signified her rejection of the marriage.[3]

In its entirety, the ceremony expressed a process of equality and balance. Both partners alternated in retrieving the broom and initiating a jump with the other. By laying the broom down with the bushy end to the north, completing a jump, and reversing its position, the couple ensured they fulfilled both directional pulls by jumping forward *and* backward in a unilateral motion, from east to west and vice versa.

The ceremony reflects beliefs surrounding the importance of the cross symbol popular among Black southerners. Forming a cross guaranteed protection, since "it pointed towards all four cardinal points; hence allowing nothing to get by it."[4] Imbedding the cross in the ritual motions of this ceremony ensured that nothing could sever the symbolic importance of the union and that the newlyweds would be protected from any malevolent forces that sought their destruction. Even if this was physically unattainable under American slavery, an institution that frequently ripped families apart, it fulfilled the psychological needs of a people whose domestic lives were consistently unpredictable.

Alternatively, these enslaved people were possibly recreating a Kalunga line, which serves as a threshold separating the terrestrial realm from the ancestral.[5] According to the religious philosophies of West Central Africans, crossing this partition allowed them to commune with the ancestors in a space that was literally inverted, even to the point that people walked with their feet pointing up in an upside-down position. The physical manifestations of this philosophy are most distinctly preserved in a Brazilian martial art called "Capoeira," in which competitors sometimes invert their bodies in both offensive and defensive strikes. Black combat traditions and religious practices throughout the Western Hemisphere also have similarities.[6] Even if the spiritual connotations are unclear in this particular broomstick ceremony, the broom's north/south orientation would require the participants to jump east/west, perhaps symbolizing the couple's links to Africa and America. By using such directions during a wedding ceremony, they were, at least symbolically, subverting the Middle Passage's devastating impact upon Black kinship ties.

The ceremony revealed its utility for the enslaved in the conclusion. No slaveowners were present, meaning that this individual tradition was free from their influence. This couple's calculated maneuvers of jumping back and forth in multiple directions safeguarded them from evil spirits, and, as they assisted each other over the broom, they accepted one another's partnership upon entering domestic life. Lacking any overt reference to Christianity, this ritual's philosophical connotations were not constrained by religious doctrine. Untroubled by slaveholders or the supernatural, these practitioners gave the broomstick wedding a cultural richness that was not always apparent in other ceremonies.

Though rich in detail, this account resembles many others in that it does not explain *why* certain enslaved people jumped over a matrimonial broom. Narratives that discuss the tradition rarely explore its origins, and they seldom comment on its symbolism with any significant detail. Either they were not interested in contextualizing its historical origins, or, more likely, they simply did not know where it came from or how it was popularized in their own community.

As a result, the ritual mystified scholars for many decades. Historical information on the broomstick wedding was largely unavailable to the public eye for much of the twentieth century, as most references were buried in the narratives of formerly enslaved people long ignored by scholars. However, by the 1970s, historians, inspired by political movements in the United States, sought to tell the story of slavery from the perspective of those in bondage. They investigated American slavery from a cultural vantage point and engaged the topic of slave marriage with unprecedented vigor. They argued that enslaved people's private lives were profoundly expressed in their intimate associations with one another, and they portrayed them as more than laborers; they were people who loved, lost, and claimed their dignity. Examining the intimate lives of people who were often voiceless was a herculean task that required a variety of approaches. In this ever-growing genre of cultural history, one finds microhistories of how the enslaved married on specific plantations, case studies of individual states, comparative histories, and ambitious attempts to encapsulate slave marriage within the broader sociopolitics of the nineteenth-century United States.[7] Though jumping the broom is mentioned regularly in most of these works, it rarely receives more than a single page of analysis, since many authors claim it was a quaint custom that none of its practitioners took seriously.[8] Many publications exploring the broomstick wedding's popular appeal lack scholarly rigor. They mention only one or two narratives from people formerly enslaved, or simply rehash findings from other secondary works. Few examine its origins across the Atlantic or the possible reasons it was adopted by enslaved people in North America.[9]

Given the broomstick wedding's importance during various periods of American history, this is not only a significant oversight in studies of slavery, Atlantic history, African American studies, and the African diaspora; it also troubles many Americans who seek to use the ritual to connect with their ancestral heritage. Engaged couples and wedding planners remain confused about the broomstick wedding's place in American history and its meaning for modern Black Americans, specifically those descended from enslaved Africans. Moreover, the fact that jumping the broom is a transnational phenomenon is largely unknown. Where did it come from? How was it acquired? Did participants ever divulge their thoughts on its purpose? What is its legacy over time? This book hopes to answer these questions, while also emphasizing that the broomstick wedding was not confined to a single group. If culturally based studies reveal anything, it is that customs in the African diaspora did not develop in a vacuum and that such traditions can be shared across racial and ethnic groups.[10]

## Precedents and Possible Origins

Popular media in the United States understandably credits the broomstick ceremony to African Americans, largely due to its contemporary appeal and its close association with enslaved people in the U.S. South. In fact, jumping over the broomstick is so intertwined with the African American experience that it has led one publication to assert, "If you're not African American, there's a fairly good chance you have not heard of jumping the broom."[11] Though such weddings occurred in European communities before they did in those of African Americans, white Americans are, with a few exceptions, largely unaware of the custom when reflecting upon their own cultural heritage.[12] The problem surely lies in representation. Until recently, questions surrounding the custom's origins were hardly explored in most popular features, and its visual representations rarely portray its multicultural roots.[13]

Perhaps surprising to those who see broom-jumping as a quintessentially African American practice, its origins are far more geographically and ethnically wide-ranging. The earliest references to jumping a matrimonial broom stem from groups throughout the British Isles, including Romani, Celts, and English laborers. Subsequently, one finds references to the practice continuing in the United States after migrants from these groups arrived. On both sides of the Atlantic, people of European descent used it for various reasons.

The transnational, multicultural dimensions of the practice might prompt a question for those seeking claims to cultural ownership: Is jumping the broom a custom of African Americans, Romani, Celts, or rural Euro-Americans? Perhaps it belongs to all of them. If so, how could these distinct communities, separated geographically by land and sea, and socially by racism, ethnocentrism and classism, all come to utilize a similar marital custom at similar moments in history? Historically, we know it was a folk practice used by groups who sanctioned their marital unions independent of ecclesiastical or governmental surveillance. Such groups were often marginalized by a ruling elite, ostracized by their surrounding communities, and/or geographically isolated. Consequently, their cultural customs were considered strange or esoteric, and they were often mocked for such practices. The historical record is not entirely clear as to how the custom gained its popularity among socially ostracized communities in the British Isles, as their oral histories do not usually speak to its origins. They simply state that their ancestors used it and provide details on how it was performed.

Although the origins of the European practice of jumping over a broomstick for matrimony are cryptic, we do know that broomstick folklore extends to ancient societies and that broomsticks were used for both practical and symbolic purposes. They are simultaneously a domestic necessity and an ominous symbol. As early as the sixth century B.C.E., Greek philosopher and mathematician Pythagoras counseled his followers to "not step over a broom," though the reason for this proscription remains enigmatic.[14] Pythagoras's rule was carried through the centuries to Roman philosophers in the first century C.E., when Plutarch explained why priests of Jupiter were forbidden to pass through paths overspread with vine branches: "Is it not of the like nature with those precepts of Pythagoras, not to eat in a chair, not to sit upon a measure . . . and not to step over a broom?"[15] While Plutarch does not expound upon Pythagoras's reasoning for avoiding brooms, he does explain how particular objects have symbolic qualities. "Now to go under a vine," he wrote, "hath reference to wine, because it is not lawful for a priest to be drunk, and they are depraved and debased thereby; whereas it is requisite that they should be above pleasure and conquer it, but not be subdued by it."[16] Thus, for Plutarch it was not necessarily the object itself, but what the object represented. Vine branches above the head of a priest of Jupiter represented an inversion of the power dynamic, and crossing underneath the branches indicated that the priest was willing to violate a sacred covenant, if only metaphorically. Crossing over a broomstick likely had similar implications, and the connection between leaping across the broomstick and entry into the domestic state evolved over time.

In 1922, Hungarian psychoanalyst Geza Roheim argued that passing over an object held cosmological significance to various groups, and he linked most of these events to a symbolic act of "coitus."[17] Roheim maintained that while the selection of objects differed from culture to culture, the connection between crossing over and fertility rites required men or women to cross over particular objects either to prevent pregnancy or to accelerate it. The broomstick likely symbolized a phallus, and a woman's willingness to "jump over" it suggested two things: first, that she was willing to invite someone into the act of procreation; second, that she was in a dominant position relative to the phallus.[18] Consequently, folklore developed around its connections to marriage and sex, as some British communities maintained that if an unmarried woman strode over a "besom-handle" she would become a mother before a wife, while others used the colloquialism "She's jumped o'er the besom" to signal that a woman had a child out of wedlock.[19] The connections between marriage, broomsticks, and witchcraft are especially apparent, as women who did not conform to the standards of patriarchal monogamy were labeled dangerous. In one example, a Polish woman in Detroit, Michigan, was accused of witchcraft in 1892, and her accusers demanded she "jump over a broomstick" to prove her innocence.[20] Her accusers likely believed she was incapable of completing the act if she was, in fact, a witch. In addition, the general practice of "leaping over" objects was also found in societies outside Europe. In the early twentieth century, for example, John Roscoe observed that the Baganda ethnic group of Central Africa believed that if a man had a young child, he was required to step over both the child and his wife prior to departing for a journey, for "should he omit these precautions, and during his journey have sexual intercourse with any other woman, his child would die, and his wife would also fall ill."[21] His failure to physically perform this act was directly tied to supernatural consequences. In these various cases, the objects could be animate or inanimate, and the only apparent requirement is that the symbol held value to the participant and their hope for positive outcomes.

The object's symbolic associations are where the connection between jumping the broomstick and the marriage ceremony is most interesting. Broomsticks are used for domestic purposes in most cultures, but the marital tradition of jumping the broomstick is most heavily documented in two locations separated by the Atlantic Ocean: the British Isles and North America.[22] Within both locations, various cultural groups practiced the ritual, including ethnically distinct Celtic groups, Romani, English sailors, enslaved people of African descent poor southern whites, and various frontier communities. While each of them shared a similar experience of social ostracism, isolation, or marginalization, they are commonly analyzed separately from one another. Very few scholars have ascertained the cultural connections among Celtic groups, African Americans, British Romani, Louisiana Cajuns, and white Americans living in rural areas.[23] Each group had its own traditions and folklore, but their use of the matrimonial broomstick is the one practice that links them together. How did their marital traditions become intertwined? The answer lies in looking beyond each group separately and scrutinizing the process of transoceanic migration throughout the early modern period and into the nineteenth century.

Oppressed people have remarkable ingenuity in forming social units to combat, or at least curtail, psychological violence. As folklorist Patricia A. Turner argues in her study of rumor in African American folk history, Black oral traditions reveal how enslaved people developed "countermeasures" to contest the enslaver's domination.[24] Similarly, historian Stephanie M. H. Camp explores how enslaved communities utilized "hidden or indirect expressions of dissent" to combat the psychological traumas of bondage, arguing it was a way for them to reclaim "a measure of control over goods, time, or parts of one's life."[25] As a form of "cultural resistance," these expressions were both defensive and offensive in nature, enabling enslaved people "to attack directly the ideological underpinnings of slavery."[26] The broomstick ceremony's most attractive feature for any marginalized group is the practitioners' ability to integrate it into their community's needs and freely adopt other components into its mix. By adopting, adapting, and reimagining the broomstick ceremony, enslaved communities throughout the antebellum South could use this custom to build community and formulate a culture. Since slave weddings were not constrained by a standard method of performance, I avoid identifying those broomstick weddings that included Christian customs as "hybrid ceremonies" formulated in the diaspora, since they were not necessarily a combination of two mutually exclusive cultural practices. In fact, many of the British ceremonies were already "hybrids" that combined Christian elements with the group's previously established folk customs. By the time the broomstick wedding was introduced to enslaved people in the eighteenth century, it likely contained aspects of Christian ceremony intermingled with folk traditions and the enslaved probably did not view these as being in conflict. For both American and British practitioners, the only requirement for the marital bond to be secured was the successful jump over the broomstick. Any additions to the ceremony resulted from the unique circumstances of the specific cultural group.

Though it is often difficult to pinpoint the precise moment of any cultural exchange, transmission, or development, historians have long argued that many cultural practices in early North America developed through the interactions between Africans and Europeans. Some practices transferred unchanged, while others were adjusted to meet the needs of the appropriating group. It is less important to locate the exact moment when a cultural practice shifted from one cultural group to another than it is to demonstrate that it did so and to analyze how its meaning and significance were likely revised in the process of such adaptation.

## Scholarly Disagreement

Jumping the broom is a relatively well-known wedding custom, but previous analyses have not comprehensively examined its transatlantic dimensions. American folklorists Alan Dundes and C. W. Sullivan III examined Welsh and Romani traditions of broomstick weddings in the mid-1990s, and while both made some comment on its use by African Americans, they were more interested in documenting its origins beyond the United States. Since the release of their pivotal articles, however, only one book pursued its cultural importance in the British Isles.[27] Legal scholar Rebecca Probert challenged the findings of folklorists who conducted research among Welsh communities in the early 1900s, arguing that many of the oral histories collected among community members should not be taken literally.[28] Probert asserts that the phrase "jump the broomstick" was simply an idiom, and the notion that couples literally "jumped" over the broom was subsequently overblown by scholars misinterpreting the evidence. However, placing the broomstick wedding within an Atlantic context allows us to realize that many such couples did take a literal jump.

Though more frequently documented in the histories of American slavery, the broomstick wedding's multifaceted dimensions are rarely explored in most works.[29] Even rarer are the studies that attempt to place the broomstick wedding in a broader narrative of transregional interaction and cross-cultural innovation. It should be noted that despite the neglect jumping the broom receives from scholars of U.S. slavery, references to the practice are most numerous in this literature for a few reasons. First, historians of slavery can use firsthand accounts from the formerly enslaved, who describe how the ritual was performed and what it meant to its practitioners. Second, scholarly interest in slave culture increased in the early 1970s as cultural historians argued that enslaved people led lives apart from their work and should not be defined as cultureless laborers.[30] The availability of ex-slave narratives and a redirected focus in U.S. slavery studies propelled dance, food, community, family, music, and more to the center of scholarly attention.[31]

Consequently, one finds glimpses of the marriage ceremony dotting studies of antebellum slavery. Despite this advancement in cultural history, most studies relegate the broomstick wedding to a few paragraphs, if that. These brief references usually include a few quotations from the formerly enslaved or authors of secondary sources who typically did not know (nor were very interested in) the custom's origins or cultural importance.[32] There are, of course, exceptions to this general rule. Sociologist Ophelia Settle Egypt's book-length manuscript "Raggedy Thorns" contains the most extensive scholarly treatment of the broomstick wedding of any work in the twentieth century; in it one finds an entire chapter on slave weddings entitled "Jumping de Broomstick." Egypt's work was ahead of its time in blending the methodologies of folklorists, historians, and sociologists, but her manuscript was rejected by university presses and never published.[33] Scholars such as Eugene Genovese, Charles Joyner, and George P. Rawick dedicated some time to analyzing the broomstick ritual's multifaceted cultural expressions in their groundbreaking books, while also attempting to explore its possible origins. Each of them argued that references found in the narratives of the formerly enslaved revealed it was a nearly universal custom used throughout the South and held ritual value for many African Americans.[34] Despite the important contributions of such works, however, most analyses omit any explanation of why enslaved people jumped the broom, when they started doing so, and what symbolic value it may have held in their community. Indeed, Rawick admitted that he was unable "to ascertain the origins of the custom." He simply knew it was "widespread" and frequently mentioned by southern African Americans.[35] In isolating the broomstick wedding as a ritual exclusively practiced by a specific group in a single area, we fail to comprehend it as a cultural phenomenon that transcends racial, cultural, and national identities.

## Unpacking a Multicultural History

The broomstick wedding is a product of the transatlantic exchange, spurred by European colonization, that spanned the sixteenth through nineteenth centuries. But one must examine the custom from more specific vantage points and consider how the interactions between gender, race, and class contribute to a group's cultural development. By viewing the custom's expressions on both sides of the Atlantic, alongside their distinctions *within* and *between* different ethnic groups, we take all groups involved seriously as cultural innovators. Analysis of the marriage traditions of Celts, Romani, and the English on one side of the Atlantic, and those of enslaved people of African descent, Cajuns, and rural white Americans on the other indicates that the custom is undoubtedly most relevant for marginalized peoples. The broomstick wedding's multicultural importance reveals how myth, memory, and history provide important paradigms in studying rituals and their impact on the cultural development and identity formations in each community. Each group uniquely practiced the custom, and its pertinence to their cultural identity was a reference point for the outsiders who judged them.

*Jumping the Broom* uses novels, newspapers, contemporary images, journals, memoirs, oral histories, and travel accounts to assess how the ritual traveled and evolved throughout various communities in the British Isles and the United States. It follows the call of folklorists to treat the oral traditions and supernatural beliefs of rural populations as serious historical sources. In 1947, J. Mason Brewer noted that folklore provides a way to reconstruct how the U.S. South's regional culture was developed, as Black and white southerners, both poor and marginalized, acquired one another's social traditions, including patterns of speech, food ways, music, ghostlore, and so on.[36] Specifically, *Jumping the Broom* follows Shirley Moody-Turner and various Black folklorists, who "tie folklore to cultural history and individual and collective identity" and use these resources to "engage in contemporary debates" and explore current trends in African American culture.[37]

In taking a broader, transatlantic perspective on jumping the broom, I begin by analyzing sources from ostracized and underrepresented groups throughout the British Isles. I then examine how the custom was transmitted across the Atlantic to marginalized communities throughout North America, and then consider the circumstances through which it was rejected or revived both by descendants and those who have no direct ancestral links to earlier practitioners. Taking the broomstick wedding outside of parochial boundaries responds to a call for historians to "demonstrate connections and explore contrasts" as different groups contacted one another at unprecedented rates in the eighteenth and nineteenth centuries.[38]

Using the broomstick wedding as a focal point, this book examines how group identities inform both historical and modern renditions of the ceremony. The subject uniquely blends the disciplines of African American Studies, Southern Studies, and European Studies to show the value in thinking broadly about transnational cultural formations. Specifically, I show how people's race, ethnicity, class, community, and/or gender greatly informs how they use rituals to commemorate their ancestors. Each chapter examines how different groups viewed the custom, and provides context for how it was adopted by each of them, why they discontinued it, and the circumstances under which it has been revived. *Jumping the Broom* uses four primary arguments to provide a comprehensive history for this dynamic marital custom.

First, I argue that jumping the broom is best understood through a historically grounded, transnational framework. Past analyses often approached this

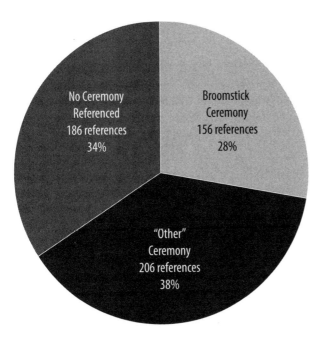

No Ceremony Referenced
186 references
34%

Broomstick Ceremony
156 references
28%

"Other" Ceremony
206 references
38%

Slave weddings compared. Based on testimonials found in Rawick, ed., *The American Slave: A Composite Autobiography* (41 volumes); Southern University's Slave Narratives Collection; Clayton, *Mother Wit*; and Perdue, Bardon, and Phillips, eds., *Weevils in the Wheat*.

custom parochially, emphasizing its impact within a single group, region, or country. Demonstrating the broomstick wedding's transnational dimensions goes some way toward explaining its multicultural appeal. This approach also identifies the parameters of cultural exchange that existed between white and Black populations during the era of transatlantic slavery.

Second, I caution readers to not presume that each ethnic group was culturally homogenous. Certain group members embraced the custom, while others rejected it. The decisions of some people to embrace a cultural trait do not necessarily reflect the choices of the whole community. This concept is generally true for each group, but it is most apparent in reviewing the sources for African Americans. In my analysis of slave narratives, I found that less than a third of the formerly enslaved respondents mentioned that brooms were jumped on their plantations.[39] Other interviewees suggested that different marital formats were used in their respective locations (such as Christian weddings or no ceremonies at all). This finding disrupts certain assertions found in the secondary literature in which the broomstick wedding is often portrayed as the *main* marital custom of southern slaves, when, in fact, it was not.[40] Such data do not negate the broomstick wedding's significance in African American history, but they do indicate a need for a more concerted effort in ascertaining its distribution amongst enslaved people and how it gained such immense popularity over one hundred years after the American Civil War.

Third, I emphasize that each group had compelling reasons to adopt the custom. Practitioners in the British Isles comprised a variety of distinct groups, including Romani, Celts, and English people, all of whom had different reasons for using it. I analyze their different motivations and how these differences reveal the custom's adaptability to specific cultural frameworks. Since there was no "correct" way to engage the custom, jumping the broom was easily transmitted to the United States through British migrants. Enslaved people probably adopted the custom since they possessed no legal protection for their domestic unions. For their descendants in the twentieth and twenty-first centuries, these historical circumstances prompt many to reimagine the custom in a mythic way, sometimes misplacing its origins on the African continent instead of in Europe. Attitudes of poor whites in North America were similar to those of their counterparts in the British Isles in the nineteenth and twentieth centuries. As the cultural descendants of migrants from there, many of these isolated white communities utilized the broomstick wedding for practical purposes, though one does find some evidence that individuals used it to resist ministers who tried to enforce marital orthodoxy.

Fourth, I examine the ways that the broomstick wedding has ebbed and flowed in popularity, inquiring why some groups stopped using it and why others revived it. Regarding African Americans, certain events directly impacted their reasons to discontinue the custom and subsequently revive it. Jumping the broom's first casualty among them came after 1865, as they could now legally marry without permission from slaveowners. Many chose to leave any vestiges of slavery behind, and, for many, jumping the broom reflected a past they hoped to forget. Eventually the custom was revived toward the end of the twentieth century as certain popular cultural movements (such as Black Power, Alex Haley's *Roots*, and Afrocentrism) encouraged Black Americans to reconnect with their ancestors. However, recent findings from internet forums and visual media cause one to question if broom-jumping will retain its popularity among newer generations of African Americans. Regarding white practitioners who jump the broom, most identify as neopagans who view it as a pre-Christian ancestral ritual. Their motivations in seeking to reject Christianity and reconnect with a more ancient past resemble those of African Americans who jump the broom in homage to their ancestors.

The chapters in *Jumping the Broom* follow a rough chronology in charting its earliest eighteenth-century references into its current standing in the twenty-first century. The timetable in the first five chapters overlap since I am examining the ceremony's importance to different cultural, ethnic, and racial groups who used it. Chapters 6 through 9 reveal how jumping the broom was gradually revived and its current expressions in popular culture. Collectively, the book examines how this ritual connects groups that, on the surface, appear disparate and distinct from each other. Similar in terms of their various degrees of marginalization, they engaged the broomstick wedding as a symbol of their subordination or as an act of resistance. The broomstick wedding serves various communities due to its cultural adaptability and its social and political significance. Consequently, some groups celebrate the custom, while others ridicule it. It is embraced by some and rejected by others. However, even if it is discarded by one generation, it can be reclaimed by descendants who reconstruct its meaning and find value in its modified symbolism. Thus, *Jumping the Broom* is as much about the contested memory and politics of the broomstick wedding as its practice. Its multifaceted cultural relevance demands that a researcher go beyond provincial boundaries and examine how race, ethnicity, gender, social status, geographical position, sexual orientation, and ancestral heritage inform a couple's choice to adopt the matrimonial broomstick.

## CHAPTER ONE

# Irregular Unions

## *The Broomstick Wedding in the British Isles*

In 1928, folklorist W. Rhys Jones discovered an interesting marital practice once used among the relatively isolated rural Welsh community of the Ceiriog Valley in North Wales. Jones found that traditional marriage among the previous generation consisted of simply laying a "birch besom" (broom) in the doorway of the cabin in which the couple was to live. The broom typically had a slight upright slant with the bushy end facing downward. Within the view of witnesses and a village elder, the groom "jumped over it first into the house, and afterwards the young woman in the same way."[1] If either of the two touched the broom while crossing over it or in any way "removed it from its place," the marriage was considered invalid by the community.[2]

It is difficult to know for certain why the groom was required to clear the broom first. Accounts from other communities suggest that the husband was also expected to assist the bride over the threshold, perhaps denoting his position of strength as protector and provider in the relationship. Apart from this requirement, broomstick weddings in this area manifested certain elements of marital equality. There were no requirements for who conducted the wedding ceremony, although they often were leaders in the local community. Nor was gender an issue in selecting an officiant: the person could be a "holy man," the "head of a tribe," or a "priestess."[3] By all accounts, Jones determined this ceremony was a "real marriage" in the community's estimation.[4] His informants further explained that women had the right to request a divorce if the marriage proved unsatisfactory within a year. To initiate the divorce, the couple performed the broomstick motions in reverse, with one or the other spouse jumping over the broom backward in front of witnesses.[5]

At the time of Jones's fieldwork, the origins of the ritual were unknown, even among the populations who practiced it. His respondents explained that it remained a popular form of marriage up to 1840, but became less common in the twentieth century. Documents from throughout the British Isles reveal the broomstick wedding was used in different areas during the eighteenth century, though it probably had roots reaching far deeper into the medieval era. Though similar ceremonies were likely used in various parts of Europe,

"The besom placed across the doorway," from Jones, "'Besom Wedding' in the Ceiriog Valley," 154.

the practice is most extensively documented in the British Isles, and migrants from there were largely responsible for spreading it across the Atlantic.

The ceremony proved especially suitable for rural communities, as they could adapt it to their unique circumstances. Though it is unclear if any particular community was the "first" to practice the ritual, as it was simultaneously used by various groups outside Wales throughout the 1800s, folklorists have credited these Welsh communities as one point of origin due to the rich oral traditions maintained throughout the region. Following Jones's findings from the Ceiriog Valley, historian John R. Gillis claims that up to 60 percent of all births in one Welsh village were from couples who wedded in this fashion. Other scholars agree that marriage over the broomstick had significant cultural currency for subaltern populations in Wales and elsewhere.[6]

It is difficult to pinpoint the moment it was first employed as a customary marital ritual in the British Isles. Most of the primary sources are oral histories passed through multiple generations, and one could understandably question the veracity of such accounts. One scholar asserts that "jumping over the broom" was predominantly a colloquial expression, like "tying the knot," and that the phrase does not denote a literal leaping over an object.[7] However, extant sources heretofore unconsidered may substantiate the custom's existence in older folk practices. One source even cites a 1598 work entitled *Quiz'em's Chronicles*, which provides the following account: "ye Bryde and ye Brydegroome, not handyely fyndeing a Parson, and being in grievous haste to be wed; they did take a Broome-stycke, and they did jumpe from one syde of ye Broome-stycke over to ye other syde thereof; and having so done, they did thinke them lawfulle Man and Wyffe."[8] The quotation suggests the ceremony's legitimacy, at least in the eyes of the couple. The ceremony was private and performed due to the absence of the parson, a problem that plagued many rural communities. Physical copies of *Quiz'em's Chronicles* no longer exist, making it difficult to comfortably verify the quotation, though another commentator known only as "Malone" suggested it was "a kind of heresy to ever doubt the authority of Quiz'em, for he is uncommonly accurate and faithful in his description of old customs." Malone concluded that if the ceremony existed, it "could have been resorted to only by the *lower classes*" and doubted whether such ceremonies were "ever admitted among people of superior birth and education."[9] In emphasizing class differences, the passage reveals that English writers knew that broomstick weddings were embedded in the traditions of populations shunned by elites. Given that literacy rates among the poor were extremely low in the early modern era, they themselves did not document their practices. Consequently, such a description of the custom and its practitioners tend to be patronizing.

The terms "jumping the broomstick" or "besom wedding" were also used colloquially throughout the British Isles and usually indicated a matrimonial practice taking place outside ecclesiastical sanction.[10] At the same time that W. Rhys Jones collected his data in the early twentieth century, folklorist T. Gwynn Jones focused on the Welsh practice. He observed that the Welsh phrase for "broom-stick wedding" was "priodas coes ysgub" and argued that in the early twentieth century this phrase could apply to any "irregular" wedding ceremony.[11] The Welsh phrase could literally mean "wedding over the broom handle," and couples leapt over a besom made of "oak branches." T. Gwynn Jones placed the practice within an ancient framework by noting similarities between the contemporary crossing over the broom with the chastity test requiring one to step over a wand found in the *Mabinogi*, a collection of popular Welsh myths.[12]

Much later in the twentieth century, C.W. Sullivan III, an American scholar with expertise in Welsh myth and folklore, would return to T. Gwynn Jones's ancient roots' thesis. Sullivan contended that ancient Welsh legal codes provided for the acceptance of broomstick weddings within Welsh culture, and agreed with Jones that a possible predecessor for the broomstick ritual is found in the Fourth Branch of the *Mabinogi*. At one point in this legend, a woman named Aranrhod is put to a test to qualify as the king's "footholder." Math, the Lord of Gwynedd, places a bent magic wand on the ground and challenges Aranrhod to "step over this . . . and if thou art a maiden, I shall know."[13] Aranrhod fails the test, for after she clears the broom a child with "rich yellow hair" drops to the floor, and when the child cried "she made for the door."[14] While Sullivan agreed with Jones regarding the possible connections between this ancient story and the broomstick ritual, he disagreed with the translation of *llathlud* as "maiden," preferring "virgin" or a "free young girl, outside all male restraints" as the more suitable translations. For Sullivan, this change suggested that the "chastity test" was more likely a test of "Aranrhod's freedom to accept this new position, a position of power."[15] If she successfully cleared the object, her position with the king guaranteed her linkage with power and the fertility of the land. In the end, however, both descriptions work since the important component is Aranrhod's inability to successfully cross over the object lying on the floor. The result of her failure resembles the nullification of the marriage ceremony if either participant fails to clear the broom.

Though the ancient tradition in the *Mabinogi* provides an imaginative origins story, not every scholar is convinced that couples physically jumped the matrimonial broomstick. Legal scholar Rebecca Probert questions the methods of her predecessors who made claims for the custom's ubiquity among different Welsh populations. Citing an overreliance on W. Rhys Jones's field research, Probert levels a heavy blow against the historiography by claiming that scholars took "an exceptional example as proof of a general trend."[16] She concludes that common rural populations practiced church-sanctioned marriages much more than "irregular unions." Her broader point suggests that previous scholarship downplayed the role of the church in framing marriage rites. She argues that the church held more sway than previously supposed and that rituals such as jumping the broom were largely outgrowths of colloquial expressions that equate broomsticks with "something ersatz, or lacking the authority that its true equivalent might possess."[17] Consequently, Probert considers most expressions describing couples "jumping over the broomstick" to be figurative.

To prove her case, she scrutinizes a thesis set forth by other scholars that the Marriage Act of 1753 solidified civil ceremonies throughout England and caused a gradual disappearance of folk marriage customs.[18] Probert further contends that most people had already been marrying in the church-sanctioned ceremony.[19] Though an excellent legal study, this argument overshoots the claim, as she sees nearly every reference to jumping the broom as either faulty or problematic. But this general contention merits one additional question. If a physical leap was used only into the mid-nineteenth century, how did such a ritual become ubiquitous throughout the nineteenth-century American South among an enslaved population of African descent whose ancestors were unfamiliar with European customs?[20] Placing such questions in a transatlantic context suggests that immigrants brought the custom over early enough to initiate a cultural transmission into communities throughout the United States. It is necessary to examine the specific ritual maneuvers used by various communities throughout the British Isles to understand how the custom was carried across the North Atlantic.

While people jumped the broom in a variety of ways throughout the British Isles, the custom transcended cultural differences among populations scorned by a dominant group, including Celtic communities, Romani, and others. Its practitioners found value in the custom and adjusted its ritual forms in accordance to their own communal needs. Migrants from the British Isles retained their marriage customs as they made their way to North America, and though the precise mechanisms by which the broomstick wedding was extended to an enslaved population of African descent remains murky, we can envision the circumstances and the context by viewing the evidence through a transatlantic paradigm.

## The Rural Welsh

W. Rhys Jones was not the only scholar to study the besom wedding—a few of his contemporaries also testified to its historical existence, primarily in North Wales.[21] However, he was one of the few observers to collect oral testimonials from the elders of these communities.

His study of Ceiriog Valley details what the ritual meant to those who practiced it. First, the house used for the broom was determined by the man's social standing or his financial independence. If he built the house or owned it, the broom was placed in his doorway to symbolize the couple's entry into their new home. If he had no permanent residence, but the couple was still determined to marry, it was placed in front of the woman's home. Second, the celebration was communal, and communal blessing of the nuptials were essential to the ceremony. Third, he noted that these weddings "outside Church and Chapel" denoted a marriage state in which "husband and wife had equal rights."[22] For instance, either partner could initiate a divorce on the grounds of "incompatibility of temper" or inability to bear children. The divorce ritual took place in front of witnesses and involved a broom, but with the marriage steps taken in reverse; again, though, if the broom was touched, the attempt at divorce was considered ineffectual, and the couple remained wed. If the couple did divorce and a child emerged from the severed union, the father was still responsible for its upkeep. Jones notes the wife kept her patronymic name and did not become the property of her husband. Even upon divorce, the "wife was held equal to a virgin or a widow" within the community.[23] He determined that the structure of marriage in these areas curtailed moral laxity, and people who jumped the besom believed they held more satisfying unions than the newer generations who embraced church weddings.

The material used to craft the matrimonial instrument—namely, birch—was also important to practitioners of the besom wedding. While birch brooms are often associated with witches, in Wales, birchwood was associated with courting. "Wreaths of birch were given as a love token. A birch twig given by a boy to a girl as a love token meant constancy."[24] One legend, dating at least to the early nineteenth century, states that a woman's acceptance of the proposal was signified by a return gift of a wreath made of birch, but if she rejected it, the wreath was made of hazel.[25] Although the importance of birchwood was continually reinforced in both men and women's expressions of love, courtship, and marriage, the marriage ceremony itself did not necessarily require a birch besom per se. One of Jones's interviewees noted that besoms made of *banadl*, translated from the Welsh as "broom," were "not unknown." Jones noted that older members of the community seemed most committed to the birch material.

Ultimately, one must admit that there are limitations in suggesting that this is a Welsh custom, or that Welsh people are the ritual's primary originators. In dealing with folklore, it is nearly impossible to specify a point of origin of a ritual within a specific group. We do not know if the custom was universal to the region, or if it was practiced in isolation by communities identified as Welsh. Jones recorded six communities in both North and South Wales that held traditions about jumping the besom, but their degree of cultural interactions outside their own communities is difficult to ascertain. We also know that similarities to the customs of the inhabitants of the Ceiriog Valley are found throughout the British Isles and across the Atlantic. Even if they were

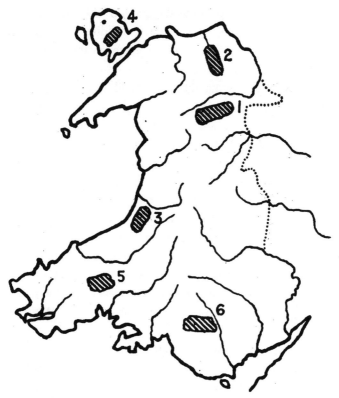

1. Ceiriog Valley, Denbighshire.  4. Anglesey.
2. Vale of Clwyd, Denbighshire.  5. Drefach, Caermarthenshire.
3. Elerch, Cardiganshire.  6. Llantrisant, Glamorgan.

Areas throughout Wales that have besom wedding traditions. From Jones,
"'Besom Wedding' in the Ceiriog Valley," 161.

not its first practitioners, they certainly adjusted the custom to fit their own
communal needs, and its importance is displayed in the way its memory was
retained by a community that no longer used it.

While other Celtic regions may have had broomstick weddings, Wales is
one of the few locations that holds a multi-generational oral tradition concerning the ritual. This circumstance suggests that the Welsh may have been
responsible for spreading the ritual to other non-Celtic populations throughout the British Isles. Considering the Welsh populations were largely rural
and on the periphery of Anglo-Saxon culture, scholars thus far have not attempted to explain how the custom may have traveled outside the confines of
the Welsh border. Welsh contact with one particular community, however,
may explain the genesis of this process. By analyzing the traditions of other

groups, we can assess the degree to which the custom traveled from one group to the other, often uniting the cultural customs of diverse peoples who were similarly marginalized by the nation state or colonial power.

## The British Romani

The Romani who migrated to the British Isles in the sixteenth-century interacted (and intermarried) with other populations, including the Welsh. These Welsh Romani used the broomstick wedding for their nuptials throughout the nineteenth century. One particular family, the descendants of Abram Wood, a patriarch of his community, has been studied by historians Eldra Jarman and A. O. H. Jarman, who note with regard to the family's practice of broomstick weddings that "the records of the Wood family probably preserve the last examples of their survival in Wales."[26] The authors' thoughts on whether gypsies held any deep-rooted attachments to broomstick weddings prior to their contact with the Welsh are far less clear. In the early twentieth century, W. Rhys Jones and T. W. Thompson noted that besom weddings did not exist among Romani communities outside of the British Isles. It was a ritual unique to the British Romani. In 1992, Alan Dundes speculated the broomstick wedding was introduced into Wales by Romani migrants. Shortly after, C. W. Sullivan offered a corrective note that more fully articulated the Welsh connections to the ritual by citing its similarities to the *Mabinogi* legends, in turn complicating the theory of Romani origins. Indeed, given that broomstick marriages were used in non-Romani Welsh populations and that no other Romani groups in eastern or central Europe are currently known by historians or folklorists to utilize the ritual, it was likely introduced into this migrant community.[27]

The "Welsh-Romani" accounts collected by folklorists divulge their assortment of matrimonial performances. Certain couples jumped a broom decorated with flowers while it was held by the bride or groom's father.[28] In a different oral account a couple performed the ceremony independently of supervision, while another reveals that a groom threw "two branches of broom" at his bride's feet, "took her by the hand and together they leapt over them. Thus they were married in his fashion."[29] Another tradition entailed a leap backward and then forward, while yet another required a grandparent to hold the sticks while the bridegroom, "de bride's girl," the bride, and "de bridegroom's man" were all required to jump over the broom in that order. In this rendition, some of the ceremony's participants beyond the bride and groom also leaped over the matrimonial object. In other instances the process was individual, and it was expected that the groom jump over first followed by the bride.[30] These oral traditions led folklorist M. Eileen Lyster to conclude that marriage over the broomstick was no myth, "but . . . a living custom among Welsh gypsies in the last generation."[31] Moreover, various American newspapers in 1912 shared a short article first published in the *London Chronicle* entitled "Odd Customs of Gypsies," which described a similar ceremony: "The besom was held by the father of the bridegroom or bride, and first the young man jumped over it, and then the young woman, whereupon the official would make some such remark as 'Now, you are married.'" Interestingly, the article also adds that "it is only within the last fifty years that that custom has been extinct in Wales."[32]

It appears that Welsh people generally stopped jumping over the matrimonial broom by the mid-nineteenth century, which explains why W. Rhys Jones did not find any living practitioners of the broomstick custom in the Ceiriog Valley of North Wales. It is unclear why this happened. A possible explanation may have to do with the influence of the Industrial Revolution upon the rural portions of Wales where this form of marriage remained most intact. Welsh historian John Davies argues that toward the end of the nineteenth century "rural Wales came to depend increasingly heavily on industrial Wales."[33] Increased contact with outside communities and ministers may have rendered the tradition unnecessary to the once peripheral rural communities. As ministers were more readily available for those who desired to confirm their marital status, it is understandable how the broomstick custom became less necessary than in previous generations. Alternatively, Welsh practitioners may have seen the use of the ritual among Romani communities as a negative reflection upon their own society and discarded the tradition.

Broomstick weddings were, in any case, associated with the Romani whose migrations extended beyond Wales, throughout the British Isles. As early as 1786, jumping the broom was assumed by some to be a "gipsies marriage ceremony, in which they set the broom on the floor."[34] Not only was this considered a strange practice, but observers usually pointed out the Romani's distinct ethnic identity, commenting on their darker complexion, eyes, and hair. One writer in the mid-twentieth century called them "dark skinned strangers" who appeared "indifferent to the rest of the world."[35] Another account even claimed that gypsy children were darkened prior to their baptisms, using "a dark liquid concocted of roots of wild plants and leaves of various sorts."[36] In essence, Romani were viewed as ethnically and culturally distinct from the surrounding populations of the British Isles, and their use of the broomstick wedding served as an additional feature of their unique identity. In the 1880s, V. S. Moorwood documented a gypsy wedding in an undisclosed location in rural England:

> Two rows of gypsies with about twelve or fifteen in each row were formed, standing face to face, being between four and six feet apart. Halfway down between these rows were two gypsies who held up a broomstick about eighteen inches above the ground. . . . In obedience to the chief's command he [the groom] came from a tent at one side of the encampment, walked between the rows of gypsies, stepped over the broomstick, turned around, and then stood with his arms akimbo waiting the arrival of his intended wife. . . . She also walked between the two rows of gypsies, tripped very lightly over the broomstick, which she had no sooner done than the young gypsy man took her in his arms and completed the ceremony.[37]

The Romani were cynically described as a "marginal, mobile, minority," suggesting their culture was predicated on their nomadic lifestyle and distinctions from surrounding communities. But this ceremony is elaborate and regimented, revealing a thoughtful manipulation of its ritual performance.[38] As with their Welsh counterparts, an elder was present to dictate the performance of the ceremony. The emphasis on community is apparent within this narrative. Considering that Romani were typically on the fringes of society, they needed to create meaningful unions sanctioned by the community. In this instance, the community served as the sanctuary, providing a human wall that guided the lovers toward the intended objective of sealing their nuptials by crossing the threshold. The emphasis on the patriarchal structure of gypsy culture is apparent, though assisting the bride over the threshold appears in other sources in the British Isles and throughout the Anglo-Atlantic.

Manfri Wood's autobiography provides additional details concerning the nuptial process and the broom's decorative features. The man initiated courtship by providing the woman with his scarf. If he later saw her wearing his gift in public, it signified her interest in pursuing the relationship. They would then jump the broomstick to test their compatibility and usually lived together for a few days. Wood notes that the besom was decorated with "flowering thorn or gorse in front of the members of their families."[39] If the two were compatible, they registered their marriage officially a few weeks later. Wood's narrative indicates that jumping the broom involved practical considerations in that it initiated a probationary period for the couple. It appears that state recognition was an option if the couple determined it was in their best interest, but divorce was far easier if government was not involved.

In the early twentieth century, newspapers on both sides of the Atlantic dismissed jumping the broom as an "odd" ritual of the Romani. "There are traditions of the marriage ceremony among certain gypsies in England consisting simply of jumping over a broom or besom. . . . The besom was held by the father of the bridegroom or bride, and first the young man jumped over it, and then the young woman, whereupon the official would make some such remark as 'Now, you are married.'"[40] The title of the article, "Odd Customs of the British Gypsies," along with its tone, suggests that jumping over a broom was considered exclusive to British Romani.

However, it does not appear to have been a universal practice among all of them.[41] In 1920, one author who identified himself as British Romani castigated the British people for their bigotry against his community and the stereotypes of thievery and violence they circulated. Interestingly, he also used marriage rituals to illustrate his point, writing, "You have read in novels about gypsies marrying by 'jumping a broomstick' and all that rot written about my people."[42] Whether or not this dismissing of the broomstick tradition as "rot" and propaganda was accurate, it does point to the fact that whereas the British Romani were often portrayed as a monolithic group, in reality, they were no such thing.

Moreover, although broomstick weddings generally took place outside the law, they were not necessarily regarded as illegitimate by the British government. In the mid-1920s at least one couple gained legal recognition for a broomstick wedding performed fifty years earlier. According to a widow named Martha Smythe, she and her husband "jumped over a broomstick at a fair" and through the laws of their own community they were considered "legally married."[43] In convincing the authorities that they had lived as a happily married couple for over fifty years, she was subsequently granted a pension by the government. Details are lacking from this brief report, and one wonders if this case was exceptional or became a general rule in the twentieth century. Perhaps it was based upon her ability to verify they lived as a married couple for multiple decades, rendering paperwork superfluous since legislators could use other measures to verify whether moral standards were upheld throughout married life.

## Irish Traditions and Folklore

While precursors to the broomstick wedding figure into the *Mabinogi* myths, brooms in general have had supernatural powers attributed to them by various communities in the British Isles. For example, in folklore collected in

1896 from North Donegal, a county located in Ireland's northwestern corner, people placed broomsticks behind the door to "keep fairies from the house"[44]—fairies that in this case could pose danger to humans if they had ill intentions. The broomstick's position in blocking these spirits is not explained in the oral tradition, but it is certainly linked to its ability to block malevolent forms of magic.

By the nineteenth century one particular group of Irish Travellers had a custom in which an engaged couple leapt over an object. A "historically nomadic" group who dwelled on the margins of society, these people survived economically by fixing metal utensils, quite literally "tinkering" with items until they were fixed, and hence were known as "Tinkers."[45] ("Travellers," an alternate designation, is now preferred.) Some observers categorized them as "a species of Gypsy," a group of dark-haired and "swarthy" people who "seldom marry out of their own caste."[46] Their nomadic existence meant that their customs involved a degree of expediency. Thus, marriage ceremonies, though communal and celebratory, had to be swift in case the group needed to relocate. The ceremony involved "jumping the budget," the "budget" meaning a bag of tools.[47] This act likely reflected the Travellers' principal focus—namely, labor. Whereas the Welsh of the Ceiriog Valley placed the broom over their doorways to symbolize the establishment of their household, "jumping the budget" placed the couple's marriage in direct relation to their whole community. Though most accounts of these weddings are from outside observers and at times are prone to mockery, in reading closely we can see how the descriptions provide an idea of how these communities interpreted their own approaches to marriage and domestic life.[48]

One rendition of the broomstick wedding, which the author calls the "Tinker's wedding," depicts a mock wedding ceremony in which two young men don wigs, and one assumes the role of a woman. In this performance, the young man pursues the woman in a "rough courtship" in which she resists the violent advances.[49] To halt the raucous escapade, "some one produces a broom, which is laid upon the floor." The couple then jumps over it "and ar [sic] pronounced man and wife."[50] After the ceremony, the broom serves a specific function for an upset wife, who uses the object to rain down blows on the shoulders of her husband who eventually flees the area. Though it is represented as a mock wedding, we can gain a few important points from this source. In many respects, this performance reflected the tumultuous nature of marriage in small, isolated communities, in which violence could be an ever-present reality. The makeshift wife's aggressive maneuvers might reflect how domestic issues were determined by such groups internally. Additionally, it may reflect perceptions of a fiercely independent Irish woman who refused to be victimized by her husband. Another account, written in 1896, notes that "a 'mode of marriage' current in Ireland, until recent times, was that of jumping over the form of a cross."[51] This account, in turn, was inspired by an 1890 collection released by American folklorist Jeremiah Curtin, who described an Irish legend in which a man found a woman alive inside a coffin floating at sea. After he rescued her, they initiated a very short, but symbolically rich marriage ceremony: "He took the stranger to his house and gave her food and drink. Then he made a great cross on the ground, and clasping hands with the woman, jumped over the arms of the cross, going in the same direction as the sun. This was the form of marriage in that land."[52] Curtin provides no commentary on the story, but a few points should be highlighted.

First, the "cross" was improvised. It is unclear if the man drew it in the dirt or assembled pieces of wood to form a cross on the ground. The main point is that the symbol took the form of a cross, which suggests that this potentially ancient cosmology was reimagined through generations with the ritualistic brand of Christianity practiced by Irish Catholics in the eighteenth and nineteenth centuries. The use of the adjective "great" also suggests some care was taken to create the symbol. Second, both partners clasp hands, which is a frequent feature of other broomstick ceremonies throughout the Anglo-Atlantic world.[53] The reference to the sun, however, is what renders this narrative unique, as it is the only broomstick wedding I have found in which the sun figures centrally. It is most likely a derivative from ancient cosmology among Celtic populations, from whom anthropologists and folklorists have found evidence of sun worship clear into the nineteenth century.[54] It seems possible that the sun may have served as an inspiration for married couples since it "crosses" the sky each day, continually overcoming the obstacle of a "threshold."

According to clergyman Henry Clay Trumbull, most ceremonies that referred to "jumping over," including the leap over the broomstick, were likely modified versions of a practice called "leaping over the threshold-stone" practiced in modified form in Belford, Northumberland, and other regions in Britain. While his thesis is speculative and tinged with a degree of ethnocentrism, his suggestion that thresholds represent hindrances to advancement is a useful idea. Trumbull believed that such objects represented "obstacles" the couple needed to overcome.[55] In order to fully engage in married life, the couple overcame the obstacle together by clasping hands and leaping over it. His speculations are useful for exploring how rural or isolated communities blended elements of tradition with innovation, creating unique practices that varied according to the individual practitioners.

Trumball's story only represents the custom in a specific area, and provides the likelihood that different groups of people in both Ireland and Britain performed similar customs with distinct cultural specifications. Regardless of its origins in this community, the element of crossing over an object appears the most important feature within the various legends. Anthropologist W. C. MacLeod found multiple societies who viewed "'jumping over' or 'stepping over' as a ceremonial [that was] variously rationalized and linked with various ceremonial complexes."[56] Throughout European societies, broomsticks held various symbolic meanings, and were most commonly associated with phallic properties and the supernatural.[57] Using the broomstick wedding as a focal point, folklorist Alan Dundes argues that these instances of stepping over various objects are metaphors for sexual intercourse, and the production of a child after clearing the broom is suggestive of its phallic properties.[58]

## The English

The few broomstick weddings recorded among the poor urban and rural English populations frequently stem from obviously biased outside observers, and sometimes they are satirical. Descriptions are often short, and the practitioners are usually condemned as derelicts.[59] An 1851 statement noting that broomstick weddings took place in Bristol illustrates the point. The report claims such matches were organized and overseen by an older woman living in lower-income housing. Since her residence was frequented by transient populations, she simply matched these strangers by having them leap over the broom. If the broomstick wedding was not performed, the "couple weren't looked on as man and wife."[60] It is difficult to gauge the veracity of this narrative. Did it simply use the broomstick wedding to mock the decadence of the industrial city, or was it explaining a specific set of individual circumstances? Beyond these questions is the problem of the extent of any broom-jumping ceremony, widespread among the English. Some scholars of U.S. slavery have attempted to track the broomstick wedding to "early Anglo Saxon villages," but frequently rely on secondary sources to make this claim.[61] Some English populations certainly used broomsticks in their nuptials, but it is unclear if the custom was used widely or on a scattered or individual basis.

The broomstick wedding could be represented as a mark of inferiority or even as a form of sacrilege. An 1882 poem entitled "The Blasphemer's Warning" includes the lines: "And unwedded maids to the last crack of doom stick / Ere [before] marry, by taking a jump o'er a broomstick."[62] The poem is referring to an aptitude among certain women to remain unmarried until the last minute, and uses the broomstick wedding to describe the abrupt nature of contemporary marriage. In a similar vein, "jumping the broomstick" became a derogatory expression for a sham marriage. Charles Dickens, for one, wrote in 1850 about a young woman who jumped over a broomstick at a bar and was fooled into believing that it was legally binding.[63] Later on, Dickens included a colloquial reference to jumping the broom in his novel *Great Expectations*, rehearsing notions about its irregular nature.[64] If nothing else, the fact that Dickens refers to marriage "over the broomstick" reveals that the broader public was aware of this form of matrimony.

Contemporary writers corroborate Dickens's report with claims that marriages over a broomstick were common at taverns where English laborers congregated.[65] In 1848, an American newspaper reprinted one story about a young man's marriage proposal that featured the broomstick wedding as an introductory statement: "We have heard of the old style of frolic marriage— namely the jumping over the broomstick—right jov[i]al fun for many a youngster of both sexes."[66] In this instance, the broomstick ceremony was an activity for the young and immature, not a legally binding marriage of respectable adults. There even exist accusations of the broomstick ritual being used by populations that openly mocked Christian sacraments. English "navvies" (construction workers) apparently used ceremonies in which they sprinkled a "stick" with holy water. After the stick was held at the appropriate level the bride and groom took turns jumping over it and into each other's arms.[67] This account is likely embellished, but it does raise the question of how diverse the ritual was among the populations that practiced it. In certain respects, this account is similar to that of the Romani account in which the bride jumps into the groom's arms. Was this a product of cultural transmission from the Romani to the English? Or were observers pushing their own understandings of the broomstick wedding upon populations they viewed as culturally inferior? In the end, such questions are difficult to answer definitively, but the broomstick wedding's association with marginalized, working-class populations is apparent in English literature.

## "Scotch" Weddings

Within the English imagination, Scotland held lax marriage laws. Young English couples historically stole away to "Gretna Green," an area on the Scottish/ English border, to obtain a marriage license too difficult to acquire in their homeland. As in other communities, rural Scots maintained folkloric practices requiring one to use a jumping action in courtship or in actual marriage

"The Scotch Wedding," from Paston, *Social Caricature*, 29.

ceremonies. In one rendition, a Scottish sailor who was forced to choose between several women who hoped to marry him said that he would marry the woman who could "jump the highest."[68] A clear victor named "Nesbitt" emerged, and in keeping his promise he married her. The news report claimed they lived happily together and reared many children.

Scotland harbored a number of Traveller communities. Though often associated with the Irish, it appears some nomadic communities throughout Scotland were described with the same name. Sometimes they were descendants of the Scottish Romani or they were ethnic Scots who led a nomadic life in the rural countryside. Given the insulated nature of the community, their identities remain shrouded in some mystery. Regarding their marriage rituals, one source suggests that the partners stood "back to back" on either side of an object such as a broom or "tongs" and jumped away from it.[69] The reason for this method of jumping away from the object is not explored in the source, and it appears to be unique to this community. Jumping away from the matrimonial item may be a way of leaving behind one's previous ties, but any interpretation is mere speculation. The use of "tongs" was probably tied to their position as travelers who repaired various items.

Another source that identifies jumping the broomstick with Scottish people is caricaturist James Gillray's "The Scotch Wedding." This 1789 image, which depicts a couple physically leaping over a broomstick, in a way that suggests the practice was commonly known by this point. The couple represented in the caricature are the Duke of Richmond and Lady Anne Gordon. It is unclear why the artist decided to attack these two figures, but looking closer at the image reveals one meaning behind it. Given that jumping the broom carried negative connotations, this appellation "Scotch Wedding" reveals a method through which the English invalidated Scottish culture during their conflicts throughout the eighteenth century. The Duke of Richmond was Scottish, and the artist was likely trying to convey the appellation of inferiority upon the person of Celtic descent, despite his noble birth. Additionally, the fact that this was a marriage performed in a bedroom with bagpipes played by the bride's mother suggests that Gillray was also depicting the ceremony's association with socially peripheral populations. No matter how privileged within the realm of politics, one could not escape ethnic stereotypes.

## Many Cultures, Many Ceremonies

Writings portraying the broomstick wedding tended to be overwhelmingly negative when referenced by outside observers, used as a literary weapon to mock the groups who used it.[70] "Marrying over the Broomstick" illustrates this feature vividly.[71] Published in the 1830s by James Catnach, an influential printer in Britain, the image was set to acquire broad distribution.[72] It depicts a man who presumably has already crossed the broom and is assisting his bride over the threshold. The bride has a strange item on her head, which appears to be an exaggerated homemade crown. Ethnicity is not mentioned, but it is possible the woman represented is Romani, since some commentators claimed they embellished their wedding clothing. However, it could simply be a broad stereotype of the groups who used it, as certain elements match those of rural Celtic communities who used the ceremony for practical reasons. On first glance, one notices a few guests are present to observe the union and a tent is placed on the side to depict the location of the marriage bed. It appears that the elderly woman in front of the couple is sanctioning the union. Such a suggestion is plausible given that folklore from Welsh sources typically claimed the union was performed in front of a village elder and that the officiant could be a man or a woman. The image used the elderly woman to demonstrate how her presence subverted the patriarchal structure of nineteenth-century Britain. Simultaneously, by depicting the man as assisting her over the broom, the picture suggests that he serves as his bride's protector, emphasizing the domestic arrangements at the inception of the union. The man's responsibility in helping the woman complete the ceremony suggests that this format emphasized gender relationships through manifestations of power. Theorist Catherine Bell argues that such forms of ritualization serve as "a strategy for the construction of certain types of power relationships effective within particular social organizations."[73] In other words, different social classes employ specific rituals to define hierarchies and the image "Marrying over the Broomstick" lends itself to different analytical conclusion.

For instance, one can find different, and overtly negative, interpretations conveyed through the imagery. First, the "guests" on the left side have interlocked arms, suggesting they are not simply observing the wedding, but are prepared to marry directly after the first couple takes their leap. By inserting this component, the artist conveyed a primary criticism of the broomstick wedding—namely, that the custom sanctioned erratic and immoral decisions. This interpretation aligns with an attached poem that renders the participants as deviants, noting that after they jumped the broomstick they became intoxicated and passed out during the festivities. Additionally, one notices that none of the women is smiling during the festivities, while the men seem elated by the nuptials. This notion of an unhappy bride who was devoid of agency aligned with contemporary English criticisms of the populations they deemed amoral and less civilized. As the British Empire expanded throughout the Americas and Western Africa, English adventurers critiqued the domestic relations of each area's inhabitants. Unsurprisingly, they often rendered them inferior to their own.

For instance, in his travels throughout Sierra Leone in 1792, physician Thomas Winterbottom criticized the marriage relations of the region's inhabitants, specifically targeting polygyny and claimed that "the female sex does not hold in Africa that distinguished rank in society which it happily enjoys in Europe."[74] Obviously, Winterbottom's critique was slanted. Many British wives were ensnared within an abusive patriarchal form of matrimony, but commentators, primarily men, preferred to look outward for domestic inequality and criticize other populations for supposedly failing to uphold the agency of betrothed women. Polygny was not an egalitarian institution, but primary sources reveal that some contemporary African women claimed that the complex institution was, in certain regards, superior to the monogamy practiced by European Christians.[75] Though they are portrayed as "European," the wedding participants in "Marrying over the Broomstick" are represented as cultural outsiders through this ethnocentric idea of marital orthodoxy. Not only does their form of matrimony render them uncivilized, but critics believed it actively encouraged licentiousness and gendered oppression. Ultimately,

## CUT III. Marrying over the Broomstick.

"Marrying over the Broomstick." Original found in James Catchnach, *The New Marriage Act* (London, 1822); courtesy of The Lewis Walpole Library, Yale University.

"Marrying Over the Broomstick" conveyed a complete inversion of an acceptable (or perhaps, imagined) form of matrimony.

As marriage was used as a form of social control by ecclesiastical authorities and aristocrats, nonconformist groups created meaningful rituals that held a quality and complexity beyond simple ceremony. [76] At the same time, persecution of a group's culture can lead its members to disavow ancestral customs, especially if they hope to assimilate into the dominant culture. As noted, Welsh communities stopped "jumping the besom" by the early twentieth century, and W. Rhys Jones only found a few elders who remembered the ancestral traditions. It is impossible to fully know if every community ceased marrying in this fashion. For a Celtic population forced to link itself to the dominant group, it is reasonable to assume that many vestiges of their ancestral traditions were actively suppressed. As older Welsh people prepared the next generation to conform to English standards, these unique ancestral customs were nearly annihilated.

In contrast, British Romani never assimilated into the broader society, remaining marginalized from and ostracized by the British public. It is unclear when gypsies stopped jumping the broom, but it seems to have vanished by the mid-twentieth century. Based on his discussions with a group of British

Romani in the 1950s, author G. E. C. Webb contended that the broomstick wedding was performed "in the past," as he did "not think Gypsies do this today."[77] Webb went further to claim it was "not . . . really a gypsy ceremony at all"; rather, it was more directly associated with Irish Travellers.[78] According to him, if a Romani spoke of a broomstick wedding, it was not meant literally. Considering their nomadic lifestyle and ethnic distinctiveness, Webb argued that claims about the literal practice were simply a point of confusion by outsiders who documented the ritual among Irish Travellers and mistakenly ascribed it to British Romani. However, many testimonials show that descendants of the British Romani claimed the custom as an ancestral tradition, even if they no longer used it. One such person named Robert revealed to his interviewer that while the custom of jumping the broom was admittedly "strange," his ancestors definitely used it: "That was quite common—literally doing that—jumping over the broomstick and that was the wedding vows—the solemn thing that they were going to carry on through life."[79] Though Robert provides no reason why it was discontinued, he understood it was valid in the eyes of the community in generations past. Interestingly, at least a few elder British Romani interviewed in 1910 believed their form of matrimony was superior to that of younger generations and claimed that husbands and wives who participated in the broomstick ritual "lived together for years without quarrelling."[80]

## Atlantic Journeys

For some ethnic minorities throughout the British Isles broomstick weddings were associated with resistance. To be sure, the resistance was not overt, nor was it always intentional, but in continuing the ritual across generations, they defied the derogatory perceptions of the practice and signified the importance of community and kinship for survival. By the nineteenth century the broomstick wedding was solidified among many working-class cultures throughout the British Isles, but its impact does not cease there. The expansion of the British Atlantic world from the eighteenth to the nineteenth centuries promoted cultural transmissions throughout various communities in English speaking territories. Exploring the transatlantic connections between migrant communities reveals that cultural practices could transcend racial or ethnic sensibilities.

Few scholars have tracked how "jumping the broom" made its long journey from the British Isles to the shores of North America. C. W. Sullivan suggests that Welsh immigration to North America was substantial enough for their customs to have had an impact.[81] But these Welsh migrants settled predominantly in the Northeast, particularly New York and Pennsylvania.[82] Historian Ronald Lewis proposed that out of 45,000 Welsh immigrants, fewer than 500 lived below the Mason-Dixon line.[83]

It should be noted, however, that "port officials did not systematically distinguish Welsh immigrants from Scottish or English passengers until 1908, and immigrants who embarked from small ports along the Welsh coast often went uncounted."[84] The Welsh presence could have been larger than the records suggest, and scholars have found that important Welsh settlements existed in Maryland, Virginia, North Carolina, and South Carolina throughout the eighteenth century, though their actual numbers are more difficult to calculate.[85] Either way, scholars should be wary of relying too heavily on migration statistics when considering the transfer of the broomstick marriage, since Welsh weddings differed from region to region, and some did not employ broomsticks at all.[86]

The eighteenth-century novel *The Journal of Penrose, A Seaman*, by Welsh author William Williams provides a representation of how the folk practice likely diffused throughout the Atlantic World. The novel's protagonist, Llewellin Penrose, becomes shipwrecked on the Mosquito Coast of Nicaragua and proclaims himself leader of a multiracial community, which includes other marooned European sailors, formerly enslaved Africans, and indigenous inhabitants. Among other things, he performs marriage ceremonies that include jumping the broom, which he describes as "a common Custome among my people when they had a mind to be merry [married]."[87] While no exact date exists for the novel's completion, Williams had finished the manuscript prior to 1776, making his descriptions contemporaneous with folk customs practiced in the eighteenth century.[88]

He himself was a sailor and traveler throughout the British colonies, and while *The Journal of Penrose* is fiction, literary critic David Dickason argues that there is evidence that "Williams did indeed share (albeit partially) in the experiences he attributes to Penrose."[89] As a seaman, colonist, and traveling artist, Williams created a character that was both semi-autobiographical and semi-fictional. The experience of Williams/Penrose helps resolve two major problems in jumping the broom's historiography, specifically regarding the timeline of when it was introduced and how it spread to other areas and adopted by different groups. First, the novel provides an early, firsthand account of the custom in the eighteenth century. Secondly, it offers a description of how the ceremony was performed and received among new cultural groups. Its introduction among enslaved African Americans was likely a similar process, in that a practitioner from the British Isles introduces it to the subaltern community and they reimagine the custom to meet their own cultural worldview. Early migrants to the Americas experienced cultural inclusion, exclusion, and/ or amalgamation.[90] The legal invalidity of enslaved people's marital rites in North America provided incentives for either continuing rituals inspired by ancestral traditions, or adopting the folk customs of the surrounding populations of white people in the southern United States.

Of course, Welsh migration was not the only prerequisite for the transmission of jumping the broom. If the ritual existed in parts of Ireland, Scotland, or England, one can postulate these immigrant populations were also responsible for disseminating its use in the colonies. Penrose's story simply exemplifies how the ritual could be reimagined across the Atlantic and introduced to non-European groups. Each group associated with the rite tailored it to its own communal needs, but while each community executed the ritual differently, all of them maintained the one essential component of the ceremony: the jump over the broom. The practicality of this custom would become particularly important for enslaved people in the rural American South who were disbarred from the benefits of a legally sanctioned marriage. Since enslaved people in the United States were categorized as chattel, meaning they were outside the contours of citizenship in British and American territories, their circumstances were unique when compared to the other groups mentioned in this chapter. Even if their marriages met the religious and civil expectations of Anglophone society, their unions were still subject to be ruptured if the enslaver decided it was more economically practical to separate a couple and sell a spouse. Though their initial motivation to adapt this custom resembles the ostracized groups in Britain, the legal status of enslaved people and the stark restrictions on their marital rights in the United States does make their experience unique and requires one to engage in a more extended study of their experiences with the broomstick wedding.

Viewing the custom through an Atlantic lens provides an important addition to previous works that largely ignored its origins and what it meant to the enslaved population that acquired it.[91] The custom's connections to the British Isles reveal many useful points for contextualizing its spread to other areas in the Anglophone Atlantic. Various group populations jumped the broom for many reasons, including necessity, levity, or a need to test the domestic compatibility of a young couple. Though it was not legally recognized, those who used it took care in how they performed the ceremony. Each group developed unique and symbolically rich ceremonies that reflected their cultural worldview. This ritual is, at its root, diverse and multifaceted. Though it is impossible to know who developed it first, we have some idea as to how it was transmitted to different groups and how its meaning was adapted by them. This understanding of cultural adaptation is helpful for contextualizing how it was carried across the Atlantic and used by a group of people who faced unprecedented restrictions on their marital liberties.

## CHAPTER TWO

# As If They Had Been Joined by a Clergyman
## Jumping the Broom and American Slavery

The earliest known documentation of an enslaved couple jumping the broom appears in an 1859 court case in Brooklyn, New York, accusing B. N. Warrick, a formerly enslaved man, of bigamy. The crux of the accusation was Warrick's 1814 marriage to Winnie, an enslaved woman, in North Carolina, and his subsequent marriage to another woman after he gained his freedom in 1828 and moved north. His migration was motivated by a law in North Carolina that threatened to re-enslave free people of African descent who lingered in the state. White authorities feared that free Black people would negatively influence the enslaved population and foment rebellion. Warrick occasionally visited Winnie in his travels back to North Carolina, as the two had twelve children together, but ultimately, he and Winnie agreed it was safer for him to stay in the North. Relinquishing hope that they would ever be legally bound, Warrick married another woman in 1843. However, Winnie unexpectedly gained her freedom in 1854 and came North to find her husband had remarried, though she still claimed him as her spouse. The state attempted to convict him of bigamy, but ultimately decided that, since marriages occurring under slavery were not legally contracted, they required no formal divorce, and so there were no legal obstacles to a newly freed person seeking a union recognized by the state.[1]

Apart from the legal questions involved, the case presents a unique account of jumping the broom. According to the *New York Times*, in 1814 Warrick and Winnie "agreed . . . to live together, and a colored Methodist exhorter read over the discipline on marriage, the parties saluted each other as bride and groom, jumped over the broomstick in the kitchen, and were pronounced married."[2] Here, several points are worth making. First, no slaveholders are mentioned, which suggests that the enslaved couple may have had some degree of autonomy in the ceremony. Second, the Black minister has a specific denomination, Methodist, which is a type of detail not usually found in the testimonies of the formerly enslaved. Third, the ceremony was performed in the kitchen, which may indicate that they were "house slaves." Though it was uncommon for enslaved domestics to embrace this custom, it did happen occasionally. Winnie and Warrick's wedding is likely not the first time an enslaved couple used the matrimonial broomstick, but the 1859 account of their 1814 ceremony is the earliest dated description of the custom. As such, this reference firmly establishes that it was known in certain communities by the early nineteenth century and that those who jumped the broom considered it binding.

Historians generally agree that many enslaved people jumped the broom, but there remains some disagreement surrounding the circumstances through which they acquired the practice. Was it an "elementary ritual" given to the enslaved by the enslavers, or was it a form of matrimonial resistance with deep symbolic and cultural value?[3] Either way, this debate is centered on the slaveowner's authority. The master's presence in many of the ceremonies has puzzled scholars who are trying to determine if the ritual should be viewed as a product of slave ingenuity or white conscription. Were slaveowner's able to coerce the enslaved into accepting the ritual? How do formerly enslaved people remember the enslaver's participation?

Determining the parameters of their involvement requires one to sift through various representations of slaveholders who inserted themselves into slave weddings. By examining the ceremony through multiple vantage points, including the intersections of gender, social position, and power, we can see that enslaved African Americans were not a culturally homogenous group. In fact, the broomstick wedding and the multiple forms it took throughout the U.S. South reveals how enslaved people restructured (or rejected) the custom based upon their own communal needs.

## The Meaning of Marriage for the Enslaved

To contextualize the broomstick wedding among the enslaved, we must examine how enslaved people understood the concept of marriage in the nineteenth century. United States law prevented them from attaining a legally recognized marriage, and their union's longevity was determined by the whims of their enslaver. These circumstances severely disrupted their abilities to form stable families.[4] Testimonials often recounted harrowing examples of forced separations. Regarding marriage, William Wells Brown, a formerly enslaved man who escaped from a plantation in Kentucky, revealed in his 1847 autobiography that it was "very common among slaves themselves to talk of it. And it is common for slaves to be married; or at least have the marriage ceremony performed. But there is no such thing as slaves being lawfully married."[5] In 1856, Brown used his novel *Clotel* to excoriate the United States for allowing powerful white people to disrupt the sacred bonds of marriage: "Marriage is . . . the first and most important institution of human existence—

the foundation of all civilisation and culture. . . . If this be a true picture of the vast influence for good of the institution of marriage, what must be the moral degradation of that people to whom marriage is denied?"[6] Brown used society's definition of marriage against itself, arguing that the marital contract was central to any righteous civilization. The deprivation of that right from any group reflected the Christian nation's deep-seated duplicity. Literary critic Tess Chakkalakal argues that *Clotel* depicts Brown's view that enslaved people, devoid of any marital protections, could still form a union "that was more lasting and loving than a legal marriage."[7] For them, marriage was a form of survival, and they were not naïve to the hypocrisy surrounding the legal parameters of their marital rights.

An individual's conception of the wedding ceremony was subjective. Though some criticized the broomstick ceremony as a fruitless activity with little cultural meaning, others contended that jumping the broom was considered a "big wedding" or a "great feat" on their plantation, especially when compared with those couples who were denied any ceremony.[8] They also had different interpretations of what it meant to form unions under slavery. Some contended the "real" wedding did not occur until after freedom commenced, believing that legal documentation was the best guarantee in protecting *and* validating their union.[9] Others asserted that their antebellum marriages were as binding as any wedding overseen by the courts and that their love was as strong under bondage as it was outside of it.[10] A review of the testimonies of the formerly enslaved shows that they had no unanimous view of marriage and that differences in their approaches to it depended on their local culture. Some enslaved couples had extravagant weddings that rivaled those of white people, while others rejected any ceremony and simply lived together.[11] Either way, enslaved people knew they lacked legal protection and faced the daily reality of forcible separation. Additionally, slaveowners attempted to regulate the domestic arrangements on their properties by enforcing curfews or rejecting a suitor's request to marry a particular woman.[12] To some degree, this neutralized the ceremonial requirements since it reflected how slaveowners ultimately determined the wedding's structure. It mattered little if a couple was married by a minister in the presence of white and black witnesses, or initiated a clandestine ceremony, so long as they were legally defined as chattel. Consequently, many enslaved communities could view the broomstick wedding on an equal basis with a traditional Christian ceremony, since neither held legal validity.

Writing in 1880, William Wells Brown echoed this sentiment by noting, "The mode of jumping the broomstick was the general custom in the rural districts of the South, forty years ago; and, as there was no law whatever in regard to the marriage of slaves, this custom had as binding force with the negroes, as if they had been joined by a clergyman."[13] Though legality was the ultimate barrier to enslaved people's marital rights, many communities were still concerned about the different meanings of rituals and how they reflected their own specific outlook on marriage. Though the broomstick wedding is the most documented folk custom among the enslaved, some sources reveal they used various ceremonies to validate their marriages. In 1847 a Boston reporter observed "two or three" slave marriages during his visit to the South and claimed they involved "kissing a horseshoe or jumping over a broom-stick."[14] "Kissing a horseshoe" does not appear in other narratives and was likely limited to this location. Outside some obscure references to horseshoes and matrimony in Anglophone folklore, I found little information on this custom.[15] The only explanation lies in the fact that horseshoes are tradition-ally considered tokens of good luck, a concept that surely resonates with mat-rimony. In a different example, one enslaved man in Georgia claimed he was "married by the blanket," which required the bride and groom to enter a cabin together and lay their blankets beside one another.[16] Though he does not elaborate, one can presume this action symbolized a couple's mutual decision to establish their household. Joining one another's blankets, a prized posses-sion for enslaved people, represented a commitment to the warmth and pro-tection they desperately needed to survive the oppression of slavery. At least one other testimony equated blankets with domesticity. A formerly enslaved person in Oklahoma used the colloquial expression "blanket married" when describing the exploits of a young slaveholder, who apparently found a woman and "just lived with her" without formal ceremony.[17] Given that In-digenous peoples were also in bondage alongside Black people, and many en-slaved people of African descent claimed ancestral ties to American Indian populations, it is possible these communities appropriated the matrimonial "blanket ceremonies" used by Indigenous peoples throughout the United States in courtship negotiations or as a gift to the betrothed couple at the ceremony.[18] Although these various wedding rituals were practiced by the enslaved, jumping over a broomstick is the most extensively documented and likely the most prevalent. However, the existence of these alternate folk customs suggests each plantation community embraced the rituals most practical to their circumstances and those most pertinent to their collective interests. It reflects how enslaved people throughout the U.S. South were not a homogenous group, but subject to local conditions that produced unique cultures. This framework, discussed later in this book, explains why the broomstick wedding was practiced in such different ways throughout the antebellum South.

The emphasis on legality caused some formerly enslaved people to deny that "marriage" existed under slavery, at least when compared to the ceremonies "white folks" used.[19] However, many expressed affection for their partners and resisted the enslaver's interference through violence or escape. For those in "abroad marriages," a term used to describe spouses who dwelled on separate plantations, men who visited their wives needed to have a pass signed by the slaveholder to escape prosecution from patrollers looking for runaways.[20] In challenging this requirement, enslaved men used various methods to escape the slave patrollers when they clandestinely visited spouses living on a different plantation.[21]

William Williams's aforementioned novel *Diary of Llewelyn Penrose* is crucial for understanding how British migrants in the eighteenth century clung to certain folk rituals and shared them with other groups throughout the Americas. Given that enslaved people and poor whites fraternized in underground networks, it is reasonable to contend that a group of Black men and women, at some unknown point, adopted the broomstick wedding for themselves.[22] Alternatively, it seems clear that enslavers who actively invaded slaves' private spaces had a role in bringing it to their plantations. It is difficult to find any clarity in this question since the communities who used it were illiterate, rendering historical documents scant. Beyond the reference to the aforementioned wedding in 1814, we simply do not know when enslaved people in the United States *first* started jumping the broom. Colonial historians Philip D. Morgan and Donald R. Wright have proposed that the origins of the broomstick wedding among antebellum slaves "may well lie in the eighteenth century, but no trace of its existence has been found."[23] Some authors, however, still place the broomstick ceremony in the colonial period through an incorrect interpretation of sources.[24]

For example, several scholars have speculated that one of the earliest paintings of a slave gathering, entitled "The Old Plantation," dated around 1790–1800, displays a broomstick wedding since one of the enslaved figures holds a long staff slightly below his knees while standing in the center of the picture. Anthropologist Jerome Handler, however, correctly dubs this interpretation "far-fetched," since no activity resembling a broom jumping is depicted in the painting.[25] Another argues that this gathering is centered in a diasporic reinterpretation of the "Juba" dance found in western Africa.[26] These past misinterpretations were understandable, as scholarship on broomstick weddings was significantly underdeveloped and its origins largely unknown. Even formerly

"The Old Plantation," Abby Aldrich Rockefeller Folk Art Museum, Colonial Williamsburg, Virginia; courtesy of www.slaveryimages.org, reference: NW0159.

enslaved people interviewed by the Works Progress Administration (WPA) in the 1930s never spoke of its origins; they simply knew it existed and attested to its reality. Thus, it is nearly impossible to know with any certainty when enslaved communities in the United States first jumped the broom or how they initially felt about it.

For the period preceding 1800, two scenarios may explain the general absence of descriptions for enslaved marriage rituals.[27] First, most comments on colonial slave marriage were written by itinerant ministers, who were more interested in discussing morality and conversion, rather than the rituals enslaved people practiced themselves. Second, white commentators in this period preferred to describe the plantation's economic viability rather than analyze slave rituals. John Brickell's travels through North Carolina in 1737 revealed that the enslaved generally performed marriages "amongst themselves."[28] He implies that slaveowners were not terribly concerned with Africans' reproductive practices, nor did they attempt to thrust Christian morality upon them. Euro-American colonists could grow the enslaved population simply through purchase. Thus, enslaved people in colonial North America remained largely unfamiliar with, or simply indifferent toward, European marital practices. These circumstances allowed Black men to draw from their ancestral homelands when courting women. Is it possible broomstick weddings were featured in some colonial slave weddings? Perhaps, but references to broomstick weddings in the United States are most prominent in the 1800s.

By 1808 the transatlantic slave trade was illegal in the United States, which forced enslavers to adjust their approach toward expanding their labor force. Some enslaved communities in North America had already yielded an American-born population through natural increase by the late eighteenth century, and enslavers capitalized on the value of Black people for both work and sale. Concurrently, areas of Virginia had exhausted the soil through overly intensive farming, causing some slaveholders to experience a net loss in their exports. The U.S. empire was also expanding to the west, and conquered territories were divided into "slave" or "free." By the mid-nineteenth century the southern "slave states" stretched from eastern Texas to eastern Virginia, enabling a domestic slave trade, in which one million people were forcibly removed from their families and communities and sold through both interregional and interstate trading.[29] Older plantations along the eastern seaboard provided bodies for the auction block, making their money by selling them to newly developed plantations in states like Mississippi, Louisiana, and Texas.[30] Though U.S. law forbade the international acquisition of enslaved laborers, no laws obstructed slave traders from selling human property within the borders of the United States. Since their marriages were not legally recognized, the severance of wives from husbands and parents from children was not just hauntingly inhumane, but entirely legal. For their part, slaveholders held a cynical understanding of enslaved people's marriages, as they understood them only through monetary benefits. Most obviously, they pressed enslaved couples to produce the children who would fill the future labor force. But as historian Tera Hunter argues, slaveholders also promoted marriage to discourage rebellion and promote a sense of contentment upon the plantation: "slave masters learned that it was to their advantage to promote marriage and families . . . it mollified the slaves. . . . It gave them incentives to remain on their plantations, as opposed to running away."[31] In essence, enslavers held little respect for Black people's matrimonial ties; all that mattered is that enslaved couples were actively breeding and not resisting. As the formerly enslaved James Curry explained, he knew that his enslaver simply viewed him as "money," and as with most slaveholders, expected a return on his investment.[32]

Lasting from 1800 to 1860, the domestic slave trade rendered familial stability especially precarious. Family members were separated and sold on auction blocks.[33] Enslaved people were forced to overcome the terror of displacement and many responded by building new kinship communities through remarriage. In certain respects, broomstick weddings served a function in quickly reestablishing familial bonds in unfamiliar areas. Emanuel Elmore recounted that when his father was sold to Alabama from South Carolina, he married another woman: "Pa just jumped the broom for both of 'em," he said.[34] Thus, not only did Elmore's father jump the broom hoping to reestablish his domestic attachments, he also carried the ritual to a new plantation. It is important to consider how the repetition of such rituals linked various enslaved communities to one another. As historian Walter Johnson argues, enslaved people had "a common culture that stretched from Maryland to Texas" as a result of the rapid displacements of the slave trade.[35] Though individual plantations were unique, enslaved migrants who carried the broomstick wedding throughout the antebellum South created cultural links among them.

## Forced or Voluntary?

The extent to which slaveowners interfered in an enslaved population's own cultural expressions is difficult to know. Each plantation was different, and the mentality of the individual enslaver largely dictated the degree to which they imposed their own values upon the enslaved. An analysis of 159 broomstick weddings discussed in the narratives of formerly enslaved Americans interviewed by both independent researchers and those employed by the WPA reveals that slaveowners did not generally have a significant role in initiating, or even encouraging, these ceremonies.[36] As will be shown, coercion certainly occurred within these marital ceremonies, but the general contention that enslavers forced this particular ritual upon the enslaved is inflated. A slaveholder's presence at a slave wedding surely displayed their authoritative position, but we must peruse the sources to determine how enslaved people adapted such rituals toward their own needs and desires. We misunderstand the dynamism of enslaved people's cultural developments if we suggest such rituals were simply produced through the owner's coercion. Though several enslavers may have introduced the custom to the plantation community, the diversity in how enslaved people performed it throughout the South suggests that African Americans tailored the ceremony to fit it to their own expressive purposes.

In reviewing the testimonies of the formerly enslaved who were interviewed in the early twentieth century, I uncovered 159 narratives that refer to the broomstick wedding in various degrees of detail. This sample collectively challenges previous arguments that maintained "the broomstick ritual was

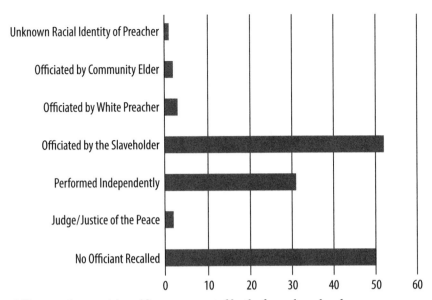

Officiants at broomstick weddings as recounted by the formerly enslaved.

almost universally imposed on slaves by the masters."[37] The imposition argument is premised upon the idea that the slaveowner's presence at the ceremony, alongside the coercive language some used when marrying enslaved people, demonstrate that the enslaved had little control over their marital rites. However, in the case of the formerly enslaved people's testimonies a few problems exist with claiming that coercive language equals a coerced ceremony. For instance, a previous study that used this method found that only twenty-three out of one hundred narratives noted coercive language, which is hardly a majority.[38] Additionally, if one reexamines these narratives closely, many of them do not contain clearly coercive language. One respondent used by this study was named Will Dill, whose testimony claimed that "his father and mother were married by a 'jack-leg' [bogus] preacher who, when told that they wanted to get married, had them both to jump backwards and forwards over a broom. He then told them that they were man and wife."[39] In this narrative the jack-leg preacher did not use any abusive language and the enslaver was not present in the description.[40] The imposition argument is based on the statement "had them jump." Similarly, Callie Williams's narrative is cited by one author to denote imposition: "When any of de slaves wanted to get married dey would go to de big house and tell marster and he'd get his broomstick and say . . . 'Jine hands and jump de broomstick and you is married.'"[41] In this case the enslaver is present, but that does not mean the custom was forced upon them. Such ceremonies hardly appear coercive, but some have argued that the words "had them jump" or the master's improvised position as minister, connotes a forced enactment. Numerous other accounts that employed identical phrases hold similar problems.[42]

Coercing enslaved people to perform a *specific* ritual was not a frequent occurrence.[43] Slaveholders were typically prone to demonstrate their authority through more assertive methods, such as forced mating or sexual violence. In one of the more revolting descriptions, Sam and Louisa Everett recalled that their marriage ceremony under slavery included their performing sexual acts upon each other while their enslaver observed: "He told us what we must git busy and do in his presence, and we had to do it. After that we were considered man and wife."[44] In this case, forced breeding is present through more sadistic methods and demonstrates that slaveowners certainly held more vicious means for imposing their wills than encouraging enslaved people to use a European folk custom. But even if coercive phrases are used as definitive evidence, only eighteen narratives out of 159 states that the slaveowners used this type of language, amounting to roughly 11.3 percent.[45] Scholars should separate the slaveholder's influence from his or her presence. In certain cases, slaveholding couples were present at the ceremony, but they appear peripheral to the actual enactment of the ritual. In the narrative of Charlie King, for instance, the "Master and mistress were present at the wedding. The broom was laid down on the floor, the couple held each other's hands and stepped backward over it, then the Master told the crowd that the couple were man and wife."[46] The owners in this case were cited as observers during the slaves' reverse broomstick jump, and the slaveholder only interjects by announcing his recognition that they were man and wife. In some cases religious figures were also involved in the broomstick ceremony. Willis Cofer remembered that a white preacher initiated the broomstick ceremony and did not attest to any other influence.[47] This does not mean the slaveholder held no influence, but it is important to note that Cofer did not feel the need to mention any interference. For most people the oppressor's presence would have been worthy of note, but the narratives do not collectively suggest they were present in many weddings.

One way to comprehend the collective testimonials is to note that broomstick weddings held different connotations depending upon the plantation's unique culture. In Hattie Cole's account, "De cullud fo'ks jus' 'gree 'twix demse'ves dat dey be man an' wife . . . [and] deys have ceremony dat deys 'ranged. 'Twas steppin' over de broom together dat am put on de flooah, wid thar hands clasped."[48] In this instance the enslaved arranged the ceremony independently and selected their partner apart from the slaveowner's approbation. Among such narratives, 39 percent reveal that a slaveholder was involved in the wedding, while the remainder narratives either suggest he was an observer or not involved or simply do not refer to the slaveholder at all.[49] In certain cases, the master's presence at the ceremony was remembered as a small detail, as in the testimony of former slave Joe Barnes: "Massa marry de folks in de broomstick style. Us don't have de party but sometime us sing and play games."[50] Wedding ceremonies ultimately depended on multifaceted negotiations between enslavers and the enslaved, and no plantation was the same. We cannot definitively say that slaveholders forced enslaved people to use a specific ceremony; nor can we claim all enslaved people wholeheartedly embraced the broomstick tradition.

What can be said is that a small percentage of the accounts suggest any forceful language was used prior to the enslaved couples crossing over the broomstick, and, with exception to those who claimed they were "civilizing" the enslaved, many slaveholders were indifferent to the actual ceremony. If slaveowners wanted to showcase the union with a ceremony, they usually opted for a Christian format. Sometimes they jumped the broom because "that was all the marriage they knowed about"; other times they preferred it above other rituals, and at certain points it was initiated through the slaveowner's encouragement.[51] Some slaveholders ensured that broomstick weddings were festive occasions, as manifested in Jeptha Choice's account of a slave wedding in Texas, where the "white folks" formed a ring around the couple prior to the jump.[52] The white audience's celebratory ring suggests that for a brief moment this group of elite whites was captivated by the ceremonial structure of a slave wedding. In another rendition, Charlotte Willis recalled that her grandparents' broomstick wedding took place on "the big house steps" in front of the slaveowner and invited guests.[53] Slaveholders had various reasons for involving themselves in the ceremony. Within the plantation they wielded their authority to restrict autonomy, functioning as a sinister intruder into enslaved people's private lives. When discussing their methods of slaveholding to the public, they often promoted slave weddings as a paternalistic humanitarian façade for outside observers.

A primary issue in trying to pin down the broomstick wedding as either an act of resistance or an example of the enslaver's imposition is that most formerly enslaved testimonials do not provide enough details to do so. In addition, interviewers rarely asked follow-up questions about the broomstick wedding to understand why or how it was performed. Specific questionnaires distributed to WPA interviewers were "often partially or totally ignored,

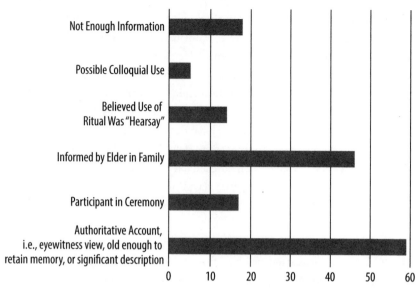

Personal testimonials about jumping the broom as recounted by the formerly enslaved.

frequently resulting in rambling or trivial comments,"[54] but they rarely pressed the respondent for additional information. WPA interviews, on the other hand, did not have pre-scripted expectations. Hence the interviews invite the researcher to engage in questions such as: Did the interviewees participate in the ceremony themselves or were they told of it by an older relative? Did they witness it? Did they use the expression "jump the broom"? Were the connotations positive, or something else?

Many reflections resemble that of Ella Booth of Mississippi: "When my mammy and daddy got married, dey just 'jumped over de broom'—den dey wuz married."[55] Booth provides little context for the ceremony, and the interviewer placed quotation marks around the phrase "jumped over de broom." It is possible she was using the expression figuratively, meaning that her parents might not have physically jumped the broom, but simply took their own vows and quietly started living together—a not uncommon practice, even if it was ineffectual in protecting their marriage from a violent rupture. Regardless, Booth's brief reference to jumping the broomstick exemplifies the difficulty in obtaining adequate details for many enslaved weddings. Since most references to broomstick ceremonies come from the memories of African Americans who were decades removed from the actual event, scholars must examine the sources providing the richest descriptions. Only by collectively analyzing these diverse references can we engage

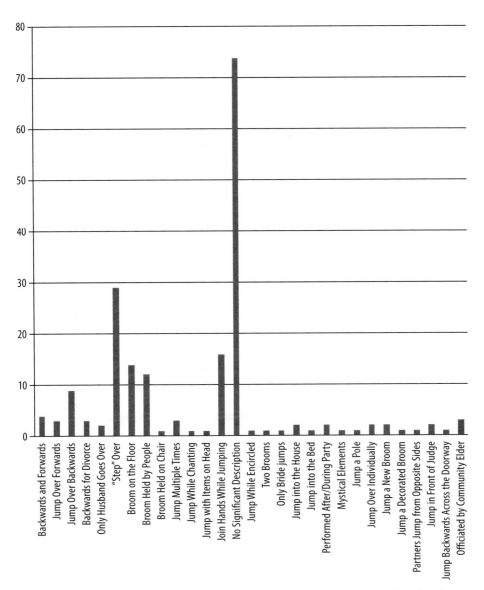

Different ways enslaved people jumped the broom as recounted by the formerly enslaved.

in a rigorous critique of the historical broomstick wedding and determine its meaning.

Enslaved people dwelled in complex, culturally multifaceted environments. To ensure their psychological survival, they created communities that thrived on innovation. If Black preachers were available on the plantations, the enslaved community could copy the Christian marriage to the best of their ability.

Some attended the weddings of white people and acquired a desire for the practices associated with elite whiteness, while others did not. Patsy Bland, formerly enslaved in Kentucky, remembered "seeing a wedding of white folks on the place in the big house"[56] Using the resources available to them, African Americans had to be innovative with practices that, on the surface, appeared to lack any meaningful qualities. Enslaved communities stretching throughout Appalachia and into the Bayous of Louisiana and eastern Texas all injected meaning into the broomstick ritual by adding their own creative novelties.

## Brooms in Life and Folklore

Though one might suspect the broom held little value outside its primary task of sweeping, the testimonies of the formerly enslaved collectively reveal that broomsticks were deeply imbedded in many facets of their cultural, folkloric, and domestic life. For many it reflected a symbol of resistance that contested the assumptions of slaveowners who assumed enslaved people's living spaces did not meet Euro-American standards of cleanliness. In one instance, Georgia plantation mistress Fanny Kemble presumed that slaves' cabins were dirty and marched over to the quarters and began sweeping their floors. After she berated the enslaved women for apparently ignoring the duty of sweeping, they cleverly retorted that white women were known to keep their homes just as dirty, "and they could not be expected to be cleaner than white women."[57] A shrewd response, it reveals how the plantation mistress's demand for cleanliness portrayed the height of hypocrisy, considering that their homes were cleaned by enslaved people who, despite a harsh and debilitating workload, were simultaneously expected to maintain their own houses. Kemble's anecdote was based upon her own assumptions and did not consider the fact that enslaved people lived in small cabins surrounded by dirt, wildlife, and a harsh climate. However, many narratives reflect a conscious effort to maintain a cleanly domestic space, and they frequently refer to the broomstick as a central tool in maintaining this standard.[58]

Historians of agriculture, medicine, and maritime culture show how enslaved people maximized their environment's potential by engaging with holistic remedies, developing innovative technologies, and harnessing the cosmological meanings of water and earth to psychologically survive their enslavement.[59] Maintaining a cleanly space provided order to a life often chaotic, and enslaved people used the surrounding materials to manufacture brooms to maintain their households. Though slaveholders provided tools for economic output, enslaved people were required to furnish their own for personal use. Frederick Douglass ranked those who made "corn brooms" as among the most "staid, sober, thinking and industrious ones of our number."[60] For her part Della Fountain recounted, "We had no brooms . . . so we made brush brooms to sweep our floors."[61] For practical purposes, members of her community independently constructed their sweeping materials when the slaveholder withheld the required materials. By using the first-person plural "we," Fountain suggests the object of her own community was distinct from the standard broom used by enslavers or white Americans more broadly. Her broom was an earthy object manufactured for the practical needs of her community. In comparing various testimonies, we find that the materials out of which broomsticks were made varied, but the means of making them were similar.

For instance, "sage brooms" appear to have been made of straws of "broom sage," which is found throughout the rural South.[62] A member of the grass family, broom sage is a high golden grass that grows in abandoned pastures or unused fields, sometimes up to five feet in height.[63] It provided the perfect material for constructing a light and effective broom, which was easy to use and easy to store. The nomenclature for such objects also depended on the local dialect. One respondent from Missouri claimed they swept their floors with "brooms made of weeds, which we called broom weeds."[64] Others simply called them "straw brooms."[65] Many used the term "broom corn" when referring to those made from sorghum, while others called them "brush brooms."[66] Solomon Lambert, formerly enslaved in Arkansas, claimed that on his plantation the brush broom served as the matrimonial object, while the brooms used to sweep the floor were made from "sage grass cured like hay."[67] While he did not elaborate on the distinction, some testimonials claimed that a ceremonial broom must be "new" for the occasion. Another testimonial indicates that the matrimonial broom was made from "sedge straw, tied with a string."[68]

In some cases, broom straws formed by tightly binding the straws together at the top and some ways down the length of the object, making a handle and pole, while leaving the remainder of the straws loose.[69] The straw was also cured before it was tied together.[70] Young people were often the ones who gathered the materials to make the brooms, and its process of assembly was more methodical than one might initially assume. Enslaved people "raised everything" they "lived on," and gathering materials for broomsticks was a crucial aspect of their work schedule.[71] Millie Evans remembered that she gathered broom sage for the community's "winter brooms" in the same way

A picture of a plantation broom. "Sol's wife, Aphrodite, is a specimen of maternal health and vigor," from Pennington, *A Woman Rice Planter*, 262.

they gathered "other winter stuff."[72] Her testimony reflects the forethought enslaved people employed by collecting larger amounts of storable items to last through the colder months. If it snowed, for instance, the frost could potentially damage the sage brush and make broom construction a more difficult process. If such approaches reflect the entire region, it is possible that the brooms used by enslaved people could be remodeled based upon seasonal needs and used in wedding ceremonies throughout the south.[73] Gathering and storing sage for future curing guaranteed that if the current brooms were lost or damaged, other materials were readily available to make new ones.

The broom was used for various purposes both inside and outside the slave cabin. Multiple narratives refer to their use on "dirt floors" inside. These floors were made by pouring mud mixed with a thickener into a foundation and allowing it to expand in the heat over a few weeks.[74] One respondent who claimed that dirt floors were the "style" upon his plantation said that the enslaved people kept their floors "clean and white." Though their cabins presented difficulties for maintaining pristine cleanliness, multiple narratives contend that enslaved people persistently cleaned their cabins and had a sense of pride in their work.[75]

The broom was also used outside. Like Black populations in the Caribbean and West Africa, enslaved people in the United States viewed the front yard "as an extension of the house, where most of the daily domestic activities outside of work occurred."[76] Annie Young, formerly enslaved in Tennessee, noted that her jobs included doing dishes and keeping the "yard clean wid weed brush brooms."[77] Though it might seem self-defeating to sweep outdoors, the fact is that domestic animals roamed plantations, especially in the areas surrounding the slave quarters. Though Young provides few details, she mentioned that she also raised chickens, which are notoriously dirty animals. Sweeping chicken feces and the feed used to fatten them was an important means for curtailing the diseases they harbored.

Despite its associations with cleanliness and marriage, the broom did not always serve virtuous purposes. At certain moments brooms were used as weapons for punishment, wielded by forces both within and outside the community. Mohammah Baquaqua noted that his enslaver was once dissatisfied with his labor and "took a broomstick" to him.[78] Josie Jordan recounted that her mistress would beat her mother with a "broom stick" if she did not quickly complete her tasks.[79] This "broomstick" was likely of the variety with a wooden handle, as this particular mistress was extremely violent and would prefer a harder weapon when punishing the enslaved. Outside direct physical abuse, some slaveowners exploited their unpaid labor force by monetizing the broomsticks created by enslaved hands. On one plantation, an "old Negro was hired to make brooms of broom corn grown on the plantation at 6¼ cents each."[80] By using enslaved labor to manufacture an object for sale, slaveholders maximized the contours of plantation capitalism. The histories of slavery and capitalism reveal that the slave labor camps functioned like machines to amplify the wealth of an emerging elite.[81] In this case, even slave-produced broomsticks held capitalist value. Sometimes enslaved people wielded the broomstick against one another for the purposes of establishing authority or inflicting punishment. A woman named "Aunt Roxy" recalled that her mother beat her with a broom upon discovering that she stole and ate a chicken her mother prepared, though Roxy claimed the culinary reward made the beating tolerable: "Us didn't keer; de brush brooms didn't hurt nigh lak de chickens taste good."[82] One could presume the broom was meant to not inflict significant damage. Broomsticks were not only widely available in most cabins, but their light weight and maneuverability made them a choice weapon for enslaved people seeking a swift form of justice without leveling bodily harm.

Given that Black southerners acquired forms of European and Euro-American folklore throughout generations, one finds they had similar ideas regarding the broomstick's association with supernatural elements, be they positive or negative. Beliefs in witchcraft and other superstitions were prevalent throughout the rural South among both Black and white populations, and brooms could be thought to block malevolent spirits. Hamp Kennedy remembered that the sound of a screech owl was considered a bad omen and that required all who resided in their cabins to throw salt in a fire and "throw a broom 'cross de do[or]."[83] Placing a broom across the door ensured evil spirits could not cross the doorstep, especially those who attacked people as they slept. In the context of slavery, one could suggest this practice provided a sense of agency, or control for the enslaved, where otherwise they had none.

A few narratives provide associations between the matrimonial broomstick and mystical forces. One interviewer noted her respondent was a practitioner of voodoo and categorized the broomstick wedding as a superstitious ritual.[84] Betty Curlett's narrative reveals the self-contradictory nature of certain beliefs in that while she noted that enslaved people often stepped over the broom to get married, she said in her next statement that "you can't get nobody—colored folks I mean—to step over a broom; they say it bad luck."[85] No further explanation is provided, making any effort to reconcile the two statements difficult. Many of the formerly enslaved did associate certain elements of the supernatural with brooms, but most interviewees focused on their practical uses. This does not negate the possibility that deeper meanings of the wedding's symbolism did not exist across the South, it simply was not frequently mentioned by the formerly enslaved.

Though important for the immediate purpose of cleaning, the broomstick's presence upon the antebellum plantation unveils a larger point about social and cultural life. It provides a reference point for understanding how enslaved people, despite being devoid of legal rights to property, independently constructed an object that allowed them to control certain areas of their environment. As Clifton Ellis and Rebecca Ginsburg argue, the ability of enslaved women to claim "certain parts of the quarter yards" enabled them to continue traditions of housekeeping and landscaping extending back to West Africa.[86] Despite a legal structure that curtailed their mobility and autonomy, broomstick makers engaged in a creative production that allowed members of their community to maintain a sense of control over their environment, even if it was only for a few brief moments.

## Ritual Innovation and the Broomstick Wedding

Conceptualizing the broomstick's unique position among enslaved southerners provides the necessary context to understand its utility for their matrimony. At certain points they opted to jump the broomstick and rejected the
ceremony sponsored by the slaveholder. Dora Roberts of Georgia explained
that her master would read a passage to the couple, declare them married, and
provide them with passes to see each other, "but de slabs dey got togedder an'
have dem jump over de broomstick an' have a big celebration an' dance an'
make merry 'til morning and it's time for work agin."[87] In this instance the
community endured the slaveowner's ostentations and afterward celebrated
among themselves. Similarly, Stephen Varner of Alabama revealed that upon
conclusion of the broomstick ritual, "the slaves would gather around and
sing and dance for the bride and groom."[88] In another instance, Amanda
McDaniel remembered witnessing a white minister presiding over a broomstick ceremony on a neighboring plantation.[89] Cross-plantation contact could
surely influence cultural exchanges between communities.[90] These variegated
approaches reveal the broomstick wedding was not a single, homogenous
folk ritual.

Thus, in one account, the broom was placed next to the marriage bed, and
the couple jumped over the broom into bed.[91] Another innovation required
the couple to balance objects like glasses of water or candles on their heads
while crossing over the broomstick.[92] Some groups would simply "step" over
the broom, while others jumped over three times, chanting "I marry you"
after each leap.[93] In the latter case, the number three likely held symbolic connotations since it encompasses the totality of the life cycle in three stages, as
one goes from beginning, to the middle, and arrives at the end. In religious
contexts, the Christian God is portrayed as a Trinitarian being, and declarations of divorce in Islamic cultures require a husband to state the phrase "I
divorce you" three times in a practice dubbed the "Triple Talaq."[94] No evidence
exists to determine whether the enslaved practitioners were conscious of
these possible linkages, but it does reveal how symbolism entered the ritual.

Although most respondents did not often elaborate on what was involved
in jumping the broom,[95] we do a have more extended commentary from a
minister named William H. Robinson in his 1913 autobiography. Noting that
in his eastern North Carolina community the "house slaves" jumped the
broom, he added that "if the couple marrying was young, the young mistress
held a broom stick knee high. If the bride and groom were more advanced in
years, older ladies held it."[96] These ceremonies were also replete with a "wedding

feast" and an "old negro preacher" who repeated a memorized script to the couple before announcing them "man and wife" following their jump over the broomstick. Though Robinson's description has some detail, it still leaves unanswered questions. Who were the "older ladies?" Were they enslaved? It appears strange that the young plantation mistress participates in one form, but is then replaced by enslaved elders in another version. It is possible that the young mistress was more interested in the marriages of those closer to her own age. Many white southern women claimed to have a kinship with the enslaved women with whom they were raised and excitedly discussed slaves' wedding nuptials in their private writings.[97] Regarding the preacher, one wonders if he was a necessary component to the ritual, or an appendage. Did his presence provide solace to the enslaved or the enslaver? In many respects, Robinson's selection ignites as many questions as it answers. What he did say a bit later was that marriage under slavery was a "farce" due to the fact that it granted the couple no legal protection.

Though the broom was widely used in marital rituals, sometimes it was replaced with sticks or poles. Annie Burton's 1909 memoir *Memories of Childhood's Slavery Days* noted, "If a slave man and woman wished to marry, a party would be arranged some Saturday night among the slaves. The marriage ceremony consisted of the pair jumping over a stick."[98] Benjamin Henderson of Georgia noted that enslavers attended such weddings and selected either a "straw broom" or a "pole" as the ritual instrument.[99] On certain plantations sweeping utensils were likely a premium, requiring an engaged couple to replace the broom in their own ceremony. Given that Burton referenced a "stick" and did not note if it was an actual broom, we can surmise that her community organized the event and substituted the matrimonial object. In their eyes this ceremony was as spiritually binding as any other.

Many brooms were jumped in the enslaver's presence, and under his direction. For example, George Womble, formerly enslaved in Georgia, witnessed a broomstick wedding at the slaveowner's house: "A broom was placed in the center of the floor and the couple was told to hold hands. After joining hands they were commanded to jump over the broom and then to turn around and jump back. After this they were pronounced man and wife."[100] Throughout his narrative Womble stated that slaveowners seemed particularly interested in pairing enslaved couples, emphasizing that a "small" man was not allowed to marry a "large, robust woman." While it is clear from Womble's description that the master took control of conjugal arrangements, it is not clear if the ritual steps of the ceremony were developed by him or by the enslaved. However, this narrative suggests that jumping the broom was practiced amidst difficult circumstances, in which enslaved people tried to determine the best approach to seal their domestic engagements.

Womble's account of the broomstick wedding includes the notable detail that upon concluding the initial jump the couple turned back and made a second leap to their original position. This goes against the modern belief that the betrothed jump into the domestic state together and leave behind their old lives. Though Womble provides no discussion of the reasons for the second leap, one could surmise that the ceremony represented the circumstances of slavery itself. Domestic attachments were never guaranteed in American bondage, even if a ceremony was performed. In jumping back over the broom and returning to their original position as one, this community ritual might convey the notion that, even if separated, they were still together in spirit. Alternatively, it may resemble the ceremony relayed at the beginning of this chapter, in which the couple jumps in multiple directions in a ritualized manner. It may simply lack the details contained in that secondhand account, revealing another difficulty in fully drawing out the broomstick wedding's intended meaning. Ultimately, it is apparent that Womble's reference unveils many layers surrounding the dynamics of culture and power upon the plantation.

Elsewhere, as in parts of Georgia, jumping over the broomstick backward to initiate the marriage was not uncommon.[101] Folklore collected from central Georgia in 1899 provides some context. People in this area commonly believed that stepping forward over a broom was "bad luck," and one must always "step over it backwards."[102] Hence it made sense to invert the customary practice. Since it was not unique to a single plantation, but spread to neighboring areas, it is likely that these different communities held increased contact with one another and spurred a cultural exchange.

Other narratives reveal definite attempts to dignify the broomstick ceremony and enhance its performative and symbolic value. One respondent from Tennessee recollected the following ceremony: "Dey goes in the parlor and each carry a broom. . . . De woman put her broom front de man and he put he broom front de woman. Dey face one 'nother and step cross de brooms at de same time to each other and takes hold of hands and dat marry dem."[103] In a slight variation, a formerly enslaved person from Baltimore County, Maryland, noted that he and his wife-to-be both jumped over the broom from opposite sides, but did not mention that they interlocked hands.[104] Another couple began by holding each other's right hands, but during the leap switched hands and interlocked them.[105] These rituals exceed the simpler form of stepping over, as detailed in many testimonies.[106] Joining hands and crossing over symbolized the deep bonds of enslaved couples. The performative value in each ceremonial step provided celebratory measure and an expression of commitment for those whose familial stability was in constant turbulence.

The wedding was often a community event. Victoria Lawson, enslaved in Mississippi, recounted that "sometimes dey would hab a crowd together and dey would put de broom on de flo and he'd jump ober it, en de girl would jump ober it. Dey would do dis sebel times and den dey was maied."[107] The ceremony recounted here resembles a few of the aforementioned ones. First, Lawson mentions a crowd, presumably surrounding the practitioners. This reflects the emphasis on one's community similarly articulated in other narratives. Second, the couple repeated the process several times, though the precise number is not disclosed. Lawson does not elaborate on the reason for the multiple leaps, nor does she describe the motions used. But when placed alongside the vignette that opened this book, in which the respondent went into great detail about the ceremonial process and their possible meanings, it is possible that enslaved couples on this plantation were enacting a ritual that was far more significant than inferred by this brief statement.

Another narrative that focuses on the broom itself indicates that it was placed at a doorway. According to Caroline Johnson Harris of Virginia, the wedding officiant laid it across the entrance of the enslaved couple's future home. The folklore surrounding this ceremony suggested it was "bad luck" to touch the broomstick, and "folks always stepped high 'cause dey didn't want no spell cast on 'em."[108] Harris further maintained that whoever "teched de stick was gonna die first." In this instance, we have greater detail surrounding the folk beliefs of this community. Whereas a few formerly enslaved people claimed that "bad luck" followed those who unsuccessfully jumped the broom, few were as specific as Harris. Though verifying this claim proves nearly impossible, the fact that some believed death was the consequence for failing to clear the broom reveals how communities aligned their beliefs with the supernatural and structured their ritual forms accordingly. One can surmise the European concept connecting brooms with negative omens was preserved through oral transmissions and conveyed throughout the southern region, and were eventually reimagined by the enslaved communities who inherited the custom.

## Gender Dynamics, Agency, and Jumping the Broom

Scholars note that gender distinctions played a key role in determining enslaved people's daily life.[109] A plantation's gender dynamics were manifested in various ways during the wedding ceremony, and jumping over the broom is particularly relevant for analyzing how enslaved people interpreted the domestic state. In certain cases, the broomstick symbolized an enslaved woman's ability to choose her spouse. Though men initiated courtship, some women used the object to gain the man's attention or affirm her desires. Sallie Johnson of Austin, Texas, noted that if a woman accepted a man's proposal, "he had to come to his sweetheart's cabin . . . and there would be a broomstick across the woman's door entrance, and he had to jump over it . . . and that act made 'em man and wife."[110] In this instance, the man proposed to the woman, but it is not clear if she was required to verbalize her affirmation or rejection. It appears the broom's positioning served as her initial way to promote a positive or negative result. One can also perceive an intentional claim of ownership for the prospective bride, as Johnson notes it was the "woman's door entrance." The suitor was invited to her space only after she affirmed her consent. This entire scenario likely alleviated stress, as the woman is often expected to make an abrupt decision following a suitor's marriage proposal.

Utilizing the broomstick during the entire courtship and marriage ritual displayed how these communities understood the gender constructions imbedded in this matrimonial process. In a similar scenario, one formerly enslaved respondent recounted, "pappy and mammy had been married jes' by havin' pappy jump backwards across a broomstick, dat was placed across de open door."[111] Though given in a secondhand, nonchalant manner, this account suggests the woman controlled the contours of the courtship by placing the broomstick at the door of her home. The man must first be approved and invited to complete the ritual requirements before he is accepted into his bride's house. The door must first remain open with the broomstick visibly placed across the threshold. The reason for him jumping backward is not entirely clear, though it is likely related to the aforementioned belief that going forward over a broom was bad luck, and one must step backward over the broom to avoid misfortune.[112]

Women sometimes presided over broomstick weddings, a fact that could suggest that certain areas have matriarchal leanings and viewed female elders as the foundation of the community. Caroline Johnson Harris recollected that on one Virginia plantation a matriarch named "Ant Sue" led the ceremony and commanded significant respect:

Didn't have to ask Marsa or nothin'. Just go to Ant Sue an' tell her you want to git mated. . . . She called all de slaves arter tasks to pray fo' de union dat God was gonna make. Pray we stay together and have lots of chillum an' none of 'em git sol' way from de parents. . . . Fo' we step over it

she ast us once mo' if we was sho we wanted to git married. 'Course we
say yes. Den she say, "In de eyes of Jesus step into Holy land of mat-de-
money." When we step cross the broomstick, we was married.[113]

The significance here is that it was conducted exclusively by enslaved people
with no evidence of white interference. The words of Aunt Sue's ceremony
were pertinent to the needs of this Virginia community, which likely feared
the destruction of their kinship ties due to the domestic slave trade that
sold African Americans from the Upper South to the slave states of the Old
Southwest.

Anne Harrison of Virginia noted that some slaveholders allowed the enslaved to have an autonomous ceremony. In this account, enslaved couples first
requested his permission, and, if granted, he simply said, "Tell Aunt Lucky to
go 'haid and marry you." Announcing the coming marriage to the community, Aunt Lucky conducted the ceremony by having the enslaved community
"form a ring" around the couple; then she "read sumpin' from de Bible, an'
den she put de broomstick down an' dey locked dey arms together an' jumped
over it. Den dey was married."[114] Women like Aunt Sue and Aunt Lucky provided psychological stability for a group of people who were in a state of constant anxiety. The matriarch's ability to lead the broomstick wedding reflects
the community's respect for her wisdom. Though not legally binding, the
prayers and blessings upon their future children at least provided the necessary consolation and empowered the couple to confirm their marriage.

In many cases where the broomstick wedding was combined with Christian elements, a preacher, usually a Black man, presided. Sometimes these
ministers were not taken seriously, as when Will Dill dismissed his parents'
officiant as a "jack-leg" preacher, though he did not necessarily contend that
jumping the broom was itself invalid.[115] Others believed the enslaved preachers were legitimate, even if they were not necessarily in charge of the ceremony. In the testimony of Tempe Durham of North Carolina, she noted that
an enslaved minister named Uncle Edmond Kirby married her and her husband, Exter. After Kirby concluded his section, however, "Marse George got
to have his little fun" by having them both jump backwards over the broom.
According to this plantation's rules, whoever touched the handle was the sub-
ordinate partner. Tempe easily completed the leap without touching it, but
Exter was clumsy and toppled over the broomstick. Following this snafu,
Marse George exclaimed that Exter would be "bossed [by Tempe] 'twell he
skeered to speak."[116] In this case, the broomstick custom seems to have been
thrust upon a community for the enslaver's entertainment. One could imag-

ine severe retribution for rejecting his attempt at "fun," especially when it was at the expense of those he enslaved. Perhaps the community was conditioned to both perform and enjoy the custom, but their enjoyment does not negate the fact that the master viewed it as a joke to be used after a solemn occasion. It was a malicious spectacle that undermined the husband's masculinity and remind him that he was not a "man," in the sense that he held no recognized control over his household. Using the broomstick ceremony was not always a conscious choice by the betrothed, and in this case the participants held little choice while the slaveholder was present.

In a final example from Virginia, told through the lens of a white northerner named Mary Ashton Rice Livermore, the ceremony was led by an enslaved elder named Uncle Aaron, a man endowed with supernatural gifts of healing and conjure. Aaron's position was determined by his wisdom of the supernatural, specifically his association with supernatural philosophies that combined Christian ideas with traditional African practices. Combined with his age, his gifts commanded significant respect from the community.[117] According to Livermore, the enslaved viewed him as a "man of many gifts—a conjurer who could raise evil spirits—and a God-man who wore a charm, and could become invisible at any moment, if anyone attempted to harm him."[118] The author carefully detailed the ritual process, noting that the ceremony was performed at "Uncle Aaron's house, and under his auspices" and he emphasized the ceremony was as "solem' as a buryin'" and commanded that all present must observe the importance of the occasion.[119] Two friends of the couple held the broom off the ground. Uncle Aaron beseeched God's mercy for the bride and groom and counted to three before imploring them to jump over the object. After they successfully leaped over the broomstick, he invited the newlyweds to enjoy their first meal together at his cabin followed by a "good send-off" to the cabin where the couple established their family.[120]

Regarding the actual bride and groom, their individual performances in the ceremony could vary greatly across plantations. In some, only one person was required to jump over the broomstick for the marriage to be effected. Such was the case on a Kentucky plantation, where it was only the suitor who jumped.[121] Benjamin Henderson recounted a more elaborate process in engaging the ritual, selecting the object, and conducting the ceremony on a Georgia plantation. There, if couples wanted to marry, they needed to obtain consent from the slaveholder: "The master of the bridegroom would then pick a straw broom or a pole and give two slaves the job of holding the ends of it. To be devilish they often held the stick too high and would not lower it until the master asked them to. After the bridegroom made the jump over the stick, the knot of matrimony was considered tied."[122] Following the ceremony, numerous attendees engaged in a "frolic" that lasted throughout the night. Henderson's description encapsulates questions surrounding the agency of enslaved people, community involvement, and how the ceremony reflected gender roles.

In this case, community members participated in the ceremony and used levity to celebrate the occasion. The enslaver was present and seemed to dictate certain terms of the wedding. Henderson noted that it was the bridegroom's master who obtained the tools used in the ceremony. By acquiring and providing the matrimonial tools it appears this was a way in which the enslaver determined the man's suitability to marry the woman. The determination was likely connected to the slaveholder's consideration of breeding possibilities, and the women in these scenarios held little choice in the matter.

Alternatively, in some cases only women completed the leap. The formerly enslaved John Ellis recounted that only brides would jump over the broom and that they did so backward. In another account, women had the choice not to jump over if they had second thoughts.[123] A very different possibility comes from folklore collected from Black southerners in the early twentieth century to the effect that "any one who refuses to step over a broom . . . is also a witch."[124] Folklorist Newbell Puckett noted this belief was a carryover from Europe and that enslaved people imitated the practice of placing the "broom across the door" to ensure one's house could not be invaded by a witch.[125] Given the similarities in how the broomstick was occasionally placed at a doorway for matrimony, it seems the broomstick's use to subvert witchcraft was in some way connected to this European tradition. Those recollecting the ritual over seven decades later might not have known of these circumstances or decided not to elaborate on the sequence of events.

Some sources reveal that the husband and wife both jumped, but did so separately. Usually, the groom jumped first and awaited his bride on the other side. The notion that the man jumps first appears to assert his position as protector and provider in domestic relations, a feature also present in the ceremonies in North Wales and among the British Romani. Under slavery, though, these attributes could be only symbolic. Broomsticks could also be used in divorce proceedings among the enslaved, as it was among the Welsh. Betty Chessier of Raleigh, North Carolina, and Cora Armstrong of Junction City, Arkansas, testified that the way enslaved people "married in slavery time" was by jumping forward over the broomstick and that the way they divorced was by jumping backward over the same object.[126] Neither, however, elaborated on who could initiate the separation nor if communal endorsement was required. Many testimonies from enslaved people discuss the contours of marriage under slavery, but rarely mention divorce procedures. If couples ever separated, it was often explained as a forced split caused by the master's interference. The formerly enslaved naturally preferred to disclose how they fought for marital dignity and critiqued the hypocrisy of "Christian" slaveholders who severed their marriages. Admitting that enslaved people willingly separated from one another potentially damaged the abolitionist cause, as it could fuel the stereotypical perception among white racists that people of African descent did not respect the bonds of matrimony. The fact that both Chessier and Armstrong mentioned divorce at all is significant, as is the fact that Raleigh and Junction City are separated by nearly 1,000 miles; the latter suggests that broomstick divorces were not confined to regional practices, but likely spread throughout the antebellum South.

## Social Divisions and Broomstick Weddings

As in all communities, enslaved people existed within a social hierarchy. One's position upon the southern plantation, usually determined by labor, influenced one's marital preferences. Rosa Starke of South Carolina recounted an elaborate hierarchy that positioned enslaved domestics at the top, followed by carriage drivers, blacksmiths, and "cow men." She noted that people in these positions had "good houses and never have to work hard or git a beatin.'"[127] Placing the "common" field hands lowest in her hierarchy, she claimed that a "house gal" would never "lower herself by marryin' and matin' with a common field-hand nigger," though she did admit an enslaved man in the house would "now and then," "swoop down and mate wid a field hand's good lookin' daughter."[128]

It was not unusual for enslaved domestics to reflect white society's expectations, particularly the idea that they were closer to "whiteness" than their counterparts who labored in the fields. Consequently, most of them claimed that the broomstick ritual was reserved for those who worked the field. William Wells Brown's 1858 play *The Escape* divulged this stratification through the characters Dolly and Susan, both domestics, who insisted they would never "jump de broomstick. Dat will do for fiel' hands, but house servants ought to be 'bove dat."[129] Author Emily Clemens Pearson similarly claimed in her 1853 novel *Cousin Franck's Household* that plantation mistresses punished disobedient house slaves by forcing them to use a broomstick wedding, instead of "a pretty wedding in the parlor" with a white clergyman.[130] James Bolton, formerly enslaved in Georgia, recollected that field hands married privately by jumping the broom, but "house servants, sometimes they married on the back porch or in the back yard at the big 'ouse."[131]

In Mary Ashton Rice Livermore's autobiography, Uncle Aaron expressed a more complicated view of marriage and status. "De fiel' han's am willin' t' jump de broomstick, but when de house sarvans gwine t' marry, dey wants a white preacher . . . but de broomstick's jess as bindin' as de preacher."[132] For her part, Livermore disagreed, observing that the broomstick wedding was a fruitless gesture since slave marriages had no legal standing and could be severed at the enslaver's whim. Nevertheless, an account from Dellie Lewis, a self-described former "house servant" in Alabama, who acquired literacy through "de white folks," confirms the extent of the practice. When asked about marriage, she said that the enslaver just "read de ceremony an' couples would step off ove a broomstick for luck."[133] Following the ceremony they engaged in merriments that included dancing and feasting. According to Lewis, it was the only known custom, rendering status distinctions void since the slaveholder controlled the ritual. Lewis' narrative is one of the few that attaches an additional meaning to the custom, suggesting it was for "luck." This could mean a variety of things under slavery. Perhaps luck indicated spousal cooperation, familial happiness, or simply believing one's spouse or children might not be sold from them. Alternatively, it might reflect supernatural beliefs in keeping away evil spirits. In any event, if a slaveowner decided to assert control over the ceremony they could determine how the enslaved interpreted it. One man noted that an Alabama slaveowner required everyone to "go to the big house, an' Ol' Master had us to jump over a broom stick, and den us was considered married."[134] Marrying on the big house steps served as one method to demonstrate the enslaver's wealth and power. Charlotte Willis of Madison, Arkansas noted, "jumping over the broom . . . was the way white folks had of showing off the couples. Then it would be 'nounced from the big house steps they was man and wife."[135] Thus, slave weddings served an important function for slaveholders who wanted to demonstrate their social prestige, simultaneously demonstrating their wealth by financing the wedding and representing themselves as benevolent patriarchs who nurtured enslaved people's physical and familial well-being.

Despite the general rules surrounding the divides between those enslaved in the house against those in the field, there were always exceptions. Though divisions between enslaved domestics and field hands were real and well documented, one finds occasional reference to those who challenged the status quo. Mildred Graves of Fredericksburg, Virginia, provides one counterpoint. In a brief statement, Graves told her interviewer about her courtship under slavery. Born in 1842, she noted that her honeymoon felt "as if it was yes-tiddy." She was a "house gal," but her suitor worked in the field, making it difficult for them to see one another. One night they snuck down to a fence post, and engaged in a conversation underneath the moonlight. He proposed, and she excitedly accepted his offer. They "stepped over de broomstick" the following day, she said. Graves noted that her mistress provided her a "cast-off" dress to wear for the ceremony, but provided no further details surrounding the master or mistress's involvement. It seemed this community held some autonomy in selecting their partners and executing their nuptials. But Graves's motivations to marry her husband make the narrative especially interesting. She stated his offer was attractive due to her boredom in the plantation home: "I was tired of livin' in de house where dey wasn't no fun."[136] Indeed, those enslaved within the plantation house were expected to imitate forms of elite whiteness, and they were forced to serve the master or mistress throughout the day *and* night. Conversely, field hands performed backbreaking labor from sun up to sundown, but at nightfall they were largely free from supervision. Many formerly enslaved domestics proudly announced their status, as this supposedly denoted their superiority over those who worked the fields. However, love (and in the case of Graves, ambition to leave her circumstances) sometimes overcame such divisions and a jump over the broom solidified such commitment.

As historian Ira Berlin recently argued, the making of African America is defined by a history of "movement" and "place."[137] Peoples of African descent in North America are trapped in a cycle of constant migration (usually compelled by outside forces), and reestablishing broken kinship and homelands. The forced movements Black people endured from 1800 to 1865 instigated unique developments in the history of the broomstick wedding. As this form of matrimony traveled with the victims of the domestic slave trade, it was reinvented and innovated in each area where it landed. Though many enslaved people "jumped the broom" in the antebellum period, one finds multiple variations in how they performed it. The fact that enslaved people transformed a wedding ritual that was nonexistent in their ancestral culture is an illustration of cultural adaptation and the resiliency of oppressed people. Accepting and implementing the broomstick tradition was born through a communal need to resist domination and subversion, and its continued use through successive generations denoted group identity and solidarity. As sociologist Erika Summers-Effler argues, "Rituals generate group emotions that are linked to symbols, forming the basis for beliefs, thinking, morality, and culture."[138] Many enslaved African Americans viewed their wedding rituals as part of their cultural identity, for good or for ill.

Of course, we should not generalize and simply call the broomstick wedding a "slave ritual," presuming it was an activity that all enslaved people practiced or supported. Both quantitative and qualitative evidence does not bear this out. Enslaved domestics overwhelmingly rejected the custom. Two-thirds of those interviewed by the WPA did not even mention it; others referred to different wedding rituals. This does not necessarily discount the custom's importance in the legacies of U.S. slavery and successive cultural patterns. Jumping the broom is doubtlessly an important component of African American history, but it cannot be represented parochially. Not only was it performed differently in multiple areas, it was not universally embraced (or even known) by all enslaved people.

Another important point needs to be made regarding the silence in the archive of slavery, especially regarding marriage and the wedding ceremony. Oftentimes formerly enslaved people were embarrassed by their inability to legally marry and likely presumed the interviewer would think them immoral for living with a partner outside legal wedlock.[139] For all those who referenced their wedding celebrations, or elaborated upon their marital relations, just as many, if not more, remained silent on the issue. The collections of John B. Cade, an educator in Louisiana who helped spur the national drive to collect and transcribe the memories of the formerly enslaved, illuminates this point. Cade and his researchers followed a general guideline for questions, including those on domestic life and marriage under slavery, and the 216 collected narratives yield the following results regarding marriage: 13 used the broomstick wedding; 29 included a white preacher or the master officiating; 18 claimed no marriage ceremony occurred; 5 suggested they were not allowed to marry; 8 recalled they were forced to marry and/or breed; 143 respondents provided no information on slave marriage ceremonies. Thus, two-thirds of Cade's interviewees did not address the question and less than 10 percent of the total interviewees referred to jumping the broom. Though quantitative and qualitative data unveil many unique facets of such wedding rituals and provide an idea of the broomstick wedding's diverse formats, we are always limited by the silence of the archive.

All we truly know is that individuals selected the broomstick wedding for different reasons, whether willingly or by coercion, and that it held a distinct meaning for each of its practitioners. Some preferred to engage in a private and symbolically rich broomstick ceremony, while others either held no other option, or they were subjected to the slaveowner's predilection. Though cultural similarities permeated many neighborhoods, narratives from the formerly enslaved collectively reveal that jumping the broom never held a single meaning across the region. The antebellum South's various plantation societies were unique in their cultural traditions and developed distinct social customs. Emerging into freedom, African Americans reckoned with the ghosts of an enslaved past. As a product of slavery, jumping the broom drew simultaneous praise and condemnation from those seeking to claim a new identity in the postbellum period.

CHAPTER THREE

# Don't Tell Things Like That
*Matrimonial Change and Continuity after the Civil War*

In 1865 four million African Americans emerged from slavery, and while plantation communities throughout the former Confederacy shared certain cultural similarities, individuals had different memories when recounting their past. Some, like Mary Harris, preferred to forget the experience. When asked, she refused to discuss it: "Slavery! Why are you concerned about such stuff? It's bad enough for it to have existed and when we can't forget it there is no need of rehashing it."[1] Harris's response is understandable. Asking her to reflect on the psychological trauma of enslavement was asking a great deal. Even when providing an honest account of the brutalities of slavery, many respondents likely did so with some trepidation. Being interviewed in the 1930s Jim Crow South, many understandably feared retribution from angry white mobs if they conveyed damning information. However, many were especially frank about punishments and hardships, portraying slavery as an overwhelmingly negative chapter in their lives. Others were ashamed of the stereotypes attached to them and hoped to provide a different framework for understanding how slavery functioned and how enslaved people found dignity within the system. These respondents often rehearsed how enslaved people were committed Christians, practiced monogamy, and met together for celebrations. Of course, most narratives do not conform to a single format, but combine elements from each category.

In a few instances, they even clash, as in the dual interview of John and Laney Van Hook. Though married to one another, each saw marriage under slavery quite differently. The narrative is lengthy and primarily features John's testimonial about his experience at various moments in the nineteenth century. John's responses generally reflected a realistic portrayal of slave exploitation, but he presented his own Master, George Sellers, as a kind man who bestowed gifts on Christmas and taught his enslaved people the Christian religion. None of them ever fled Sellers's plantation, but he knew of those on a neighboring plantation, owned by Tommy Angel, who did. John was likely speaking in coded language, as one gains an impression that every white person he knew, with the exception of his own master, abused and mistreated the enslaved. This caveat allowed him to explain the brutalities of enslavement without directing attention to his former owner whose family presumably still held power over him. Despite the clandestine messages scattered throughout his narrative, an untrained eye might interpret his statements as reflecting the benign nature of southern enslavement. In this scenario, it may appear that slaveowners were benevolent paternalists preparing enslaved people to integrate into Eurocentric civilization. However, John's testimony alluded to the broader problems of enslavement, including the gross brutalities of racialized chattel bondage.

Originally, the interviewer expected to interview only John, but on a return visit to his home, he met John's wife, Laney, who participated as well. Although the couple had met after slavery ended, they were still asked about slave marriages, specifically about slave rituals and the degree to which enslaved people remained in committed relationships. This question triggered one of John and Laney's most direct disagreements, reflecting a divide surrounding how marriage occurred under slavery and how it was remembered in the present.

John answered first, claiming that enslaved people viewed marriage as a "solemn" occasion and that they never willingly separated from one another.[2] He applied this notion as a counterpoint to the modern era (1930s) and criticized the decadent youth who consumed "hard liquor" at their wedding parties. At this point, Laney "interrupted" John and divulged her thoughts. Noting she had never witnessed an actual slave wedding, as she was still quite young when slavery ended, Laney claimed that her mother's community "used to make up a new broom and when the couple jumped over it, they was married. Then they gave the broom to the couple to use keeping house." Perhaps Laney interrupted because she believed John's narrative was incomplete, or at the very least, there were different experiences on other plantations. However, John interjected before she could continue, in turn displaying how the concept of "forgetting" is relevant to historical memory: "Laney, that was never confirmed. It was just hearsay, as far as you know, and I wouldn't tell things like that."[3] He then continued to discuss his own recollections of a wedding party, and his perspectives dominated the remainder of the interview. Laney occasionally interjected, but any further conversation about the broomstick wedding did not occur. Still, the question arises, why would John demand Laney not "tell things like that," when others seemed to have no problem mentioning the ceremony to interviewers? John was undoubtedly aware that white American society associated slave customs with marks of immorality and cultural inferiority. Even if John knew about the custom, he wished to withhold such knowledge to an outsider. Instead, he hoped potential readers would view enslaved people as good Christians who were as morally virtuous as the free, white population. John's own experiences with slavery are relatively unclear, as he knew more about Reconstruction than the antebellum period. Like Laney's, his stories were based on his parents' experiences, neither of whom had been a field laborer. His mother was the personal servant of the mistress who seems to have lived in the plantation house. His father was a "carpenter and mechanic" who performed any required tasks, revealing he also avoided field labor. Such backgrounds validate John's contention that enslaved people, at least those he knew personally, did not jump the broom. Considering it was overwhelmingly used by field hands, it seems reasonable John's parents never utilized the custom and possibly shunned it. If one hoped to present African Americans as good Christians, any ritual outside that standard needed to be denied or erased from the narrative.

Though John silenced any further discussion, Laney's brief comment provides important context for the preparations that went into broomstick weddings and how such ceremonies were commemorated by those who used them. Laney's account is the only one to divulge that brooms were made specifically for these events, noting it was a gift from the community that symbolized entry into a new household. Crafting this domestic tool was the community's ways of providing a "housewarming" gift from the items available to them. Slaveholders cared little for the random broom straws scattered throughout the landscape, and enslaved people capitalized on this indifference to mold a meaningful gift for the betrothed. Harnessing their environment, enslaved people crafted domestic items from freely available materials. In the case of broomsticks, a person "cut hickory poles and made handles out of dem fer de brooms."[4] The symbolic gesture knit the community together in a unique way, a way that John, though once enslaved himself, was unwilling to validate.

Comparatively speaking, Laney's account prefigures those of modern Black heritage weddings, in which the broom is a gift to the couple from a relative who specially crafts it. She was excited to discuss the unique nature of slave matrimony, viewing the ritual as a transcendent moment for couples entering domestic life. Unfortunately, we receive no further elaboration on how the ceremony was conducted, but her brief intervention provides further context for understanding how memories of the ritual resonated among individuals in the early twentieth century. It allows us to explore why the ritual was largely discarded and discredited by Black Americans for over one hundred years following emancipation, while simultaneously analyzing how its legacy and influence survived in subsequent generations.

## The Meaning and Impact of Freedom

In May 1865 Congress created the Bureau of Refugees, Freedmen, and Abandoned Lands under the jurisdiction of the secretary of war. One of its aims was to ensure that freed people in Maryland, Washington, D.C., West Virginia, Kentucky, and the eleven Confederate states could obtain legally recognized unions. One of the first declarations by the "Freedmen's Bureau" was that "in places where the local statutes make no provisions for the marriage of persons of color, the Assistant Commissioners are authorized to designate officers who shall keep a record of marriages, which may be solemnized by any ordained minister of the gospel."[5] Many African Americans exercised their freedom by heading to the courthouse or chapel to receive the coveted marriage license.[6] The vigorous emphasis on legal, Christian matrimony prompted folk rituals like jumping the broomstick to fall out of favor with many newly free African Americans trying to advance in society.

Black couples knew that officially sanctioned marriage was a crucial factor toward securing their rights to one another and their children. Obtaining legal acknowledgment was an important step toward gaining citizenship, and many former slaves secured legally recognized unions from either a justice of the peace or a registered minister. Having been barred from the legal institution of marriage for several centuries, African Americans recognized its value. Though the Jim Crow era curtailed various expressions of freedom in the United States, Black people recognized that legally registered marriages were essential to legitimating their familial units and ensuring their property could be inherited by their descendants.

Accessing governmental recognition after 1865 was not always a streamlined process for African Americans, as the circumstances of slavery complicated the transition to freedom. As one individual from Tennessee explained, the wives of deceased Black soldiers found they were ineligible for a pension "if they married by jumping over the broom stick."[7] The testimonial reveals a postbellum dilemma that many Black women faced. Slave marriages were not legally recognized at the time they were performed, and it was not uncommon for formerly enslaved couples to separate either during slavery or after 1865 and settle with other partners. Some women were embroiled in legal battles as they sought to prove that they were the lawful heirs of their husband's possessions and government benefits. But if their marriage was never formally recognized by the state, their claims were typically rejected by the governmental representative.

Emerging from slavery and facing the harsh conditions of a makeshift free-dom, African Americans used their expansive familial structures to survive the physical and psychological oppression wrought by postbellum Ameri-can racism. But they often ran against government legislators who refused to bend on their commitment to monogamy. Many of the formerly enslaved re-married for love and practical purposes, assuming their former partners were either impossible to locate or perished during the war. Ministers were unsure how to approach betrothed couples who married after slavery's end. The Freedmen's Bureau passed laws recognizing all formerly enslaved couples liv-ing together as man and wife and required that an ordained clergyman, em-powered by the state, to assess the couple's fitness for Christian matrimony.[8] It is impossible, however, to place any particular standard on African Ameri-cans' marital preferences when they emerged from slavery, as their attach-ments were in a constant state of flux due to death and forced separations. These domestic ruptures were so prevalent that former slaves published ad-vertisements in local newspapers describing children or spouses in the hope that someone would know of them.[9]

Though white government officials held their suspicions about Black Americans' marital patterns, matrimonial heterodoxy was hardly unique to any racial group in the nineteenth century. Cases of bigamy, desertion, and undocumented common law marriages were typical among rural popula-tions throughout this period. Historian Beverly Schwartzberg notes it was viewed as a fluid institution among the working classes who largely rejected the middle-class model of a lifelong, permanent union. Various people used a "pragmatic flexibility" when negotiating their relationships, either eschewing the state's legal parameters or ignoring the consequences of severing their unions outside legislative structures.[10]

## Marrying under Jim Crow

In the decades following slavery, many African Americans recognized that domestic stability relied upon state recognition, and many of them conse-quently secured monogamous unions. A revealing study spearheaded by W. E. B. Du Bois in 1890 provides a useful reference point for understanding the value African Americans placed on legal marriages and nuclear families. The tables revealed that marriage rates were roughly equal across races. For instance, 55 percent of Black Americans were married compared with 55.4 percent of white Americans. One decade later the statistics revealed that African Ameri-cans' marriage rates exceeded those of white Americans: 58.9 percent compared

"Marriage Ceremony of Former Slaves, Vicksburg, Mississippi, 1866"; courtesy of www.slaveryimages.org, reference: HW0043.

with 55.9 percent. In only one generation after slavery, Black people in the United States were exceeding whites in their commitment to legally recognized marital bonds.[11]

Historian Tera Hunter argues that "as the economy goes, so goes marriage."[12] Considering that most Black Americans resided in the rural South and worked as sharecroppers, their high marriage rates correlate with the demands of agricultural work. The labor of all family members was required to survive the oppressive conditions of the Jim Crow South. As occurred under slavery, these circumstances led to a more expansive definition of family among Black populations in the South. Although most African Americans embraced the concept of the nuclear family by the end of the nineteenth century, statistics in 1880 nevertheless reveal that 22.5 percent of Black family units included "other kin," a category usually called "extended," while 19.5 percent of white families lived in a similar situation. Thus, African Americans did not approach marriage and family life in an especially abnormal manner throughout the last half of the nineteenth century, but largely conformed to societal expectations that linked monogamous marriages to American citizenship. However, Black people living in the Jim Crow South had unique dilemmas when attempting to nurture the matrimonial ideals of the United States.

Jim Crow's restrictive laws were especially toxic in destabilizing Black marriages and separating families. African Americans were exploited by the predatory system of sharecropping upon the plantation, as well as by the convict-leasing system, which preyed upon Black men, who were discriminatorily sentenced to prison for minor legal infractions. Black men were especially susceptible to vagrancy laws and could be arrested upon the suspicion that they were unemployed and without a domicile. In the early twentieth century, the Georgia Equal Right Convention asserted that the vagrancy laws and convict-leasing system threatened the stability of Black families. The convention claimed these laws stunted "the development of 'honesty, sobriety, industry and chastity,'" and their "unjust application left black women in 'a defenceless condition.'"[13] In effect, Black couples faced a unique set of external pressures that prevented them from conforming to expectations of citizenship.

Wedding ceremonies served a critical function for African Americans surviving the Jim Crow era. Not only did they link families in a broader network of extended kinship, but they provided respite from the arduous labor of sharecropping and brought communities together in celebration. As many African Americans in this period were only a generation or two removed from slavery, the ability to pursue a marriage relation and select their own decorations, minister, and ceremonial format without the enslaver's interference was especially rewarding. Though a couple's economic circumstances determined the scale of festivities, the historical record is replete with testimonies of lavish weddings and communal revelry.

The importance of legal and legitimate marriage was embedded in American social thought since the colonial period. The fact that enslaved people were prevented from engaging in legally recognized marriages was one of the most demoralizing experiences of enslavement. At the dawn of emancipation in 1865, the formerly enslaved were thrown into a world rife with laws adjudicated by people who remained unfriendly to their existence. An important exception, however, was the ability for Black couples to obtain a legally protected marriage and for the head of household to lay legal claim over dependents. Though many areas throughout the South enjoyed a brief respite between 1866 and 1877 from the ubiquitous racism of slavery and Jim Crow, northern whites and progressive southerners still believed the formerly enslaved were incapable of practicing morality through their own volition. Many politicians and legislators specified that African Americans needed to register their marriages, deaths, and births to ascertain familial relations and the legitimacy of children and spouses within the nuclear family unit. In 1873 congressional representatives introduced a bill specifically targeting the formerly enslaved, requiring them to register births, deaths, and marriages to allow states to track the progress of integrating "the ignorant classes" into the requirements of citizenship. Reports on the bill argued it was a good idea, contending that if people knew the "terrible morality" that existed amongst the Black population, they would understand the "necessity of teaching" them how to raise their children and remain true to their marital commitments. They argued that Black Americans who registered their partnership would naturally understand the "solemnity of the marriage tie," adding that they must encourage them to embrace wedding ceremonies conducted by registrars or preachers, for actions like "jumping over the broom stick will not satisfy the confiding fair."[14] Not only did many politicians lack faith in Black people's natural attachments to one another, they did, in some cases, point to rituals like jumping the broom for evidence of this moral failure. Like the rhetoric of slaveowners, the paternalistic language assumed that people of African descent were incapable of independently obtaining moral standards, at least in the way Euro-Americans saw them.

## Divided Memories and the Broomstick Wedding's Impact

Nearly fifty years after the Civil War ended, the *Hartford Herald* reported that 103-year-old Timothy Griffin and 73-year-old Lucy Woody were wed by a minister after having been "slaves on the same plantation in North Carolina before the war . . . having entered into the connubial state by the old slave custom of jumping over a broomstick."[15] Griffin and Woody waited an exceptionally long time to have a legally sanctioned marriage because of their belief that the broomstick wedding was sufficient to secure their personal commitment to one another. However, for the sake of inheritance and proving legitimacy of one's children, even the most defiant couples were compelled to register their marriages. Thus, one couple who were wed in an antebellum broomstick ceremony and never registered their marriage for forty years, did so once the husband laid "on his deathbed."[16] It is likely that most newly free African Americans acted in accordance with the testimony of Tennessean Jon Moore, who noted his parents jumped over a "broom handle" held by two guests under slavery. Though the custom was "taken seriously" by the entire community and his parents always remained "true to their vows," they later remarried in a legal ceremony to secure and document their union.[17] George

Leonard went even further, claiming that Black couples not only clung to the symbolic value of their previous broomstick weddings, but that certain communities continued to jump the broom "long after freedom came."[18] Indeed, at least one couple obtained a marriage license from the courthouse and then "jumped over the broom handle" later in the day.[19] There is some visual evidence that Black couples continued to use folk customs into the early twentieth century, as one extant picture shows a married couple who "crossed sticks" at their wedding ceremony to symbolize their new bond.[20] However, references to folk ceremonies are infrequent in the historical record. For various legal and cultural reasons, many formerly enslaved people eventually engaged in legally recognized unions, even if they were belated by many decades.

The opportunity to obtain a minister, white or Black, through their own volition was surely attractive for many African Americans previously unable to organize their own ceremonies.[21] According to Bongy Jackson, once enslaved in Louisiana, the broomstick wedding was the primary form of marriage on his plantation, but "after the Cibil War, soon's they got a little ole piece of money they got a preacher and had a real weddin.'"[22] For Jackson, a "real weddin'" reflected a free person's ability to exchange money for matrimonial services and governmental recognition. In addition, however, the notion that a postbellum wedding devoid of antebellum customs was the "real" or "right" type of ceremony devalued former slave customs. In many respects, the involvement of government officials and zealous ministers led many formerly enslaved people toward a degree of cultural amnesia, in which the embarrassing components of chattel slavery were either denied or relegated to memories that died with the individual.

Nevertheless, as the formerly enslaved journeyed to churches or courts to register their marriages, they found it difficult to escape the legacy of jumping the broom, since white Americans still associated them with the custom. A 1918 report noted that many formerly enslaved people flocked to Washington, D.C. searching for employment opportunities and to purchase farmland. The author noted the difficulties men faced in registering their marriages, as they were married by the broomstick custom under slavery and often remarried if their wife was sold or they parted ways after the war ended. Called "broomstick husbands," they were said to take additional wives without apology. Since Congress passed laws to retroactively recognize the marriages of those who jumped the broom, the author claimed that "every broomstick husband" now must account for the multiple spouses who could claim a legal union with him.[23] The author suggested that their land purchases would lead to wives and their respective children sparring over who can legally inherit the land. Though written in a condescending tone, often mocking the morality and work ethic of the Black population, the article provides a unique glimpse into ideas of marriage after the Civil War and how the legacy of slave marital customs transferred into the early twentieth century.

One possible reason the broomstick wedding did not survive wholesale into the postbellum period is that not enough people were familiar with its symbolic importance. One respondent said of broomstick weddings and couplings across plantations, "Dey'd 'low us to get married dat way, and dat wuz all dere wuz to it."[24] Mark Thrash made a similar statement when responding to his interviewer: "You want to know how us jumped the broomstick? Well, you lay the broom on the floor and jump forward and then backward holding hands. That's all there was to it."[25] In stating "that's all there was to it," both respondents reflected an attitude that the broomstick ceremony was a simple practice that did not need extended description, either due to their own associated embarrassment, or their belief that it held little symbolic value in their own community. Ephom Banks of Mississippi went further in stating that "the master would sometimes make a couple step over a broom and when they did that they were married but they all didn't even have to do that."[26]

Another reason for the decline of the custom is that some simply didn't know about it, as in the case of, Abner Griffin, who said he "never seed no broomstick wedding."[27] But insofar as African Americans were aware of the custom, those reckoning with the memory of slavery could detach themselves from the experience by performing the orthodox ceremonies of an institution that they were legally denied for over 200 years.

Though a few aforementioned testimonies suggest that the broomstick law resonated in a few communities in the postbellum period, we do not hold enough resources to catalogue its cultural impact with the same precision as the antebellum period.[28] Some African Americans simply refused to register their marriages after the Civil War as they claimed the broomstick wedding was sufficient, despite federal and state regulations to the contrary.[29] But the prevalence of broomstick marriages among enslaved people forced state legislatures to adjust their preconceived notions of "legal" marriage. In 1915 an Arkansas court ruled that people's antebellum broomstick marriages retroactively qualified as legal marriages, given the circumstances of legislative proscription before 1865.[30] Two years later, Missouri followed suit and recognized jumping the broom as a valid marriage, specifically citing a case concerning "a marriage performed back in slavery times, when broomstick weddings were popular among the negroes."[31] Ultimately, many African Americans needed to secure a legally recognized union from either a justice of the peace or a registered minister. As one formerly enslaved person from Tennessee explained, those wives of deceased black soldiers found they were ineligible for a pension "if they married by jumping over the broom stick."[32] Having been barred from the legal institution of marriage for multiple centuries, formerly enslaved people recognized the value of attaining a legally protected union. In the postbellum period, they recognized this was the only way to legitimate their familial unit and ensure their property could be inherited by their descendants.

While most African Americans embraced more orthodox forms of marriage after the Civil War, this should not necessarily be interpreted as a concerted attempt to completely disregard the symbolic value the broomstick wedding under slavery. In an 1890 celebration commemorating emancipation in Richmond, Virginia, African Americans used the broomstick wedding to exemplify their moral advancements, showing the juxtaposition between "how they used to marry by jumping over the broom and how they marry now."[33] Though its legitimacy was rejected for postbellum matrimony in this exposition, its use as a visual symbol of antebellum matrimony ensured subsequent generations remembered their ancestral customs. In other instances, some nostalgically reflected on the ease of marrying over the broomstick and resented the notion they had to "pay good money for a license" merely for a justice of the peace to say a few words.[34] Others attested to the moral superiority of slave matrimony as compared with the marriages of Black Americans in the 1930s, contending that slaves stayed with their partners for more extended periods than the decadent youth of the early twentieth century.[35] Thus, while legislative requirements and cultural transitions gradually phased out these folk customs from the view of the general public, the recollections from many African Americans suggest they believed these rituals were important for providing psychological comfort in times of oppression.

## Rejection and Denial of the Custom

Many formerly enslaved interviewees likely felt obliged to offer a counternarrative to the idea that they did not marry in accordance with American standards. Like John's saying to Laney "don't tell things like that," some contended the broomstick wedding should be actively suppressed in public memory, as it was a tool wielded by slaveowners. In a sermon given in 1892, a minister argued that slaves' morality was at the disposal of the master and that "marriage consisted in simply jumping over the broomstick, and then going to bed."[36]

By connecting the custom to the immoral actions of slaveowners, he discounted its ceremonial legitimacy, especially when compared with Christian matrimony. Lizzie Johnson insinuated that despite the tendency of some African Americans to continue broomstick weddings after slavery, her mother "really got married and didn't jump no broomstick."[37] For her, couples who eschewed slave rituals were morally superior.

Johnson's use of "really" to denote legitimacy resonates with other narratives. Rena Raines asserted that as soon as freedom came to North Carolina, her parents went to Raleigh "and were married right."[38] Her assertion that the postbellum legal wedding was "right" implies that the slave wedding was invalid or, at best, that it was a gesture that reflected the couple's unrealistic desire to commit to one another free of outside interference. In this interpretation, legality is equated with validity. But Raines also said that the broomstick ceremony was unchristian and reflected the uncivilized nature of enslaved people in the South. Others personally disavowed it. Ella Belle Ramsay argued that on her plantation they "never had none of dat jumping over de broom foolishness you hear 'bout in other places."[39] Respondents such as Johnson, Raines, and Ramsay likely viewed the legally sanctioned marriages, replete with religious overtones, to be a ritual Black Americans should embrace. They rejected resurrecting aspects of the slave past that dehumanized Black people in American society.[40]

Denying the reality of the custom in the postbellum period allowed the formerly enslaved to suggest that, despite popular opinion, their antebellum marriages mirrored those of white people. The only aspect lacking was legal recognition. In a 1938 interview, journalist Sarah Singleton King noted that "Aunt Lelia Wood" hoped to use her own testimony to counter the contemporary beliefs surrounding slave marriages, stating, "No honey, I didn't have no license, but we had a preacher. Marriage at our house wasn't as some people say it was, just jumping over the broom. We had a real ceremony."[41] Again, her emphasis on a "real" ceremony reflects a few realities of antebellum memories. First, in rejecting the broomstick ceremony she reveals that it is a well-known custom associated with slave marriages, and by responding to the assumption that all enslaved people jumped the broom, Wood counters any preconceived notions that the ceremony dominated slave life and culture. Second, Wood proposes that marriage under slavery was as valid as any other. Not only did she commit to one man her entire life, but their ceremony mimicked several aspects of one accepted by the Christian nation.

Wood reflects the attitudes of many formerly enslaved people who attempted to gain dignity through matrimony—only seven decades removed from slavery. Amanda Oliver used the broomstick wedding as a reference point to emphasize the importance of marrying with a preacher: "We went to de preacher and got married. We did more than jump over de broomstick."[42] Presumably, Oliver did not *need* to mention that she and her husband "did more than" jump the broom, but her ultimate point would still reflect the broomstick wedding as a reference point for invalidity by identifying the centrality of the preacher in determining legitimacy. Her notation suggests a cognizance that certain stereotypes persisted about slave marital rites and the lack of seriousness in which they were undertaken. In many ways, she reflects the attitudes of some postbellum Black communities that emphasized that enslaved people mirrored the marital patterns and ceremonies of the white majority. In using orthodox marriage rituals it is evident that Black communities imitated not only the legal and social norms of white Christians, but their moral standards as well.

Paul Laurence Dunbar, a noted Black author in the postbellum period, recreated an antebellum wedding of a southern mistress in his short story "Aunt Tempy's Triumph." The piece rehearses certain elements of the popular narrative of benevolent masters and mistresses interacting with loyal slaves, but Dunbar portrays "Aunt Tempy," an elderly house slave, as managing the wedding preparations. In one conversation between Aunt Tempy and the slave owner, the prospective bride's father, she demands that her "baby" have a "big weddin'," to which her enslaver replies: "Of course, what else do you expect? You don't suppose I'm going to have her jump over the broom with him, do you?"[43] Tempy vigorously insists it must be grander, and eventually intimidated her master into allowing *her* to give the bride away, as she was a more legitimate parent to the child than him. Beyond the unique, and rather unbelievable conclusion to this story, it suggests a notion in the popular memory that jumping the broom was reserved for those considered unworthy of a large wedding. The denigrating tone that surrounds the broomstick wedding in this story reflects its position as a counterpoint to Christian weddings officiated by ministers. Tempy served as a symbol for portraying this aspect of respectability. By noting that she was enslaved in the plantation house, Dunbar reveals how people like her believed jumping the broom was beneath the station of her mistress or anyone familiar with respectable society. Consequently, Dunbar portrayed a popular belief about the ceremony's connections between class and race rehearsed by many African Americans both during and after slavery.

African American author Charles W. Chesnutt's "A Deep Sleeper," an 1893 short story set in the Old South, used a similar idea as Dunbar by noting that a Presbyterian slaveholder did not allow his enslaved people to jump over the broomstick. He insisted that weddings were a religious service requiring a minister to preside over the couple. Chesnutt's story suggests the broomstick wedding resonated in the popular memories of antebellum slavery, but it was considered to be an irreligious farce. Formerly enslaved people dismissed it as well. Josephine Ryles, enslaved in Galveston, Texas, claimed to "hear some of 'em say somethin' bout jumpin' over de broom an' bein' married dat way, but it ain't true. No'm, dats jus' a story. I seen a lot of marriages, an' dey was married regular."[44] Similarly, Partheny Shaw testified that jumping the broomstick "was just a sayin', they didn't jump over nothin.'"[45] Another respondent "heard tell of 'em" and described his understanding of the ceremony before quickly transitioning into the post-emancipation celebration that featured a minister who wed his parents "according to the law."[46] These and similar passages might initially cast doubt upon the ceremony as a legitimate marriage ritual, since it is always discussed apart from questions of legality.[47] But legal recognition was not a reference point in validating its symbolic meaning to the enslaved people who used it. The number of formerly enslaved people that affirmatively spoke about the custom far outnumbers the doubters, suggesting that the ritual should not be dismissed as something the formerly enslaved simply erased from memory.[48]

## Oral History, Tradition, and the Process of Forgetting

Even after the practice fell out of favor, oral traditions ensured that certain customs were remembered long after the community ceased practicing them. Into the twentieth century African Americans retained the idea that jumping the broom was associated with southern slavery, as revealed in a poem entitled "Slave Marriage Ceremony," which circulated after emancipation:

> Dark an' stormy may come de wedder;
> I jines dis he-male an' dis she-male togedder
> Let none, but Him dat makes de thunder,
> Put dis he-male an' dis she-male asunder.
> I darfore 'nounce you bofe de same.
> Be good, go 'long, an' keep up yo' name.
> De broomstick's jumped, de worl's not wide.
> She's now yo' own. Salute yo' bride.[49]

In its entirety, this verse reveals "the poetic and symbolic language and concepts . . . by which even those who were enslaved lived and communicated on special occasions."[50] It reveals the historic centrality the broom held in sealing the ceremony. For after the broomstick was jumped, enslaved couples were eligible to begin their lives together. It ensured that descendants recognized the importance enslaved people placed upon marriage, though they knew their marriages were tenuous under the law. Despite the persistence of traditions performed through specific patterns, the specific function of the broomstick ceremony decayed over time.

Folk histories can reveal how Black communities lost knowledge of their traditions over generations of disuse. Though they knew a form of the broomstick ritual existed, recalling specific details decades later proved difficult. One respondent said, "I have heard of it all my life. I never seen it done. I was a little kid, you know."[51] The gradual process of communal amnesia is found in the oral traditions of an isolated Black community in Coe Ridge, Kentucky, studied by folklorist William Montell in the early 1960s. Montell interviewed the descendants of its original settlers, which at its inception provided refuge for Black Americans after the Civil War. His lengthy transcriptions provide considerable information on the history of Coe Ridge and how the descendants viewed its place in Appalachian history. The respondents rehearsed the history of slavery in similar fashion to those interviewed by the WPA, discussing foodways, dances, and methods of escape employed by the community's ancestors. Respondents casually mentioned certain events, such as the marriage of Zeke and Patsy Coe, the original progenitors of the community, who they claimed were married by "jumping over the broomstick."[52] Deeper into the interviews, Montell requested further information about the ritual. The responses reveal uncertainty among those being interviewed, suggesting they had never seen it firsthand. It was a ritual performed "way back then" among their ancestors.[53] Regarding its performance, they knew only that both individuals jumped over the broom backward. When pressed for information concerning who used the broomstick ceremony, an exchange between two respondents, Sarah Coe Tooley and Ruthie Coe Anders, reveals an interesting interchange between history and memory:

TOOLEY: Well, did my grandfather and grandmother get married that
way?
ANDERS: Unhu.
TOOLEY: Jump the broom?
ANDERS: Jump the broom? I don't know just let me see now whether she jumped the broom or not. Well, now, all them . . .
TOOLEY: Now, since you've named that, I believe they did.

ANDERS: . . . all them old people of that age, when they got married, they
jumped the broom. . . .
TOOLEY: Daddy told me that before he died. I'd forgot about it.
ANDERS: That's the way they got married 'cause I remember that.

Both Anders and Tooley attempt to recollect the history transmitted through
their elders, relying upon each other to validate one another's information.
Tooley suggests she "forgot" about the ritual until the interviewer requested
additional information, while Anders, though initially unsure, ultimately
cited oral history as her authority. The exchange highlights how rituals can
physically die within one or two generations, even if they persist in the oral
traditions. Neither respondent was particularly far removed from the custom,
citing it was her grandparents who married in this fashion.

Montell notes that when Ruthie Anders first mentioned the broomstick
wedding, "heavy laughter" ensued. He did not investigate the matter further,
but the fact in itself is notable. Laughter can be a way to deflect attention from
one's anxiety or to calm one's nerves. It is possible both respondents felt some
embarrassment at the notion that their ancestors did not get married in a traditional Christian ceremony. For them, outsiders could not fully comprehend
the folkloric origins of the matrimonial broomstick, and fearing judgement,
they burst into laughter to regain composure before continuing their descriptions of enslaved life.

## Colloquialism and Cultural Preservation

If African Americans largely rejected the broomstick custom in the postbellum era, it does appear to have survived in folk speech. Like "tying the knot,"
"jumping the broom" was a colloquialism. Some enslaved people used the
expression to describe marriages devoid of ceremonies, suggesting that certain plantations used "jumping the broom" to describe either a literal leap
over the object or an irregular marriage. Shade Richards of Georgia noted
that enslaved men "courted" women from other plantations and gained permission from both slaveholders before they formed an attachment. Richards
noted "there was no ceremony if both masters said 'alrigt' they were considered married and it was called 'jumpin' the broomstick.'"[54] For her part, Dora
Franks of Mississippi eschewed the idea that the phrase was associated with
marriage and contended that it "was what they called going to see a woman."[55]
In this version, "jumping the broom" simply conveyed one's participation in a
sexual tryst that may, or may not, have held promise for lasting commitment.

The perpetuation of the phrase ensured that descendants of enslaved people retained a reference point for an ancestral tradition, even if they did not fully understand the implications of the statement or how the literal ceremony functioned. The phrase appears to have survived for an extended period, as some references are found among Black southerners into the late twentieth century. For example, Jerry Rice, a noteworthy wide receiver in the National Football League, stated in 1987 that he was hoping to "jump the broom" and explained that "it's one of those Mississippi terms that means to get married."[56] Rice's statement suggests that, for him, the term was less racial than regional. The folk speech of the rural South preserved the memories of traditions used by their ancestors. It does not appear Rice meant he would take a literal jump over the broom; rather, he associated the phrase with his southern heritage. The expression was mutually understood by both Black and white southerners. Paul Jenkins, formerly enslaved in South Carolina, recalled that his mother died in the late 1870s and his father, Paul Sr., was not concerned with remarriage. His lack of interest attracted the attention of white men he befriended in the area, who once approached him to ask when he was going to "jump the broomstick again."[57] Paul Sr. lightheartedly revealed he had no woman in mind and was not actively in pursuit, to which the men replied, "Just wait 'til the right girl come along."[58] Considering this conversation occurred decades after slavery's end, it seems likely the men were applying the expression figuratively and did not anticipate that Paul Sr. would enact a literal jump over a broom. Regardless, all understood the meaning of the colloquialism in this case.

On a similar note, Nashville band Alvin Gaines and the Themes first performed "Let's Jump the Broomstick" in 1959, acquiring the lyrics from songwriter Charles Robins. Though members of the group were African American, the song does not detail the actual ceremonial performance or even suggest it was a racially specific custom, but reflected its use for a shotgun wedding by a young couple marrying against the wishes of their respective families. The song is fast-paced and meant to initiate motion in the crowd, but does not provide extended context on the custom. The most constant theme revolves around the chorus, which simply states, "Come a little baby lets jump the broomstick come and let's tie the knot."[59] Here we see both colloquial expressions used in the same sentence, providing different phrases that conveyed the same request. Though the band obtained some mainstream success they never pursued this song after this first performance. The song did not receive significant attention until Brenda Lee, a white artist from Georgia, covered the song to significant acclaim. It is unclear why they stopped performing the song or how they conceptualized its message, but it does suggest they were familiar with the term and anticipated their audience also understood the expression.

Following the Second World War, Black middle-class families generally modelled their celebrations in accordance with the "white wedding." They used public engagements to "demonstrate adherence to clearly defined gender roles and acceptable displays of heterosexuality."[60] Though Black couples adapted certain aspects of the wedding to fit their own cultural distinctions, including public recognition of family and friends who assisted with food preparations, adopting the white wedding countered the negative stereotypes espousing Black promiscuity and hypersexuality common under slavery and Jim Crow.[61] Announcing nuptials in African American magazines such as *Ebony* and *Jet* countered America's racialized conceptions of beauty and purity, suggesting that Black Americans were just as capable of performing respectability as their white counterparts. By eliminating folk ceremonies associated with slavery, and simultaneously embracing Euro-American forms of matrimonial celebration, the expanding Black middle class propelled itself beyond memories of slavery and into the consumerist culture of middle-class America. It is possible that those who actively suppressed the broomstick wedding from the descendant community accomplished their goal in nearly eradicating its use, but vernacular speech rooted in the region preserved it in some form. Its revival in the African American community toward the close of the twentieth century was ultimately born through a greater attention to Black history and the ceremony's preceding connection to the colloquial expression.

## CHAPTER FOUR

# Into the White Mind

## Jumping the Broom and Social Divisions among White Americans

Like their British predecessors, some white Americans used the broomstick tradition to mock their opponents or disparage their adversaries. Targets for ridicule could include politicians, state legislators, or individuals who simply had different moral philosophies. In 1856, Chauncey Shaffer ridiculed Millard Fillmore's nomination to the American Party, suggesting that a few powerful delegates made the decision without the consent of the people. As a prominent member of the American Party, Shaffer asserted the nomination was not binding, and he elicited cheers and laughter when he quipped, "If that is a nomination, then jumping the broomstick is marriage."[1]

Stating an event was no better than a broomstick wedding also allowed a critic to mock someone's social station and character. For example, an 1831 article attacked an unnamed politician considered an enemy of religious gathering, and noted that he was nominated "to the Vice Presidency and to the Presidency of the country." The article's author specifically ridiculed his domestic attachments, noting that he was married to a "colored woman" and wondering whether his marriage was "on the book, or by . . . jumping the broom." It also noted that he fathered children with his wife.[2] Though unnamed, the politician in question is Robert Mentor Johnson, a Kentuckian who lived in an openly publicized relationship with an enslaved woman of mixed-race named Julia Chinn.

Scholars suggest that one reason Chinn remained enslaved, rather than being freed by Johnson and then taken as his legally recognized wife, was that Kentucky's manumission laws required all newly freed people to leave the state after emancipation. Rather than move from the state where he held a prominent political career, Johnson could maintain their domestic attachment by retaining the status quo. Since slaveowners had nearly unbridled control over their chattel, Johnson could also protect her and any children they bore together. Johnson remained faithful to her for over twenty years and never hid his relationship from the public.[3] He did not marry her, however, and it is not likely that they jumped the broom. Regardless, as far as the author of the article was concerned, asking whether Johnson jumped the broom was enough to impugn his character.

As we will see in the pages that follow, popular conceptions of the broom-jumping tradition tended to be derogatory. Sometimes white commentators associated the tradition with enslaved people and used it as a racist trope when criticizing their supposedly crude folk customs. At other times, racism was not so much at play as classism and other negative attitudes regarding marginalized populations who practiced the custom, as was the case in the British Isles. Hence, in the United States, attitudes toward jumping the broom speak to intersections between race and social status.

## White Conceptions of Slave Weddings

Historian Emily West correctly notes that finding references to broomstick weddings in the documents of slaveowners is difficult since they had no reason to record them. They were instead more "concerned with the betrothals of their favored slaves," who typically did not jump the broom.[4] Slaveholders usually portrayed slave weddings as grandiose affairs, using their anecdotes to contest the rising tide of abolitionist criticism and prove that enslaved people lived superior lives to those of other oppressed populations. While abolitionists accused southern slaveowners of breaking the most sacred tie in Christian civilization, southern apologists claimed their outrage was exaggerated.[5] Slave weddings were an especially popular apologetic, as they manifested the purported interracial comradery of antebellum race relations. In these ceremonies, white families and enslaved laborers shared a celebratory space that reiterated slaveholder's claims that enslavement was a benefit for Black people. However, one does find a few references to slaveowners' conceptions of the broomstick wedding in their private correspondence.

For example, in 1830, A. Burwell, a slaveholder in Alabama, wrote a poem that he enclosed in a letter to his sister recounting the courtship of a "coal black" enslaved woman named Kate by the "stout square shouldered" Mingo. The poem is incredibly long and portrays Kate as "broad-footed, flat nosed and thick lipped," but "tho' black she be, he calls her his sweet dove."[6] The piece expresses some admiration for the extended courtship of the enslaved couple in admitting that "for love does also darkies grieve." The poem ends with a reference to an undefined ceremony, noting "no more has been revealed of maid or lover / Whether they were with ceremony wed / Or jumped a broom and then popped under cover / The muse does not disclose—My pastoral's over." Written in 1830, the poem speaks to a slaveowner's perception of a slave wedding a generation before the Civil War, as it reflected the traditional classism of Anglo-American society while implementing the anti-Black racism rampant throughout the antebellum United States. Both Mingo and Kate were represented as unattractive people according to standards of white society, and their attraction to each other reflected the lowest form of love. Compounded with the legal structure that prevented recognition of their union, Burwell's reference to their broomstick wedding highlighted the elementary simplicities of the ceremony. Though many American slaveholders did not have the multi-generational wealth of British elites, southern whites mirrored these conceptions of social class through the paradigm of racial slavery.

Just as elites in Britain disparaged others for jumping the broom, slaveowners who witnessed this ceremony among the enslaved likely reflected these same ideas. Other fictional works produced by white authors before and after the Civil War portrayed the interactions between master and slave when preparing to jump the broomstick. In John Jolliffe's 1858 novel, *Chattanooga*, a disagreement emerges between a slaveholder and an enslaved woman named Huldah who refuses to marry her prospective husband, Abe, claiming she "hates him" and would "die before I'll have him." Attempting to curtail her insubordinate behavior, the enslaver shouts, "You shall marry him. I'll let you know who's master on this plantation," and then explains that the ceremony will be conducted by a Methodist minister and that there "shall be no jumping the broomstick wedding."[7] In this rendition, the slaveholder portrayed his social power over the enslaved woman by asserting his position, and he simultaneously demonstrated a façade of his concern for her Christian soul by procuring a minister for the ceremony and rejected the broomstick custom. Similarly, southern writer Ruth McEnery Stuart's postbellum novel *Moriah's Mourning* dedicated five pages to enslaved people discussing a slave wedding. The crux of Stuart's portrayal examined the nuanced perspectives of Black people who knew their marriages under slavery were not legally recognized, but who nevertheless took them seriously. The broomstick wedding was a central piece of such discussions, exploring conversations around broomsticks being borrowed amongst the community for marriage ceremonies and the degree to which marital commitments taken over the broomstick were legitimate, or if the couple needed to remarry in a church ceremony.[8]

## Mockery of Jumping the Broom

Scrutinizing the broomstick wedding was not merely about satisfying the author's own curiosity; it also often led to mockery, as in an 1883 article referring to jumping the broom as one of "the oddest and most reckless harum-scarum marriages ever perpetrated in any country or among any people."[9] In the 1890s, newspapers celebrating the achievement of emancipation in civilizing African Americans used the transition from "jumping over the broom" to the legally sanctioned marriages as one of their focal points.[10] As states pushed for legally sanctioned marriages, folk rituals were contrasted with appropriate marriages. The broomstick wedding seemed securely placed in the colloquialisms of white America, as the *Daily Globe* claimed in 1878 "women of the present day think no more of marriage than they do of jumping over a broomstick."[11] The reference reveals how Americans in the late-nineteenth century were developing a lax attitude toward the marriage covenant, and used the symbol of "jumping over a broomstick" as a reference point.

Perceptions of the custom were generally informed by one's social position in society or their location. For elitist writers, it was often connected to supposedly deviant communities. In trying to place its geographical origins, one finds such claims were blatantly contradictory. As early as 1831, a publication in Washington, D.C., speculated that two people were married by the "northern mode" of jumping the broom.[12] Although what is meant by "northern" is unclear, it might be referring not to the northern United States, but to northern British Isles. Conversely, in 1913 a guest columnist from New Jersey called it a "southern ceremony," though a writer from the *Florida Times-Union* claimed no such ceremony was found in the South.[13] Again, the discrepancy might be explained by the time of writing. In 1913 the rural South held a distinct regional identity from the industrial North. Perhaps the New Jersey writer regionalized the broomstick wedding to mock southern culture as backwards, rural, and uncivilized, in the same way the English press mocked rural Celtic and gypsy groups who used the matrimonial broomstick. Broomstick weddings were typically used by people in rural areas who could not access a minister in a timely manner, and not necessarily limited to specific regions. However, the South was the last region of the United States to become an "urban majority." Whereas most of the populations in the North, West, and Midwest had urbanized by the 1910s, the South did not do the same until the 1950s. In holding a far larger rural demographic than the rest of the country, these communities were more likely to use practical folk customs than their counterparts elsewhere. Thus, the writer for *Florida Times-Union* was wrong, as the broomstick wedding was most prolific in the South due to its adoption by African Americans, Louisiana Cajuns, and white Appalachians. Indeed, each group's broomstick traditions are some of the most extensively documented among populations in North America. As an easily transferable ritual for populations inhabiting various geographical areas, the broomstick ceremony could be described as "southern," "northern," or "western" depending on who practiced it and where they lived. Given the negative associations of the broomstick wedding among the educated classes, the writer for the *Florida Times-Union* may have rejected its existence because he was embarrassed by his region's link to the custom.

As a means for denouncing others, the broomstick trope carried over into the sectional conflicts of the mid-nineteenth century. In defense of Southern society and its attachment to slaveholding, social theorist George Fitzhugh wrote: "The people of our Northern States, who hold that domestic slavery is unjust and iniquitous, are consistent in their attempts to modify or abolish the marriage relation. Marriages, in many places there, are contracted with as little formality as jumping over a broom, and are dissolved with equal facility by courts and legislatures. It is proposed by many to grant divorces at all times, when the parties mutually consent."[14] Fitzhugh evidently forgot that most of the enslaved population also experienced "as little formality as jumping over the broomstick" in their own marriages, as noted in the testimonies of the formerly enslaved. Similarly, such references entered pro-Confederate literature following the Civil War. In *Bertha the Beauty: A Story of the Southern Revolution*, Sarah Whittlesey recounts two Southern slaveholders criticizing Yankees who created laws that alleviated obstacles to divorce, with one saying: "The marriage-vow up there is about as binding as the one our darkies make when they jump over a broom into the uncertain state of matrimony."[15] By suggesting northern marriages were as "binding" as those of enslaved people who jumped the broom, she claimed Yankees were even less moral since they chose to separate at any sign of marital trouble. As seen in Fitzhugh's critique, such notions portrayed the moral superiority of the Proslavery cause. It contended that enslaved people lived in circumstances far superior to poor whites in the decadent, urban North.

Its associations with slavery made it a popular reference for postbellum writers seeking to mock marriage laws that did not fit their worldview. In one instance, a journalist used the broomstick ceremony to criticize the contemporary standards of marital laws in Georgia, writing in 1919 that if such laws remain a "farce" the citizenry should do away with the laws and "adopt that old-time method of marriage that was used by slaves . . . that of jumping over a broomstick on Saturday."[16] The reference suggests that by the early twentieth century white Americans associated jumping the broom with antebellum slavery, and they used it as a comparative example to warn others who went against the accepted standards of Christian marriage. But some journalists held other motivations and used marginalized communities to dismiss the broomstick wedding's value for other populations. *Broad Axe*, published in Chicago, Illinois, contended that the expression "jumping the broomstick" was "derived from an old gyspy superstition to the effect that by literally jumping a broom one can ward off evil influences."[17] By suggesting the colloquial expression "jumping the broom" was a relic of superstitious thought, this author claimed it was a past vestige of a pagan group, effectively discrediting its cultural value to the broader American public. Finally, despite its multigenerational resonance in various communities, many authors considered it an "old" way to get married.[18] Obviously, this description connotes something reserved for a previous generation, making its modern use abnormal.

## Abolitionists and Jumping the Broomstick

The few white abolitionists who spoke of the broomstick wedding viewed it unfavorably, linking it to the degradations forced upon the enslaved. The informal nature of the ceremony was equated with indifference on the part of the enslaver who cared little for reverence in the ceremony, as his only interest lied in the promise of reproduction. John Hawkins Simpson's 1863 book, *Horrors of the Virginia Slave Trade*, portrayed broomstick weddings as akin to factory lines where enslaved people were rushed through a marriage ceremony and encouraged to bear children. In Simpson's account, thirteen enslaved couples were brought into the "big house" and lined up in front of a magistrate. The magistrate then "took the hand of a girl and put it into that of a man, repeating the action till all were paired. Then one of the young ladies laid a broomstick in the doorway, and to each couple as they jumped over the stick, the magistrate said 'You are man and wife.'"[19] As the ceremonies ended, the newly betrothed were ordered to dance and make merry, largely for the white guests' enjoyment. Simpson apparently obtained this narrative from Dinah, a fugitive from Virginia who migrated to London. As with most abolitionists, Simpson made no links to the custom bearing resemblance to rituals in the British Isles, but linked it to the dominance of American slaveholders. For educated whites inclined to antislavery sentiments, the ritual held no dignity or value. The enslaved were captive to the slaveowner's capricious ceremonies.

A few antislavery authors went into greater details surrounding the dynamics of plantation weddings. In her antislavery novel entitled *Cousin Franck's Household*, Emily Clemons Pearson describes a fictional wedding between two enslaved people and provides a depressing image of the ceremony. Writing under the pseudonym "Pocahontas," she used her novel to detail the system's brutalities.[20] According to the text, the enslaved woman, Mima, initially refuses to jump over the broomstick with a man named Juniper, whom she was forced to marry. The broom is unceremoniously placed on a stool and a chair to mock the entire proceeding, as it prevented others from Mima's community to actively participate. When Mima refuses to jump, Juniper is bewildered, and Rose, the plantation mistress, becomes enraged. Amidst a flurry of curses, Rose slaps Mima's ear and eventually forces her to jump over, but Mima still exclaims, "It's des' no marrying 'tall, to jump over de broomstick," which prompts Rose to chastise her once again: "Shut up, it's more than you deserve!"[21] Regardless of whether or not Mima and Juniper's story was based on actual events, or simply a reflection of how Pearson interpreted southern slavery, she was correct in claiming that enslaved women often fell victim to others on the plantation, including slaveowners and enslaved men.[22] Through the eyes of an abolitionist, this marriage ceremony was one of the more revealing elements of exploitation within the southern system because it withheld a Christian ceremony from a downtrodden population.

The ambiance of the image is gloomy—displaying Mima as a sulking bride, her fellow enslaved people as nervous observers of the ceremony, and the mistress as an angry tyrant raising a shoe to strike her. The broom is placed upon a stool and chair, while a cat scoots across the center of the image and approaches a piece of clothing messily draped over a piece of furniture. The unkempt scene reflects a chaotic domestic space that entraps Mima and her fellow Black women. As historians Thavolia Glymph and Stephanie E. Jones-Rogers note, Black women confined to plantation houses were frequently victimized by the white women they served.[23] The only smiling face in this entire image is that of the enslaved man, Juniper, who seems to have gained the woman he desired through an agreement with the mistress. A white figure leans over the staircase and examines the scene nonchalantly. This rendition of the broomstick wedding mocks enslaved agency and their capacity to pursue romance, especially enslaved women who confronted abuse from multiple directions. Mima's facial expression, filled with the deepest sadness, alongside the abusive action frozen within the image, encapsulates the omnipresent violence of domestic enslavement.

"A Forced Broomstick Wedding," from Pearson, *Cousin Franck's Household*, 168–169; courtesy of www.slaveryimages.org, reference: BROOM.

Another depiction provides a more empowering rendition of the ceremony, though the white abolitionist author comes to a similar conclusion about the validity of the broomstick wedding. Entitled "The Broomstick Wedding," the image portrays a community free from white surveillance: the couple is dressed for the occasion, actively involved in the nuptials, and an enslaved minister presides over the ceremony. By not including white attendants and centering the ceremony at the forefront of the picture the image suggests that the participants held some agency in the ceremonial selection, as no one is forcing them to marry in the broomstick fashion.[24] The minister's authoritative posture, with his right hand raised dictating the ceremonial format, displays a power and prestige absent from the previous image of Mima and Juniper. Though the marriage was not legally recognized, the ceremonial format ensured the occasion was celebratory and sanctioned by the community, its elders, and its spiritual leader. The cabin is also free of clutter, which conveys reverence for the occasion. Unlike the disheveled domestic space of the previous image, "The Broomstick Wedding" reveals how enslaved people maintained an internal respect for marriage and domestic partnership, even if their unions were not respected by the legal structure.

"The Broomstick Wedding," from Livermore, *The Story of My Life*, 257; courtesy of www.slaveryimages.org, reference: Livermore257.

The image comes from the 1897 work of Mary Ashton Rice Livermore, a white northerner who was recollecting the "broomstick wedding" of an enslaved couple, Pompey and Susan. She attended this ceremony in the antebellum period when she served as a governess on a Virginia plantation. Rice carefully detailed the ritual process, noting that the spiritual leader emphasized the ceremony was as "solem' as a buryin'" and he implored everyone present to recognize its sacred nature.[25] After two friends of the couple held the broom off the ground, the enslaved minister asked God to have mercy on their souls and counted to three before entreating them to jump over it. After they successfully leaped over the broomstick, the newlyweds enjoyed a meal and received a "good send-off" to the cabin where they established their family.

Despite the empowering sermon of the enslaved elder and the community's participation in the nuptials, Livermore still concluded that the ceremony was a frivolous gesture that displayed the perversions of American slave law. Since slave marriages had no legal standing in American law, she concluded the event was a futile attempt to bring solemnity to an institution that the antebellum South made inaccessible to the enslaved. According to Livermore, the officiant announced, "De fiel' han's am willin' t' jump de broomstick, but when de house sarvans gwine t' marry, dey wants a white preacher . . . but de broomstick's jess as bindin' as de preacher."[26] It seems the statement was designed to contest the social divisions within the community, as field hands challenged the insinuation that house servants' weddings made them superior. Enslaved people defined their social stratifications along similar lines as antebellum whites, in that the pomp and display of their social gatherings denoted their position within the society. However, even if the enslaved held a specific viewpoint, white observers from outside the community found no dignity in the ritual and used it as a trope to point toward the horrors of the system. Livermore interpreted the ceremony through a legal lens, collapsing the validity of all slave weddings under a legal framework. Whether married by a white minister or a broomstick ritual, Livermore concluded both ceremonies were equalized by the law since enslaved partners could still be forcibly separated: "[The preacher] was right. No marriage was binding among the slaves . . . I could not enjoy their gaiety and merriment; their very happiness made me sad."[27] Despite her firsthand observation, Livermore was still a white northerner who was ill-prepared to understand the dynamics of slave culture and the ways through which communities found meaning and purpose while under bondage. Her conclusions on American slave codes were correct, but her pessimistic developments caused her to overlook the cultural genealogy of this ceremony and how this particular community adapted it to meet their needs. As a firsthand observer, Livermore was positioned to uncover how the broomstick ceremony was adopted and adapted by this group of field hands, but her fixation on law over culture prevented her from entertaining the idea that this ceremony held any validity to its practitioners.

The above selections from abolitionists portray three separate forms of literature: one is a second-hand account published as a biography of the formerly enslaved Dinah, the second is a novel based upon stories and accounts of people formerly enslaved, and the third emerged from the writer's past observations of a slave wedding. The circumstances of each ceremony were distinct and their ritual processes differed. However, each white author came to the same conclusion: the broomstick ceremony, as a slave custom, had no broad societal value and was a mockery of marriage in a Christian nation. For two of them, it was a ceremony imposed by the master. But even when the enslaved used it themselves, Livermore still dismissed it due to its having no legal standing. Much of the criticism was, appropriately, wrapped into the politics of the antebellum period, in which antislavery activists believed the most horrifying feature of the system, beyond its sheer physical brutality, was the inability of enslaved couples to obtain a legally recognized, and protected, marriage. Thus, from the perspectives of white observers the broomstick wedding's connection to slave customs represented the institution's most blatant hypocrisies. In many respects, these portrayals reflect the methodological problems of relying upon outside observers to unpack the dynamics of slave culture. Even white people who were sympathetic to the plight of enslaved people were unprepared to take their culture seriously, and consequently, these same white people did not further explore the otherwise rich symbolism such ceremonies might contain.

## Minstrelsy, Popular Culture, and Racist Tropes

A white American's hesitation to accept the broomstick wedding as a serious ritual was likely structured by the racial parameters of the antebellum period. By the 1830s minstrel shows gained popularity in the United States and found a significant audience in the North. Minstrels were typically white men who appropriated slave culture for comedic entertainment, oftentimes portraying it as a joke for white audiences. Consequently, jumping the broom was lambasted in popular culture towards the close of the antebellum period and remained so well into the early twentieth century. Antebellum minstrels often employed jumping the broomstick in their mockeries of slave life, which exposed white audiences in the Northeast to the custom and likely influenced their low opinions of enslaved people's cultural patterns.[28]

A popular song used in minstrel shows called "De Nigger's Wedding-Day" reveals the stereotype in unsettling detail:

> I came from ole Virginia, and I'm a nigger of some game
> I lubs a yallow gal called Dinah, and she lubs me de same;
> I'm always dare and neber away,
> So, niggers, we'll have a dance, for dis am my wedding day
> . . .
> We'll go to Deacon Peabody, and get him for to say,
> You now both tied togeder, and dis am your wedding-day
> . . .
> Den I turn my pocket inside out, an' gub him all my money,
> Den ole Deacon kissed de bride and said she was sweet as honey;

An' as we both jump'd ober de broom and wed widout any boder,
Now I'll go to my massa's house and you go tell your modder.[29]

The song exposes a variety of stereotypes employed by whites in the antebellum era that reverberated in postbellum racial discourse, including the liberal use of the word "nigger," the exaggerated imitation of speech patterns of Black southerners, and the supposed promiscuity of enslaved people who married "widout any boder." Minstrels exposed audiences to the stereotypes of southern slave culture and reemphasized white assumptions that the enslaved were promiscuous and lacked the intellectual faculty for civilized living.

By the mid-1850s, minstrel shows adapted and modified Harriet Beecher Stowe's bestselling 1853 novel *Uncle Tom's Cabin* to fit their performances. Using a cast of characters who represented the depravities of southern slavery, including two lovers seeking to save their union by escaping North, an enslaved Christian who loyally serves his enslaver, a depraved slave hunter, and even sympathetic white southerners, Stowe's work ignited a transnational debate about the morality of slavery and bolstered antislavery sentiment in the United States and abroad. Minstrels, however, took creative license in reconstructing the characters, scenery, and overall message of the book for live performances. These "Tom Shows" could reiterate the antislavery sentiments of Stowe's novel, but others drew from certain elements of the text to portray enslaved people as docile, loyal, and happy in their circumstances. Consequently, white audiences otherwise unfamiliar with the systemic brutalities of slavery could potentially sympathize with white slaveowners.

Regardless of intent, white actors in blackface provided exaggerated representations of Black life for the consumption of white audiences. Minstrel actors regarded themselves as accurate interpreters of slave culture, and believed their movements, speech, and showcasing of specific customs authenticated their authority upon the subject. But they were entertainers, not scholars, and their audience composed of white Americans who readily consumed stereotypes of African American culture. Such creative license allowed them to add cultural rituals that were not included in Stowe's book, but were well known as customs used by the enslaved. At least two American performances added a scene where the characters George and Eliza jump the broom at their wedding.[30] However, *Uncle Tom's Cabin* never refers to the broomstick custom. In Stowe's original novel George and Eliza are presented as a married couple, but few details are provided about their wedding. It is reasonable to assume that the minstrel performers believed the broomstick wedding was an authentic representation of a "slave wedding," though they likely did not consider the different classifications to which enslaved people subscribed. George and Eliza are not field laborers, as George usually works skilled tasks and Eliza is enslaved within the plantation house. According to the typical stratifications of the plantation, neither of them would likely select the ceremony, preferring a grander affair that fit the parameters of Christian orthodoxy. The fact that the broomstick wedding is foisted onto George and Eliza by outside interpreters, however, demonstrates the cultural weight it carried throughout the nineteenth century.

## Broomstick Weddings and Social Divisions

Broomstick marriages in southern white discourse usually connoted either shotgun weddings performed on a whim, or a form of marriage employed by populations considered inferior by both cultural or racial standards. In Missouri lore it was a "simple and crude" ceremony that gave young couples permission to consummate their marriage in "absence of the clergy."[31] In the journal of Margaret Ann Morris Grimball, she recorded that an acquaintance's father "is said at a gay party in Ireland to have jumped over a broomstick with one of the young ladies, and they were pronounced man & wife."[32] In many respects, this reference resembles the aforementioned references to broomstick weddings performed at English taverns. The liveliness of the party, and the likely presence of alcohol, may have caused the man to initiate the wedding without inhibition. The young woman's friends were so incensed by the event that they "had a divorce procured so that he was divorced before he was married."[33] The statement is somewhat unclear if they considered the broomstick marriage as valid and binding. On the one hand, the procurement of a quick divorce suggests they viewed the ritual as a serious commitment, requiring them to act before the relationship continued. On the other hand, the statement that he "was divorced before he was married" could mean that he was divorced before married in the United States, since Morris later mentions that marital separations were especially difficult in the man's home state of South Carolina. It is apparent this form of marriage disturbed many respectable adults, and one gains the impression it was popular among lively young people.

Both the custom and phrase carried negative connotations. Just as certain groups in the British Isles endured stinging criticism of their marital rites on one side of the Atlantic, marginalized groups throughout the United States endured similar treatments. Those who jumped the broom were condemned as "marriage simplifiers" by certain moralistic commentators.[34] Horace Greeley, noted statesman and editor of the *New York-Tribune*, sarcastically wrote those who married hastily would not "need even so much ceremony as that of jumping the broomstick."[35] Ultimately, broomstick weddings were presented as a silly form of nuptials that had no binding authority for the couple.[36] Perhaps unsurprisingly, broomstick weddings also signified pacts with demons, as revealed in the play *Jurgen: Comedy of Justice*, in which the main character Jurgen and his Vampire bride "were duly married. First Jurgen's nails were trimmed, and the parings were given to Florimel. A broomstick was laid before them, and they stepped over it."[37] Though a significant component of American popular culture, it was used by commentators to reflect those cultures that lived on the periphery of acceptance.

Indigenous Americans were also subjected to such attacks concerning marital morality. In a collection of satirical tales entitled *The Knights of the Horseshoe*, published in 1845, a conversation emerges between two of the characters concerning the marital rites of Native Americans. When Squire inquires if they have any such rites, his friend, Jarvis, replies, "Oh, as to that, they may jump the broom stick, or the likes o' that, but cuss me if I think they're even so much christenated as that comes to."[38] For Jarvis, those who "jump the broom stick" have no affinity for Christian ceremony. The conversation between the two characters continued to detail the general lack of Christian morality among the Indigenous population. The tone of the statement suggests that Anglo-Americans believed that broomstick marriages resonated among populations that were not only devoid of Christianity, but also rejected its rituals. Ethnocentric ambitions to Christianize Amerindian populations through appropriate forms of marriage were relatively familiar to early Americans. This statement was likely not meant to convey that Indigenous people jumped the broom for marriage, but more to dismiss their non-Christian ceremonies as irregular unions. Using the broomstick wedding as an analogy for heathenism reveals the negative connotations the phrase carried into the middle of the nineteenth century. Despite this association, however, white Americans utilized the broomstick ritual for a variety of purposes both before and after the Civil War.

Descriptions of the practice reveal familiarity with it as both an action and an expression for irregular unions. In one memoir, Nelly Jones, the daughter of a cotton speculator in East Feliciana, Louisiana, was married in a mock ceremony to her "suitor" Captain Prince in the 1840s. The ceremony largely functioned as an amusement performed before guests, but the ritual's description is strikingly similar to those employed by enslaved couples on southern plantations. Within the account, the officiant, Major Bee, first asked for a prayer book. Despite one not being available, Major Bee proceeded with the ceremony, holding a broom a little off the floor with a command of "Jump over!" Nelly and Prince both "stepped over in a business-like manner," which was followed with Major Bee's exclamation "I solemnly pronounce you husband and wife, and I hope and trust that you will dwell together lovingly and peacefully until you die. I have at your request tied this matrimonial knot as tight as I possibly could, under the circumstances."[39] The broomstick wedding appears initiated as a coy gesture without the seriousness of a legally binding contract. If one looks closer, however, certain statements reveal that the practice held a degree of legitimacy within certain white southern communities.

In the initial phase of the ceremony, Captain Prince approached Major Bee to perform the ceremony, who in turn seemed completely willing "to take part in this dangerous pastime."[40] After the ceremony was performed and the "mock bridal couple" sat to entertain their guests, Captain Prince exclaimed, "My dearest, I fear when your mother hears the news she will say 'Poor Nelly, she has thrown herself away.'"[41] The narrative explains that Captain Prince gained a sense of satisfaction at the thought of upsetting Nelly's mother with such surprising news. Even if the ceremony was not legitimate by legal standards and performed as an activity to entertain guests, it held symbolic qualities that are illustrative of southern marital culture. For one, many white southerners were familiar with the broomstick ritual, be it through cultural transmission or observation. Second, it provides one example of the ability of young southerners to control their spousal selection even in the face of the parent's "disapprobation." Since broomstick weddings could be undertaken on a whim and without official approval, denoting them as a "dangerous pastime" suggests that young couples used these ceremonies with some regularity and such unregulated practices needed to be curtailed. Even if Nelly Jones and Captain Prince performed the ceremony only as a mock gesture, such performances may not have been unusual for those of marriageable age who did not wish to wait for either parental approval or ecclesiastical sanction.

In American fiction jumping the broomstick is a figure for weddings performed in haste. Walter Sawyer's 1899 novel, *A Local Habitation*, depicted a conversation between two people who could not marry in a church since they were members of different Christian denominations. One of the partners suggests they find any way to obtain ceremonial endorsement, including procuring a priest, rabbi, parson, or even locking hands and jumping the broom.[42] A short story published in 1848 in a magazine entitled the *Rural Repository* depicted an attempted broomstick marriage between a young woman named Delilah and a French suitor. After Delilah's friends "united their voices in commendation of his gallantry," the "giddy girl" requested that her cousin Jack "bring a broom . . . and let me prove my gratitude by jumping the broomstick with him."[43] Delilah's cousin prevents the activity, however, and convinces her that a "young traveler" could "play a parson for once" with a feast to follow. As with the previous scenario, the remainder of the story reveals that the entire ceremony is a mockery, which Delilah performs to make the Frenchman "the ridiculous hero of a joke."[44] It appears that the French guest committed some form of "impudence" during his stay, causing Delilah to exact revenge upon him by requesting his hand in marriage. Throughout the ordeal, he appears convinced of the ceremony's legitimacy. The story was designated "polite literature" in its title. Thus, a literary work caricatured the marriage methods of marginalized populations by rendering it a game or a practical joke meant for entertainment.

Conceptually, "jumping the broom" retained its utility as a marker of social divisions in the United States, in which self-important writers used it to denigrate the social mores of those deemed culturally inferior, primarily people of African descent. "Jumping the broom" was referenced in every sphere of American popular culture in the nineteenth century and early twentieth century, including politics, stage performances, and literary fiction. Those who jumped the broom in the United States, be they Black or white, were regarded in similar terms as the ethnic minorities of the British Isles: primitive and downtrodden groups who clung to odd customs.

## CHAPTER FIVE

# Better than Nothing

*Broomstick Weddings in European American*
*Ritual Practice*

From 1956 to 1958 the American Broadcasting Corporation aired *The Adventures of Jim Bowie*, based on the novel *The Tempered Blade*, which reimagined Bowie's life in the Louisiana Territory about a decade before his death at the Battle of the Alamo in 1836. The series is in the tradition of the classic American Western. Bowie is an adventurer who fights wicked antagonists, evades danger, and assists those in need, even strangers. In the sixth episode of the first season Bowie finds himself aiding a young woman from a Louisiana community. The series' narrator introduces the episode by explaining that in 1829, Louisiana, despite its annexation to the United States, was still influenced by the "Spanish and French rule of the previous century, and this particular story shows how Jim Bowie, an American, confronts the two heritages of Louisiana: Spanish Catholics and 'Cajun women.'"[1] Through a series of misunderstandings and betrayals, he is introduced to a Cajun community that practices an unusual form of matrimony.

The episode begins with an exchange between Bowie and an acquaintance named Raef Bradford, who is fleeing from trouble. After significant persuasion on the part of Bradford the two exchange horses, promising to meet again to return the animals to their rightful owners. Unbeknown to Bowie, Bradford is being pursued by Cajun vigilantes, who claim he dishonored a Cajun woman by kissing her and leaving. According to the woman's uncle, it is the custom of his people that "a kiss is a promise to marry." In the eyes of this community, Bradford has deserted her and should be forced to marry her. Based upon the description of Bradford's horse and saddle, which Bowie is riding, the Cajun vigilantes mistake him for Bradford and detain him at gunpoint. He then ventures into their "clannish . . . fishing village," where he is viewed as a "foreigner and . . . curiosity" by the isolated community. The beguiled woman eventually proves him innocent, claiming he was not the man who kissed her. Bowie is then invited to a wedding party in the village, and engages in a revealing conversation with her uncle:

BOWIE: Isn't it a little unusual, a wedding at night?

UNCLE: We do not have enough priests to serve all of the villages in the bayou. . . . Sometimes it is months between their visits. For the young people in love we have the broomstick wedding. It is like your civil ceremony. Then when the priest comes, they are married again with the full rites of the church. I think you will find the ceremony . . . charming.

Following this conversation, the viewer learns that the original woman's mother has plotted to frame Bowie by having her daughter lead Bowie into her home and exchange a kiss with him. Following their romantic exchange, the Cajun leaders storm into the house and declare: "There is only one honorable path for you to follow tonight, Monsieur, [that is] the broomstick wedding!"

The viewer then witnesses a rendition of a Cajun broomstick wedding. A young couple stands at one end of two parallel rows of guests who are chanting, "over and over and over you go, Jump the Broom!" At the other end are two individuals holding each end of the broom. After the couple are pronounced man and wife by the officiant, they run between the two rows and leap over the broomstick; the man lifts his bride in the air and carries her to their new residence. Prior to Bowie's jump, the show's narrator notes that while this ceremony might seem like a "quaint" tradition to outsiders, it was nonetheless a "binding ritual . . . [for] couples who jumped the broomstick were married in the eyes of Cajun custom." Through a mutual agreement with his potential bride, Bowie escapes the ceremony without jumping the broomstick. He then finds Raef Bradford, beats him into submission, and brings him to the Cajun community where he jumps over the broomstick with the woman he originally kissed.

Not surprisingly, the episode portrays Bowie as a forgiving hero who simply hopes to make matters right. What is noteworthy about it is the accuracy of the portrayal of the broomstick wedding, which aligns with oral traditions gleaned from Cajuns and other communities. It is true that rural communities used the broomstick wedding as a temporary substitute for a church wedding, allowing young couples to cohabit without giving into their premarital carnal desires. As will be discussed later, the method of performance is also validated by various testimonies in which couples describe wedding guests surrounding them while they jump over a broom held by their friends. The episode's accurate portrayal of this tradition suggests that enough information was available in the mid-twentieth century to enable the show's writers reconstruct it for television.

Although European Americans perceived and practiced the broomstick tradition in many ways, scholarly research on this subject is less robust than it is on that of slave matrimony.[2] The omission is understandable, considering that many references to jumping the broomstick come from Black interviewees of the WPA. White narratives of the WPA usually do not mention living during the time of slavery and rarely describe their marriage ceremonies, but typically reflect upon aspects their lives in the late-nineteenth and early twentieth centuries. There are, however, scattered references to the broomstick wedding in white communities in other sources, and these can shed some light on the ritual, the motivations for its performance, and the functions it served for those who did.

## The Social Meanings of the Broomstick Wedding

The choice to use the broomstick wedding is somewhat of an anomaly among white southerners in the antebellum period, since, unlike enslaved peoples, they had access to legally recognized marriages, no matter their social status. At the same time, though, while the law prescribed marriage as the only acceptable form of cohabitation, it did not formally denounce any particular ceremony. An 1853 report in South Carolina claimed there was no law prescribing a marriage ceremony: "If Mr. A and Miss B jump over a broom, the former saying I take this woman to be my wedded wife, and the latter I take this man too be my wedded husband, and go to housekeeping they are legally married."[3] Poor southern whites' rural locations certainly made it difficult for them to sanction their marriages through church services or legal formalities. Jumping the broom was convenient for populations that lived on the periphery of southern cultural norms. As will be seen, broomsticks and the supernatural connotations of "crossing over" an object influenced the worldviews of many white southerners.

For some southern whites, the broomstick ceremony signified both luck and a safeguard against witches. In their folklore a bride could "secure good luck by jumping over a broomstick after the wedding."[4] In another variation practiced in early twentieth-century Illinois, "to keep from being bewitched, a newly married couple should step over a broom on entering the house for the first time."[5] Though a twentieth century source, it has counterparts across the Atlantic as well as the antebellum South, where, in one version of the ritual, an enslaved respondent explained the master and mistress stood "inside the house with a broom held crosswise of the door and we stands outside . . . and we steps over the broom into the house."[6] The difference is that protection from witches appears to have been an important aspect of the ritual for many of the rural whites who used it: "If you see a witch coming, run and put the broom down in front of the door and say, 'Kiss my a . . .' three times; and she will not be able to step over the broom."[7] In Tennessee, "A broom was laid across the doorway before the bride and groom entered the house so as to keep out witches."[8] Due to a lack of primary sources outside of folklore, it is difficult to know how many people believed these traditions, but the broomstick was connected to supernatural elements. In one Halloween tradition, ghosts and witches could not enter the world of the living unless they first jumped over the broomstick."[9] In a somewhat different variation on this theme, a woman accused of witchcraft in 1892 had "quantities of salt [poured] down her breasts," and she was forced to "jump over a broom" by her accuser.[10] In addition to the broomstick, salt also served as a safeguard against witches, as it was usually sprinkled over one's doorstep to prevent a witch from entering the home.

The similarities in folk practice should not be surprising. Ex-slaves remembered itinerant white laborers on their plantations who worked for a day's wage before returning to their communities.[11] Even when slaveholders banned the "poor white trash," some narratives reveal that the enslaved fraternized with them outside.[12] Cultural transmissions and interchanges obviously occurred, but illiterate whites left no documentation. Enslaved people may have acquired it from these associations, and, in certain cases, could have introduced it into white communities that did not previously practice it. But the source base rarely discusses origins, and finding the broomstick wedding's American originators is less important than analyzing why groups used it and how they felt about it. The ritual's influence in white American folklore suggests that broomstick marriages were not simply "slave marriages," but became a custom largely identified with marginalized and isolated populations of various ethnic and regional identities.

## Social Class and the White Southern Family

Marriage and family formation were crucial aspects of antebellum southern culture, as they served as methods of networking and establishing social capital. Elite families, for instance, "rejoiced at marriages to wealthy heirs or heiresses," and middle-class farmers, while less assertive in selecting who their children would marry, "took steps to encourage men whom they considered good potential husbands for their daughters."[13] Marriage was ideally both a civil contract and religious commitment that needed sanction by both God and the community. While the unifying nature of marriage was certainly important, ritual expression served as a definitive method of distinguishing social classes. As noted in previous chapters, the pomp and display of a Christian ceremony that included food, festivities, and guests was a coveted feature of slave weddings. If only for a moment, a select group of enslaved people could mimic the ritual functions of elite culture through the sponsorship of their master and mistress. The enslaved, however, were not the only group to suffer under the aristocratic rule of southern society. Evidence in the antebellum period suggests that wedding rituals and ceremony greatly distinguished the region's social classes. The broomstick wedding's popularity among antebellum whites further shows class distinctions among them, as well as cultural commonalities between poor whites and antebellum slaves.

Folk customs, traditions, and cultural patterns were certainly carried across the Atlantic by the early colonists. In *Albion's Seed*, David Hackett Fischer tracks various British folkways to specific locations in colonial North America. Fischer briefly mentions the "ancient pagan practice" of jumping over the broomstick in Europe, but does not find any references to colonial Americans using the ritual.[14] Documents prior to the antebellum period provide few details of the marital traditions of the early inhabitants.[15] The difficulty in finding references to the practice in colonial America likely stems from a combination of the rural locales of most settlers and of the individuals doing the reporting. Much of the literature on marriage in eighteenth-century South Carolina, for example, stems from the writings of itinerant missionaries in African and Indigenous American populations, who were usually less concerned with describing the specifics of their wedding ceremonies, as they were with reporting how they adjusted them to the Christian standard.[16] Like their forebears throughout the British Isles, colonists in North America lived in a world culturally peripheral to the elite class and created cultural patterns that went largely undocumented, save in a few descriptions by missionaries and adventurers. As the cotton belt expanded into frontier territories, however, descriptions of common whites in the nineteenth century suggest how they shared similarities to both the enslaved and the enslaver, but could never identify with either one.

Broomstick ceremonies were known to have transatlantic origins, as an Alabama newspaper reported in 1829 notes, one couple who cut "a tremendous caper over a long hickory pole, probably in imitation of the old English custom of jumping over the broomstick."[17] But as with most southern cultural patterns, the variegated methods of jumping the broomstick in the U.S. South were produced through undocumented interactions occurring between poor and common whites, slaveowners, and the enslaved. The similarities in how each population envisioned broomstick folklore and the supernatural speaks to these cultural exchanges. A popular practice among both white and Black southerners was to place a broomstick over one's doorway to prevent witches from entering. Indeed, a white southerner from the Smoky Mountains of North Carolina bluntly claimed, "Anyone who refuses to step over a broom is a witch."[18] In his fieldwork of 1909, folklorist Tom Cross claimed that the superstitions of "witch-lore" were not only popular among Black southerners, but "also current among ignorant whites."[19] Cross's inclusion of "ignorant" in his description of the white population suggests that beliefs in folklore were typically associated with marginalized groups that lacked access to formal education, even though evidence suggests that some slaveowners both believed and feared enslaved people who claimed to wield power from the supernatural realm.[20]

## The North

In his 1976 book, *The Black Family in Slavery and Freedom, 1750–1925*, historian Herbert Gutman observed that white Americans also jumped the broom in the rural North. While citing a report in New England's *Lowell Offering* that an engaged couple, "Johnny S. and his sweetheart Molly," jumped over the broomstick in a simple ceremony,[21] Gutman did not broadly explore the ritual's use among white Americans and concentrated his research on its connection to African Americans. Since his study, scholars have not examined the ritual's use outside the U.S. South. Though documentary evidence is less robust for this region, a few references prove that couples throughout the North occasionally employed the tradition. In one case in 1869, the *Saturday Review* reported on a "short and simple" wedding in New York, in which the husband and wife jumped over the broom "in succession."[22] The ceremony matches other narratives that required partners to jump separately, suggesting it shared a common root with previous examples of successive leaping. However, given that many groups who used the custom rarely documented their own experiences, we have a far smaller sample to illuminate its diverse array of performances. But a children's story published in 1867 provides especially useful details in how certain white communities viewed the ritual as a cultural practice. Written by "Aunt Fanny," the story tells a fictionalized version of her experience with a broomstick wedding in antebellum New York. At a young age, the author developed an adolescent crush on a much older, married man named Mr. Carson. Knowing of her infatuation with him, her relatives set up a mock wedding ceremony in the form of a broomstick wedding. The broom

A mock wedding. From "Aunt Fanny's First Marriage and Its Tragical Ending," 30–31.

is laid on the floor at a tilt, and after counting to three, both partners leap over to seal the "marriage."

Reflecting on the experience, the author was critical of her elder relatives' actions, claiming that as a child she held a perfect "conviction that jumping over the broomstick was the only way to be married."[23] When young Fanny discovered the entire ceremony was a façade (and her pseudo-husband was previously married to another woman) "all her faith, truth, and devotion [was] struck down, crushed at one blow! With wild eyes, as if she were gazing at some fearful apparition, the child gave a piteous cry, and fled from the room."[24] The author's story served as a warning to parents to not mislead children for their own amusement, but taken with the other evidence the story is much more revealing. The association of the broomstick wedding with childlike simplicity reveals many white American perceptions of the custom's associations with uneducated and illiterate populations. The essay included an image depicting the ceremony, illustrating the general lack of respect elite and middle-class societies held for populations that used the broomstick ceremony. Showing a young child preparing to leap into matrimony with a grown man reflected the broomstick wedding's status as an amusing joke for those who had access to an official ceremony. The story seems to have received rather wide circulation, as the volume that included it was reviewed favorably in the *North American and United States Gazette* in 1866.[25]

## White Appalachians and Geographical Isolation

Referring to the Ohio Valley, folklorist Lawrence S. Thompson argued, "Perhaps no household instrument is the subject of as many superstitions as the broom."[26] Thompson linked the American tradition to European precedents, noting that countries in both eastern and western Europe had oral testimonies portraying broomsticks as safeguards against witches and sorcery. It often served as a way to determine practitioners of evil magic, since witches and other malevolent spirits apparently refused to step over brooms.[27] As noted, communities in Tennessee placed the broomstick over the doorway as protection against witchcraft, believing a witch could not enter the house due to her inability to step over it. In his 1970 essay on folk traditions throughout the Smokey Mountains, Joseph Hall claimed this tradition "alluded to . . . the common expression, 'They jumped the broom' . . . meaning that a broom was laid across the doorway before the bride and groom entered the house."[28] Hall's quote suggests that by 1970, "jumping the broom" was understood as a colloquial expression that referred to a literal practice once used by these isolated communities. In slight variation on this idea, folklore extending from North Carolina to Kentucky in the early twentieth century claimed it was bad luck to haphazardly step over a broom, and if one hoped to reverse the effect, one had to "step over it again backwards."[29] Utilizing ancestral concepts that connected brooms with domesticity and matrimony, Euro-Americans in isolated areas engaged different forms of this folkloric practice for reasons of practicality and to preserve their cultural traditions.

"Appalachia" designates the mountainous areas that range from states in the Deep South, like Georgia, Alabama, and Mississippi, up to the northern states of Ohio, Pennsylvania, and New York. Though a huge swathe of land, the region's cultural cohesion stems from the similar lifestyles harnessed by living in the mountains. Historians suggest that European settlers, comprising Celts, the English, and Germans, amalgamated their ancestral cultures with the indigenous populations. Throughout southern and central Appalachia, enslaved people of African descent contributed heavily to the region's social and cultural identity. Though Appalachians were connected to larger markets through toll roads, few Americans traveled into the mountain communities.[30] Those who did were viewed as strangers and worthy of distrust. Thus, Appalachian culture became a distinct subset of the American Southern identity, and for those outside the region it became "known better by myth and legend than by history."[31] Its inhabitants possessed a unique set of customs, rituals, and dialects nurtured by their isolation. Unsurprisingly, the broomstick wedding became a defining aspect of the white inhabitants' marriage ceremonies.

While the broomstick ceremony touched various portions of this region, the mountainous sections of Kentucky were associated with a "pan-Appalachian" identity and its unique wedding culture.[32] The Kentucky connection to broomstick weddings extends into the antebellum period. In 1848, the *New York Evangelist* criticized Kentucky marriage law as being "not a bit more binding upon the parties than jumping over the broom-stick."[33] Nearly thirty years later, one politician's career was ruined when the press discovered "that his original marriage was a sort of 'broom-jumping' Kentucky affair of which there is no record."[34] The designation of broom-jumping as a "Kentucky affair" served to stereotype a population that was considered politically and culturally backward when compared with an increasingly industrialized North America. Similarly, Eleanor Kelly's 1916 novel *Kildares of Storm* depicts a revealing conversation between a local Kentucky mountaineer and an inquisitive outsider named Channing. When Channing assumes that jumping over a broomstick is the common form of marriage in the mountains, the local man replies: "Well, stranger, a broomstick's better than nothin', I reckon . . . It kinder stands fer law and order, anyway. I've knowed folks down around these parts, whar they's a-plenty of preachers, to take up with each other 'thout'n [thought not] so much as a broomstick to make things bindin'-like."[35] In this instance, the nomadic respondent explains that certain couples decided to forego the minister's ceremony, even though it was available to them. In fact, the broomstick wedding attains a higher caliber in this rendition, since some couples did not even avail themselves of that ceremony.

A recorded oral tradition suggests the broomstick ceremony was discussed in Appalachian folklore, revealed by songs sung at weddings in the early twentieth century. One verse implores the couple to jump the broom following their ceremony: "Now you have one of your own choosing, be in a hurry— no time for losing / Join your right hands, this broom step over, And kiss the lips of your true lover."[36] As in other folkloric sources, this selection provides no context for its use within the community or what it meant to them. It was certainly a pragmatic resource for an isolated population—like those who lived in Appalachia. But in looking outside this region and into the deep South we find one community who viewed it for both its practical applications and as a symbol of resistance.

## Louisiana Cajuns

Due to their isolated position in the broader narratives of American colonial and antebellum history, Cajuns' cultural contributions and connections with other populations are often overlooked.[37] The Cajun community's historical trajectory in the United States is one of struggle and discrimination. Cajuns were initially known as "Acadians," the name stemming from the French-Canadian territories of Acadia, where they lived in the eighteenth century. During the French and Indian War, Britain annexed Acadian territory for itself, ultimately leading to an event known as Le Grand Derangment, or The Great Expulsion, after the Treaty of Paris in 1763.[38] Acadian exiles were shipped to a variety of French, English, and Iberian territories, many of them perishing from the harsh climates while also dealing with various enactments of discrimination in their host communities.[39] Those who migrated to the predominantly Francophone territories of Louisiana, however, established a vibrant community in the deep South.[40]

Some Acadian immigrants migrated directly to Louisiana during English expulsion, while others toiled in the harsh conditions of other Atlantic colonies awaiting their ability to join their kin on the west bank of the Mississippi River. By 1770, about 1,000 Acadian immigrants arrived in Louisiana; they were joined by another 1,500 to 2,000 in the last quarter of the eighteenth century.[41] By the mid-nineteenth century Acadians became "Cajuns," a name typically claimed to be an Anglicized corruption of their French-Canadian original. Cajuns intermarried with other European and Indigenous American populations living in the Louisiana bayous, but the isolation of the swamp allowed them to keep much of their culture intact. Such isolation had also characterized life in French Canada. In both locations, the Acadian/Cajun identity became consolidated around common French origins, distinctive language, social solidarity, and neglect by the governing body, an extended kinship system, and frontier mentality.[42] Cajuns used the maritime skills their ancestors acquired in both France and Canada to navigate the harsh bayous of the Louisiana swamp and develop a fishing culture. By the antebellum period Louisiana Cajun were reported to practice a wedding custom known as "sauter l' (le) balai," or "to jump over the broomstick."

It is unclear if Cajuns jumped broomsticks prior to arriving in the U.S. South. For such an isolated community, it is somewhat surprising to see Cajun folktales that emphasize broomstick marriages as legitimate forms of union since the custom is not currently known to have been practiced in seventeenth- or eighteenth-century France. Cajuns, however, were willing to blend with other populations, which strongly distinguished them from their Anglo-American counterparts. In his 1897 history of "Acadia," James Hannay stated that the Acadians were "a darker people than the majority of their ancestors were."[43] Hannay denies that this darker complexion was produced through interracial relationships and suggests instead that "different modes of living and differences of food are potent influences in changing the complexions of people."[44] Interestingly, Hannay dismantles his own case by including instances of intermarriage between Cajuns and the indigenous population. Though scholars note that French legislators interpreted miscegenation as a sign of social disorder in the colonies, citizens throughout the French colonies were less opposed to sexual contact with non-Europeans.[45] At any rate, the first half of the nineteenth century saw an influx of African American slaves from the upper South in Louisiana. As Cajuns migrated throughout states that maintained and expanded chattel slavery—eventually settling in the slave-importing state of Louisiana—it is reasonable to assume this wedding ritual is one cultural tool they took (or, at least adapted) from another group they associated with—namely the enslaved.

Cajuns and enslaved people shared common experiences, in that both were forcibly expelled from homelands, forced to labor in various locations like Charleston, South Carolina, and were largely ostracized, at least initially, by the slave-owning class. In his classic work, *Negro Folk Music*, Harold Courlander argued that "as landless immigrants the Acadians [Cajuns] had a lower social status than the old French settlers" and that "there seems to have been a considerable cultural exchange in some areas between the Negroes and Cajuns."[46] It should be noted, however, that being "Cajun" in southern Louisiana was not a monolithic identity. While many Cajuns isolated themselves deep in the bayous, others emerged as powerful sugar cane planters, using the system of slavery to generate economic and political prowess in the early nineteenth century; in turn, they identified themselves as Creole planters of French colonial Louisiana, in a way that mimicked the cultural capital of the emerging "economic kingpins" of south Louisiana, who were Anglo-American planters.[47] Most Cajuns, however, practiced small-scale farming, ranching, and fishing. The enslaved people who were brought to the region had their own creolized cultures drawn from mixture of western and central African and European traditions. Increased contact between enslaved people of African descent and Cajuns of French and Amerindian descent surely initiated cultural interactions and transmissions between the two groups.

The influx of enslaved people into the Louisiana markets likely introduced broomstick weddings to rural Euro-American populations who, prior to this point, had less interaction with the enslaved minority.[48] Throughout the early nineteenth century, slavery rose rapidly throughout southern Louisiana, and the number of enslaved people imported to Acadian sugar parishes exploded.[49] The isolated and rural settings of bayou life prompted rural Cajuns to adapt their former cultural expressions to the new environment. Though scholars are unable to point to a specific date in which the custom was adopted by Cajuns, it seems likely that it was used by the early nineteenth century. Folklorist Elizabeth Brandon argues that priests were largely unavailable in the swamp regions of Louisiana and that "in the absence of the priest, the young couple . . . held hands and jumped together over the broom that had been placed on the floor . . . when the priest finally arrived, months later, he performed the religious ceremony."[50]

A folktale named "Le Bon Dieu [The Good Lord] Leads Trumps" further reveals the complexities of Cajun matrimony. The story relates the account of Cleophas, an aging fisherman who informally adopts a fourteen-year-old girl named Titine upon the death of her parents. Through the suggestions of his friends, Cleophas and Titine marry, so as to not offend Cajun sensibilities of a grown man traveling with a young woman who is neither his daughter nor his wife. Eventually, due to Cleophas's failing strength and realization that he cannot provide for Titine much longer, a young man named Leo joins the group and quickly falls in love with her. Cleophas supports the union and asks a priest to dissolve his own union with Titine, to which the priest replies: "Oo! Oo! Impossible. Only death can dissolve your bonds."[51] A few months later Cleophas is sitting in his skiff when "*le bon dieu* took a hand and led trumps. . . . Suddenly a bolt descended. The hand was played out."[52] In the minds of Cajuns articulating this story, God intervened to overrule an uncompromising priest.

Seeking to marry, Leo and Titine approach the priest, Pere Thome, who remains unsympathetic, adamantly maintaining the entire process of courtship and marriage was blasphemous in its irreverence. After Thome refused to marry the couple, Leo unleashed a threat that quickly changed the priest's mind: "We don't want to be *placer* [cohabitation without marriage] but want a good ceremony of the Church. Very well, we make [like] one of the marsh people, *sauter le balai*, before the grave of a good man to have him for our witness. If you want to bless our wedding, *tant mieux* [that's good]; if you don't, *tant pis* [nevermind]." After the priest demands they leave the cemetery, Leo responds, "We make it on the public road, in the sight of the grave, lay a stick on the ground instead of a broom."[53] After this final threat, Thome begrudgingly relents: "Come back; I'll marry you. But this is terrible; no banns, no nothing. Only two hard heads."[54] This brand of folklore reveals a resistance to authority, and likely represents difficulties Cajun people experienced exercising church functions while isolated in the Louisiana swamps.[55] Leo and Titine desire a church wedding, revealing the deeply religious sentiments most Cajun Catholics maintained within the Louisiana swamp. The reference to the "marsh people" reflects the ritual's utility for geographically isolated populations and how the ritual was attached to their cultural worldview. The rural nature of the bayou and unavailability of itinerant preachers made the church wedding both a desired objective and slow process. Such conditions required them to adapt to a rather harsh environment, and the ability to marry and form kinship networks was pivotal to their survival. When the conservative priests prevented the desired unions, young couples like Leo and Titine threatened to perform the heathenish ceremony of the "marsh people" to seal their union.

If one looks closely at the above folktale, Pere Thome is not necessarily upset that they are threatening to jump over a stick; he is more irritated by the fact that they are threatening to perform the ceremony so abruptly, which would in turn force him to marry them—according to the laws of the church. While the priest begrudgingly submitted to their demands, the ritual process of their potential broomstick ceremony provides some fascinating clues to Cajun understandings of the marriage covenant. First, the couple feels that the broomstick union is not sufficient if performed without witnesses, but then also claimed that performing the ritual next to a dead man's grave fulfilled the requirement. Second, the element of "crossing over" into matrimony is the main requirement, and the couple threatens that they will not even take time to use a broom, but find a random stick to complete the ceremony. Lastly, they desire a church wedding, but Leo's retort "tant pis" reveals that, in the end, Cajun couples recognized God as a higher power than the church. Thus, *sauter le balai* represents a temporary substitute for a church wedding. Interestingly, *sauter le balai* is not mentioned often in French literature, and it is unclear if the rural French ever used the custom in any significant way.[56]

Cajun communities also possessed diversity in their ritual choices beyond the antebellum period. Some accounts in the early and mid-twentieth centuries reveal witnesses holding the broom a foot off the floor. Others described brides wearing "tennis shoes," and said that after the broom was jumped, "an 'official' wrote a brief statement in French to which others attached their marks."[57] "Cajun" is a term that describes a diverse collection of communities, many of which practiced the broomstick wedding. Among Louisiana Cajuns the phrase "jumping (over) the broomstick" survived into the twentieth century and it denoted a marriage not formally sanctioned by the church. In her excursions into the Louisiana bayous throughout the 1950s folklorist Carolyn Ramsay found the phrase used frequently among Cajun men.[58] Ramsay determined this practice of irregular marriage was used most frequently among isolated groups in the bayou interior: "The people here 'no like' the words the priest has to say over the couple; they prefer to *sauter l' balai*, the 'jump-the-broom-stick' method which was the way of their fathers. . . . From the few outsiders that know these people, I learned later that their marriages stick. They don't jump the broomstick but once and family life is a very stable affair."[59] Ramsey later suggests that no physical leap was required by the 1950s. The term became a colloquial expression that denoted the couple's rejection of the priest's ultimate authority. Regarding one couple named Jacques and Marianne, Ramsay reports that for them to marry simply required "Marianne go to Jacques' home to live and den dey are married."[60] It appears that this group of Cajuns utilized the concept of *sauter le balai* not as a literal activity, but a rejection of clerical authority. Though they maintained that the couples who married in this way took it seriously.[61]

## Moving West

Various political, economic, and cultural incentives led to mass migrations to the American West.[62] The various immigrant groups brought their own worldviews to their new locations. Just as people from the British Isles and Atlantic Africa brought their customs to the British colonies of the eastern United States, and enslaved people displaced from the Atlantic seaboard invigorated the culture of the Deep South, pioneers moving West brought their traditions to these new environments. Unfortunately, sources for marriage ceremonies are scarce, but the available references do suggest that jumping the broom was practiced by certain rural cultures. An 1889 reference in Superior, Wisconsin stated that "the old settlers" in that region "didn't get married in those days- only jumped the broomstick."[63] Into the 1950s isolated communities in southeastern Illinois maintained that a woman needed to "walk over a broomstick immediately after marriage to be [a] good housekeeper."[64] Moving farther West, an early twentieth-century wedding in Oregon reveals that jumping the broom was an auxiliary ritual that followed the actual ceremony. The couple renewed their vows with a ceremony that "consisted principally of numerous stunts, such as jumping the broomstick, etc."[65] Like writers in other areas, this outsider dismissed the practice as a "stunt." However, this criticism does not suggest the couple did not take the custom seriously.

As far West as California, some newspapers believed it was a custom per-formed in "the East," perhaps recalling its prolifically documented use across the Mississippi. *The San Francisco Call* reported that a woman named Mary Viola was required to produce evidence of her marriage when issues surfaced surrounding her late husband's last will and testament. The controversy centered primarily on the question of whether the couple had legally married. After a rather confusing explanation of their many forms of marriage (some due to the woman frequently switching her religious affiliation), an examiner asked her how the previous wedding officiant prepared the marriage certificate, to which she replied, "I thought it would be well to have it prove the marriage. In the East all that is necessary is to jump over the broomstick to get married."[66] The use of the term "jumping over the broomstick" in the West reminded these communities of the cultures many of them hailed from, and seems to have served as a distinguishing feature of how groups began to view themselves in opposition to the culture they left behind.

Though it was a ritual some Californians claimed to reject, one group residing along Mission Road in Los Angeles County reportedly did jump the matrimonial broomstick. In 1906, the *San Jose Mercury* highlighted the nuptials of Maria Leon, the leader of a local "Romany" group. Maria Leon's marriage was newsworthy due to a postnuptial riot that erupted between the families, when the bridegroom did not pay the promised bridewealth. Her parents required a group of horses worth $1,000, but found that their new son-in-law only possessed "three raw-boned, decrepit horses."[67] They immediately demanded their daughter be returned to them, but he refused and cited the marriage was finalized through the ceremony. The two factions physically quarreled for multiple days until police quelled the violence.

Though the brawl did not paint an endearing picture of the community, it did capture attention from reporters who provided a few details about the wedding ceremony: "The party stood together in the moonlight in the midst of a circle of gypsies and went through the quaint ceremony of leaping over the broom. Then followed feasting and rejoicing as it does everywhere when people are married in the bosoms of their families."[68] A similar report from the *Los Angeles Herald* provided an additional detail, specifying that only "the bride jumped over the broomstick in approved fashion" and was subsequently led to the tent by her husband.[69] In yet another article, an additional detail reveals that her jump over the broom "acknowledged her marriage" to her suitor.[70] All accounts could be correct, portraying separate parts of the same whole. It was not uncommon for only brides to make the jump, and the combined accounts hold similarities to British Romani ceremonies. Indeed, the event's most noteworthy feature is the community's retention of an ancestral custom. By maintaining the broomstick wedding as their preferred form of matrimony, this group of Romani linked a western European folk tradition to the North American West. Just as the rural conditions of many Southern states fostered the need for broomstick weddings to remain a functional alternative to both church and state-recognized weddings, the cultural isolation they faced in the U.S. West prompted Romani migrants to utilize jumping the broom as a meaningful alternative to legislated requirements.

One example from the Colorado gold mines, however, provides rich details regarding a community's role in the process. The broomstick ceremony in a Boulder, Colorado, mining town ensured women were appropriately treated. Women were scarce in the Colorado gold mines, but the article notes "if it got about that one was not handsomely treated by her husband a miners' meeting was called and the case considered."[71] The decree for divorce was usually granted, and the process of divorce followed a familiar method: "Two honest miners were detailed to hold the broomstick in a horizontal position, and the parties to the suit were required to jump it in token that their divorce was an accomplished fact. The good morals of the camp required that the woman marry immediately, and as one after another of the elect men fell from luck it would happen to the lady to have had as many husbands as she of the scriptures."[72] The narrative displays many connections between this Colorado mining community and their broom-jumping counterparts elsewhere. First, the miners viewed the ceremony as an appropriate alternative to church weddings. Second, the broom was jumped in the presence of "honest" witnesses, signifying the seriousness with which the group viewed the ritual. Lastly, it allowed women a certain degree of autonomy that church officials were less willing to grant. If a woman was mistreated by her husband, she understood her value to the rest of the community, and could appeal to them for a divorce from an abusive (or perhaps infertile) husband. This rare glimpse into how communities in the U.S. West viewed jumping the broomstick provides further evidence that allotting voice to the populations who practiced it reveals many new insights surrounding the cultural paradigms of rural and frontier communities.

## Colloquialisms and Popular Culture

Even if jumping the broom was not literally practiced, it remained a colloquial expression. In a poem written about the marriage of Adam and Eve, a minister used it to complete his rhyme scheme:

It was a private wedding, too
As we may well presume
No gazing guests were gathered there
To watch them jump the broom.[73]

As late as 1960, folklorist Wayland D. Hand stated that "from folk speech, and . . . our proverb collections, comes the phrase 'to jump over the broom.' This means 'to get married,' and is still encountered in many rural areas of America. There are even children's games in which the broom is held for the young lovers to step over."[74] Though it is not always evident if "jumping the broom" refers to a literal act or a phrase describing marriage, certain statements hold enough context to interpret the differences. Descriptions of a literal ceremony oftentimes provide some elaboration on the features of the ceremony, or they add a few words to detail the physical activity. The phrase "jump over the broomstick" sometimes provides an important distinction between the shorter phrase "jump the broomstick" in American folk speech, as the latter is easier to use in casual conversation. Including the word "over," especially when conveying information through the written word, helps the reader visualize the ceremonial format. The distinctions are never absolute, but they do provide one approach for determining the difference between literal and colloquial statements. For example, a newspaper in Missouri used the colloquialism by proposing that one man would "jump the broomstick" on his forty-fifth birthday.[75] The report was in a section called "Missouri Notes," intended to provide short sketches local events. The colloquial phrase provided a quick way to postulate a pending marriage without having to describe the festivities. Similarly, one woman wrote her friend in rural Michigan that all the young people in the area just "jumped the broomstick."[76] It seems unlikely she intended to convey everyone literally jumped a broom, since the folk expression revealed the swiftness in which everyone married and moved away. Given that the custom was intended to be a rapid action undertaken by rural populations, it seems the colloquial phrase conveyed circumstances through which people married abruptly.

Rural whites also used colloquialisms and music to preserve their traditions, as depicted in a popular 1959 rendition of the song "Let's Jump the Broomstick," sung by Brenda Lee, a native of Atlanta, Georgia:

Goin' to Alabama back from Texarkana,
Goin' all around the world

. . .

My father don't like it, my brother don't like it,

My sister don't like it, my mother don't like it
Come a little baby lets jump the broomstick,
Come a lets tie the knot.[77]

This rendition of a broomstick wedding is likely employing the colloquialism. Often used as a synonym for an informal marriage, this verse suggests that the partners were motivated to marry despite familial disapproval. Lee's use of the term "tie the knot" suggests that both phrases were equally known to designate a wedding, and it is likely they did not engage a literal tying of the knot. The song simply employed two well-known folk expressions connected to marriage. Similarly novelist and playwright Truman Capote wrote the lyrics for songs featured in his 1950s play *House of Flowers*, which followed the romantic trials of a Haitian woman named Ottilie. One song is entitled "Jump de Broom":

Take de broom all a-roun',
Sweep us de room, sweep up de groun'

. . .

Time has come to JUMP DE BROOM,
First de bride an' then de groom.[78]

Thus, even if certain rural couples did not perform the literal broomstick wedding in the mid-twentieth century, the tradition was kept alive through terminology in folk speech and memory. As one rural southerner bluntly claimed in 1957, "Jumpin' the broom means to get married."[79] One finds numerous references throughout the late-nineteenth and early-twentieth centuries linking the broomstick wedding to "irregular" marriage or to predict two people were going to marry abruptly.[80] Even Amelia Earhart, the first female aviator to fly solo across the Atlantic Ocean, wired her sister that she and future husband, George Palmer Putnam, were going "over the broomstick" on that same day.[81] At the very least, many white Americans in the twentieth century were familiar with the phrase, even if they knew the action was performed only by marginalized or geographically isolated populations.

## CHAPTER SIX

# No Expression as Prevalent
## Civil Rights, Black Power, and Alex Haley's Roots

The 1976 publication of Alex Haley's *Roots: The Saga of an American Family* awakened interest in American slavery and its residual cultural impact on African Americans. Haley's novel was advertised as a historical fiction that depicted his ancestors' travails in North America, beginning with his eighteenth-century West African forebears and concluding in the twentieth century with Haley himself. *Roots* vividly illuminated the African experience in the United States as a narrative distinct from traditional Anglo-American histories. Haley personified this experience through his initial protagonist, Kunta Kinte, a character who unabashedly resists the system that placed him in chains. Despite Kunta's fortitude in refusing to denounce his Muslim Mandinka heritage, he begrudgingly assimilates certain parts of slave culture. Kunta's marriage, in particular, represents a pivotal shift. At the behest of Bell, his American-born bride, they jumped the broom, despite his initial thoughts that the custom "seemed ridiculous . . . for such a solemn occasion."[1] Despite his reservations, Kunta and Bell marry in the slave quarters, where they entered "into de holy lan' of matrimony" surrounded by festive observers and an approving master.[2] The shift between Kunta's initial attitude toward jumping the broom to his participation in a slave wedding represents the shift from an "African" to an "African American" identity that so many captives experienced. For Black Americans, Kunta was the quintessential representation of their ancestral struggle.

The impact of Haley's novel and subsequent television miniseries was nothing short of explosive, as African Americans grappled with a historical depiction of slavery many felt was previously hidden from them. Popular among audiences throughout the country, Haley's depiction of an enslaved people's cultural resilience ignited African Americans' interests in furthering their knowledge of their ancestors' cultural traits. The enigmatic broomstick ceremony eventually became a focal point in defining Black American heritage, especially among those seeking deeper cultural and intellectual connections with the past. Not surprisingly, *Roots* was studied and debated by academics trying to ascertain its historical accuracy and its impact on white and Black viewers in the United States.[3]

One effect of *Roots* was to encourage African Americans to embrace racial pride, cultural solidarity, and an appreciation for the resiliency of the ancestors. Subsequently, broomstick jumping gained significant attention in American popular culture. Given the nature of enslavement and its destruction of the family, the televised manifestation of two enslaved people marrying provided the cultural pride many viewers sought. Due to this increased attention, "jumping the broom" was inducted as an auxiliary ritual in African American "heritage weddings." Popularized in the 1980s, these ceremonies combined traditional Christian rites with components of the past, including rituals connected to both West Africa and American slavery, and designed for Black couples seeking to pay homage to their ancestors. Haley essentially reintroduced the descendent community to a practice featured in many slave weddings. Various authors have cited *Roots* as the primary reason for the broomstick wedding's resurgence among African Americans. The argument has validity, but this chapter shows it is a slight overstatement.[4] As previously noted, the broomstick custom resonated in rural American communities into the 1950s and was even used in visual media to represent the cultural expressions of isolated Euro-American communities. Though its popularity was surely curtailed throughout the twentieth century, it never fully disappeared. Jumping over the broom was just confined to a cultural demographic that was not well-represented in the American mainstream. In one example from a 1972 interview, Mississippi civil rights activist Ruby Magee recalled "seeing movies when I was a child where the white master would take ... a black male slave and a black female slave and let them jump over a broom and they would be considered married." The visual depiction appears to have made an impact on Magee, but her testimony suggests these enslaved people possessed no agency in determining the marital process. Magee further explained that the tenuous nature of the enslaved reunion invalidated the custom, and maintained that the ceremony looked "farcical" due to the ability of the slaveowner to forcibly separate families.[5] If the enslaved remained passive victims in cinema, literature, and television, their folk customs were dismissed as products of the plantation regime.

*Roots* appeared in the aftermath of the civil rights movement and the rise of Black Power, both of which contributed to a newfound pride in Black identity in the United States. The assertive spirit of such social movements inspired a generation of scholars to view people of African descent as active agents from slavery's inception in the Americas up to its conclusion. Scholarship emerging from the 1960s and early 1970s stressed the resiliency of enslaved people in forming cultural communities that resisted the slaveowner's encroachments, contesting previous scholarship that portrayed slaves as remaining in a state of "cultural chaos."[6] Haley's book was produced through the author's years of dedicated research and his capacity for imaginative storytelling, as well as an engagement with secondary works that sought to rescue African American history from narratives that portrayed slaves as cultureless laborers utterly degraded by their experiences in the United States. The emerging literature argued that enslaved people had a culture that was both vibrant and distinct from their Euro-American counterparts. Customs that appeared ubiquitous in the narratives of the formerly enslaved, such as those associated with social gatherings and family life, helped demonstrate that they had not been defined solely by their labor. Consequently, jumping the broom gained increased attention in African American popular culture.

The resurgence of the broomstick tradition in African America was produced by the impact of cultural movements that occurred before, during, and after the publication of Alex Haley's *Roots*. Haley is rightly credited with popularizing the slave marital ritual through *Roots'* extensive influence in literary and visual expositions. However, one must recognize that his work relied upon the contemporaneous revisionist scholarship in American slave studies, alongside assertive social movements that reclaimed Black history for Black Americans. This cultural renaissance was amplified by the dissemination of such ideas through venues more readily available to the public. Popular magazines such as *Ebony* and *Jet* published articles that investigated slave culture and family life alongside tracts dealing with celebrity news, gossip, and events relevant to Black people. Additionally, Haley operated within a tradition of Black novel writing that promoted a curiosity in genealogy and folk history. Without these pivotal intellectual and cultural transitions undertaken throughout the 1950s and 1960s, it is likely that the historical content that propelled *Roots* to the center of American popular culture might have been less apparent.

Throughout the 1970s and 1980s, broomstick weddings gained exposure in the press and through marketing campaigns for newly conceptualized African American heritage weddings that implemented components of the enslaved past. The broomstick ceremony was elevated to the preeminent custom used in slave marriages within African American historical memory. Imaginative interpretations of the broomstick wedding's mysterious origins quickly filled African American literature. Some examinations were heavily speculative, but they were effective in solidifying the ritual's position as a physical representation that defined the uniqueness of African American culture, as were the entrepreneurs who capitalized on the publicly recognized pride in racial heritage. Ultimately, the broomstick wedding's revival in the last quarter of the twentieth century was produced through an intertwined web of influences that were all, in many respects, linked to the impact *Roots* held in popular culture, though they were never solely reliant upon it.

## Precedents to *Roots* in Reviving the Custom

The civil rights movement confronted the intertwined components of violence, resistance, and protest in American society, and encouraged a new generation of historians to reexamine how Black people confronted their recurring oppressions under slavery. In particular, it sparked interest in the residual influence of slavery and racist oppression in the African American psyche and a desire to explore enslavement from an enslaved person's perspective. The struggles of African Americans nearly one hundred years removed from plantation slavery reoriented popular conceptions of how the past resonated in the present. In 1968, for instance, *The Negro Digest* featured a short piece titled "The Black Woman's Soliloquy," in which the author imaginatively recreates a first-person narrative concerning the experiences of African American women from slavery to freedom. After tracing her journey from Africa to the antebellum South, the author describes her slave wedding: "I met a man, a slave like me, and according to the white Christian law of that time, I married him by jumping over a broomstick among our friends. I would have liked a preacher, but this was not to be allowed."[7] An enslaved person's inability to access the accepted marital tradition illuminated the contradictions imbedded in an American society dominated by white elites. Though enslaved people were expected to follow Christian moral law and its traditions, they were unable to access a preacher. This symbolic trope of past discrimination exposed modern circumstances of inequality. Such musings symbolized the contemporary hypocrisy of the democratic American Republic as it withheld citizenship to Black people well into the twentieth century.

The broomstick wedding in "The Black Woman's Soliloquy" is represented as a negative feature of slavery, though the description also divulges the communal sanction it received amongst the similarly enslaved. Surviving slavery and oppression required collective support, and an individual's participation in community-sanctioned rituals socially validated such traditions among those whose opinions mattered. The enslaved community's approval was paramount in confirming the ritual, even if it appeared frivolous. In a militant essay concerning the residual influences of slavery on the image of Black people in the early 1970s, folklorist Kathryn Morgan placed the broomstick wedding on similar grounds as enslaved people eating "hog guts," arguing that these cultural practices reminded Black people "that their entire existence depended on the affluence and disposition of their enslavers."[8] Morgan was certainly attuned to the prominence of the broomstick wedding through her readings of the ex-slave narratives. While she categorized the marital custom as a "rite of passage," she contended that the "marriage ritual exemplifies a meaningless rite which has neither legal nor moral sanction."[9] She interpreted the custom as an adverse feature of slave life that belittled the marital customs of African Americans. The notion that it lacked "moral sanction" is certainly subjective, as enslaved communities often determined their own moral codes apart from their enslavers. Though pessimistic, Morgan's understanding of slave life was influenced by scholars such as Bobby Frank Jones and John Blassingame, both of whom argued (through different interpretative methods) that the available Black voices for the antebellum period were requisite if scholars hoped to conceptualize the brutality of slavery and the resiliency of the ancestors. Nonetheless, since few people knew of its origins at the time, both Jones and Blassingame interpreted the broomstick ceremony as a trivial cultural tradition that Black people left behind after slavery.[10]

Despite these negative views, certain activists used the broomstick ceremony as an expression of solidarity and survival. An early poem by noteworthy civil rights poet and activist Mae Jackson portrayed the ceremony in a setting where past meets present:

> And you know,
> once when I was here before
> I fell in love with don l lee
> we picked cotton and stole kisses beneath the blossom trees
> and marvin x and I got married
> by jumping over a broom.[11]

The notion of "picking cotton" connects the speaker of the poem to the legacy of slavery that resonates with her marriage to "marvin x," a name likely connected with the Nation of Islam, which used "X" to (symbolically and literally) reject the surnames forced upon their ancestors by white slaveowners and display the anonymity of the names stolen from them. Jackson's poem blends slavery, marriage, and modern nomenclature to represent the perpetual inequality Black Americans have faced in the United States, while representing the custom of jumping the broom as a meaningful one that the couple initiates through their own volition. Such literary commemorations of slave heritage in the mid-twentieth century literature allowed the largely forgotten custom of "jumping the broom" to gain exposure within African American popular consciousness, and ultimately led to its position as a primary cultural identifier within a few decades.

The broomstick tradition's entrance into African American popular culture, however, would not attain its full potential until it was displayed through other venues. An important component of Black academic writing throughout the early to mid-twentieth century was the use of publications started by Black people that were accessible to Black people, such as the *Journal of Negro History*, rather than publications that celebrated only white achievement. Black academics participated in historical forums dedicated to educating the African American public, which was intensified by the looming presence of segregation throughout the United States. In illustrating the erasure of Black history from the Eurocentric curriculum, historian and educator Carter G. Woodson contended that while white publishers "may not be prejudiced" they were certainly "not interested in the Negro."[12] Historical exclusion from white American journals, museums, national parks, and other forums caused Black scholars to publish research in collections devoted to the African American experience.[13] Such publications provide a crucial resource for tracking the evolution of slavery in African American historical memory.

*Ebony* and *Jet Magazine*, two of the most popular African American publications, delineate a shift toward focusing on Black family life and its historical context. Until the 1970s, both magazines were generally silent on broomstick marriages. While some African American marriages in the late 1960s contained elements of African-centered practices, as couples dawned traditional garb and included West African symbols, it is not until the 1970s that one sees the phrase "jumping the broom" appear in these publications. In November 1971, Gerri Majors's "Society World" column in *Jet* described an "African inspired wedding" that utilized the broomstick custom, suggesting that traditions stressing homage to ancestors through ritual symbolism were growing among African Americans, even prior to the publication of *Roots*.[14] As early as February 1971, social historian Lerone Bennett Jr. published "The World of the Slave" in *Ebony*, which briefly highlighted jumping the broom as a method of slave marriage in the U.S. South.[15] The selections were extracted from Bennett's work *Before the Mayflower: A History of Black America*, and published while he was senior editor of the magazine.[16] Bennett's book was incredibly popular, as it was one of the few works to trace the experiences of African peoples from West Africa up to the civil rights movement. First published in 1962, it was reissued five times, with the final version including information on Black life in the 1990s.[17] Knowing the value in using multiple outlets, he disseminated his findings on slave marriages through a magazine that was highly popular among African Americans. Subsequently, the topic of jumping the broom was revisited by the publication. The colloquial expression "Broom Stick Jumping" even appeared in the title of an article discussing aspects of modern marriage legislation.[18]

Bennett's decision to publish extracts of his work on slave marriage was praised by *Ebony*'s readers. In one letter to the editor, a subscriber responded that he "could only marvel at its power and impact," and even claimed the article's superiority over a publication written by historian Eugene Genovese, a white scholar who wrote important work on slave culture in the 1970s, on a similar topic.[19] In 1981 Bennett submitted a second article called "The Roots of Black Love" to combat the historiographical trend that highlighted the failure of the Black family in America. His work exemplified the enslaved community's resiliency in maintaining their kinship connections.[20] Academic and political concern for the stability of the Black family was popularly traced to slavery, which in turn increasing scholarly interest in slave family patterns and marital customs. Bennett entered this debate as both a scholar and a popular author and was able to reach a demographic for which such issues were deeply personal.

## Genealogy, Historical Fiction, and Margaret Walker's *Jubilee*

Amid the emergence of historical revisionism promoted during the civil rights era some African Americans pondered the possibility of finding direct links to enslaved ancestors within their genealogy. Due to a lack of documentation, traditional methods of genealogy proved a frustrating task for the descendants of enslaved American people. The appreciation for oral histories and folk traditions, however, kept customs like jumping the broom alive in the conscience of many Black Americans, even if they were not widely observed. In 1981, centenarian Charity Mae Wallace recounted that her mother told her "how she and papa jumped the broom in Tennessee when they were married."[21] Similarly, Gospel singer Bessie Jones recollected in 1970 that she learned to sing from her grandparents, "who were slaves in Virginia and . . . married in the old slave ceremony of jumping over a high broom together." Jones's references to the broomstick wedding was peripheral to the immediate question of her musical pedigree, but the quote effectively demonstrates how the social practice was implanted in her memories at a young age. Despite this tangential detail in her musical genealogy, Jones felt the ceremony deserved further explanation, noting that "they practiced and practiced beforehand because you only got two chances, and if you missed you had to go back to courting again for a while."[22] It is difficult to verify how common this ritual performance was throughout Virginia plantations, since none of the WPA narratives include a similar description. Familial and cultural genealogies were important features for Black families across generations, particularly among those born in the rural South. The oral transmission of ancestral folk traditions was another component that contributed to the resurrection in the 1970s of marital folk customs that were previously discarded or denied by those who were once enslaved. Historical fiction, genealogical interest, and marketing campaigns through visual media in the last quarter of the twentieth century generated a concerted interest in African American folklore that survived in cross-generational oral histories, though they had largely disappeared from the public eye.

Although tracing the ancestral past was a frustrating experience for most African Americans, novels such as *The Autobiography of Miss Jane Pittman* by Earnest Gaines and *Jubilee* by Margaret Walker provided imaginative representations of the lives of one's formerly enslaved ancestors. In many respects, both works provided the possibility that African American genealogies could be reconstructed through fiction. Gaines's work capitalized on a tradition of Black novel writing that sought to recapture the past through combining imaginative storytelling with historical events. *Jane Pittman* was not entirely about slavery, but it did depict an enslaved forebear caught in the transition from slavery to freedom during the Civil War era. The work most explicitly portrayed the similarities in the social conditions of plantation slavery and sharecropping, in turn suggesting that the Black experience in the United States was one of continuous strife and resilience in the face of oppression. In various interviews, Gaines explained that his research involved a combination of oral traditions from his rural upbringing in Louisiana and an intensive study of the ex-slave narratives published through the WPA.[23] Though fiction, *The Autobiography of Miss Jane Pittman* was simultaneously marketed as an accurate representation of rural southern life and neo-slavery in the twentieth century.

It was Gaines's contemporary Margaret Walker, however, who directly promoted the notion that she could accurately recreate her genealogy through scholarly research and oral tradition. Born in Birmingham, Alabama, in 1915 Walker was initially better known for her works of poetry, but *Jubilee*'s unique premise captured the attention of many Americans seeking links to a largely undocumented past. *Jubilee* is a historically informed, fictional biography of Walker's ancestors and their experiences in the nineteenth-century South.

Film director Phyllis Klotman notes that *Jubilee* emerged "from the tradition of the slave narrative, and Walker uses the research into this unique Afro-American literary genre to support the oral tradition of the black family."[24] Having come of age when pride in her "folk heritage as a Negro was . . . very much the rage," she was connected to noteworthy authors such as Langston Hughes and Richard Wright.[25] These intellectual connections helped her develop her skills as a literary scholar and poet, but she did not become a recognized novelist until the 1960s.

*Jubilee* was published in 1966, when the civil rights movement was gaining legislative victories in the United States. In assessing its contribution to the African American canon, Roger Whitlow noted that it served "especially well as a response to white 'nostalgia' fiction about the antebellum and Reconstruction South."[26] Walker said that her fascination with genealogy began in her adolescent years, when she listened to her grandmother's stories of slavery in antebellum Georgia. She wrote down ideas for a story as early as the fall of 1934, when she was a senior at Northwestern.[27] At the age of twenty-nine, she recorded specific plans to "write a historical novel about Negro life in America that begins in 1830 in Georgia and ends in 1915 in Alabama. The big character is my great grandmother, whose life-span covers these 85 years."[28] Due to life circumstances of teaching, marriage, and having children, Walker would not complete the manuscript until the mid-1960s. The chronological setting of *Jubilee* represents Walker's original intentions to begin her narrative in the antebellum period and then assessing the impact of Reconstruction on newly freed Blacks in the South. For Walker, each character reflected modern philosophies of Black resistance, showing that both militant and restrained ideas of liberation always existed among African Americans. The main character, Vyry is based on Walker's great-grandmother, a biracial woman who was a product of a white slave owner raping an enslaved Black woman. Walker later wrote that Vyry should be seen as a "product of the plantation," and her story reveals how the confinement of slave life is manifested through her more reserved outlook on the transition from slavery to freedom.[29] In contrast, the more militant character Randall Ware, a free Black artisan based on Walker's great-grandfather, is characterized as more aggressive and assertive in the face of oppression. Prior to meeting Ware, Vyry had never imagined what it meant to be free, believing such an event would occur through a divine intervention. However, his encouragement eventually caused her to attempt to escape the plantation, though she was captured by the overseer.[30] Ware's societal viewpoints resonated with the contemporary Black political activism of the 1960s. Walker's main characters helped her audience understand that Black people were not the docile and submissive laborers that popular history portrayed them, but were a multidimensional group who held ideas that flowed contrary to the oppressive systems that attempted to silence them.[31] In Walker's own words, her novel was "a canvas on which I paint my vision of my world."[32] Walker's "vision" specifically relied on folklore, especially the folk sayings and beliefs that resonated through oral traditions into the late twentieth century.[33]

Within *Jubilee* Walker distinguishes between Black and white conceptions of love and marriage in the plantation South. White people's weddings were elaborate celebrations. The context of the white southern wedding served to remind enslaved people that they could never mimic such ceremonies through their own initiatives. This distinction is portrayed in the moment when Vyry expresses to "Marse John" her desire to marry Black freedman Randall Ware:

> "Marster, I wants your permission for me to get marriaged."
>
> "Well, now that's no trouble, lots of gals are getting married around here every day, how do you say, 'jumping the broom'?"
>
> And he laughed, but she did not crack a smile and she remained silent. Between them arose a silent question, but Vyry waited for him to speak first.[34]

The disagreement was rooted within the form of marriage one used, as well as the mate they selected. Marse John's laugh reemphasizes the ritual inferiority of the enslaved custom, and since Vyry desires to marry a free Black man, she also considers the broomstick wedding unsuitable for such an important event. Even Randall Ware's assurance that they could have "Brother Ezekiel 'marriage' them in the way the slaves called it" does not satisfy her.[35] Walker's novel definitively shows that the main character considers slave marital customs to be inferior. It is likely that the biographical representation of her grandmother prompted Walker to portray Vyry as the exception within the enslaved community, as the text states that people usually "jumped the broom" on her plantation. The actual ceremony, however, is not described. *Jubilee* does not divulge if the statement was meant as a reference to a literal custom, or a colloquialism that denoted how they informally engaged their marriages. The wording, however, is significant since Walker does use the phrase to distinguish the slave marital ceremony from those of the surrounding white society.

It is unknown at what point Walker was exposed to the phrase "jumping the broom," as she never elaborates on whether the custom figured into her family history. Additionally, her reference to it within *Jubilee* has not garnered significant attention in subsequent literary studies or interviews discussing her work.[36] One could surmise that her exposure to the expression began as early as the mid-1920s, when Walker listened to her grandmother's recollections of plantation life, or she may have heard it during any one of the numerous visits she made to various research institutions during the thirty-one years she was considering this project.[37] The most likely scenario is that "jumping the broomstick" survived the postbellum period in colloquial usage, and Walker, rooted in Black southern traditions, was wholly familiar with the expression. In *Jubilee* it was "the way that slaves called it," but readers do not receive a description of the ceremony.[38] Despite this caveat, Walker's use of the term indicates how the idea of jumping the broom was known to Black southerners well before Alex Haley's book was published in the 1970s. Walker's claim to authoritative interpretation eventually led to her conflict with Alex Haley, whose work *Roots: The Saga of an American Family*, eclipsed *Jubilee*'s influence in Black America's interpretation of the enslaved past.

## The Development and Success of *Roots*

*Roots* portrays the broomstick wedding as a fundamental component of slave marital culture. The wedding between Kunta Kinte and Bell literally enacts jumping the broomstick, which "Bell had forced him to practice over and over the day before."[39] Even after the ceremony, jumping the broom serves as an idiom for the marriage between the two.[40] Kunta's grandson Chicken George also performs the ceremony with his wife, Matilda, though it is initiated at the behest of Matilda's "missis," who combines "some of the white Christian wedding service with jumping the broom afterward."[41] Thus, after George and Matilda "locked arms and jumped the broom," he declares, "De Lawd is my shepherd ... He done give me what I wants!"[42] *Roots* also uses the phrase "jumping the broom" as a colloquial expression. In one example, Matilda's reflections upon her courtship process with Chicken George depicts his reaction at the notion that she would not engage in premarital sex provides one example: "When he foun' out weren't no man gwine have his way wid me 'fo' we'd jumped a broom, Lawd, he had a fit!"[43] Similarly, a secondary character named Virgil is noted as having "been in a daze ever since he had jumped the broom."[44] Thus, even if the physical enactment was not referenced, *Roots* illuminated the cultural value the expression held for African Americans.

The only character in the novel who foregoes the broomstick ceremony is Kunta's great-grandson, Tom, whose wedding to Irene featured "members of both the white and black Holt and Murray families" held at "the Holt big-house front yard, with their minister performing the ceremony and Massa Holt himself giving away the bride."[45] The absence of broomstick jumping from this ceremony manifests a generational evolution: whereas Kunta's broomstick ceremony is performed within the view of residents in "slave row," and Chicken George has a hybrid ceremony that implemented white Christian preferences with those of the enslaved, Tom's wedding is entirely devoid of folk rituals. This trajectory suggests that the desire of enslaved people to perform Christian rituals that mirrored those of the white population increased as the antebellum period drew to a close.

Tom and Irene participated in a full-fledge Christian wedding, but the pages of *Roots* never entirely divulge the reason for this.[46] In an earlier version of his manuscript, Haley portrays Tom as being content with a "simple quick wedding" that includes jumping the broomstick among slaveowners, family, and friends. Irene, however, according this early manuscript "would have none of that . . . As a favored servant, Irene was given a 'dress-up' wedding, even with waiters and a white preacher."[47] The published novel does portray Irene as a favored domestic who feels an attachment to her owners, "Missis and Massa Holt," but it provides little description of the wedding's ceremonial format.[48] In the earlier, unpublished edition, the ceremony includes religious instruction concerning the sacredness of the marital vow, a Bible reading, a prayer, and an exhortation to always remain faithful. The ceremony ends, however, with the couple's leap over the broomstick "after muttering among the slaves that unless so, they wouldn't be really married."[49] The last point reveals Haley's considerations of the importance of folk ritual in slave matrimony, as it is not so much Tom and Irene's belief that this is a crucial component of their wedding, as the broader community's. Haley may have decided to delete the ceremony due to his advancing knowledge that slave marriages were based upon distinctions in status among the enslaved. Haley's description of Irene as a "favored servant" may have ultimately reoriented this representation, as his readings of the slave narratives made him aware that enslaved domestics, like Irene, generally refused to engage in the rituals of field hands. Other drafts divulge Haley's initial attempts to portray each engagement as a broomstick ceremony, but the published version denotes the gradual evolution of marriage ceremonies and his belief that enslaved people increasingly preferred the Christian ritual later into the antebellum period.[50]

A dizzying amount of both favorable and pessimistic reactions immediately propelled *Roots* into the center of discussions considering American slavery, race relations, and ancestral research. Within seven months of its release, *Roots* sold over 1.5 million copies, and spent twenty-two weeks at #1 on the *New York Times'* bestseller list.[51] Perhaps as a method to bolster sales, the *Times* touted *Roots* as a work of nonfiction. A contemporary review by historian David A. Gerber noted it was "accepted generally as if it were nonfiction," despite the realization that the book contained "novelized aspects" to accommodate the gaps in the historical record.[52] In its focus on genealogy, *Roots* promulgated the possibility that Americans of all races and ethnicities could (and should) investigate their ancestral heritage.[53] *Roots* even inspired creative projects among grade school classrooms, in which young people developed fictitious biographies of their ancestors in the same narrative structure that characterized the novel.[54] Black school teachers and intellectuals were enthusiastic at the prospect that "the black experience will be depicted with insight, compassion, and understanding."[55] *Time* magazine anticipated that dialogue on race relations in American history would benefit from the release of the nationally televised miniseries.[56]

The *Roots* television miniseries ensured that it maintained cross-cultural preeminence in America. To make it palatable to white American audiences, however, the visual representation of *Roots* was "transformed from a critique of slavery and exposition of white cruelty and indifference into one that diluted, in many ways, the horror, complexities, and seriousness of slave holding."[57] Despite the diluted material, emotions ran high among white and Black high school students after the content was visually disseminated to a diverse American public. One anonymous respondent in a sociological survey noted: "I was the only white person on my school bus.... And these people would take it out on me. We cannot help what happened 100 years ago. I can only hope it never happens again."[58] In reflecting on the impact of the miniseries versus that of the novel, historian John E. Wills Jr. contended that its cultural resonance was profoundly demonstrated "in the extraordinary performances of its black actors and in reaching and moving of huge numbers of people who don't read books at all, it went far beyond the book as a national political and moral event."[59] In a questionnaire sent to local chapters of the National Association for the Advancement of Colored Persons throughout the United States assessing the impact of the *Roots* television series, *The Crisis* reported that each area's community, white and Black, responded enthusiastically; exceptions were in Savannah, Georgia, and St. Louis, Missouri, where some viewers preferred to move beyond the depictions of violence and/or the guilt associated with America's slave history.[60] Another sociological study complicated previous conclusions, finding that southerners were least likely to watch *Roots*, and contended that most Americans "watched this epic program for reasons other than mere enjoyment."[61]

The miniseries resonated differently with each demographic, but its ability to stir emotions contributed to its popularity. Studies found that the program was discussed at homes and workplaces in interracial environments.[62] Black Americans viewed the program most consistently and enthusiastically, and *Roots* was shown to have stimulated an increase in Black pride and solidarity.[63] However, despite the pride one felt in their ancestors surviving slavery, the visual depictions of punishment and subjugation evoked emotional responses. The reaction of columnist Marvin Kittman summarizes this impact: "The really different thing about watching Roots compared to the other TV novels I've seen, has been that it slowly makes your blood boil. . . . Nothing upset me like the first episode of Roots."[64]

## Criticism and the Plagiarism Controversy

*Roots*'s popularity put it in the crosshairs of critics who questioned Haley's research methods, particularly his archival and field research.[65] Haley dismissed the charges, and he had a core group of noteworthy defenders ranging from trained historians to lay viewers of the miniseries.[66] Though he survived these accusations, his largest legal and financial difficulties came from plagiarism accusations, and the content of Margaret Walker's lawsuit was directly connected to comprehending "jumping the broom" as a category of intellectual property. It is important to note that prior to the conclusion of Walker's case, Haley settled a simultaneous suit brought by folklore novelist Harold Courlander by paying him and his legal team $650,000.[67] Courlander's suit is more familiar in American memory, as he successfully proved that Haley lifted passages from his novel *The African* when describing Kunta Kinte's homeland of Juffureh. Due to Courlander's well-publicized legal victory, his trial gained more notoriety than the case filed by Margaret Walker. Walker's suit predated Courlander's by a few months, but lasted much longer.

Walker sued Haley on grounds that he copied terms, phrases, and concepts from *Jubilee*. After more than a year of litigation Judge Marvin Frankel ruled that his "review of the alleged similarities points unmistakably to the conclusion that no actionable similarities exist between the works."[68] Walker's defeat contributed to her gradual fading from American memory, and her lawsuit has largely been peripheral in secondary literature.[69] Still, the diversity of reactions to the lawsuit at the time show how slave customs such as "jumping the broom" increasingly resonated among African Americans throughout the 1970s.

News reports following the trial noted that Walker's claims centered on Haley's portrayal of enslaved culture, which she argued were copied from *Jubilee*, "especially the 'jump the broom' sections."[70] By the time of the lawsuit, Walker was a formidable opponent. *Jubilee* had sold over one million copies and was translated into multiple languages.[71] She oversaw Jackson State University's Black Studies Department and was a nationally renowned authority on the African American experience. There were even hints that Haley admired her work prior to *Roots*, though he did not "recall" ever reading *Jubilee*.[72] Walker's private journals note the inconsistencies in Haley's work, stating that even his details of the writing process and research methods mirrored her own accounts.[73]

Walker's accusations became personal, condemning him of being "greedy for white people's money."[74] In her personal journal she wrote that *Roots* manifested "the kind of black caricature full of sexism and violence that the American public swallows whole, and with glee."[75] Such passages were certainly written as the stress of the trial weighed upon her, but her claims reveal several legitimate complaints. Walker held that Haley plagiarized *Jubilee's* representations of "birth, death and marriage" and that his copying was evident in the overlapping of "familiar" customs, specifically "jumping the broomstick."[76] Both novelists were roughly the same age, and each of them surely grew up hearing their elders use the expression, but Haley's description of the ceremony ultimately positioned his rendition of the ritual at the center of historical memory. It is difficult to prove who first knew of the custom, since the references in *Roots* are admittedly much different from that of *Jubilee*. *Roots* depicted characters who physically leapt over the broomstick, while *Jubilee* only used the colloquial phrase. Such creative differences prompt speculation concerning the point at which Haley came to believe this ritual enactment was an important component of the community.

Walker cited well over one hundred instances of possible plagiarism, but she specifically highlighted a few phrases and concepts.[77] The prosecution's trial notes reveal that the phrase "jumping the broom" (along with the expression "Newnited States") was a primary point of examination.[78] The defense countered that the renderings of "jumping the broom" in *Jubilee* and "jumpin' de broomstick" in *Roots* amounted to nothing more than "trifling similarities in phraseology . . . which would appear in any literary work concerning slavery" and cited previous cases to show that such similarities were not subject to copyright infringement.[79] When questioned by the prosecution concerning his decision to include the broomstick wedding, Haley testified it was a ritual deeply imbedded in his cultural memory as both a Black American and a southerner: "If we come to the expression 'jumpin' de broomstick,' it was common. I don't think there is any expression as prevalent. I can't even think of one that comes close, in the light of the idiomatic way slaves express the act of marriage. It was called 'jumpin' de broomstick.'" Outside his own cultural genealogy, Haley explained that "the actual ceremony involved the couple literally jumping over a broomstick. And it was spoken of, the act of marrying, as 'jumpin' de broomstick,' so that's why I used it. It's to be found throughout the slave narratives, for one source."[80] The defense corroborated this testimony by presenting three examples from the narratives in which people spoke of the ceremony and concluded that "Alex Haley did not copy the passage . . . from *Jubilee*."[81]

Multiple news venues reported the rumors surrounding the lawsuits and accusations of dubious research methods. Soon after Walker filed her injunction against Haley for plagiarism, the *Washington Post* reported that the combined pressures from Mark Ottaway, a journalist who questioned Haley's research methods shortly after *Roots'* release, Walker, and Courlander caused Haley to declare it was "open season on *Roots*."[82] With a degree of levity, Haley dismissed the accusations that he copied *Jubilee* to produce *Roots*, citing the notion that "it took me 12 years to do the book, and if I were copying I'd type faster than that."[83] While he settled outside of court with Courlander, he resisted Walker's accusations and successfully defended his case after a lengthy trial. On September 1978, Judge Marvin Frankel stated "the review of the alleged similarities points unmistakably to the conclusion that no actionable similarities exist between the works. Nobody writes books of purely original content."[84] As opposed to the Courlander suit, in which it was effectively demonstrated that paragraphs were lifted from *The African* and copied into *Roots*, Haley's defense team used his research notes to claim that each contested concept or phrase in *Roots* held a source independent from Walker's novel. Even if it held similarities with *Jubilee*, Frankel ruled that her specific accusations of plagiarism were not protected under copyright laws.

The question of whether Haley plagiarized portions of *Jubilee* when he crafted his manuscript can never be answered definitively. We know that Black academics and lay readers, especially men, criticized Walker's lawsuit and accused her of jealousy. Consequently, she believed that the overt dismissal of her claim and the wholesale acceptance of Courlander's revealed how the intersections of class, race, and gender operated against her throughout the trial.[85] Regardless of the speculation, the campaign against *Roots'* inclusion of the broomstick ceremony does reveal the politicized connotations for reviving (or reimagining) cultural traits. Who can tell the story? Does it matter who tells it first? The more noteworthy dimension of this entire debate involves Haley's publishing methods, which differed distinctly from Walker's. While *Jubilee* was widely read, critiques of the work stayed predominantly within the academic realm, and the only visual portrayal of her novel came in the form of an opera of the same name.[86] In contrast, two of Haley's favored publishing venues were *Playboy* and *Reader's Digest,* both of which allowed his voice to be disseminated far into the public space.[87] Walker noted this popular appeal and privately wrote that stories on Haley and *Roots* appeared "in *Ebony* and *Jet* and he has been in every magazine imaginable in the country."[88] The expanding popularity of *Roots* actually caused Walker to face the ire of the Black community at different points in her life. During a radio debate on the plagiarism case, callers to the program accused her of being "selfish" and believing "she is the only one who can tell our history or our story." One might assume such actions were provoked by the common belief that "Black people ought to stick together and not be divisive."[89] Even more importantly, however, Haley's largest impact on Black identity came during the moment his vision came to American television. It is at that point in the late-twentieth century that jumping the broomstick had a remarkable resurrection.

*Roots* visually displayed that West Africans hailed from culturally rich societies, such as the Mandinka community of Juffureh Village in what is now modern day Gambia. Haley's portrayal of African Americans' links to Africa, in the words of one contemporary reviewer, had "given us back our ancestors and our land."[90] Connecting one's "roots" beyond the plantation and toward West Africa appears to be the key difference between Haley and many of his popular predecessors and successors. The *Roots* miniseries proved attractive for visual media since it went beyond the southern plantation in tracing Haley's family history. The issue of timing, of course, factors into this dynamic considerably. The portrayal of a broomstick wedding on television in the 1970s was a significant catalyst in exposing the custom to the 130 million viewers of the *Roots* miniseries.

The importance of television on late-twentieth century American culture cannot be understated. Geographer Paul Adams argues, "Culture and television are clearly involved in reciprocal relations: television affects culture, but culture also affects television in regard to interpretative strategies and social attitudes toward viewing."[91] Haley brought depictions of enslaved life to the homes of individuals who, while interested, might not have had the time or ability to read the dense historical works that form some of the basis of his historical fiction.[92] Haley's opportunity to disseminate his ideas beyond the written word secured the increased popularity of the broomstick wedding in African American culture. The miniseries spurred interest in slave folk customs, and after it aired in 1977, the broomstick ritual was increasingly represented in Black American weddings throughout the 1980s, and even more into the 1990s.[93] In one example of *Roots'* impact on young viewers, the personal journal of African American wedding coordinator Danita Rountree Green displays the value of *Roots* availability via television. Her entry reveals how the miniseries resonated with young African Americans: "'Roots' was on again last night and I can't get anything done. Kunta and Bell got married and jumped the broom just like those old folks used to talk about. I thought they were joking."[94] For Green, *Roots's* depiction of the ceremony validated her family's oral history and encouraged her to seek her ancestral rituals.

## Televising the Culture of the Enslaved

*Roots's* commercial success reframed American conceptions of the broomstick wedding, but it was not the only production to display the ritual. On December 1978, Cicely Tyson starred as Harriet Tubman in the two-part miniseries *A Woman Called Moses*, based on Marcy Heidish's 1976 novel of the same name. The work follows the life of Harriet Tubman from her days as an enslaved teenager to the woman who led thousands to freedom. Heidish noted her novel was "a fictional work" grounded in historical facts gleaned from her research in archives and published sources. Both the novel and miniseries feature a broomstick wedding, and both renditions provide a unique vantage point for considering how the ritual was imagined differently by Heidish and Alex Haley. It is unclear if she knew of *Roots* prior to her own book's publication, as both novels were released in the same year. Like other novelists of slavery, Heidish detailed her source base by including a bibliography. It comprised an array of scholars ranging from Black intellectual W. E. B. Du Bois to noted historian Eugene Genovese, alongside archival material from Howard University, the Library of Congress, and the Schomburg Collection of the New York Public Library.[95] The miniseries was highly anticipated, as Cicely Tyson previously received an Emmy in 1974 for her leading role in *Miss Jane Pittman*, based upon Earnest Gaines's iconic novel, and an Academy Award nomination for her work in *Sounder*, a story depicting a family of southern sharecroppers.[96] By all accounts, the series was well received.

Cicely Tyson's performance as Harriet Tubman was lauded by critics, and both episodes gained a respectable viewership.[97] Though it never drew comparable numbers to *Roots*, its success did reveal that Black leads could draw viewers and revenue on network television, especially roles that provide "meaningful portrayals of the black experience."[98]

In the novel, Harriet meets John Tubman when she is rented out to another plantation. Though she believes that "no one would ever jump the broom with me,"[99] John Tubman's courtship proves her mistake. John is a free man, a position to which Harriet aspires. She has spent much of the previous summer weeding, planting, and "sweating" to harvest crops to sell in the market and has gradually gained a surplus that she hopes can buy her freedom. Amid her efforts, John Tubman courts her by engaging in jibes and questioning her about various topics. As their relationship blossoms Harriet overlooks John's lack of ambition, as Heidish describes Harriet's vivid sexual dreams when she lay alone in her cabin.[100] She initially doubts that John is serious, assuming he will "jump the broom" with a "pretty yellow gal" he was "known to favor."[101] But he does not, and when they eventually marry, Harriet deliberately rejects a ceremony at the "Big House," noting that they were no more lawful than those performed in the slave quarters. They also allowed the enslaver to usurp the ceremony's format, forcing the preacher to omit statements about separating families. By marrying in "the Quarters," Harriet assumes a degree of control over the ceremony. The ceremony follows a sequence of events before the broom jumping: her mother places a wreath over her head, an elderly Black preacher named Amos gives a "short" and forgettable sermon on marriage, and she receives a homemade ring from John. Then, her two brothers step forward and hold the broom "a foot above the ground," and, as Harriet recalls, she and John "joined hands, shut our eyes, and jumped over, clearing it easy. And Amos said: Now you are married."[102] In this rendition the broomstick wedding is empowering, a ritual kept by the enslaved community to provide dignity outside the master's gaze. This is a private affair that allows enslaved people to celebrate matrimony with authentic displays of "music-making" while consuming "cider jugs and loaf cakes."[103] The broomstick wedding symbolized resistance to the indignity of American laws that prevented slaves from obtaining legally protected unions.

Though the miniseries follows the general narrative provided in the book, it eliminates Harriet's sexual fantasies and focuses on Harriet's ambitions to accumulate money while interacting with John. In the wedding scene, the slaveholder's young son attends the function and participates in the postnuptial dancing. Though this sequence does not appear in the novel, historians note that young white men frequented the slave quarters during parties to escape the monotony of southern white civility.[104] Additionally, the plantation mistress observes the wedding from a distance while standing on the Big House steps with two enslaved domestics. Harriet receives a crown of flowers, and the broom is held by two men. The main distinction stems from the miniseries providing words to the sermon that Harriet ignored in the novel, although, as in the novel, the ceremonial words are brief and not especially compelling: "Now the Lord says a man is a man, and a woman is a woman, and they are supposed to live by the words of Lord, as husband and wife, without sin. [Looking at John] Now, you got the ring? Well put it on her boy, put it on her! Now, take your walk!"[105] After they walk through two rows of wedding guests they leap over the broomstick and the merriment commences. Though similar to the novel, the scene lacks the accompanying narration provided in Heidish's text that explains why the custom was important. Just as the *Roots* miniseries does not examine Kunta's initial apprehensions surrounding the broomstick ceremony, the televised adaptation of *A Woman Called Moses* does not explore the nuances of the broomstick ceremony. Both visual depictions render the custom as one that enslaved people practiced without any forethought or discussion. Accordingly, Americans who acquired their knowledge of slave culture through cinema and television were not invited to consider the nuances surrounding folk customs. Absent an origins story, one could easily assume that enslaved people robotically performed the ritual without reflection.

## Revitalization and Expansion

Outside television and audiovisual media, the broomstick wedding's introduction into popular culture came through its induction into African American "heritage weddings." Coverage of such events emerged in the 1980s by *Jet Magazine*, *Ebony*, and various Black-owned newspapers. In 1980, Gerri Majors's "Society World" section in *Jet* reported that "Reginald A. Oliver and Stephanie Jo Stokes of Seattle 'jumped over the broom' into the land of matrimony in the traditions of their slave ancestors."[106] "Society World" was largely responsible for the broomstick ceremony's increased popularity throughout the decade, as the column not only reported on weddings employing the custom, but featured photographs of the ceremony. In 1981, it reported that "Monroe C. Nash III and Jo Ann Weaver Brown 'jumped the broom' recently, becoming Mr. and Mrs. Nash."[107] The attached photograph displayed the bride and groom in mid-jump, though the broom is only partially visible. *Jet's*

July 1983 issue highlighted a lottery winner's $50,000 wedding and showed the couple in traditional white marriage garb jumping over a decorated broom during a rather extravagant wedding.[108]

The ceremony's widespread attention in Black cultural forums increased its associations with African American popular culture. While precedents for the custom's revival date back to the 1960s and 1970s, the exposure it received among the public led to its wide scale reintegration into Black popular culture. Noticeable embellishments, such as a decorated broom, were highlighted in its photographic depictions. This dissemination through both descriptive and illustrative methods allowed it to penetrate African American communities throughout the United States, particularly in urban spaces. Another image published by *Jet* in 1987 showed "Mr. and Mrs. Carl L. Morgan of Las Vegas" combining "traditional rites with the ancestral custom of jumping the broom during their recent nuptials in the city."[109] In the attached photo the couple jumps over a lavishly decorated broom. While a plain broomstick would have provided the same functional qualities, African American couples increasingly preferred a decorated broomstick that highlighted the unique stylistics of their ceremony. By 1988 *Ebony* referred to jumping the broom as one of the "latest trends in tying the knot."[110]

Outside *Ebony* and *Jet*, local Black-owned publications like the *Los Angeles Sentinel* prominently featured the new matrimonial trend. As early as 1979, one report included a photo of a couple's leap over the broomstick, and described the ceremony as "an old Afro-American rite" that was used during slavery.[111] In most earlier references it was portrayed as an ancestral custom and considered a novel addition to the modern weddings. In 1981, a couple "added a different touch" to their wedding by jumping over the broom, which the paper claimed "was the only form at one time of marriage of slaves."[112] Though not entirely accurate, as there were other ceremonies, the American descendants of enslaved people now used the broomstick ritual to symbolize the ingenuity and resilience of their ancestors who molded a legacy that challenged oppression and broke the bonds of victimization. Consequently, the ceremony was rendered "quite meaningful" to this couple and many others.

In recognition of its novelty and the likelihood that not all attendees were familiar with it, many wedding officiants provided a statement explaining the ritual's symbolic meaning and historical importance for Black Americans. A high-profile wedding in 1984 vividly reflects this scenario. The ceremony not only included "hundreds of guests," but several of them were considered "distinguished," including Tom Bradley, the first Black mayor of Los Angeles. Prior to the actual jump, the couple's friend explained that the enslaved "invented" the ritual because they were "not permitted to have wedding ceremonies."[113] Channeling the audience's emotional and cultural attachments to it, the guests were invited to "renew their marriage vows" by jumping over the broom. Accordingly, many of the guests participated. Though elaborate, this wedding was not alone in its ability to introduce a large audience to the custom. A 1983 wedding featured in the Maryland-based *Afro-American* newspaper noted that "four hundred guests" were captivated by the broomstick ceremony, described as "a highlight of the reception and a surprise to all."[114] News reports and magazine features disseminated the custom nationally, but word-of-mouth within local communities should not be underestimated. Reports even circulated in the mid-1980s that Black families reenacted slave weddings at reunions held at their ancestral plantations.[115] Given that this ceremony often reached "hundreds of guests" at such gatherings, one can assume they were inspired by its symbolic importance and spread this newly acquired knowledge to their various social circles.

By the mid-1980s publications added more description to the ritual process, briefly explaining the motions used and the decorations that adorned the broom. One broom was "decorated with trimmed streamers of ribbons and flowers," illustrating it was not a plain, disposable item, but one that was central to the ceremony and could function as a keepsake for the couple.[116] Prior to one broomstick wedding in 1989, the report noted that the "best man put down a broom" and the bride and groom jumped over it.[117] Unfortunately, the account provides no further description. It remains unknown why it was the best man's responsibility to initiate this process, as there is no documented example of this format in oral histories. Oftentimes, two of the wedding guests would hold the broomstick in the air as the couple jumped, or the ceremony's officiant would lay down the broom prior to the leap. Presumably, this was a personal innovation on the couple's part. As displayed throughout its history, there was no orthodox method to jumping the broom at this moment, as each couple took creative license to enact the ceremony the way they felt it was most applicable.

Largely suppressed and/or forgotten in the most American communities, the custom's rapid revival unsurprisingly brought speculation surrounding its origins. Most people simply knew it was performed by enslaved people, but few ventured to guess its origins beyond that population. But as it gained more exposure after *Roots*, some writers assumed its popularity throughout Black America held origins beyond the Atlantic, not in western Europe, but in Africa. Writing in 1978 for *Essence Magazine*, a publication specifically designed for Black women, Stephanie J. Stokes hoped that her own wedding would combine her "Black American culture" with her "African slave ances-tors" by jumping "'over a broom' at my Baptist church wedding."[118] In this case, Stokes does not directly place the broomstick ceremony upon the conti-nent of Africa, but suggests that tradition is something distinct from, and more ancient than, African American culture. This implication was chal-lenged in a later piece submitted by a reader who would "resent the fact that" Stokes did not mention jumping the broom originated in Europe. In fact, the reader argued, "the slightest bit of research would have shown there is *no* evi-dence that jumping the broom is of African origin." The reader asserted its origins were in England and that it was the slaveowners who forced slaves to perform it, because they felt that "Blacks were unworthy of a Christian mar-riage." The letter concluded by stating that jumping the broom was an impor-tant piece of Black America's cultural heritage, but it was imperative for those jumping the broom to "understand *why* it came to be so."[119] In 1986, a piece in the *New York Amsterdam News* similarly criticized the ceremony, arguing that masters "ordered" slaves to use the "cynical, burlesque exercise of jumping the broomstick" to demoralize their perceptions of morality and kinship.[120] While some knew of the ritual and its origins and felt compelled to caution people against adopting it without further research, most African Americans yearned for cultural symbols that tied them to their ancestors. Due to its pro-lific appearance in oral histories and presence in the cultural productions of Black artists, the broomstick wedding served the purpose. Its role in commu-nal practice simply needed to be reinvented.

It should be noted that, though the visual display was a primary catalyst in reviving the broomstick wedding, the *Roots* miniseries departed from the novel by downplaying Kunta's thoughts about the custom. In the novel, Kunta has severe reservations about its use for matrimony, but his love for Bell forces him to swallow his pride and, together, they jump the broom. Prior to the event, Haley writes that the couple repeatedly performed the jump to en-sure it was executed perfectly on their wedding day.[121] The 1977 miniseries has no equivalent representation, nor does it provide a preamble to the couple's decision to jump the broom. After Kunta Kinte declares his intentions to marry Bell, the scene immediately cuts to the plantation quarters where a crowd of enslaved people stand around Kunta, Bell, and an older woman who waves a broom above her head while requesting that God blesses the couple's union. Following the oration, the couple jumps the broomstick in view of their friends, as well as the slaveowner, who observes them from a distance. There is no dialogue between Kunta and the enslaved community about whether or not it is legitimate. Rather the broomstick wedding's inclusion within the miniseries is taken for granted, as there is no discussion surrounding its origins, its prominence among American slaves, or the diverse attitudes enslaved people held about wedding ceremonies. Consequently, people who never read the book, but watched the miniseries, left the feature with a belief that jumping the broom was an unquestionable piece of enslaved matrimony that was never challenged or rejected. In many respects, the miniseries left the ritual open to interpretation. Those who felt a cultural pride in the story of Kunta Kinte's survival, but held no other frame of reference for the ritual's history, could speculate on its origins and importance for people of African descent. Since Kunta simultaneously "jumped the broom" while unapologetically espousing pride in his African heritage, one could (as many later did) presume the ceremony held cultural ties to Western Africa. Various authors subsequently explored this mythic connection and minimalized the custom's roots in European folk practice, ultimately developing a thesis of "African origins" that became especially prominent in the 1990s.

## CHAPTER SEVEN

# Every Black Person Should Do It

## *The Rise of the "Heritage Wedding"*

During the concluding months of 1992 news circulated through the Black press that Harriette Cole, at the time a fashion editor at *Essence Magazine*, wrote the "definitive manual" on jumping the broom, underscoring the "folk-loric/historical significance of the African wedding ritual."[1] Geared toward African Americans seeking to include African-centered elements into their ceremonies, it was deemed by one reviewer as the "first 'how to' wedding planner of its kind" and by another the "first comprehensive guide written and designed expressly for African-Americans."[2] Harriette Cole's *Jumping the Broom: The African American Wedding Planner* was an immediate success not only in terms of sales, but also in its ability to disseminate the information to engaged couples seeking to blend ancestral traditions into their modern cer-emonies.[3] As one review noted, it provided the necessary blend of African and American traditions, and such a work was long overdue for Black couples who held no previous reference point for organizing a Black American wed-ding.[4] In only a few weeks after its publication it underwent a fourth printing, and by 1995 one source suggests it sold over 70,000 copies.[5] Cole was invited to discuss her work at many public events, where she often elaborated on her impulse to write it and enable African American couples to include jumping the broom in their ceremonies.[6] Fulfilling an abiding hunger for Black-centered wedding ceremonies, her book became the primary reference point for heri-tage weddings for over a decade, and by 2004 a second edition was reissued.

For Cole, concern over Black America's divorce rates was one reason for promoting an African-centered approach to marriage. She claimed that Afri-can couples on the continent "hardly ever get divorced."[7] The statement im-plies that African Americans had lost crucial pieces of their moral compass under slavery, segregation, and Americanization and that they needed to reach deep into their pasts to reclaim their identity as African people whose ancestors were forcibly displaced. By drawing from the ancestral well, African Americans could reclaim their domestic attachments from reliance on Euro-centric principles and, if they chose, could combine African and Euro-American marital philosophies in ways that most benefited them. The broomstick wedding's centrality in Cole's work became a topic of intense discussion, largely centered on its origins and how to navigate its mysterious history.

Though her book was advertised as a wedding planner, many readers viewed Cole as the authority on the historical origins of jumping the broomstick. Her work certainly inspired many Black couples to embrace the ritual. Shortly after *Jumping the Broom* was published one sees a relative explosion in references to couples jumping the broom at African American weddings.[8] By the mid-1990s, use of the broomstick ritual far eclipsed its earlier advancement in the 1980s, since it was now spotlighted in national news venues and not solely confined to Black publications. Such views are predicated on the first part of her work, in which Cole uses anecdotes, folklore, and select slave narratives to show how Black people in the United States viewed broomsticks, and how such philosophies connected them to Africans on the continent. She hoped to challenge the idea that African American culture was subsumed by Euro-American perspectives regarding love, romance, morality, and family. Using the Kgatla ethnic group of southern Africa, she notes, "It was customary . . . on the day after the wedding for the bride to help the other women in the family to sweep the courtyard clean."[9] She claimed this ritual process signified the bride's integration into her husband's family, as well as the broomstick's centrality in the domestic arrangements of certain African peoples. Thus, Cole never claims that jumping the broom itself is African in origin, but notes that certain ethnic groups used broomsticks in their nuptial processes. Building on this perspective, she suggests enslaved people, barred from legal matrimony, became inventive, and "out of their creativity came the tradition of jumping the broom."[10] Cole does not, however, provide any reference to the custom's connections to the British Isles. Presumably, she believes that enslaved people combined the broomstick's central importance in their ancestral homeland with idea of "crossing over" into the domestic state, a common belief in many folk cultures.[11] The connection was certainly tempting, as it redirected portraying slaves as cultureless laborers to a community that created a vibrant, autonomous culture despite their oppression.[12]

Cole's book provided her readers with a mythical link to jumping the broom's possible connections to Africa. Building on *Roots*'s literary and visual display of the custom, she effectively convinced a younger generation of Black Americans to reconsider their ties to their ancestors and to revise Black America's matrimonial culture. This occurred at a time when the rise of the wedding industry was bolstering Americans' interests in ethnic traditions. By analyzing a diverse selection of primary sources, including newspapers, magazines, wedding planners, and even children's literature, I show how they helped establish the broomstick weeding in Black matrimonial life throughout the United States.

## The Rise of the African American "Heritage Wedding"

Jumping the broom followed four intersecting cultural movements that helped propel the "heritage wedding" into Black popular culture in the late twentieth century. First, Americans of various ethnic groups garnered an intense interest in genealogy, hoping to locate the geographical origins and customs of their ancestors. Curious about their "hyphenated" identity, they explored what it meant to be an American of Irish, Italian, or West African descent.[13] Second, the 1970s, 1980s, and 1990s witnessed an upsurge of "Afrocentric" thought among many African Americans. Though it is expressed in various forms, the Afrocentric philosophy generally asserts that Black people "have a distinctive way of doing things, a set of cultural values and practices that are unique to their African heritage."[14] Essentially, it shifts Black American identity away from a country and culture that historically oppressed them and encourages them to reconnect with African philosophies outside of the Eurocentric canon. It also prompted many descendants of enslaved people to examine the "Africanized" aspects of slave culture, including their foodways, music, dance, and notions of kinship.

In defining Afrocentrism as a distinct movement, historian Mia Bay notes that "Afro-centric," which was originally developed in the early 1960s by Black sociologist W. E. B. Du Bois, means "focused on Africa."[15] Within a few decades, however, the term was linked to a new intellectual movement, largely encapsulated by scholar Molefi Kete Asante's 1980 work *Afrocentricity: The Theory of Social Change* and his 1987 follow-up *The Afrocentric Idea*.[16] Bay argues that Asante's work was the first to provide "guidelines" for Afrocentric thought, "advocating the rejection of Western/European forms of knowledge and analysis" in favor of African-centered beliefs and values. The problem, according to Bay, is that such ideals and values were difficult to summarize as Asante moved to different points of emphasis in developing his theory, ultimately just placing "an increasing emphasis on the wisdom of ancient Kemet (Egypt)" as a foundational model for Afrocentric theory.[17] Afrocentrist intellectuals considered the philosophies of Egypt and "Africa" as "inborn characteristics" of African Americans. The problem here is the assumption that Black people throughout the continent of Africa were united by a common cultural worldview—that people living in such a massive, diverse geographical area all subscribed to a homogenous set of cultural ideals as defined by Asante and others.[18] Opponents of this vantage point argued that an African heritage must be more specific and that to understand the cultural lineages of African Americans one must analyze the ethnic identities of the people taken through West African ports during the transatlantic slave trade.[19]

Even if most Black Americans were not avowed Afrocentrists, many related to the movement and its vision for their autonomy. Though birthed by academics and intellectuals, Afrocentric concepts became highly influential among lay readers by the 1990s. As Bay notes, by then, Afrocentric publishing had become a "cottage industry," in which "paeans to black America's glorious ancient past and Egyptian ancestry" were never "more numerous" than during this decade.[20] A 1991 article published in the *New York Times* maintained that "the ever-changing black experience in America is being assessed with a new intensity. Skin color, how you talk . . . and how you live your life are examples of the tests being used to determine what it means to be black in the 1990's." The author noted that "not since the tumultuous 1960's has there been such an intense focus on blackness."[21] By 1996, historian Andrew Hartman added, most Americans became familiar with Afrocentrism through the debates over a "so-called Ebonics resolution" in Oakland, California, in which the school board tried to mandate that its "mostly white" faculty learn their Black students' brand of English.[22] The resolution was mired in controversy, but it thrust the idea of Black-centered learning into the national spotlight. For many, mandating Ebonics as a recognized form of English was an "Afrocentric response" to the Eurocentric curriculum.[23] While critics accused Afrocentrists of idealizing African cultural history as unchanging and "enclosed . . . by a grand narrative" of uninterrupted progression, as well as questioning the methodological approaches and apparent lack of empirical evidence in many publications,[24] many Black Americans appreciated Afrocentric works as they sought narratives that did not place slavery as the genesis of Black American identity, and rather glorified the African past.[25] Consequently, the community's need to acquire and reclaim their unique cultural rituals, even those with spurious origins, helped solidify and unite an ethnic identity of American blackness that was distinct from white America's standards.[26] For example, historically Black colleges and universities created to educate African Americans barred from entry to traditionally white institutions, gained higher enrollments by the mid-1990s. Television programs such as *A Different World*, a spin-off from the immensely popular *Cosby Show*, highlighted the unique social and cultural features of such institutions, the plethora of Black professionals produced through them, and their rejection of Eurocentrism. Enrollments increased through this positive representation in popular culture.[27]

Third, the Black middle class in the United States continued to expand following desegregation policies of the mid-twentieth century, and by the 1990s independent communities of the Black middle class formed outside the lower-income areas where they previously resided.[28] Consequently, there was a rise in expendable income for many households, which allowed a greater investment in American consumer culture. Increased consumerism directly ties to the fourth and final development: the contemporaneous expansion of the wedding industry and the promotion of lavish wedding ceremonies. Various racial and ethnic groups embraced the lavish white wedding, both in terms of tradition and increased financial investment, toward the close of the twentieth century. For African Americans, this wedding format reflected a uniquely American form of consumerism while also emphasizing a respect for "tradition," which encouraged the betrothed to embrace their pre-Christian African cultures. According to Katherine Jellison, Black Americans used the white wedding as a "hallmark" of their middle-class status, though they also included "Afrocentric themes," including libations and kente cloth, beside such traditional trappings as the white bridal dress.[29]

Sociologist Chrys Ingraham's seminal work *White Weddings: Romancing Heterosexuality in Popular Culture* noted that the wedding industry capitalized on the projection of marriage in popular culture in the same decade, especially following the release of the comedy *Father of the Bride* in 1991.[30] Ingraham termed the new development the "Wedding Industrial Complex," an economically powerful industry that many economists deemed recession-proof due to the social pressures surrounding its ritualistic and cultural importance.[31] Many engaged couples even went into debt to maintain the pomp and display associated with the ceremony. Sociologists Erika Engstrom and Beth Semic argue that televised depictions of the white wedding in the mid-1990s, especially shows deemed "Reality TV," bolstered its mass appeal and popularized the use of religious and culturally specific rituals in American matrimony.[32] However, Ingraham also notes that the *look* of such weddings was not equally distributed across all racial demographics and that until the late 1990s Black women were vastly underrepresented in, if not completely absent from, mainstream bridal magazines.[33] The absence caused many Black couples to look toward Black-owned publications and wedding planners who could provide them a traditional American wedding in their church intermingled with aspects of their African heritage. Thus, the exclusionary practices of the predominantly white wedding industry of the mid-1990s bolstered the demand for African-centered themes for a growing Black middle class who desired to participate in the wedding industry on their own terms. Consequently, jumping the broom catapulted to the forefront of heritage ceremonies. Though its links to Africa were spurious, at best, the broomstick wedding symbolized the transatlantic migrations that defined Black American culture. Reviving this cultural icon provided an additional "test" of blackness for engaged couples seeking to fuse their American and African identities.

In essence, each of these cultural tendencies combined to form the unique brand of matrimonial celebration championed by Harriette Cole and other wedding planners: the African American "heritage wedding."[34]

Like Harriette Cole, wedding planner and coordinator Danita Rountree Green actively promoted the broomstick wedding to Black couples in the early 1990s.[35] In one event she claimed that jumping the broomstick provided a way for enslaved people to seal their unions since they "were not allowed to be married as Christians." Juxtaposing the broomstick tradition with a Christian wedding was a common way of reframing the ritual's history under slavery. Presumably, these authors linked marrying as a "Christian" with legality. This became a common trope among officiants seeking to explain the ritual's significance under slavery, though they never explained if the two ceremonial formats were mutually exclusive. As shown earlier, some groups saw no inconsistency in professing love for Jesus Christ while marrying over the broomstick. Green went on to claim that "it is the oldest, uniquely African American ceremony of love."[36] One can certainly argue that African Americans reinvented the ritual and innovated its performance, but they still comprise only one of many groups that used it.

Perhaps most significantly, Green promoted the "African origins" thesis in her *Broom Jumping: A Celebration of Love*, where she proposed that Moors brought the custom to the British Isles and introduced it to the local populations. These British broom-jumpers then brought the custom to North America and apparently reintroduced it to enslaved people. While adamantly maintaining that jumping the broom is African in its origin, she is nevertheless admits: "There is no recognized documentation . . . proving this theory."[37] Much of her book relays what "folklorists" or "scholars" have suggested, noting the broomstick ceremony was practiced by various cultural groups in both the United States and the British Isles, but one rarely gains a definitive statement from the author. However, one gets the impression Green is most inclined to believe its African connections, as she rehearses the notion that Ghana is the most likely point of origin for enslaved Africans using the nuptial broomstick.[38] Despite the obscure description of the ceremony's origins,

Green's public expositions and her position as an officiant for heritage weddings secured her authority as an interpreter of both its origins and importance in modern African American social practice. She regularly performed ceremonies and discussed her book and garnered national attention from Black press outlets throughout the country.[39] Consequently, the broomstick wedding's popularity only grew in the mid-1990s. Alongside its increased exposure in popular culture, the wedding industry expanded massively in the 1990s. Combined with a rise in African-centered discourses throughout Black America, the rise of the "heritage wedding" had commenced.

## Marketing the Broomstick Wedding

Young African Americans coming of age in the 1990s had access to a far more extensive collection of literature and material culture that, according to Michael Eric Dyson, demonstrated "an attempt to celebrate the spirit of ingenuity and survival in the face of suffering."[40] When placed in its cultural context, the success of Cole's *Jumping the Broom* is not surprising. Both its content and timing were spectacularly on point, as it emerged through the confluence of the wedding industry's unprecedented expansion and the rising popularity of Afrocentric philosophy. If one reviews the literature on both topics it seems self-evident that heritage weddings would be born from these contemporary movements. Afrocentrism provided Black Americans with cultural tools distinct from the white American majority, and provided aspects of cultural reclamation for a descendant community that believed much of its ancestral culture was whitewashed over generations of oppression and marginalization. Integrating traditions that fell outside the middle-class weddings of white America was a deeply important aspect of this cultural reclamation.[41]

With the need to create a uniquely African American ceremony many celebrants looked toward a custom that appeared uniquely associated with their enslaved ancestors. Consequently, the broomstick wedding also gained increased exposure through television and literature, and by the 1990s entrepreneurs began manufacturing decorated broomsticks to capitalize on the developing fashion. The marketing of "heritage brooms" expanded throughout the 1990s, reorienting the original emphasis on "heritage" to representing them as objects of fashion. Of course, fashion and ancestral heritage were not mutually exclusive categories, and the boom in marketable heritage brooms was lucrative for some designers. Some broom-makers tapped into the booming business to supplement their income, while others developed businesses focused on African American wedding trends. One designer provided "custom brooms and favors, broom bouquets and DIY broom kits."[42] Some observers called this new craft "broom artistry," and manufacturers offered different forms of matrimonial broomsticks specially designed for Black weddings. Certain brooms were of the "loose straw variety," bearing similarity to the string-tied straw brooms enslaved people used for cleaning. The other version resembled modern broomsticks designed to reflect older materials, including a "solid handle" made from wood.[43] One report in 1999 noted that the surge in the broom-making businesses occurred around the mid-1990s, due to a demand to have "a broom that looks like the slave brooms of history but is ornate enough to be considered a keepsake."[44] Such brooms could range from as low as $35 to as high as $200, as each broomstick-maker carved out his or her niche for the product. Ms. Butcher, an independent broom-maker in Pennsylvania, claimed that her brooms were "made from materials that slaves once used in their daily lives," including "feather-like straw" and "stiffer straw that serves as a handle." Additionally, her shop was apparently located "atop what historians believe was a stop on the Underground Railroad," a detail that further added to the "folkloric allure of her brooms."[45] The marriage between historical memory and contemporary fashion solidified the appeal of broomstick weddings for those who previously had little interest in remembering the enslaved past.

The heritage broom provided a way for the diaspora to connect itself with the continent, even if its African roots were questionable. One finds references to people donning "African attire" when leaping over the object, pouring libations beforehand, or even wrapping the broom itself in traditional kente cloth,[46] which denoted pride in one's African heritage.[47] While the aforementioned broom-makers developed unique strategies in marketing the concept to various customers, wedding planners were most directly linked to the ritual's ubiquitous revival. This group of predominantly African American women specialized in heritage weddings designed to promote commemoration and admiration for both enslaved and African ancestry.

In addition to the television adaptation of *Roots* in the 1970s, some columnists believed the 1999 film *The Best Man* helped to further interest in the custom.[48] Starring many prominent Black actors and actresses, including Sanai Lathan, Taye Diggs, Morris Chesnutt, Terrence Howard, and Nia Long, the film is a hybrid comedy drama that displays the rocky circumstances under which four men reunite for their best friend's wedding and how they navigate love, romance, and relationships from the past to present. After a raucous series of events, the groom and his bride are pronounced man and wife by a minister and they both leap over a broomstick lying on the floor. No indication of the reason for including the ritual is given—a circumstance that suggests that Black audiences watching the film were already familiar with the custom and that no explanation was needed. Either way, this visual representation in a major motion film certainly ignited further interest in the ritual, which was further disseminated by the Learning Channel's multi-season reality show *A Wedding Story*. The series followed the wedding preparations and ceremonies of various American couples and explored their different religious and cultural expressions in the ceremony. Two couples in the series included the broomstick tradition in their weddings.[49]

Alongside Danita Green's proposal linking the custom to Ghana, Cole's interpretation, partially influenced by Afrocentric concepts, initiated a chain reaction. African American–centered wedding manuals consistently reiterated, and built upon, either the notion that enslaved people created the ritual on their own or the idea that they imaginatively recreated an African precedent. Ingrid Sturgis's 1997 work *The Nubian Wedding Book*, which noted that scholars were unsure where it originated, examines folklore that offers a possible African link, even claiming that some individuals from Trinidad and Tobago witnessed broomstick weddings on the island before the popularization of *Roots* in the 1970s.[50] Six years later, Thereze Fleetwood's *The Afrocentric Bride: A Style Guide* celebrated the reintegration of jumping the broom into Black weddings, noting it was the enslaved who invented it as their "own" form of matrimony.[51] By 2007, Thony C. Anyiam's *Jumping the Broom in Style* forcefully asserted that jumping the broom was "specifically West African" and that "enslaved Africans (African-Americans) practiced broom jumping as a celebration of their African heritage."[52] Imagining the development of African-American culture from this framework caused some pushback from certain scholars and public intellectuals, though it seems for entirely different reasons.

## African Origins and Other Myths

Ascribing mythical origins to this folk custom occurs for various reasons, including a misreading of the available texts; generalizing the lives of enslaved people; romanticizing the brutalities of the institution; viewing slavery from a parochial, nationalistic perspective; or projecting one's present assumption upon the past without engaging the nuances found in the historical documents. Some writers promulgate the romanticized notion that enslaved people's marriages were free of internal abuse or disruption, a notion encapsulated by the statement: "The jumping process was so important for our ancestors. . . . You can't ever jump back. You have to jump forward."[53] Beyond the fact that some historical documents noted enslaved people *did* jump "back" to initiate a divorce, this premise of unbroken marital commitment denies the enslaved an important element of humanity, in which they are subjected to human passions of disagreement, irritability, and anger. Historian Jeff Forret shows that as in contemporary situations of domestic abuse, whether emotional or physical, an enslaved person's intimate partner or child could be the primary victim of his or her rage.[54] The reinvention of jumping the broom is not alone in this scenario, and scholars of memory studies note that "whether deliberately or not, individual or group memory selects certain landmarks of the past—places, artworks, dates; persons . . . real or imagined—and invests them with symbolic and political significance."[55] Indeed, reimagining the broomstick wedding's sociocultural origins is likely not done with malicious intent; it simply reflects a desire for cultural ownership among a people who already had so much stolen from them.

A common myth asserts that enslaved people had no other choice but to "jump the broom," assuming they did not practice other rituals or that such rituals were withheld from them. An oft-cited statement from many journalists and cultural critics surrounds the idea that jumping the broom was the "only" ceremony available to enslaved people.[56] Not only does this assertion withhold creativity and ingenuity from the enslaved, but it also incorrectly generalizes their collective experience. Despite the odds against them, enslaved people still elected to make choices regarding who they loved and how they confirmed their commitment. Suggesting that the broomstick wedding was their "only" option misrepresents the dynamic creativity under which enslaved people developed their cultures. We know that they married in various formats, and, though difficulty ensued, used some agency in doing so. One article from the *Los Angeles Sentinel* noted in 1993 that jumping the broom "was the only formal ceremony signifying marriage in which blacks could partake."[57] Granted, it was far more difficult for enslaved people to acquire ministers if none was available on their plantation, but as noted earlier, enslaved people used various forms of matrimony and broomstick weddings did not comprise a clear majority. Additionally, we know this ritual was largely rejected by those enslaved in the plantation house who hoped to differentiate themselves from field hands. As it gained more exposure in popular media, its seemingly exclusive association with Black Americans caused it to overshadow the diverse forms of matrimony that enslaved couples practiced.

Different outlets claimed the broomstick ceremony was the sole option for enslaved people who were "forbidden to marry," explaining "couples jumped over a broom before friends and family in secret ceremonies."[58] The main problem with this argument is that it again generalizes the richly diverse historical experiences. Not all broomstick ceremonies were secret, and many slaves did refer to the master's presence at the ceremony. Additionally, the language is very slippery. Enslaved people were not "forbidden to marry." They married quite frequently, and many believed their unions were as legitimate as those of free people. The more accurate phrase would read, "their marriages were not legally recognized," which made their bonds especially tenuous under threats of separation. Some heritage weddings include a "broom mistress," who serves as a spiritual elder presiding over the ceremony.[59] Historically, older women did sometimes lead the ceremony, but no narratives include the title "broom mistress" in their descriptions. In one of the more prevalent assertions, many argue that enslaved people developed the custom themselves due to the government's unwillingness to legally recognize their marriages.[60] It would be correct to claim that enslaved people reimagined the custom for their own purposes, but no evidence suggests it was developed without a precursor or that it was solely unique to enslaved southerners. Jumping the broomstick served a variety of purposes for individuals, and writers must be more cautious when attempting to explain the depth of its meaning for these various communities.

The notion of "African origins" is arguably the custom's most persistent myth.[61] Though wedding specialists such as Danita Green and Harriette Cole note the broomstick ceremony's direct African origins are difficult to confirm, others relentlessly pursue its imagined connection to African roots. Tolagbe Ogunleye, a former professor of Africana Studies, even attempts to connect every aspect of ancient matrimonial culture in the British Isles to an African root. Much of her argument has little historical substance, and her citations reveal a preference for a few secondary sources written by Afrocentric scholars. She primarily asserts that the British Isles were populated by people of African descent in the ancient period, and if these Africans were already engaging in matrimonial broomstick rituals prior to their migrations, the true origins of the broomstick wedding would lie in Africa, not Britain. This claim is not based in any empirical research, and it is worth noting that none of the British "Africans" in Ogunleye's book "jump the broom" until they arrive in the antebellum South as enslaved people.[62] No precolonial documents from West Africa reveal anyone engaging matrimonial broomstick rites throughout the duration of the Atlantic Slave Trade. In other words, she provides no evidence it was ever performed on the African continent, but, somehow, this supposed African ritual is practiced by a small percentage of people taken in the transatlantic slave trade. Though the primary sources invalidate her assertions, these ideas hold remarkable staying power as they continue to spread through-out venues dedicated to African American popular culture. Bereft of deep pri-mary source analysis, many publications in the twenty-first century still promote the African origins of jumping the broom.[63] Hence, the African origins thesis remains prominent in popular culture. In the 2005 season of *Bridezillas* a Black woman discussed her interest in including the broomstick custom, cit-ing it as an "African tradition."[64] As entrepreneurs invested in the wedding industry, specifically promoting an Afrocentric approach to their clients, re-taining the broomstick wedding's mythic African origins was important for preserving its symbolic value for those seeking an empowering experience.[65] The politics behind group identity transformed a custom once employed by various cultures into one that manifested cultural homogeneity.

If evidence discredits the African origins thesis, however, why is it perpet-uated? Researcher Imani Strong explains that both literally and symbolically Africa represents the ancestral roots of Black Americans, which are detached "from the historic pain and oppression of American citizenship, and, thus, cultural continuity and connection are desired in a quest for place and accep-tance."[66] Essentially, the literal connection to Africa is less important than the psychological attachment to an ancestral practice. For many social commen-tators, refusing to jump the broom was an insult to the ancestors. Conversely, if the broomstick custom has no African roots, it is more easily dismissed as a relic of slavery that has no value for modern practitioners.

Perhaps the greatest paradox in the custom's revival is that while Haley's *Roots* is cited as the prime motivator for revisiting the place of jumping the broom in Black culture, Haley never claimed African origins for the wedding. Kunta Kinte initially shunned the ritual. In fact, the novel specifically repre-sents slaveowners being present at the ceremonies and sometimes even spon-soring them, and he never mentions any clandestine elements surrounding its performance. This is not to suggest that such ceremonies were not, at times, performed privately, or even secretly, but popular writings have per-petuated many such exaggerated claims that remain unsubstantiated by the primary sources.[67] Enslaved couples were certainly creative in how they prac-ticed the ritual, but the historical record shows that the earliest documented practitioners of the ritual lived in western Europe, not Africa.

## Jumping the Broom in Children's Literature

Black cultural movements, novels, and media propelled jumping the broom's modern revival, and children's literature helps sustains the practice across generations. With regard to the latter, in 1994, author Courtni C. Wright released the first juvenile publication visually displaying the ceremony. The tale is narrated by Lettie, the younger sister of the bride, Tillie, who is set to "jump the broom" with her fiancé Will. The story centers on the preparations for the wedding, men fishing, women sewing and cleaning, and the enslaved community at relative leisure in their anticipation for the big event. The harsh realities of slavery are subtle: for instance, Lettie notes that her father makes visits from "Master William's plantation" and that her oldest brother, Sam, will not be attending because "Master sold him away last year."[68] These references are not dealt with, however, and remain relatively subliminal within the larger narrative that stresses the autonomy of enslaved laborers. In many ways, Wright's work revisits the academic literature of the 1970s and 1980s that depicted enslaved communities through paradigms of agency and individuality.

This trajectory, however, caused some criticism of the work. While most reviewers were impressed with the stunning visuals, Wright was criticized for failing to "establish the historical context" by not matching Lettie's descriptions with the visual images.[69] One reviewer noted that the artist Gershom Griffith's depictions of slaves' spacious cabins, decoratively patched clothing, and abundant food contradicted the less comfortable parts of the text.[70] In one example, Lettie reveals the forced rupture of her family, but the visual depiction features "a beatifically smiling protagonist being teased by her other two brothers, and there's no textual development or resonance of sadness."[71] English professor Gerald Early noted that while it was "heartening to see children's books like 'Jumping the Broom,' . . . a reader is likely to come away from this book thinking that slavery wasn't too bad at all."[72] In fact, *Jumping the Broom* was cited in other reviews as an example for how slavery should not be illustrated.[73] Despite these criticisms, reviewers generally believed it was step in the right direction, and Wright achieved her goal of visually displaying the custom as it might have been practiced in slavery.[74] By the end of the book the climactic ceremony is undertaken. Since there is "no minister in the quarters," an elder gives a few words of counsel, and Tillie and Will jump over a broom placed on the ground. This is followed by an explanation from Lettie's elders that the broom was for sweeping away the past and evil spirits. Thus, Wright injected small amounts of enslaved folklore into the book that would inspire two decades of African American children's literature about the broomstick tradition.

In 1997 Candy Grant Helmso, a "self-taught children's book author," produced the second depiction of the ceremony, though this time it does not take place among enslaved people on a plantation. The story's protagonist,

Tyrick, based on Helmso's childhood friend, witnesses the marriage of his older sister in a church ceremony generations after slavery's demise. Tyrick remains a relatively casual observer, his uncle places a broom on the ground and the newly wedded bride and groom clasping hands and jumping over it. When he inquires about the ceremony's meaning, his mother explains that enslaved people in the United States were unable to legally wed and developed a "secret" ceremony to marry, and that the contemporary broomstick ceremony represented a way to bless the marriage and honor the ancestors.[75] As in Wright's depiction, there is no reference to slaveowners or certified ministers. Unlike Wright's Lettie, however, Tyrick is not exposed to the darker components of enslaved life, such as the rupture of enslaved families. Helmso's work conveys the importance of continuing the tradition in homage to the ancestors. The broomstick ceremony here symbolizes triumph for enslaved Americans, as it provided them an outlet from otherwise oppressive circumstances. Due to the popularity of *Jump the Broom*, a Spanish version was released one year later, a fact that suggests that publishers believed children's literature held potential for cross-cultural impact.[76]

Mississippi storyteller Diane Williams's work *Annie Mae Jumps the Broom* was published in 1999. Williams' story is more text heavy than the previous works and concentrates almost exclusively on the slave couple, Annie Mae and Buster. The work vividly describes their courtship and wedding, as well as the role of An't Minnie, the "leader of the plantation." After Buster proposes, An't Minnie orders them to wait a few days to ensure they were adequately prepared to wed. Upon their decision to go ahead, Buster gives Annie Mae "a ring he had fashioned from a piece of brass the blacksmith gave him." The actual wedding features a meal heavy in pig meat and dress inspired by "African" backgrounds. An't Minnie officiates the ceremony, which includes features noted in former slave narratives, such as couples jumping over three times, or the belief that bad luck follows those who stub their toe on the broom. Williams even includes the suggestion that the master's permission was not necessary, which is consistent with some testimonials. Unlike in Wright's and Helmso's books, the slaveholder does appear briefly to enjoy the cake served at the wedding, but he still remains largely peripheral to the overall narrative. Williams apparently engaged in some focused research on the enslaved ceremony, but in a concluding note she leaves her readers with a cliffhanger: "No one really knows where 'jumping the broom' originated, except maybe An't Minnie, Annie Mae, and Buster." It appears the author hoped to promote curiosity in the African American past and encourage descendants to use the ancestral customs. Williams's book is, in many respects, consistent with the previous works in displaying enslaved cultural autonomy, but differs from them in focusing more exclusively on the ritual performance of the broomstick wedding and the social dynamics of the bonded community.

Taking the broomstick wedding in a different direction, Connie Porter's *Addy's Wedding Quilt* is set during Reconstruction and focuses on Addy, who is coming of age directly after enslaved people were emancipated. Porter emphasizes Addy's relationship with her grandmother, M'dear, and highlights the position that elders occupied in their communities, where they were often viewed as the ultimate sources of wisdom.[77] After her parents announce their plan to legalize their marriage in a church ceremony, Addy, a gifted seamstress, makes them a quilt, but is unable to decide upon its designs. Through M'dear's oral histories she discovers that her parents were married by jumping the broom twenty years earlier upon their owner's plantation, and she gradually learns more details through her confrontations with a bully named Harriet, who discovers that Addy's quilt is an intended wedding present.

After discovering that Addy's parents were not legally married, Harriet taunts Addy with the accusation that her parents were living out of wedlock. Infuriated, Addy retorts that they were married in slavery by jumping the broom and would soon marry in freedom. Addy even reveals plans to jump the broom at her own wedding ceremony. Harriet retorts that jumping the broom was "a slavery way of doing things. Slavery ways should be left in the past. . . . Nobody jumps the broom these days, . . . It never meant anything."[78] The dignity of the ceremony is only rescued by an emotional conversation between Addy and her mother, in which she explains the precarious nature of enslaved matrimony, as well as emphasizing the personal commitment of couples who jumped the broomstick. Encouraged by her teacher, Miss Dunn, Addy uses the broomstick as an applique on the quilt, and continues to combat Harriet's remarks concerning her "slavery quilt." Overhearing the discussion, Miss Dunn chimes in with the book's intended message: "Slavery is over, Harriet. It is in the past, but memories like these are about who our families are, who *we* are. Addy's right to cherish them."[79] The story concludes with the quilt's presentation at the wedding party, and both parents' appreciation of the gift. Porter provides an instructional appendix to the story explaining the historical backdrop of matrimony before and after emancipation and uses selections from ex-slave narratives to illustrate the point. Porter's story provides a generational synopsis of divergent viewpoints. Harriet represents the view that slave customs should be abandoned if Black Americans were to attempt to socially advance in American culture. Addy represents a different perspective, that of African Americans in the late-twentieth century who believed the revival and cultural recognition of enslaved customs commemorated ancestral resiliency.

Sonia Black's 2004 work *Jumping the Broom* attempts to depict the ceremony's usage in a "heritage wedding." The young protagonist, Erin, becomes emotional at her inability to afford a wedding present for her sister, Simone, and seeks consolation from her grandmother. During the conversation, "Nana" reveals the wedding practice of "jumping the broom." In this rendition, the broomstick itself was a family heirloom, as Erin's mother had jumped the same broom used by Nana, and it was anticipated that Simone would also use the broom. Upon asking Nana why they jumped a broomstick, Erin is told that when people were brought from Africa, "it was against the law in some states for blacks to marry in church. So we made up our own ceremony. . . . It meant that they were jumping the broom into their new life together."[80] The description inspires Erin to decorate the broom with "cowry shells" and "little bells."

While Black's ancestral heritage hails from Jamaica, not the United States, she notes that her motivation in writing *Jumping the Broom* was that its "origin is important to our heritage. . . . I feel it is vital that we pass on information so age-old traditions can live on."[81] While most would agree with the sentiment, her claim to a shared culture with Black Americans represents a pan-African perspective on racial identity. Jamaicans have no documented tradition of enslaved people using broomstick weddings, but Black's evocation of the first-person plural designates that, for her, racial unity provides a venue in which an author of Jamaican descent raised in the United States can lay claim to a shared culture with African Americans. Ultimately, one of the work's triumphs is that Erin is a thoroughly relatable character to most children in the twenty-first century, and she exemplifies a young person "honoring her roots" through connecting with the elders.[82]

*Ellen's Broom*, a 2012 children's book by Kelly Sterling Lyons, focuses on a young child during the Reconstruction period who confronts the harsh realities of her ancestors' enslavement. During a church service, Ellen and her family discover that the government is prepared to legally register the marriages of freed people, which prompts a special family trip to the courthouse to legitimize her parents' union. The broomstick used at their antebellum wedding still hangs over the fireplace, reminding the children that their parents "did the best we could with what we had."[83] Ellen's father elaborates on the precarious position of enslaved couples: "Before freedom came, the law wasn't on our side. . . . Husbands and wives could be ripped apart, sold away at any time. It didn't matter if they cried or even begged to stay together." In response to this revelation, Ellen's "eyes burned and her heart ached" at the thought of separation. The image that follows this exchange features two slave traders and four enslaved people, with one enslaver forcibly dragging away a woman as her husband is led away by a white man with a whip and club. The gritty scenario contrasts sharply with Courtney Wright's jovial community.[84]

The climactic point comes when Ellen's parents arrive at the courthouse to attain legal validation for their ceremony. Having brought the broom along, Ellen compares her mother's homespun dress to the more expensive clothing of the women around her and decides to decorate the broom with red and pink flowers from a garden she spotted near the courthouse. After the registrar validates the union, they stop for a picnic beneath a shade tree, where Ellen asks her parents to perform the broomstick ritual. Ellen's father initially hesitates, explaining that "broom jumping is in the past, Lil' Bit. We're married, official." The interjection of Ellen's mother, however, testifies to the need to the importance of connecting the past to the present: "It will always be a part of who we are. Come on, Papa. Let's show these young folks how it's done." After they do, Ellen discloses her plans to jump the broom at her own marriage, and after slight hesitation, her father suggests that would be "might fine." The newly decorated broom is subsequently rehung over the fireplace directly above the marriage certificate, symbolically legitimizing and linking both ceremonials.

According to one reviewer, *Ellen's Broom* "expresses the poignant significance of our 'jumping-the-broom ritual,'" and, alongside its beautiful illustrations, it provides a "perfect expression of the enduring power of Black love."[85] Another suggests it was useful for elementary school children, as the story was "depicted in lovely linoleum block prints."[86] Though its illustrations bear similarity to the brightness of Courtni Wright's 1994 book, *Ellen's Broom* provides a realistic interpretation of life under slavery by not romanticizing the institution or depicting perpetually happy slaves. Kelly Lyons, who gives a brief note at the end of the work explaining the story's origins, explains that upon her discovery of an 1866 Cohabitation List of Henry County, Virginia, she came to understand the tenuous nature of enslaved marital relations. Having jumped the broom at her own wedding, Lyons describes the ritual as "a symbol of our commitment and a tie to the trials our people have overcome." Lyons' autobiographical sketch demonstrates the most concerted attempt to place her research in a coherent children's narrative displaying the horrors of slavery, while also acknowledging the triumph of her ancestors.

The six works discussed here have several commonalities in the ways that they engage discussions of slavery, marriage, and history in children's literature. With the exception of Helmso's protagonist, all the others are young women. All books, however, make an explicit connection between femininity and marriage, for even the young man, Tyrick, is attending the wedding of his sister. Each work focuses upon the wedding ceremony or marital aspirations of young women or girls, which prompts one to wonder how the social value of the broomstick ceremony resonates across genders and how a modern author should depict it. Similarly, each work uses maternal figures to explain, and ultimately salvage, the practice, while fathers remain indifferent to the custom's value, at least initially. Dimensions of historical memory are fully displayed in each work, with the periods of slavery, Reconstruction, and the post–civil rights era represented. In many respects, each work functions as an apologetic for the value of jumping the broom, defending its importance as a necessary component of African American cultural history. Regardless of whether the realities of slavery can ever be displayed through children's literature, each work seeks to ensure that jumping the broom will not be forgotten by subsequent generations.

## Juvenile Literature and the Preservation of Historical Knowledge

Juvenile literature on slavery also demonstrates attention to jumping the broom's dominance in popular representations of American slavery. Anne Kamma's 2004 book, *If You Lived When There Was Slavery in America*, depicts various aspects of slave life and includes sections on recreation, labor, and even the differences between "servants" and "slaves" in colonial America. The book dedicates two pages to exploring slave marriage, first explaining that while enslaved people had no legal protection for their marriages, slaveowners encouraged marriage to prevent their slaves from being tempted to run away. In a subsection that asks, "What Was 'Jumping the Broom'?" Kamma explains that the broomstick wedding was a "special way" to get married and notes that if either partner touched the broom during the leap it was "bad luck." The attached picture, illustrated by Pamela Johnson, features a couple inside a large room jumping over a broom placed on the floor, as their wedding guests clap and dance around them. Ultimately, the book rehearses the idea that in being "special," jumping the broom was the only option for marriage and that it was wholeheartedly embraced by the enslaved. It is the only wedding ceremony that merits any description or representation in the book, a circumstance that highlights its cultural dominance in the post-*Roots* era.

Similarly, Bobbie Kalman and Amanda Bishop's *A Slave Family* focuses on familial units. The work provides a grittier portrayal of the domestic rupture many families experienced, explaining that enslaved people possessed no legal protection against forcible separations of husbands from wives and parents from children. In the section on "Marriage and Children," the authors illustrate a broomstick wedding, correctly noting that the ceremony held "different meanings to different people," and describe how communities in different areas interpreted it. They note that marriage could take many forms on each plantation, be they Christian ceremonies dictated by the slaveowner or those led by elderly slaves or spiritual leaders. The work verifies the broomstick wedding's important position in U.S. enslavement, and arguably one of its most distinctive cultural traits.

Other forms of juvenile literature use the broomstick wedding to imagine the lives of historical figures. The reconstruction of Dave the Potter, an enslaved man who left notes and messages on his artwork, is one such example. Known as "David Drake," he was a skilled potter enslaved in Edgefield, South Carolina, a location famed for its stoneware. Scholars have identified him from the notes he left on each piece he crafted. His messages, which range from clever rhyme schemes to simple signatures and dates, indicate that at some point in his life, he became literate, and the snippets of information he left behind provide glimpses of his life. They also provide an impetus for imaginatively reconstructing his life.

For example, Andrea Cheng's 2013 work *Etched in Clay* consists of short stanzas of poetry written in similar style to Dave's inscriptions and intended to provide lessons about American slavery. Sometimes these poems are attributed to Dave, other times they represent the thoughts of his friends or love interests. Though we know little about his personal life, Cheng uses historical events associated with the antebellum period to contextualize Dave's position as a skilled slave. Regarding his personal life, she uses the broomstick wedding to reflect how enslaved couples approached courtship in a poem entitled "Jumping the Broomstick, Eliza, 1820." Leonard Todd's biography of Dave suggests that a woman named Eliza was listed alongside him at a young age and may have been his first wife, though documents reveal their owner sold her shortly after the listing was produced.[87] Cheng's story produces a fictional conversation between Eliza and her slaveowner. The latter asks if Dave is "good enough" for Eliza to marry, to which she replies that he is a bit young and too skinny, but that she admires his skills with earthenware and he is generally a kind man. Eventually, she agrees to the proposal and describes the wedding:

> I put on my dress,
> blue as the sky,
> with white dots like cotton
> ripe in the fields.
> Dave is standing there
> in black pants
> and white shirt.
> We jump the broomstick,
> and the minister says
> we'll be together
> 'till death or distance
> do you part.[88]

Cheng attempted to encapsulate the multifaceted meanings of slave weddings by adding details of the anticipation felt during courtship, the clothing worn at the ceremony, and the ever-present reality that one could be sold at the master's whim. In another section, Cheng recreates another courtship involving Dave and a woman named Lydia, who produced children with Dave after his forced separation from Eliza. In this rendition, Lydia is privately musing that she and Dave share a common plight, as they have both lost a spouse through sale, but she wonders if they are compatible. She views him as the best option for her current circumstances, since her children love him as a father. She knows Dave wants to marry her, and she concludes with an affirmative decision: "the broomstick is waiting, and I will jump."[89] Cheng correctly depicts the psychological dilemmas imbedded in slave matrimony, though one could challenge the sole reliance on the broomstick wedding as the primary way to represent the ceremony. However, Cheng operated in a paradigm where popular writers and academics asserted the broomstick wedding was the *primary* method through which slaves married, which renders her decision understandable.

The association of remarkable historical figures with the broomstick custom took place in tandem with its increased popularity. It is no surprise that popular works analyzing Harriet Tubman, arguably the most famous formerly enslaved person in American history, also abound with references to broomstick weddings, including one reference to Harriet's own broomstick wedding with John Tubman. The author follows the African-centered interpretation, claiming the ceremony stemmed "from the Ashanti tradition in

Africa."[90] Considering that prominent figures such as Frederick Douglass, Booker T. Washington, Solomon Northup, and Harriet Tubman are not associated with the custom in their biographies, the matrimonial practice's inclusion in this depiction of Tubman is used to reflect a theory of Black cultural homogeneity. While such marital traditions certainly influenced enslaved laborers throughout the U.S. South we must be careful in attributing certain practices to individuals who never mention their own participation in such events. Such claims hinder further comprehension of the diversity that existed in the antebellum South and how enslaved people used various strategies to survive an oppressive system.

In another example, the story of Harriet Jacobs, who recounted her escape in her autobiography, *Incidents in the Life of a Slave Girl*, is reimagined in Mary E. Lyons's *Letters from a Slave Girl*, which, though fictive, intended "to retell portions of Harriet's story . . . social occasions, meals eaten words spoken."[91] In one letter dated 1827, addressed to her "Daddy," Jacobs notes that her "friend Chloe, who belong to Mrs. Gardner, jump the broom with Moss McDonald at Christmas, and now she expecting a baby in March."[92] If one is to honestly represent the realities of enslavement, Jacobs is certainly an attractive choice for juvenile readers. Indeed, *Incidents in the Life of a Slave Girl* bolstered the abolitionist cause by vividly exposing the treatment of enslaved women and the precarious state of slave matrimony upon the southern plantation.[93] By combining Jacob's story with the popular slave ritual, the author is reemphasizing its importance for young readers who seek to connect with their past.

## Pride or Embarrassment? The Debate

Jumping the broom's cultural revitalization did not emerge without some controversy. Conflicting views of the enslaved experience pitted some public intellectuals against one another. Cole's proposal that the broomstick ritual was produced through the ingenuity of enslaved people ignited various reactions from her opponents. In one response, Kwaku Person-Lynn, a lecturer and public intellectual in Los Angeles, California, proposed that African Americans should use caution in reenacting such rituals. Though the broomstick ritual might seem "innocent" or "fun," he argued that Black people did not need to be "saddled with a slave tradition" and that they should avoid duplicating "something we thought was part of African or American African heritage, no matter what movie it appeared in."[94] Maulena Karenga, an activist and professor of Africana Studies, went even further by publicly mocking

the ritual in 1994, asserting that it stemmed from enslavers manipulating marriage rituals: "What's the purpose of jumping over a sweeping utensil? . . . It's
an obscene thing for those people to lecture us on morality."[95] A few years
later, he went further, arguing, "It doesn't come from African people. It comes
from people who enslaved us. . . . It reduces our commitment to each other
with a physical act over an instrument of labor."[96] For Karenga, the revival of
the custom revisits a past of violence, oppression, and exploitation.

In this interpretation enslaved people did not willingly appropriate the ritual; they were forced to use it for the enjoyment of their oppressors. Since the
custom did not originate with African Americans, Karenga sees no value in
their using it. Afrocentric philosopher Molefi Kete Asante concurred, arguing that enslavers created the ceremony through their lack of respect for Black
culture: "It's a degradation of marriage. . . . I'm tired of African Americans
participating in it."[97] Writing for an Afrocentric audience, Karenga and Asante were suspicious of the custom's ties to slavery and tried to articulate the
need for Black people to reject European traditions and embrace Afrocentric
paradigms. But Harriette Cole's access to popular publication venues secured
the custom's revitalization. She responded by asking why slaveowners would
waste their time worrying about how slaves married, considering that labor
extraction and profit were the supreme motives for owning slaves: "It doesn't
make sense to me that slave masters would try to figure out a ritual for slaves
to get married."[98] Ultimately, her way of reimagining the ritual took hold among
African American couples seeking to reconnect with their ancestral heritage.

In many respects the arguments were academic in nature. Even if one accepted the interpretation that enslavers imposed the ceremony upon the enslaved, both Karenga and Asante neglected to note that captives could modify
a slaveowner's imposition and create something meaningful. Harriette Cole
and Danita Green's propositions relied more upon a somewhat preternatural
connection to the past. Cole's assertion that it did not "make sense" for a master to impose a ceremony upon his slaves reveals an appeal to logic that, while
not based upon intensive research, is highly effective in public forums. The
novelty of the tradition in the 1990s might explain how both sides drew such
stark conclusions. For scholarly purposes, the exchange certainly reveals how
jumping the broomstick was a product of contested memory among African
Americans.

Criticism of the custom was not limited to Afrocentric authors however,
as academic folklorists challenged claims to African origins. In 1997, folklorist
Alan Dundes responded to the African origins thesis in the *Journal of American Folklore*, arguing that wedding planners used speculative evidence in their

arguments and contended the available documents pointed to a European origin, specifically the British Romani. He bluntly pointed out that it was neither "invented" in the United States, nor derived from an African ritual. Instead, "It is an undeniable borrowing from European folklore."[99] Dundes claimed that enslaved people were "forced" to use the ritual, denying them any agency in reinterpreting its meaning. Shortly after, folklorist C. W. Sullivan published two articles analyzing the ceremony's possible Welsh origins and pointed toward the ways through which it arrived in North America through immigration.[100] Such a focus on Europeans as agents of the practice speaks to Karenga's and Asante's arguments that it is offensive to encourage Black people to integrate these foreign customs acquired by the enslaved into their modern celebrations. Misunderstanding the parameters of enslaved people's abilities to make choices is likely at the heart of this debate.

## Persistence and Distinction

Broomstick weddings and decorative broomsticks dot the landscape of African American culture throughout the United States, ranging from cinematic features, to its display on the designs of local Kansas City quilter Sonie Ruffin, and even into the courthouses of cities with Black majorities.[101] In 2006 a news report noted that Herman Marable, a Flint, Michigan, judge, was conducting broomstick ceremonies "that are personalized and reflective of the cultural heritage." Not surprisingly, the article promoted the popular idea that "the tradition of jumping the broom . . . has been thought to have originated in West Africa."[102] Courthouse weddings serve various functions, but couples often choose them for their low cost and the privacy they provide. Though many couples hold a reception after the marriage certificate is secured, rituals tied to the ceremony (such as jumping the broom) are typically skipped in exchange for the expediency of moving through the courthouse. Marable's decision to include the broomstick ceremony reveals two important points. First, it allowed people engaging in a civil ceremony to still perform a ritual connected to their ethnic heritage. Second, it affirmed the broomstick wedding's unique association with Black Americans.

In the 1990 stage play *The Piano Lesson*, August Wilson uses the tradition to display the importance of heritage and commemoration for African Americans. Set in Pittsburgh, Pennsylvania, directly after the Great Depression, the plot revolves around the Charles family's disagreement over the practicality of selling the family piano. Indicating its importance as a family heirloom, the character Doaker interprets the carvings etched on its side, "See that? That's when him and Mama Berniece got married. They called it jumping the broom. That's how you got married in them days."[103] The engravings were done by Doaker's "granddaddy" Willie Boy, the Charles family's common ancestor, who carved the pictures to preserve the memory of his family after they were sold from the plantation. Thus, the piano and its carvings were the nucleus of their familial heritage. It was first owned by a man named Robert Sutter who enslaved Willie Boy, and it remained in the Sutter family until Willie Boy's descendants stole the piano from them in the early twentieth century. For the Charles family, it was a tangible symbol of their freedom and family heritage. As long as the Sutters possessed it, they still symbolically owned Willie Boy's descendants.

Wilson intended that the family exemplify the experiences of African Americans who took part in the Great Migration. Due to the social and economic conditions of the Jim Crow South, many migrated to urban environments in the Northeast and Midwest, as well as to West Coast to escape the oppression of the white southern political regimes.[104] In this case many members of the family understood the importance of remembering their ancestors' experiences under enslavement, though they experienced tensions when some appeared willing to sell the important family item to attain socioeconomic advancement. *The Piano Lesson* remains an important piece in depicting African American sociocultural history to wider audiences since it held prominence as both a stage play and feature film. Though the reference to jumping the broom is subtle, it is central to Wilson's broader discussions of kinship and the legacies of slavery in Black American life.

Recent works of historical fiction continue to depict the ceremony as the premier ritual of slave matrimony. Kathleen Grissom's 2010 *Kitchen House* describes a broomstick wedding in which the master leads the ceremony, advises the couple, Jimmy and Dory, and tells them to jump over the broom. They then clasp hands and leap over, but the groom stumbles to the ground to raucous laughter. The master then quips, "Well, Jimmy, we know who will be the boss of this family."[105] The sequence rehearses the idea of the broomstick's centrality in determining domestic authority. As with most works of fiction, substantive explanations on the ritual's origins or its meaning for the enslaved are missing from the work, but its inclusion does reflect its resonant popularity in widespread conceptions of southern slavery. Even Nat Turner, who led one of North America's deadliest slave revolts, is associated with the tradition in cartoonist Kyle Baker's 2008 graphic novel. Baker's work outlines the process of slave matrimony, providing a "five page silent sequence" depicting the journey from courtship to marriage, and then an eventual sale at the auction block.[106] In the final graphic, Turner and his wife jump over a broomstick held by fellow slaves, as others celebrate the union. While the wedding is portrayed as a festive event, the next sequence illustrates how their children are violently ripped from their grasp.[107] The broomstick ceremony is associated with the joys of marital bliss and familial formation, though such happiness is destroyed by an institution predicated on the monetary valuation of human beings. Baker uses this sequence to suggest that this familial disruption was a climactic point in which Turner decides to revolt against the system.

Likewise, cinema and television continue to display the broomstick wedding in various capacities in the post-*Roots* era. The 2015 miniseries *Book of Negroes*, based on the novel of the same name, is one example.[108] The story concerns the struggles of Aminata, an enslaved woman who had been kidnapped as a young girl from West Africa in the mid-eighteenth century. During her march to the coastline she meets Chekrura, a young boy used by the slave traders to oversee the captives and prevent their escape. Chekrura is eventually betrayed by them and sold on the same ship as Aminata, and the two form a bond throughout the passage. The ship eventually arrives in Charleston, South Carolina, and the two are sold to different slave owners, but promise to never forget one another.

As she grows older, Aminata gains a reputation both for her beauty and her intelligence, especially her ability to learn various languages and dialects. Chekrura finds her through inquiries sent along a system of maritime passages on the coastline of South Carolina used by Black men. They begin meeting at night in secret. Her master, Mr. Appleby, discovers their trysts. Angry at her constantly rejecting his own advances, and her refusal to unveil Chekrura's identity, he rapes her in the big house. She continues to see Chekura and the two grow closer romantically. At one point the series shows them gathered at night deep in the forest surrounded by fellow enslaved people from the plantation. In the background one hears traditional African drumming (not played in the actual field, but as part of the narration), and they simultaneously jump forward over a broom with arms locked. Aminata immediately begins dancing and everyone celebrates. She then narrates the following words to the viewer: "Appleby doesn't let his negroes marry. Some jump the broom secretly, while others just live together or visit at night."[109] Here, the ceremony represents an act of resistance, which is consistent with the portrayal of Aminata's resilience and eventual escape from slavery. She reflects agency, resistance, and an eventual triumph over the physical and psychological brutalities of American slavery.

In Nate Parker's 2016 *Birth of a Nation*, which portrays the life of Virginia's Nat Turner, who instigated one of the bloodiest slave revolts in American history, viewers witness a broomstick wedding. The ceremony begins with soft drumming as background music and shows the enslaved couple, Hark and Esther, jumping the broom in front of the community. After the leap, the enslaved community begins clapping to a beat, moving counterclockwise and repeating the phrase "you got a right to the tree of life."[110] The celebration resembles the ring shout, which was common on plantations in North America. The ring shout infuses African styles of body movement and vocal repetition with Christian theology (i.e., the "tree of life" evoking the concept of salvation so important to the unique brand of Christianity developed by enslaved people.)[111] In this ceremony, the enslaver is not present and the enslaved seemingly performed the nuptials outside a white gaze, allowing Parker to visualize how a Black-centered ceremony might look if the community was left to its own devices. However, the message imbedded within the film ultimately revolves around racialized violence and white domination over Black men and women. A few scenes later Esther is raped by a slaveholder from another plantation, her body having been offered by her owner as a way to gain favor with his company. Despite knowing the information beforehand, Hark is unable to protect her. Thus, the joy and serenity of their broomstick wedding is juxtaposed by the terror of sexual violence, which served as a daily reminder that enslaved people's commitments to one another were overruled by white lasciviousness.

In addition to literature and visual media that introduce and preserve the enslaved past, historic sites are increasingly spotlighting the lives of Black people who lived there, especially on southern plantations. Journalist Eugene L. Meyer wrote in 2001 that plantation museums faced dilemmas in presenting the experiences of enslaved people, including issues of nomenclature ("enslaved" versus "slave"), the degree to which the experience is sensationalized, and accurately reflecting the unique experiences of people in specific areas. Part of the issue was the novelty of representing the enslaved experience, although there were exceptions.[112] In the early 1990s Colonial Williamsburg, an interpretive site of early American life in Virginia, featured representations of slave life and culture, including a broomstick ceremony, which elicited various responses, ranging from sorrow, to indifference, to admiration, from viewers. One claimed that witnessing the reenacted slave wedding "had a far greater impact on me than reading about 18th century slave life could ever have had."[113] Under the guidance of Rose McAphee, a historian, educator, and training specialist on historical research, Colonial Williamsburg recovered the names of the site's enslaved laborers and hired actors to re-create aspects of enslaved people's social lives. Including a visual representation of the broomstick ceremony for eager visitors reflected a substantial shift in how historic sites display slavery publicly and reflects the important of the custom for comprehending slave marriages and families.

Though broomstick weddings are often shrouded in myths or presented as one-dimensional events, McAphee used careful research methods and formed nuanced conclusions about the custom.[114] When asked for information on its cultural origins, McAphee opined that connections to brooms and weddings did possibly exist in West Africa, but noted that the only migrant groups to North America who claimed an ancestral broomstick marriage across the Atlantic came from the British Isles. For the reenactment, she drew on the slave inventory of Nathaniel Burrow, owner of the plantation, and selected the names Esther and Manuel for the couple, and Bristol for the enslaved minister. Unsurprisingly, the details of their actual wedding are not documented in Burrow's daily logs, but using the actual names not only brings some authenticity to the reenactment, but also places Esther, Manuel, and Bristol at the forefront of historical representation, instead of simply confining their experiences to their labor. Regarding the wedding itself, McAphee notes, "Whether those two individuals jumped the broom, I can not say, but they were enslaved people who lived on Nathaniel Burrow's property in 1775."[115]

The ceremony generally follows the mainstream depiction of the broomstick wedding, but it adds additional elements prior to their leap. The bride and groom exchange gifts, the elderly minister admonishes the community in attendance, and he encourages them to produce children. Regarding this representation, McAphee was careful to note that ex-slave narratives reveal multiple ways to perform the custom and that any one of them was as valid as another. In essence, there were no "written rules," and enslaved people creatively adapted the ceremony to their needs. Once unseen by the public, this reenactment of the broomstick wedding helped beckon America to reckon with its original sin. Though descriptions of slave labor and its link to American wealth gained exposure, many tourists were interested in enslaved people's private lives and how they loved, lost, and survived under bondage. Marriage was an especially salient topic in this regard, and witnessing a reenactment of such a wedding between actors identified by the names of people once held on that plantation is an experience difficult to duplicate in print or on a screen.

For over four decades the broomstick wedding was gradually reintegrated into African American cultural memory. Through the interventions of civil rights activists, Black authors, and wedding coordinators history and memory collided as the ritual became more widely practiced by African American couples seeking to pay homage to their ancestors. Lack of knowledge about the origins of the custom does not seem to have detracted from its popularity. On the contrary, mystery surrounding the ritual made it more enticing to some authors and gave more room for speculation. It also led to a degree of politicization by various authors who wrapped jumping the broom into political discourses of cultural triumph or demoralization. The battles between academic Afrocentrists and Afrocentric wedding planners ultimately demonstrated the power of media and advertisement. Just as *Roots* trumped *Jubilee* in representing the African American experience, the ceremonies combining African-inspired dress with enslaved broomstick weddings silenced outside criticism by retaining significant popularity among wedding planners and betrothed practitioners.[116] In both cases, the "African" link appears to be an important element of seeing one's heritage in a broader perspective, beyond the borders of the United States, even if aspects of that heritage are only imagined.

Regardless, the late twentieth century saw a revival of the broomstick wedding among African Americans, and its popularity persisted into the early decades of the twenty-first century. Black couples who married prior to its widespread popularity even expressed disappointment that they did not know of the ritual beforehand, as they would have implemented it to honor their ancestors and portray an authentically Black tradition.[117] The revival of a custom that was once widely rejected by the formerly enslaved and their immediate descendants reveals the power of media in the late-twentieth century. It also attests to the capacity of African Americans to reinvent traditions to reflect their own realities. For a people simultaneously tied to and distinct from broader U.S. society, jumping the broom provided a unique departure from white cultural norms of matrimony.

## CHAPTER EIGHT

# To Create Our Own Rituals

*Same-Sex Marriage and the Symbolic Value
of Jumping the Broom*

Throughout November 2008 the film *Noah's Arc: Jumping the Broom* premiered at select movie theaters across the United States and was released on DVD by February 2009. The cinematic feature served as a conclusion to the *Noah's Arc* series that ran for two seasons on the LOGO television network. *Noah's Arc* was the first TV program to focus on the unique experiences of Black gay men, whom they identified as a "discernable community" within the broader LGBTQ collective.[1] The film follows the pending nuptials of two Black men, Wade and Noah, who travel from Los Angeles to Martha's Vineyard to celebrate their love. The film examines issues pertinent to many gay Black men, including the "diversity of queer black manhood . . . femme-phobia, HIV, same-sex marriage," and the struggle of "coming out" to one's family and friends.[2] By including "jumping the broom" in the subtitle, the writers hoped to convey that the film's social and cultural allusions were specific to gay Black Americans and their unique experience in the United States.

The show's raw and honest portrayal of each character's life earned it many accolades from cultural critics. Writing for the Toronto-based *Xtra! West*, Natasha Barsotti opined that *Noah's Arc* promoted visibility for queer Black men in the same way the *Cosby Show* did for the Black American middle-class in the 1980s.[3] Each character reflects the diverse attitudes and experiences imbedded within his identity. Discussions about sex, love, and commitment are frequent. While one character named Ricky contends that "monogamy for men is a contradiction,"[4] Noah and Wade's friends collectively doubt that their union will last, perceiving that both men are using each other to fill a relational void. Their interactions reveal the tensions between them, specifically in how each man fulfills a role within the group. The film conveys the importance of mentorship for younger, often closeted men, who may feel at a loss navigating relations with family and partners. The film examines how the marital commitments of Black gay men hold both similarities and departures from heteronormative unions. They face typical marital issues such as consistent sexual attraction to one another and the need for quality time, but as

Black men, they are a threat to white America, and their queer identities are condemned by many both outside and within their community.

Toward the end of *Noah's Arc* two characters briefly address the broomstick's symbolic importance during preparations for the ceremony. In one scene, Brandon, a college student, asks Chance, a university professor, "So what's the deal with this whole broom thing?" Chance responds, "When our ancestors were slaves they weren't allowed to marry legally so they created this ritual to symbolize a wedding. It's a way for us to honor our history," to which Brandon casually replies, "Cool." While Chance provides the usual explanation for Black couples using the ritual—namely, that enslaved people created it through their own ingenuity and that it is now used by descendants to honor their ancestral struggle—he does not bring in anything about this couple's sexual identification or the legal status of gay marriage at the time. At the film's conclusion Noah and Wade jump over a broomstick held slightly above the ground by the pastor, and that is the entirety of the ceremony. Though the broomstick wedding is featured in the film, it appears relevant only in terms of the couple's African American ancestry, not their queer identity.[5] But for African American couples who identify as gay or lesbian, the broomstick tradition can, in fact, be doubly meaningful, given that they are historically twice-barred from legal matrimony, once as enslaved people and then again as queer-identified.

In the context of the broader LGBTQ struggle to obtain recognition for same-sex marriage, many same-sex couples have seen the broomstick wedding as a symbol of resistance. At the same time, however, there are important differences in how the custom is understood and practiced, especially across racial lines. As legal theorist Kimberle Crenshaw argues, any analysis of identity politics must account for intragroup differences. Thus, by employing an intersectional framework, in which we account for how one simultaneously embodies various socially constructed identities, we can provide a focused analysis of how the broomstick wedding is used differently by people within the LGBTQ community and understand its cultural significance before and after the Supreme Court extended marital rights to same-sex couples in 2015.

Throughout the early 1990s and into the 2000s, jumping the broom was linked, both literally and symbolically, to the LGBTQ fight for marriage equality.[6] In California, an op-ed published in April 2000 used the broomstick ceremony from the *Roots* miniseries to illustrate America's long history of marital discrimination, equating the legal proscriptions against slave marriage with laws forbidding miscegenation and the disenfranchisement stemming from California's Proposition 22 law enacted in March 2000, which defined marriage in the state as an institution comprising only one man and one woman.[7] Barred from legal marriage at the federal level and throughout most of the states, gay men and lesbians enacted their own commitment ceremonies, which usually comprised a communal gathering that recognized and validated the couple's union. In an acknowledgment of the plight of the enslaved, some used the broomstick ceremony to symbolize their struggle,[8] while others who were affiliated with neo-pagan communities used the broomstick tradition in homage to pre-Christian practices, framing their resistance to modern heteronormative standards predicated on Christian traditions. In the neo-pagan renditions, the broomstick is part of an elaborate cleansing ritual, in which it is used to sweep clean the space of matrimony and is then laid at the feet of the couple who jumps over it together. One priestess who officiated same-sex ceremonies had the couples jump east, denoting it "the corner of new beginnings," in which the couple began their life anew.[9]

## Theatre Rhinoceros

Introducing the matrimonial broom jump to a broader audience required an approach that drew inspiration from the historically marginalized communities who used the ritual. In 1993, the San Francisco–based group Theatre Rhinoceros staged the production *Jumping the Broom*, which featured a "series of vignettes on the marriage and domestic partnership question."[10] It explored the "conflict, contradictions and creativity of lesbian and gay weddings," using the fight for marital equality to highlight the plight of gay couples who are prevented from sharing the same benefits as straight couples who marry legally.[11] *Jumping the Broom* was released alongside vigorous debates within the LGBTQ community surrounding whether or not same-sex couples should fight for legal marriage, as many were suspicious that legalization would encourage gay couples to conform to heterosexual standards of marriage. Opponents worried that reliance on government endorsement could potentially mainstream the institution and deplete the creative energy attached to same-sex weddings. Others disagreed, arguing that legalization was a significant step toward enjoying their full benefits as citizens and would reduce homophobia over generations.[12] Various vignettes address this issue throughout the production, some of which examine how dress, food, and ritual might problematically mirror heteronormative traditions, while others provide scenarios where Christian-inspired ceremonies might be useful in gaining societal acceptance and marital equality.

Theatre Rhinoceros's production envisioned the broomstick wedding as a force connecting different populations barred from legal marriage. Though *Jumping the Broom* had an activist agenda, exploring the political, social, and legal connotations of same-sex marriage, the production shied away from addressing race, ethnicity, or the cultural distinctions permeating within LGBT communities, and the cast for the initial workshop series was overwhelmingly white.[13] Though it appears that the collection of actors diversified as the productions made its entry to the broader public, it is noteworthy that none of the advertisements showcased a couple of African descent. The available clippings show four couples used for the advertising campaign, two of them completely white, and the other two interracial Black/white. In what appears to have been a colorblind move, the ads positioned the broomstick ceremony as a symbolic ritual that was first used by American slaves and then translated into the current struggles of gay men and women, regardless of race or ancestry.

Programs distributed during the play provided a brief description of the ceremony, which stated that the tradition's origins were unknown, but that it was used by enslaved people in the nineteenth century and revived in the United States through the popularity of Alex Haley's *Roots*.[14] If the intent of the note was to link the current illegality of same-sex marriage to a longer struggle extending to American slavery, the vignettes in *Jumping the Broom* never directly address slavery, nor do they explain the various ritual processes enslaved people used to marry outside the law.[15] Only a few preliminary scripts even mention a broomstick being used in a modern same-sex ceremony, and the sole piece exploring the custom in any detail, entitled "The Handfasting," did not make the final cut.[16] Interestingly, initial drafts of the project contain a private note from an anonymous reviewer who marked over an early version of the program's section on the custom's links to *Roots* and American slavery, stating that jumping the broom was also found in northern European ceremonies and now used by modern Wiccans, a neopagan religious group that was formed in the early twentieth century and revived pre-Christian traditions of Europe.[17] For reasons unknown, this information was not included in the program's final description. However, it does appear in two separate monologues delivered by a Celtic priestess named Morgan at the production's opening and closing acts.

Dressed in a Celtic, Wiccan-styled robe, Morgan enters the stage and lays a broom down before retreating to the background. Shortly after, two men

approach the broom, lock hands, leap over it, and embrace one another before they exit the stage. She then returns to the center and explains how the
broomstick wedding unites so many distinct cultural groups, noting its use in
the "camps" of Romani, throughout the Highlands of Scotland, and on the
"plantations of Dixie."[18] Morgan hopes to convince the audience that jumping the broom is the one universal symbol shared by these marginalized communities, and since same-sex marriage is illegal in the United States, that it
can symbolize the modern fight for marital equality among gay and lesbian
couples. She then disappears for the duration of the production, which consists of a series of short plays and vignettes exploring how different same-sex
couples conceptualize ritual, romance, and heteronormativity in U.S. marriage
culture. Following the last segment, Morgan reappears and provides concluding thoughts, holding the broomstick to the ceiling and reemphasizing its
centrality in understanding historical and contemporary marital inequality.

Critics were generally thrilled with the production's political message and
the comedic execution of certain sketches. They especially appreciated how
it showcased local talent, as most of the vignettes were written by artists and
creatives residing in the Bay Area. Each of them explained how the title,
*Jumping the Broom*, was based upon the slave custom, but, curiously, only one
mentioned that the entire event never addressed how or why the play was
based upon the ritual.[19] The primary linkage appears to be the broomstick
wedding's connection to marginalized communities, with specific emphasis
on the inability of enslaved Black people to contract legal marriages. Seeing a
legislative parallel with the modern fight for same-sex marital equality, a note
"From the Director," located on the program, emphasized how attendees
should take inspiration from enslaved couples who jumped the broom to ensure their "weddings were still held and still celebrated."[20] Despite its short-
comings in not addressing the custom's deeper importance, the production's
appropriation of the phrase reflects its appeal for marginalized groups as it
catapulted to popularity in the early 1990s.

## Intersections of Racial and Queer Identities

The broomstick ritual remained a point of reference for same-sex marriages
into the twenty-first century. Although scholars noted that the specific legal
and social barriers to slave marriage and same-sex marriage were different,
gay rights activists were inspired by the tenacity of enslaved people who never
surrendered their fight for marital dignity. Hence, when jumping the broom
was introduced into various LGBTQ communities, it was framed as an act of

resistance against bigotry and marginalization. In 2007, historian Randolph W. Baxter noted some gay couples were "following the lead of slaves" by integrating the broomstick jump into their nuptials, though he observed their ethnic identities were not disclosed.[21] The focus on a couple's sexuality, without reference to their ethnic identities, was a prominent feature in the gay rights movement that favored the voices of gay white men, though it was often presented as a colorblind struggle.

An April 2000 report from the *Washington Post* noted a gathering of same-sex couples seeking to marry in Washington, D.C., in an event billed as "the largest mass 'wedding' of homosexuals in the world." At the time, same-sex marriage was illegal in Washington, D.C., and in forty-nine states, and this mass wedding served as an appeal for lawmakers to legalize it. The 385-word article summarizes the movement and similar events preceding it, but its first sentence is especially pertinent to the position of rituals among people of same-sex attraction. According to journalist Phuong Ly, various couples brought decorative outfits and bouquets to enliven their nuptials, and one couple "carried a broom in the African American tradition of 'jumping the broom' after taking vows."[22] Including reference to the custom is important, but the quotation is most revealing for what it does not say. What was the racial identity of the couple? The author simply states that the broom was used "in the African American tradition," but does not relay if the couple themselves were African American. The article flattens the movement's racial diversity into an undefined whole solely predicated upon same-sex attraction, but in this case one can argue that distinguishing the member's racial heritage is crucial since the ceremony reflected different meanings for individual couples. On the one hand, it might serve as a symbol of resistance for all same-sex couples who feel a spiritual kinship with the enslaved, as both groups were disallowed a legally recognized union. On the other hand, one could argue it holds a dual meaning for Black couples in the LGBTQ community, who understand their ancestral struggle on a much more literal level. Despite the expansion of marital privileges to the formerly enslaved in 1865, gay, lesbian, and genderqueer couples still felt the impact of discriminatory laws that deemed their love unworthy of governmental recognition and protection.

The phenomena of white same-sex couples using the ritual is imbedded in controversies surrounding cultural appropriation, the idea that one group is inappropriately performing the rites and customs that hold specific meanings to another, often marginalized, group. Thus, for example, in an op-ed in the *Washington Post* a contributor noted that she married her partner in 2002, which meant their domestic partnership was only granted "partial marriage rights." To commemorate the historical struggle for legal recognition, they included "the African American tradition of 'jumping the broom' in the ceremony."[23] She then provided a brief account of its symbolic importance to the enslaved, asserting that the broomstick wedding "finalized the emotional and spiritual bond of marriage."[24] Although she did not disclose her ethnic identity, in writing about the broomstick ceremony she portrayed herself as an outsider who practiced the custom in solidarity with another oppressed group. In this case, oppression was colorblind under the presumption that one form of mistreatment impacts members of different groups in the same way.

By the mid-1990s advocates for same-sex marriage used jumping the broom and the slave trope to promote their colorblind ideology of marriage equality. As one op-ed stated in 1996: "Maybe lesbians and gays should consider 'jumping the broom' after getting permissions from the 'plantation master' rather than engaging in 'radical' behaviors such as legal marriage."[25] According to this iteration, the "plantation master" is the government that restricts one's legal rights, and lesbian and gay couples resemble enslaved people who are unable to obtain governmental recognition for their union.

In the 2015 memoir *And Then I Danced*, Mark Segal, a prominent journalist and gay rights activist, gives a personal account of his involvement in the movement for marriage equality prior to the Supreme Court's overturning of the laws prohibiting same-sex marriage in 2015. Among the incidents described is Segal's attendance at a "domestic partners" ceremony for two gay men who could not legally marry in their state. One of the men was a staffer for Philadelphia Mayor John Street, who offered to officiate the ceremony. Formerly an outspoken opponent of same-sex marriage, Street explained that he considered his staffer, Micah Mahjoubian, a friend "and if this is something he would like for me to do, then I'd like to do it for him."[26] Segal notes that the ceremony concluded with Street, who is African American, bringing out a broom and explaining its symbolic importance in the past and present. "Since it is outlawed for LGBT to marry in our country, like it was for slaves," he said, "it is appropriate for you, Micah and Ryan, to jump the broom."[27] According to Segal, the broomstick jump was an emotional moment for everyone present. Both Micah and his partner, Ryan Bunch, are white, but Street linked their struggle to the historic disbarring of enslaved people from legal marriage. Because it did not showcase examples of marginalized white populations who used the broomstick wedding, such as rural Celtic populations or poor white Americans, Street's explanation reveals how Black America's connection to jumping the broom dominated historical memory in the United States and became the primary reference point for marginalized groups who felt a kinship with them.

Thus, for example, one scholar observed a wedding between a lesbian of African descent and another of European descent, who jumped the broom to make a political statement in the 1990s: "Just as it was illegal for slaves to marry, it's illegal for lesbians to marry."[28] A couple running a website dedicated to finding locations friendly to the LGBTQ community posted a picture of themselves jumping the broom in 2010 at their Arizona wedding.[29] Though little commentary is provided, the use of this custom was firmly linked to marital equality for same-sex couples, as the caption for their photo read "Jumping the Broom at our 2010 Wedding. Not legal in AZ but that didn't stop us!"[30] The broomstick's attachment to a group's historical disenfranchisement inspired this couple to harness its cultural value. Neither groom identifies as African American, nor do they provide details surrounding the broomstick's meaning in their nuptials.[31] Stripped of its historical context, the broomstick primarily functioned as a signpost for a political message. The public comments attached to the image, however, were overwhelmingly supportive, and none of them revealed any discrepancies in the two using the broom-jumping tradition.

Writing in 2000 in the *Gay and Lesbian Times*, Kevin Isom noted that two grooms jumped the broom in front of an African American minister. Isom noted the ritual's links to slavery, but did not comment upon the ceremony's racial connotations. He simply stated, "as in the time of slavery, we gay folks mostly create our own rituals to formalize our relationships—our jumping over the broom."[32] Instead of noting if the ritual held an additional meaning to the couple using it, he suggests "gay folks," broadly conceived, all face the same dilemma in that their marriages were not legally sanctioned. Some might be cautious about this colorblind approach to a cultural ritual that holds a deep meaning for the descendants of enslaved people, and it should be noted that the circumstances of gay marriage before 2015 were not entirely the same as Black people before 1865. The laws against marriage only applied to the enslaved. Free people of color, in both the North and the South, married in similar forms as white Americans, and their unions were recognized by law.[33] Furthermore, there was no specific law *banning* Black people from matrimony. Enslaved people's unions were not recognized because they were considered human chattel and could not engage in a contract as autonomous citizens. Such circumstances granted slave owners complete control over enslaved bodies, and they could separate family members from one another and sell them at whim. Same-sex couples in the millennium never shared the same legal category or social circumstances, and for many, the final barrier to full legal equality was the right to marry. In contrast, enslaved people in the antebellum period faced far more obstacles to gaining full citizenship in the United States. These distinctions suggest some attention to the intersections between race, law, and heritage are important to consider before problematic comparisons are drawn between the two groups.

Still, wedding planners actively encouraged their clients to use the broomstick wedding, since many same-sex couples wanted to infuse forms of symbolic resistance into their ceremonies. Tess Ayers and Paul Brown's *The Essential Guide to Gay and Lesbian Weddings*, first published in 1994 and reprinted in 2012, listed the broomstick wedding as an African American tradition that has ancient roots. Ayers and Brown's description of the ritual, however, mirrors those of neopagans and pre-Christian Celtic groups in that it involves sweeping circles before the ceremony and the couple jumping toward the east. At the same time, they give no indication of the custom's associations with marginalized European communities, and the only image they show of a couple jumping over a broomstick includes two white men in traditional American wedding attire (tuxedos) hopping over a decorated broomstick with a long handle.[34] Once again, LGBTQ advocates framed whiteness as the primary representation of same-sex attraction.

Comparatively speaking, one can surmise that jumping the broom, and the general concept of marriage, is a different experience for two white, cisgendered people than it would be for the descendants of enslaved people. Sociologist Siobhan Brooks notes, "Black LGBT scholars critical of marriage point out the anti-Black bias within the gay marriage movement, which frames Blacks as 'bad queers,' or anti-gay, and white middle-class gay and lesbians as 'good queers' and thus deserving of equal rights."[35] Whether one can definitively state that anti-blackness is a prevalent attitude among white people in the LGBTQ community, people of color within the movement do sense a tension between white and nonwhite members.[36] Discussions surrounding how white gay men appropriate the elements of Black women's culture cites their use of exaggerated verbal pronunciation (for example, saying "YASSS" instead of "yes"), certain dance styles, and nonverbal cues to communicate their feelings.[37] Representation within the community also remains fraught across racial lines. White individuals in the LGBTQ community demonstrated such divides by contesting the addition of a brown and black stripe on the rainbow flag. Supporters of the additions intended to critique their exclusion from leadership roles and to highlight how their experiences with heteronormativity were different than those of white people. As journalist Michael Arcenaux contends, "Simply sharing a difference from heteronormativity and/or the rigid gender binary does not make us all one big happy family."[38] The divisions primarily revolve around the differences in their ultimate goals. For many white lesbians and gay men, marital equality and legislative change were the culmination of their civil rights movement, as they believed full legal privileges would eventually mainstream LGBTQ issues and gradually erode social exclusion. Sociologist Colin P. Ashley explains that gay liberation was once a radical movement, but that its "self-depiction as a middle-class, mostly white struggle for mere acceptance" made it otherwise, as well as preventing coalition-building with other, specifically Black-centered, movements.[39] After same-sex marriage was legalized in all fifty states, people of color in this community noticed that white lesbians and gay men could now enjoy nearly identical privileges as straight, cis-gendered white people in America. Such privileges included greater access to economic advancement, representation in popular culture, and a nearly unquestioned social acceptance as equal citizens. In contrast, people of color, especially those of African descent, remained minorities in a country perpetually hostile to their racial, sexual, and gendered identities. Legal scholar Dean Spade notes that the marriage campaign actually overshadowed pertinent issues afflicting gay people of color, and many believed that using funds and energy to obtain civil rights was more useful when directed to health care, housing, and the fight to end police brutality.[40] Additionally, Black men and women are stereotyped as "hypersexual" compared with the supposedly more reserved sexuality of middle-class whiteness.[41] Though white gay men and lesbians can potentially understand the ritual's value for recognizing America's troubled past, queer-identified Black men and women directly comprehend how the broomstick wedding is tied to America's legacy of slavery, racism, and sexual violence. Jumping over the broom is a far more emotional experience for queer people who descend from enslaved people, and they have a direct precursor for performing a ritual that symbolizes their modern sociopolitical disenfranchisement.

## Rituals and Symbols

Symbolic reflections on jumping the broom and its meanings to captive people arguably find their most literal expressions in the modern prison system, where some inmates practice the custom to secure an informal marriage. Researcher Omar Padilla, a student in New York University's Prison Education Project, observed two men jumping over the broom in a facility in upstate New York, noting the ceremony was openly conducted in the prison yard. After the union, the couple held hands and walked around the yard while their supporters cheered and encouraged their partnership. Padilla notes that he knew many couples who were "partnered in this way," including men and transgender women.[42] Though he notes that the custom's origins lie in "England," he recognizes that most Americans who jump the broom are of African descent. Except in the case of one inmate he calls "Big Black," who jumped the broom with a transgender woman named "Moët," Padilla usually avoids disclosing the racial identities of his respondents, nor does he mention if they felt any ancestral connection to the custom. However, due to the disproportionate representation of Black men incarcerated in the U.S. prison system, and the ceremony's deep cultural resonance among African Americans, we can reasonably assume incarcerated Black men primarily employ this ritual for practical reasons, alongside its important symbolic meanings to them as descendants of enslaved people. Though scholars disagree on whether the modern prison system mirrors antebellum slavery in its entirety, chattel bondage certainly has had a lasting impact on the modern penal system.[43] Even as the Thirteenth Amendment made incarceration as the only acceptable form of bondage in the United States, imprisoned men and women still perform uncompensated labor, have many of their rights stripped, and are stereotyped as moral and social deviants. One can imagine that prisoners who descend from enslaved people would realize the similarities between themselves and their ancestors. Whether confined to a plantation or a prison yard, people of African descent repurpose the broomstick wedding to affirm their attachment to another human.

But one does not have to be formally incarcerated to feel trapped within society, especially for gay and lesbian couples who lived openly before the legislatives changes of 2015. For these couples, engaging in the broomstick ritual within their own community still provided a similar source of psychological stability and symbolic confirmation. Sociologist Krista B. McQueeney's 2003 study of lesbian commitment rituals illuminates the dual meanings of the broomstick wedding for Black lesbians. McQueeney gathered her data from August 1998 to September 2001 from a "65-member LGBT-affirming Christian congregation in the South," of whom 70 percent were African American.[44] McQueeney contends this ritual held multiple meanings that reflected the couple's intersectional identities of being Black, female, and queer and suggests that jumping the broom "served as both an assertion of their racial identities and an allusion to the subversive nature of their own self-marrying rite." In describing one ceremony, McQueeney notes that the officiant provided a short history of the broomstick wedding, beginning with slavery and tracking its use into the present. The officiant compared the circumstances of the modern wedding to a slave wedding, in which everyone gathered in a shared, protected space to offer their blessings to the couple and their union. Just as enslaved people on the plantation offered mutual support, every participant in this commitment ritual was part of the couple's "family" and provided them with "sustenance amidst systems of oppression."[45]

Despite its popularity as a custom that people performed, not everyone discussed the broomstick wedding in such literal terms. At times, it served as a colloquial phrase to make a social or political point about the experience of being Black and gay in the United States. Debra A. Wilson's 2006 documentary, *Jumpin' the Broom: The New Covenant*, interviews four Black lesbian and gay couples. She asks them to explain their reasons for marrying and the difficulties in navigating homophobia within the Black community, in tandem with homophobic and racist rhetoric from non-Black people. Outside an opening statement from Georgetown University professor and public intellectual Michael Eric Dyson, *Jumpin' the Broom* does not explore the ritual's symbolic value for Black same-sex couples in the twenty-first century. It simply states that "jumping the broom" was the way enslaved people signified and solidified their marriages, and it occasionally displays photos of certain couples leaping over the broomstick.[46] The respondents do not actually comment on using the broomstick custom, nor do they elaborate upon its personal meaning to them.

Similarly, jumping the broom indicates the political divides between social conservatism and progressivism throughout Black America, especially as it relates to same-sex marriage. As a people whose ancestors were once barred from legal marriage, African Americans view marriage as a protected right, though divisions persist within the community regarding how it should be protected.[47] The 2005 publication *Jumping the Broom: A Black Perspective on Same-Gender Marriage* was jointly released by the Equality Maryland Foundation and the National Black Justice Coalition. The booklet tried to answer the primary concerns about same-sex relations among socially conservative African Americans and hoped to convince them that gay marriage is as much a civil rights issue as any other. Representative John Lewis, who once marched with Martin Luther King Jr. and supported the message of the publication, is quoted as saying, that he had fought "too hard and too long" against discrimination and that it was time to forthrightly say "the government's exclusion of our gay and lesbian brothers and sisters from civil marriage officially degrades them and their families."[48] Seven years later the state of Maryland was bitterly divided over the issue of same-sex marriage, as campaigns on both sides of the issue drew from the historical experiences of slaves to make their case for or against it. One group called "Jump the Broom for Marriages" distributed flyers encouraging residents to vote against legalization of same sex marriage.[49] They used biblical verses to support their position and encouraged all who agreed to donate, volunteer, and organize against legalization. Conversely, the Center for American Progress published *Jumping Beyond the Broom*, which pointed out marriage was not the only issue impacting the Black queer community, contending that "black gay and transgender Americans ... experience stark social, economic, and health disparities compared to the general population and their straight black and white gay counterparts."[50] Thus, for African Americans the relationship between enslaved people's practice of the ritual and modern same-sex marriages were far more historically complex, and even divided the community alongside religious lines. The use of "jumping the broom" as a symbol by both opponents and supporters of same-sex marriage within the Black community unveils its prominence as a reference point in their long history of political, social, and cultural struggle.

The broomstick wedding's pertinence to discussing the inequalities of marital legislation and its impact on Black Americans also found a place in the performing arts. Black choreographer David Rousseve used the custom to link historic marital discrimination with present circumstances. In 2004 he created a short narrated dance solo entitled "Jumping the Broom" that begins as a slave narrative and gradually evolves into a modern testimonial about the devastating psychological impact of the illegality of same-sex weddings in the modern era. Performed by soloist Gesel Mason, the piece vividly reflects the problems surrounding marital issues for all LGBTQ people, but in centering a Black woman on the stage, it hints at the double impact for Americans of African descent.[51] Thus, in the first segment, Mason takes the role of an enslaved wife as the voice of her enslaved husband recounts the story of their "secret ceremony" of jumping the broom, followed by the slaveowner's discovery of their secret affair, and, ultimately, selling the wife to punish the couple. Dancing throughout the monologue, Mason becomes a woman grasping for life as she is being sold. As the enslaved man's narrative ends, the voice of a modern lesbian takes over, describing her disappointment when she and her partner were blocked from registering their marriage. Though the woman's race is not disclosed, she ends her monologue by describing a dream in which enslaved people jumped over the broom and says, "But I suppose I was really dreaming how far this hatred could go." As the monologue concludes, Mason, with her hands still bound, inches toward a woman sleeping on the periphery of the stage. Though she tries to jolt her awake, the woman remains limp, as Mason repeatedly says, "I just wanted to love you," before the spotlight shuts off and the stage darkens. The performance reflects a violent struggle for marital equality that is never obtained while people were enslaved, and it is compared to the disappointment experienced by Black gay and lesbian couples who were also forbidden to marry.[52]

The LGBTQ community in the United States continually reckons with its internal differences in race, gender, and class. Sociologist Elena Kiesling notes how the popular adage "gay is the new black" collapses LGBTQ issues into a problematically colorblind politics that places it within a sea of whiteness.[53] The phrase implies that members of this group are part of a homogenous, colorblind counterculture predicated on historical oppression alongside their influence on popular culture. But what about Black gay men and lesbians? By equating homophobia with racism, white men erased, or at the very least, trivialized, the historical experience of what it means to be both Black and queer. By generalizing the experiences of gay men and lesbians across racial lines, the movement's spokespeople made a critical mistake in trying to unite the group around a misinformed identity politics: they ignored, conflated, or did not account for "intragroup differences."[54] The marriage question was at the heart of this divide. By stating that they adopted a ritual used by the enslaved, white lesbians and gay men hoped to encourage social change by establishing their link to the most horrific period of American history. However, by assuming their marital circumstances were similar, they generalized the harsh realities of slave marriage and family life, leaving Black men and women voiceless in the process. Though LGBTQ groups were united in the purpose of gaining full legal rights to marry, federal recognition of same sex marriage after 2015 reveals the socioeconomic and racial divides among them. Tellingly, references to white lesbians or gay men jumping over broomsticks nearly disappear after June 2015. Perhaps they concluded the ritual served its purpose in symbolizing legal inequality. Conversely, many people of African descent within the LGBTQ community still use the ritual to reflect their heritage, viewing it as a ceremony that is deeply personal to them and reflects their own long road to marital equality, domestic dignity, and societal respect.

## CHAPTER NINE

# Beyond Black or White
## *The Broomstick Wedding's Expanding Meaning*

.

In 2016 the blogger "Aleta," a self-described "wife, mother, and philosopher," published an essay titled "Jumping the Broom: An Anarchist Perspective on Marriage," which detailed her decision with her partner to marry in front of their own community without seeking state recognition.[1] She explained: "We believe that 'Marriage' is a commitment between two people who have a deep and fulfilling love for each other, along with common goals and values. . . . We do not believe that government has any business in marriage, and we choose to leave it out of ours."[2] The couple challenged the notion that only the state can claim a union as "legitimate," after paperwork is filed and that the government holds discretion in recognizing that spouses are legally bound by law. The notion is useful to consider, and bears resemblance to the enslaved people who refused to register their marriages following the Civil War, determining their commitments under slavery were as binding as anything a piece of paper might provide. Aleta's essay acknowledges the connection. Noting that enslaved people and Romani in the British Isles used the broomstick wedding, she claims that the broomstick ritual was a way to reject state authority that it is the wedding guests who truly validate the union.

Aleta and her partner "jumped the broom" primarily for this purpose, arguing that rejecting formal legislative restraints is the only way to be truly free. Registering a union with state and federal governments suggests that one is seeking outside approval from an immensely powerful entity. In discussing anarchist views on matrimony, Aleta explains her evolving conception of "gay marriage": "I used to think I was pro–gay marriage. It seemed so obvious to me that an individual has the right to marry whomever he wants, regardless of gender. But I am not for gay marriage, not as it is defined by the state. . . . That doesn't mean I don't believe in a gay man's 'right' to get married. The right to marry is an inherent right—as you own your body you alone may choose who you spend your life with." Thus, her main criticism with being "pro-gay marriage" is that the appellation is always imbedded within governmental approval. When one claims to fight for the "right" to marry, one is usually seeking government recognition for a union, not one's ability to experience romantic love and form a partnership. Aleta notes her views have very little to do with religion, but opens the possibility that legitimate claims to matrimony should come from God, if one is spiritually or religiously inclined. In the end, she writes that her espousal of marriage independent of the state is based on her complete commitment to her husband and the family they hope to build. If that bond is secure, then governmental approval is irrelevant.

The article proposes many reasons to reconsider the government's intervention in marriage, but it is arguably most compelling for what it does not say about the couple's attachment to the broomstick ceremony. It is noteworthy that Aleta claims no ancestral connection to the custom, and she does not treat it as a quaint addition to the ceremony. Nor does she claim it holds any spiritual significance. For her and her partner, the meaning and value of the custom was strictly ideological in that they identified it with groups ostracized and oppressed by the state, and therefore saw it as symbolizing a form of resistance to governmental overreach. In many respects, this aligns with the historical groups who practiced the custom. Consider the Romani in the British Isles, who lived outside the bounds of a culture that determined the parameters of a "legal marriage." Additionally, some Cajuns used it to confront church authority in the isolated swamps of the Louisiana Bayou, and some enslaved people of African descent adopted it due to their inability to marry legally. The historical trajectory of oppressed groups employing it for purposes of nonconformity, creativity, or subversion has led historian Lesley Skousen to claim that white couples can appropriately jump the broom if they wish "to add a subversive element to the tradition-heavy life event of a marriage."[3] Though she claims the activity should not be determined by a modern practitioner's racial identity, Skousen implies that couples should not jump the broom if it does not hold cultural importance in the ceremony. One's motivation is a determining feature, and modern couples of European descent should practice it in the same spirit that historically marginalized communities did.

Aleta's essay suggests that the broomstick wedding continues to be influential among various groups who, on the surface, appear to hold few cultural similarities with one another. Throughout the broomstick ritual's history, its appeal broadened and it was adopted by different groups, some of which held no ancestral attachment to the custom. The pages that follow show how the ritual must be examined through a diasporic and multicultural lens, questioning how it has recently gained acceptance from people who do not hold genealogical ties to its original practitioners. News reports unveil that broomstick weddings are taking place among some Caribbean peoples, despite no documented evidence of it being practiced in the West Indies during slavery. African

American brides and grooms who are deciding whether they will jump the broom with a non-Black partner are finding that the decision is more complicated than they initially assumed. Modern white communities who identify as Romani, Appalachian, Cajun, and neopagan also jump the broom, and one must ascertain how and why the custom is revived and/or continued in these groups.

## Jumping the Broom and the African Diaspora

In addition to the African Americans who have "destination weddings" throughout the Caribbean, some groups in the region who have no connection to an enslaved North American heritage adopt the broomstick wedding. Identifying with pan-Africanist philosophy, in which people of African descent throughout the world are united in a common struggle, some Jamaican couples adopted the broomstick wedding either by observing Black American wedding rituals or consuming media that describes the ceremonies. Some commentators wonder if its adoption among Black people outside the United States reflects a new way to interpret the custom, as revealed in a question posed by literary scholar Faith Smith: "In what sense are Caribbean residents who 'jump the broom' in 'Afrocentric' ceremonies in the Caribbean distinct from African American tourists who do the same thing when they visit the region to get married?"[4] Smith's question is framed within an essay on Caribbean identity and the difficulties of navigating one's ancestral history, especially for West Indians who acquire cultural traits generally associated with African Americans. If one believes jumping the broom holds African origins, as some reports suggest, it is much easier to validate its adoption. The fact that Smith described these weddings as Afrocentric ceremonies suggests that its association with Black people in America provides an automatic kinship through their shared West African heritage, especially for those outside the community with no other frame of reference. Concerning jumping the broom, however, it is important to note that there are (as yet) no documented cases of it ever happening on the island during slavery, nor do statements from white observers or the formerly enslaved recall its existence in their cultural history. The fact that some West Indians use the custom in the post-*Roots* era merits further attention.

Jumping the broom is unique to enslaved people in North American, particularly in its sheer volume of practitioners and the enduring legacy it retains within the United States. The custom is not found in areas colonized by the French, Spanish, or Portuguese. Places such as Haiti, Cuba, and Brazil imported far more enslaved people than the United States, but none of their descendant populations claim ancestral links to the tradition. More to the point, mentions of the custom are not found in the British-colonized sugar islands of the Caribbean. The only other locale holding a possible link to the ritual is Bermuda, a small island in the Atlantic, as historian William Zuill wrote in the 1930s that it was once used there. The date is important: Zuill was referring to the practice well before African Americans began repopularizing it in the 1970s–1980s. According to oral tradition, couples clasped hands and jumped over the broomstick "three times, the stick being held at an easy height by the groomsmen."[5] The specifics are similar to those found in accounts of formerly enslaved people in the United States,[6] but the fact is that we have no testimonials from enslaved Bermudians or their immediate descendants attesting to the practice. However, even though the extent to which it was practiced by enslaved Bermudians is not quantifiable, there are a few reasons to believe that some people on this island used it.

First, Bermuda was a British colony, which meant that certain cultural traits were transferred from white British colonists to the Black population, and vice versa. One can imagine that these slaveowners or mariners were familiar with folk rituals like jumping the broom and transmitted them to the enslaved who, like their counterparts elsewhere, reimagined them for their own social benefit. For one, the archipelago's size (about 21 square miles) provided a related social geography that facilitated cultural exchanges.[7] Just as enslaved people in Bermuda acquired aspects of European Christianity and became proficient in the maritime business of "whaling," Kevin Dawson shows such transmissions worked in the opposite direction, as the European population actually adopted the captives' swimming traditions.[8]

Second, Bermuda's economy was not based on sugar, which ensured that the enslaved population's growth was not determined by continuous imports from West Africa.[9] In fact, Bermuda significantly minimized imports in the early 1700s. The largely nonfatal form of enslavement allowed Black Bermudians to form families at higher rates and reproduce on the island, which ensured they were influenced by a combination of West African and British cultures. While slavery was valuable to the Bermudian economy, it was mainly in the form of maritime labor, and life at sea meant that some Black sailors could have some degree of autonomy on the ship and become acquainted with different societies when they docked at port cities. Compared with colonial economies elsewhere in the Atlantic, the Bermudian economy was not based on mass agricultural production, and thus did not demand continuous imports of enslaved people from Western Africa who often perished in the arduous and fatal labor regimes that characterized the sugar economies of the West Indies.[10]

The third, and final point, is connected to the second, in that the enslaved Black population of Bermuda was never significantly larger than that of the white, and, when compared to other island colonies in the British Atlantic, neither group ever gained a significant majority throughout the duration of the system.[11] One census taken in 1749 revealed the white population at 5,290 and the Black population at 3,980, suggesting the white population held a larger percentage of the island's inhabitants in the colonies' earlier history. The Black population would grow to equal those of European descent, but throughout the latter half of the eighteenth century most estimates declared that the Black and white populations were more or less equal.[12] British migrants preferring a cooler climate continued to migrate toward the North Atlantic colonies, including areas of the U.S. South and Bermuda, resulting in their higher demographic representation in these societies. As a semi-tropical island, Europeans seemed to prefer Bermuda's weather. Consequently, a larger percentage of European migrants translated into a wider dissemination of European cultural traits in the colony. Even as the Black population eventually gained a slight majority in the nineteenth century, an 1844 census reveals that Bermuda's Black majority was only 57 percent by mid-century.[13] Thus, Black Bermuda's culture evolved and became a mixture of the populations inhabiting the island. For this reason, Bermuda is unique as an island culture that seemingly holds a legitimate claim to using the broomstick wedding, though it is impossible to know if it was widespread throughout the island or only contained in a few isolated cases.

Nonetheless, Bermudian author Joy Wilson Tucker's writings reveal that she believed it was a practice linked to her ancestors. In her essay, "Weddings—Old and New," she prompts the reader to "imagine jumping a broom into the field of matrimony," and uses two fictive characters to illustrate the ceremony.[14] It is unclear if the participants are enslaved, however, as Tucker entitles the ceremony "a Negro Wedding," instead of the more common "slave wedding." The only clue is that the bride is described as a "shy house nigger," which is often a description for enslaved people who labored inside the slaveholder's home. Regarding her groom, "Cupid," described as a man with a "strong, handsome face," readers know little about his responsibilities or attachments. The two are passionately in love, preparing to take the leap under a clear blue sky and hot sun. After their vows, they both "jump over the broom into the land of matrimony"—the language echoes the matrimonial description in Alex Haley's *Roots*. The wedding is portrayed as a ceremony independently undertaken by Venus and Cupid, but it remains unclear whether the couple was enslaved. All Tucker says is that jumping the broom was a part of the "old-time weddings" that were deeply important to the ancestors of Black Bermudians. By imagining the ritual in a wedding that was independently organized, performed, and celebrated by Black people, she reveals the tradition held importance to those in the diaspora outside the United States. Considering that both the historical references and Tucker's 1983 essay predate its wide scale reemergence through African American heritage weddings, one is apt to believe that Black Bermudians can lay claim to jumping the broom as a piece of their cultural heritage.

Conversely, the use of the ritual in modern Jamaican society appears to be a byproduct of their interactions with African American tourists, many of whom hold philosophies of Afrocentrism and pan-African solidarity. Certainly, some free Black Americans made their way to Jamaica throughout the nineteenth century, mainly as Christian ministers seeking to establish churches and attract converts.[15] However, even if these missionaries left traces of Black American folk culture on the island, in the absence of known documentation, it is impossible to say whether jumping the broom was or was not one of them. The modern acquisition and implementation of an African American wedding custom amongst Jamaicans appears to be an instance of "Afro-cosmopolitanism," whereby diasporic groups seek cultural meanings of blackness from other African-descended groups, often privileging the traditions of African Americans.[16] Though many diasporic groups have their own distinct cultural identity, scholars note that many outside the United States imagine themselves within a global Black community that has adopted the language, dress, and modes of civil rights activism of Black Americans.[17] With African Americans being cultural innovators in a globally influential country, their customs are disseminated throughout the diaspora, largely by the media and African American tourism. In 2012, for instance, a Black lesbian couple wed in Jamaica by jumping over the broomstick. The marriage was not legally recognized on the island, which is notorious for its open homophobia. After securing the legal paperwork required by the U.S. government, the couple performed the actual ceremony in Duncans, Trelawny, in front of family and friends. It marked a return for one of the partners who was a Jamaican national before migrating to the United States.[18] Though associated with the unique circumstances of African American slavery, the Jamaican partner's decision to leap over the broomstick reflects a pan-African consciousness that suggests that Black unity can override Black cultural differences. In another case, a Black lesbian couple ignited debate about same-sex relationships throughout Jamaica when the media spotlighted their wedding. Given that the couple jumped the broom to symbolize the intersection of their "race and sexual orientation," one could assume it promoted some curiosity amongst observers previously unfamiliar with the ritual.[19] If the tradition is viewed as a phenomenon unique to Black people, non-American observers might overlook cultural differences and assume it applies to their own circumstances as African-descended people in the diaspora.

Such conceptions of Black unity and cultural affinity appear to inspire these other diasporic groups to practice the ritual. For example, Lennox Lewis, a former heavyweight champion boxer born in London, England, to Jamaican parents, included the ritual in his wedding to Violet Chang, even though neither is an African American.[20] A marriage report from the *Jamaica Gleaner* reveals that myth and memory are powerful tools in remaking cultural perceptions. According to the *Gleaner*, the "high profile wedding" of Pearnal Charles II, son of veteran Jamaican Labor Party politician Pearnal Charles, and his bride Eleasia Lewars "incorporated the African 'jumping the broom' ritual."[21] The persistence of the African origins thesis permits individuals to mold the broomstick wedding into a pan-African custom that enters into a collective historical consciousness. In a similar vein to its eighteenth and nineteenth century predecessor, jumping the broom is now being carried in the opposite direction of the Atlantic Ocean, and is in many ways redefining Black identities as it continues to migrate. Populations of African descent, however, are not the only ones remolding the ritual for themselves.

## Interracial Marriage

The 2010 film *Our Family Wedding* provides one reflection on marrying across cultural lines by following the travails of an African American man named Marcus (Lance Gross), and a Mexican American woman named Lucia (America Ferrera). *Our Family Wedding* revolves around the marriage preparations of Marcus and Lucia who return home to Los Angeles and abruptly reveal to their families that they plan to marry at the end of the academic year. The crux of the plot is framed through a clash of cultures, as the couple's respective patriarchs, Brad (Forest Whitaker) and Miguel (Carlos Mencia), espouse negative stereotypes of the other. The film was not well-received by critics, who claimed that a very talented cast was wasted by the film's regurgitation of ethnic stereotypes and lackluster character development. Regardless, it was profitable, ultimately securing over $21 million against a $14 million budget.[22] Thus, people did watch the film, which includes jumping the broom in its exploration of crossing ethnic and racial boundaries in marriage.

In one scene, the families meet at Brad's home to discuss the format for the ceremony, and it becomes evident that neither family expects to cede control to the other. After Lucia and Marcus reveal they want a small wedding, her family interjects by stating it should be a traditional Mexican wedding that showcases her ancestral heritage. Viewing this as a threat to his own culture, Brad interrupts by explaining that African Americans held many "great" wedding traditions that should be considered. Brad's friend, Angie, played by Regina King, provides a foil to his character by casually asking him, "Like what?" After a period of nervous hesitation, Brad answers, "I can't believe you forgot, Angie. Y'know jumping the, jumping the broom." Following this reference, he then lists the "electric slide" as an integral piece of Black weddings and recommends they sing "Lift Every Voice," often called the Black national anthem, during the ceremony.[23] This scene's exchange reveals a cynicism in how some Black Americans conceptualize the broomstick wedding. Brad refers to it only to counter another group who seemed fully equipped to display their distinct and rich cultural heritage. His initial pause reveals that he is unsure what unique matrimonial traditions African Americans held and that he likely has no intention of following them unless doing so would prevent Lucia's family from claiming cultural dominance over the ceremony.

The young couple, for their part, wanted to jump the broom together, nonchalantly saying, "Yeah, we can do that" before Brad continues to explain additional features unique to African American weddings.[24] Despite their positive response Brad's brief lapse in listing his culture's unique wedding rituals illustrates a stereotype that the American descendants of enslaved people lost their West African cultures to the influence of (white) Americanization. In this case, he reveals a feeling that Black ceremonies mirror those of white, largely Anglo-American, weddings. Whereas all people of color have collectively experienced forms of white supremacy and domination in the United States, *Our Family Wedding* suggests that anti-Black racism is unique, and in many respects, more severe than its counterparts. Brought as captives to the shores of the United States, Black people were forced to adapt to the oppressive circumstances of a foreign land. Scholars once believed this amounted to cultural annihilation, but recent histories propose that enslaved people preserved certain features of West African traditions and combined them with other cultural forms in North America.[25] It was not cultural loss, necessarily, but cultural evolution over generations. In contrast, other communities of

color can remain more closely tied to their ancestral homeland through continued migration of people from that country, an ability to visit and reconnect with relatives in specific locales, and the freedom to perpetuate traditions
across generations without the gaze of an ever-present master class.

The disagreements in *Our Family Wedding* reflect one primary difficulty in
celebrating bicultural weddings, in that both partners know every aspect of
their respective cultures cannot be included. As sociologist Cele Otnes argues, "Splashing just a few customs onto the lavish wedding canvas may leave
either the bride or groom (or their families) feeling dissatisfied."[26] While cultural differences between people of color cause friction in determining the
performance of group customs, the deepest divisions persist between Black
and white couples seeking to integrate both of their cultural patterns into the
ceremony. Such a division is reflected in a 1993 ceremony observed by anthropologist Ellen Lewin, who documented the contours of a commitment ceremony used by a lesbian couple, one African American and the other Jewish.
Though the couple believed their love transcended the color divisions per-
petuated in U.S. identity politics, they noted that a few of their friends were
uneasy not only about the complications surrounding an interracial marriage, but also the difficulty in ensuring each cultural group was equally represented. Lewin observed that the ceremony was replete with Jewish traditions,
but the couple also went to great lengths to incorporate an imaginative rendition of the broomstick ritual. They used two brooms decorated in colors reflecting their ancestral heritage, one in white and blue representing the Jewish
state of Israel, and the other decorated in black, red, and green to symbolize
the colors of Black power and pan-Africanism. The process of jumping each
broom was framed as showing a mutual respect for each partner's culture, as
the couple noted: "We were to [first] jump over our own culture so that we
stay in our own cultures, and then jump over one another's cultures. There
were two brooms tied together making one broom."[27] While attendees generally appreciated this mutual respect, a few believed the plethora of Jewish traditions overshadowed Black traditions. A mutual friend serving as the guest
officiant for the ceremony's broom jumping section even announced to the
audience that the Jewish traditions were lovely, but the African American
bride's roots "were somewhat subordinated by what she perceived as the
predominantly Jewish character of the ritual."[28] Such difficulties of inclusion reflect the reality of the conflicts rehearsed in *Our Family Wedding*, in
which families and friends of the betrothed may never be wholly satisfied
with the cultural representations of interracial wedding ceremonies. Despite the couple's openness in embracing one another's customs, it is the

surrounding community that presents the most difficulty in navigating the cultural divisions.

Given the history of the broomstick wedding and its deep importance to white and Black populations in the United States, this divide might seem surprising. One might imagine this multicultural custom could easily translate into the ceremony without offense to either family. However, polls and blogs reveal these divisions persist through continual misinformation surrounding the ritual's cultural history. In her forum "Ask Dr. Sherry," clinical psychologist Sherry Blake answered the query of a Black woman who was engaged to a white man, noting her fiancé had expressed his support for jumping the broom at their wedding if she desired it. She revealed, however, that certain "cousins and aunts" held a "huge issue" with her performing the tradition with a white man, given its association with slavery. Disinviting her unsupportive family members was not an option, and so she wondered if inclusion of the ritual would be "weird or uncomfortable" for the wedding guests. In a supportive tone, Sherry Blake encouraged the woman to disregard any such criticism, citing that there is "no rule that 'white men can't jump!'"[29] Sherry Blake's encouraging response is typical in most public forums, but one still detects a hesitation from couples seeking to include multicultural wedding customs. Evidence suggests the primary fear is not often found within the couples themselves, but in the potential criticisms leveled by their respective communities.

Under presumptions this is an "African" ritual exclusive to Black Americans, blogs and internet forums contend that white people using the ritual are committing cultural appropriation. Consequently, brides (both Black and white) ask if it is appropriate to jump the broom if one partner is white, fearing the action could be interpreted as "disrespectful" to the sacred tradition.[30] However, in one post from WeddingWire.com, most comments were from fellow interracial couples who either themselves embraced the tradition, or witnessed other interracial couples perform it. They were resoundingly supportive, explaining that a blessing from the Black in-laws could prove helpful in easing one's discomfort. Gaining permission helps the white partner affirm and embrace his or her partner's "history, culture, and family."[31] Other forums held similar explanations, with many exclaiming that couples should not allow others to dictate the customs they use.[32]

Christelyn D. Karazin, a relationships expert and author of *Swirling*, a book designed to encourage and advise people who date interracially, jumped the broom with her white husband. Entitled "Jumping the Broom with a White Boy," Karazin noted that her mother insisted she use the ritual to remember her roots.[33] She provides little detail on the ritual or the groom's thoughts on the custom. The omission is possibly deliberate, as Karazin asserts that interracial marriages work if both partners accept and celebrate one another's cultural differences. In this case, it symbolized only their entry point into the matrimonial state. If they allowed it to be a source of contention, it would distract from the celebratory process of their engagement. Harriette Cole's 2004 revised edition of *Jumping the Broom* tackled the same issue, specifically at the request of an African American woman engaged to a white man. The woman noted her husband was "apprehensive" about practicing the ritual, though she did not elaborate on the reason for his discomfort. Cole responded by noting that she and her fiancé needed to realize their wedding ceremony was blending different cultural traditions, and she must explain that the simple act of jumping over the broom provides a blessing from the ancestors. Cole generally believes each partner should consider the other's views, but does not necessarily assert the broomstick tradition should be surrendered. Ultimately, she ends her response by stating, "If your fiancé continues to be uncomfortable, you will have to decide if the ritual is more important than your marriage."[34] Though her recommendation appears reasonable, it does not address the degree to which white participation in the broomstick wedding is acceptable when marrying someone of African descent. Afrocentric fashion designer Thony Anyiam says that interethnic traditions are perfectly appropriate, so that, for example, a Jewish American and African American couple should both break a glass and the jump the broom at their wedding.[35] Similarly, a 2003 article described the wedding of a Norwegian man and an African American woman where they shared one another's cultural traditions throughout the ceremony, including a jump over a broom crafted by the bride's friend.[36]

Despite positive support, however, other spaces hesitate to fully endorse couples hoping to share the ritual. On the website Lipstickalley.com, described as "The Internet's Largest African American Forum," one writer inquired about jumping the broom's relevance for modern African Americans. Answers were split, but one woman stated bluntly that she would not jump the broom if she married outside her race: "I'd only want to share that experience with a black man."[37] The comment is interesting for what it reveals about the need to protect the uniqueness of certain cultural customs, even if they are historically shared across groups. The writers were responding to an article by journalist Jacob Shamsian that detailed the broomstick wedding's British origins, its importance to enslaved African Americans, and the persistent myths that surround it.[38] Their responses reveal that, despite similar methods of performance between communities of African and European descent, jumping the broom can still mean different things to its white and Black participants, and, for some, a white partner's participation can denote cultural insensitivity.

A 2018 interview featured on *The Nod*, a weekly podcast that interprets various facets of Black history, life, and popular culture, illustrates the point. On February 19, 2018, the show's co-host, Eric Eddings, presented the history and meaning of "jumping the broom" as gleaned from various authors writing on the subject, and to personalize the episode, he interviewed an engaged interracial couple, a white man and Black woman. He relayed the tradition's history throughout the segment, explaining his own surprise at discovering its roots in Britain, and that Black Americans once rejected the custom after slavery before reviving it in the late twentieth century. When he asks the couple if they will jump the broom at their wedding, they both reply "no" and explain that the tradition's intimate tie to the African American experience makes it inappropriate to share the custom with a white American. A cross-racial adaptation would be an appropriation. Anticipating the answer, Eddings explained that broomstick weddings were also practiced in rural white communities in the United States, especially in Appalachia. Noting the prospective groom had roots in Kentucky, he again asked if this new information adjusted their thinking. Both partners maintained their original stance, and the groom explained his reasoning: "I'm still a 'no.' . . . I think that no matter the origin of it, through our perspective of history it is completely inseparable from Black identity, and for me to participate in it would be performative and it would be appropriative. . . . I think there are a lot of traditions and a lot of festivals that belong to one people that came from somewhere completely different. So I don't think it takes away from it being a Black tradition at all."[39] His response is understandable given that, despite his heritage, he apparently has no ties to any recent family members using the custom. If his Appalachian ancestors performed it, he is unaware of any direct oral traditions surrounding its symbolic value to their community. Additionally, there is no Appalachian equivalent to *Roots*, in which the custom is popularly linked to one's regional identity and revived by the descendant community. Thus, the broomstick wedding's position remains unclear when considered across cultural and/or racial lines, especially for those concerned about diluting its importance for a specific ethnic group. Though many embrace the custom as a way of appreciating, respecting, and embracing their partner's heritage, it has specific historical resonance for African Americans that is difficult for other groups to fully understand, even if their own ancestors once practiced a version of it. However, this groom's statement does lead one to ask if white people still jump the broom in the twenty-first century, and, if so, what their motivations are for using the ceremony.

## Do White People Still Jump the Broom?

White practitioners of the broomstick tradition lay claim to many centuries of history, but its modern renditions only recently expanded from regional customs linked to specific ethnic groups, to becoming a matrimonial phenomenon often used for religious purposes. Compared with African American heritage weddings, however, pinpointing the motive for its revival among Europeans and Euro-Americans is more difficult. Despite the existence of "jumping the broom" found in the folk histories of rural white Americans, modern white practitioners do not generally espouse literal ancestral links to the custom.[40] The white populations associated with it stem from groups that are ethnically and regionally diverse, and there are no inherent characteristics that bind neopagans with Cajuns or white people in Appalachia. Whereas for African Americans *Roots* was a watershed moment in reviving and reinventing an ancestral custom tied to slavery, these disparate white communities have no equivalent event. Indeed, if they practice it at all, each employs the ritual for different reasons that are tied to their group's unique social, legal, and cultural experience. For many white couples, the tradition is now usually performed for two reasons. First, white Americans became fascinated by the mystery of the tradition and its deep history in African American cultural practice, and they integrated the custom into their own weddings to celebrate, or appropriate, different cultural traditions. The second, and more common, reason is that it serves as a symbol through which the participants pay homage to their own religious or ethnic heritage, specifically that which predates Christianity. Both reasons can be traced to what Mathew Jacobson calls the "Hyphen-Nation," in which Americans of European descent in the post–civil rights period invoked ethnic identities to complicate the racial divides in American history and portray America as a multiethnic nation comprised of various ancestral groups.[41] A passion for genealogy inspired many Americans to look overseas for identities that transcended the cultureless "white" racial category and initiated an interest in claiming the folk customs of their ancestors.

As jumping the broom moved beyond its limited definition as a "slave tradition," white Americans revisited the utility of using it to assert their religious and ethnic heritage. Cajun communities were arguably its most consistent Euro-American practitioners, as their traditions were occasionally publicized throughout the twentieth and twenty-first centuries. In 1960, one media outlet still reported about the "odd" marriage customs of the Louisiana Cajuns, in which a bride and groom leapt over a broomstick held "a few inches from the floor" by two members of the community.[42] In 1989 a newspaper noted that one couple jumped over a broomstick in their Cajun-themed wedding, which suggests a recognition that the custom is tied to both the history and future of their community.[43] Columnist Bill Ellzey stated in 2001 that jumping the broom ceremonies formed "a whimsical part of this year's Downtown on the Bayou Cajun Wedding." Having some familiarity with the broomstick's associations with African American weddings, Ellzey introduced his article with a pointed question: "Whose custom is it anyway?"[44] As manifested in the previous chapters, the fluid nature of cultural exchange prevents any group's "claim" to the custom. It is significant, however, Cajuns have practiced the ritual from the mid-twentieth century, a time when few Americans did, into the twenty-first.

One Cajun author even used children's literature as a method to introduce young people to cultural customs that define unique features of their heritage. The *Cajun Alphabet*, published in 2003, uses "Gaston the Alligator" as a tour guide through the alphabet to introduce readers to different vernacular and cultural traditions. Jumping the broom appears twice in the work. The first involved a "charivari, for the fine bride and groom / Some good natured hazing, after jumping the broom."[45] A charivari was a European tradition in which crowds would gather around the home in protest of a recently married couple, banging pots and pans to voice their disapproval of the union. Rural American communities continued this tradition throughout the nineteenth and early twentieth centuries, though the American variant was known to be based less upon humiliation and focused more on reintegration.[46] Perhaps unsurprisingly, the second reference follows the letter "S" in which a young couple engages in "sauter l' balai," the colloquial equivalent to jumping the broom, noting that when the priest was away it would "join bride and groom."[47] By evoking the broomstick wedding's use as a community tool that validated relationships in the absence of a priest, the work suggests that Cajun practitioners held a unique understanding of the custom's ties to their cultural history.

Using a different approach, the descendants of Appalachian whites retain its memory through language. Adrienne Young, a bluegrass singer, noted in 2004 that her song "Jump the Broom" was inspired by a phrase her grandmother used to describe "folks that wanted to get married" when there was "no preacher around 'cuz they lived up in the mountains or down in the valleys."[48] Officially released in 2005, Young's "Jump the Broom" tracks the courtship of a young couple eager to marry and escape their circumstances. The song begins with a festive rhyme describing the ceremony's format: "Join two hands, this broom step over, / Take a sweet kiss from your own true lover." It then launches into the actual song, beginning with the description of the young woman as a "Kentucky wonder" whose head was "full of curls." The song's lyrics reflect the courtship of two young lovers, Pearl and Corey, as they dodge family members and steal away at night to marry in haste:

> Now young Corey's waitin' down by the gate,
> Can't call the preacher,
> It's much too late.
> But that don't stop his bended knee,
> No no, Pretty Pearl girl, marry me!

The reference to the preacher's unavailability reflects the reality of Appalachian history, though in this case the band takes liberty with the story by suggesting the broomstick tradition provided an outlet for young couples trying to escape their parents or the religious authority. Doubtless such events occurred, but since most broomstick weddings were left undocumented it is difficult to know if this was a primary way it was used or an offshoot of the process.

Though Romani communities generally stopped using the broomstick custom by the mid-twentieth century, one can imagine such ceremonies continue in isolation. Researchers are captive to documentation, and one finds very few references to Romani groups jumping the broom past 1950. For modern descendants, an appeal to tradition sometimes compels them to reintroduce it in their nuptials. In 2006 a couple in New Zealand, who said they were Romani "by choice rather than blood," cited Romani traditions as inspiration for their decision to jump over the broomstick in a "hybrid ceremony."[49] This hybrid event aligns with traditional Romani practices that were based largely on practical needs.

Twenty-first century depictions of Romani weddings reinforce the negative stereotypes of immorality and irresponsibility, but they do not feature the broomstick ceremony. In 2010 The Learning Channel aired *My Big Fat Gypsy Wedding*, a show documenting the marital excesses of Romani and Traveller communities throughout the British Isles. Subsequently, the network produced an American variation entitled *My Big Fat American Gypsy Wedding*, which documented similar issues specific to nomadic groups living throughout the United States. Generally, the portrayals of Romani communities are overwhelmingly unfavorable, featuring celebrations of underage drinking and sexual harassment committed by men against women. Romani journalist Jake Bowers was unsurprisingly troubled by such depictions. In a 2012 piece, Bowers argued the show had done nothing to advance the interests of Romani groups who hoped to gain acceptance in Great Britain. Instead, it gave "the old myths about gipsies being immoral, flashy thieves a glitzy tv makeover."[50]

He also notes the unique historical trajectory of the British Romani, citing their origins in India, unique language, deep respect for family and community, and their cultural contributions to British society, and adds that, "until recently gipsy weddings were created by 'jumping the broomstick.'" Though a brief reference, it speaks volumes to the circumstances of damaging stereotypes leveled against modern Romani communities. In this respect, Bowers suggests the televised decadence of Romani weddings does *more* damage to societal perceptions of Romani culture than a folk ritual that was once mocked and despised by outsiders. In a unique turn, the custom now reflects a nostalgic element of a past much harder to find, but when compared to modern depictions, it is comparatively preferable.

The largest group of European descendants who currently use the broomstick wedding are those affiliated with neopagan communities, often consolidated under the term "Wiccan." It is unclear exactly when such groups reintroduced the broomstick custom into their marriage rituals, or how ubiquitous such adoptions were, but we do know that white people who viewed *Roots* were interested in the broomstick ritual, and that when they pursued further research, they discovered it held European origins.[51] Since its Black cultural connections were dominant in the United States, most Americans of European descent initially considered themselves as cultural outsiders and were unsure how they should conceptualize the ritual's symbolic importance. A guest at one such wedding even expressed confusion when told it was an "African" tradition. But the attendee noted the bride and groom were white; the ceremony had no expressly African elements; and apparently, the officiant never explained their reason for engaging in the ritual.[52] However, as more people of European descent rejected Christianity and revisited pre-Christian traditions in the late twentieth century, folk customs like jumping the broom were integrated into their cultural worldview.

Regardless of their motivations for integrating the broomstick wedding, by the early 2000s different news outlets noted that more white couples with neopagan connections were jumping the broom during their marriages. The custom is most prevalent in white-majority, Anglophone countries, including Australia, Canada, Britain, and the United States. One finds scattered reference to broomstick ceremonies and "hand fastings" throughout the 1990s, as neopagan authors elaborated on the customs for those desiring pre-Christian forms of marriage.[53] The open practice of the ceremony, however, was halted by the passage of various "anti-witchcraft laws" in these Christian-majority countries. In Canada, for instance, a Wiccan priest in 1988 applied to be the "first Canadian witch" to perform marriages for the country's Wiccan population, but was denied through the country's "Marriage Act" law that did not recognize pagan ceremonies.[54] Even outside the legal apparatus, many kept their faith private in fear of social ostracism or persecution.[55] By the mid-2000s such laws were overturned, and one finds couples openly performing the ceremonies. In September of 2004 a couple jumped the broomstick in Scotland's first legalized pagan wedding.[56] In Australia, one report found "witches and warlocks legally tying the knot" by jumping over the broom in 2005, coinciding with the legalization of pagan ceremonies in the country.[57] Ireland did not legalize pagan weddings until 2010; afterward, a report suggested that many couples soon utilized the broomstick custom upon legalization.[58] The United States largely left such issues to individual states, and most of them recognized pagan ceremonies by the 1990s. There were exceptions, however. For instance, a "hand fasting" ceremony, in which the couple pledges their love for one year and a day, electing to repeat the process the following year, may not be recognized as a marriage by a particular state or legislature since marriage is defined as a lifelong commitment that can only be severed by legal proceedings.[59] But many neopagans eschew legal recognition where it is unavailable and unite through common law after performing commitment ceremonies surrounded by friends and community members.

Though jumping the broom is prominently displayed in neopagan ceremonies, these events take various forms depending upon the practitioners' spiritual affiliations. The sources of their deities range from ancient Celtic mythologies to those of Egypt, and each community holds its own philosophies surrounding the place of magic, nature, and spiritual authority. Some meet in the nude, while others wear robes and various associated forms of regalia. Sometimes the ceremony is held outside in a designated sacred space.[60] But the available descriptions suggest that pagan weddings do have some universal customs and symbols, including a blessing by a priest or priestess, a fastening of the groom and bride's hands to denote they are "tying the knot," an exchange of gifts such as crowns or rings, and a jump over the broom to denote household unity.[61] In many cases the couple is surrounded by their community in the form of a circle, symbolizing completion and protection of the union. Practitioners believe these rituals resemble ancient rites used by European populations throughout the pre-Christian era. Like African American newlyweds, some couples retain the broom and display it in their homes.[62]

Though it is difficult to know how or when modern pagans reintegrated the custom into their ceremonies, it is enjoying a public renaissance as legal barriers to non-Christian traditions are gradually knocked down in various Anglophone countries and practitioners' beliefs become more socially acceptable. "Pagan weddings" even enjoy some exposure through popular television programs. In season two of *The Originals*, a show that explores the supernatural, two white characters discuss the origins of "jumping the broom" as a regional practice. When a woman named Hayley approaches her fiancé Jackson's rural residence in southern Louisiana, she notices people in his community were leaving broomsticks on the porch at each of her visits. In his discernibly southern accent, Jackson explains, "Back in the day it wasn't easy getting a preacher out here. So if you were engaged and you couldn't wait, then the community would let you jump the broom." The segment concludes with a comic moment in which Haley realizes that their inability to "wait" equated to sex, to which she responds, "Oh, ahem. I would have been happier with a panini press."[63] He laughingly responds, "It's just a tradition." In this case, the ritual reflects a combination of rural white traditions in Louisiana with those of supernatural figures that exist outside the orthodox Christian tradition. The broomstick wedding held important symbolism in the community even if it was no longer a necessary component for marital consummation. Though such a reference does not match *Roots* in its magnitude, its appearance in a successful television miniseries recognizes it holds cultural relevance for certain Euro-American cultural groups.

Still, given the controversies surrounding who has the right to use the broomstick custom, and the suspicions some Black Americans hold against white people who adopt it to mimic their culture, it is worth returning to Aleta's "anarchic" notion of marriage and ask if using the custom fits the definition of cultural appropriation. Usually, accusations of cultural appropriation revolve around the lack of accreditation by those using the cultural product. If a white couple jumped the broom in a flippant manner, lacking appropriate context and pretending the custom holds no deep, symbolic value, one could legitimately criticize their appropriative tendency. However, Aleta and her partner selected the ritual in the spirit of resistance to the state, allying themselves with historically marginalized groups on the both sides of the Atlantic

Ocean. When viewed within the framework of cultural transmission, Aleta and her partner adopted the ceremony with profound respect for its symbolism, and by crediting its originators they did not embellish its historical function.

The broomstick wedding's modern use amongst such a disparate, multifaceted collection of people reveals its continued relevance for current matrimonial practices. Each of them holds different reasons for integrating it into their traditions. One unifying feature seems to be the popular belief that the broomstick wedding is subversive, a way to challenge the conformity of marital traditions. Though it is not entirely clear whether historical figures always viewed the broomstick wedding from this vantage point, many modern practitioners embrace the custom for a number of reasons. Indeed, the broomstick wedding's contested history and continual adoption by various groups reveals its malleability for those who identify with its symbolism. Like those who used it in the past, modern practitioners attach various meanings to the ceremony. It simultaneously functions as a way to reject one's culture, as in the case of neopagans and anarchists; a way to embrace it, as it does for African Americans and marginalized whites; a way to share it, as found in interracial marriages; or a way to reenvision it, as found in its diasporic reimaginings. Adopted and adapted across cultures for multiple centuries, each rendition reveals its continuous utility. None of these groups *needs* to jump the broom, per se, but its modern use reveals its continual relevance for sanctifying a couple's unique bond and in many cases validating their need to connect with those who preceded them.

# Whose Heritage? Whose Culture?
## *The Uncertain Future of Jumping the Broom*

In 2016 the History Channel released a new version of the *Roots* miniseries hoping to reintroduce Alex Haley's iconic story to a new generation. The revived *Roots* follows the basic premise of the original story, showcasing Kunta Kinte's capture from the shores of West Africa, the trials of his daughter, Kizzy, and the moment his grandson, Chicken George, gains his freedom following the Civil War. Some content was sacrificed, as the newer version was condensed to four episodes instead of the original's eight. At the same time, the visuals and dialogue are updated to reflect recent turns in slavery studies and representations of slavery in film. Responding to depictions of racist violence displayed in films such as *Twelve Years a Slave* and *Django Unchained*, the revamped *Roots* vividly showcases the brutalities of capture, enslavement, and punishment. In one noteworthy example, the camera fixates on the protruding blood from Kunta Kinte's foot as it is hacked off by slave catchers, leaving viewers with a haunting memory of how Black people faced bodily mutilation for daring to attempt an escape. Beyond visual updates, however, the new *Roots* uses the characters to engage in current debates about African American culture.

The broomstick wedding's cultural relevance is central to these dialogues. In the wedding scene, Kunta Kinte, Bell, and Fiddler disagree on the meaning behind jumping the broom for enslaved people in a way that positions the conversation within the social politics of the twenty-first century. As Bell and Kunta excitedly agree to take one another as partners, Fiddler, who is leading the ceremony, throws the broom in front of them and says they must jump the broom to make the marriage "official." Bewildered, Kunta asks how the broom makes a marriage official. Fiddler stares at him blankly, as Bell interjects:

> BELL: Well, we jump together, just like in Africa.
> KUNTA: No people in Africa jump brooms.
> FIDDLER: You don't know every people in Africa. Every Negro on every plantation say that jumping the broom when you get married come from the old way.

KUNTA: The old way is from Europe, must be, passed down from master to slave. Bell, they are making fun of us. Won't let us marry under their laws to remind us we belong to them, not each other.

FIDDLER: (Whispering in Kunta's ear) Either you jump over this broom, or I'm gonna swat you upside the head with it.[1]

Eventually, Kunta relents and jumps with Bell, deciding that her happiness is more important than his pride. In the background one sees the overseer roaming around the slave quarters, though he is not involved in the ceremony and allows the community to hold its internal discussion. This sequence was likely used to reflect cultural constructions of the 1990s that sought to situate Black America's cultural origins to Africa. Fiddler's response that "every Negro on every plantation" claims the tradition stems from Africa represents how mythic ideals are transmitted to the broader community and accepted through generations. Pieces of information possibly linking a slave custom to western Africa are disseminated to those seeking evidence that dignifies their ancestral culture. In the case of the new *Roots*, oral claims were authoritative history, despite their generational distance from the African homeland. Kunta Kinte disrupts this narrative as one who is directly from the continent. By declaring that no brooms are jumped in Africa, Kunta subverts the myth publicly, leaving the surrounding community speechless. As the community's de facto leader, Fiddler is the only one to contest the claim, exclaiming that Kunta can speak only to his own experience, not all people in Africa. However, Kunta remembers the transition from freedom to slavery and the slaveowner's attempt to annihilate his cultural memory. He argues the broomstick holds more nefarious undertones, claiming it was a tradition from Europe passed from the slaveholder to the bondsperson designed to mock enslaved people and their inability to access legal marriage. By this logic, he believes that convincing the enslaved to unquestionably accept the broomstick wedding and even reimagine it as an ancestral custom from the other side of the Atlantic Ocean, was a way to socialize them to accept their servitude.

From my own reading of the available slave narratives, none of the formerly enslaved was especially concerned with the broomstick wedding's origins, let alone its connection to Europe. They simply knew it existed, and if they held firsthand experience, they elaborated on how their own community performed it. Given that the series was based upon a novel, its writers were not as concerned with displaying a factual conversation among historical figures, but used the characters to reflect the Black community's contemporary impressions of the custom and its place in their heritage. Fiddler's final warning was a playful threat to assault Kunta if he did not comply with the tradition, as he was embarrassing Bell on their wedding day. However, it still reflected a form of his intellectual surrender. Fiddler had no solid proof the tradition was African, though he maintained it was important to use it since enslaved people, stripped of legal matrimony, held no other concrete traditions in their wedding celebrations. For Fiddler, it was an enslaved couple's best option for cultural distinction since they knew of no other racial group who used it. His private threat toward Kunta was an appeal for him to drop the issue, at least publicly, so he and Bell could enjoy the ceremony without controversy. Kunta's reluctant acceptance of the ritual reflects the mentality of some modern practitioners. Despite its associations with slavery and its possible introduction through the slaveowner, the happiness of one's spouse, family, or community can erase their initial reservations.

The wedding scene in the new *Roots* departs significantly from that of the original miniseries. In the 1977 version Kunta and Bell also marry in front of their community, but the wedding is led by an enslaved plantation matriarch, not Fiddler. She marches around the couple with the broom turned toward the sky, emphasizing her hope that neither of them will do anything to get sold away and they will be blessed with "good healthy young'ns." She then asks, "Y'all sure you wanna get married?" After their affirmation, she exclaims, "In the eyes of Jesus jump over the broom into the land of matrimony." Though the master is present in observing the ceremony, he is peripheral to its functions, suggesting it was an affair the enslaved largely controlled, and he leaves once they begin dancing. During this entire sequence Kunta gives no opinion of the ceremony, but does become despondent when he thinks about his village, his family, and the realization that he will never be free. The 2016 *Roots* is closer to the novel, since it expounds upon Kunta's initial reservations.

In the novel, Kunta thinks that "jumping the broom" is "ridiculous" for such a solemn occasion.[2] This brief insertion suggests that Haley was cognizant of the broomstick wedding's origins outside of Africa, while simultaneously confirming it was a fundamental component of slave culture that needed exposure. The original miniseries represented the broomstick wedding as a liberating activity, in which the community surrounds the couple and the plantation's matriarch led the ceremony. When told to jump the broom, both Kunta and Bell do so without hesitation. The newer version exemplifies Kunta's reservations through dialogue, using him and Fiddler to symbolically reflect different sides of the issue. Why did the original miniseries erase Kunta's misgivings? It is possible that the original producers and writers wanted to avoid disparaging slave culture and believed negative comments might distract from the dignity that enslaved people placed upon the wedding. Considering that studies of slave resistance and agency dominated the scholarship of the 1970s and 1980s, the original *Roots* hoped to display a triumphant narrative where it was available. That enslaved people still married under restrictive and violent circumstances reflected their resiliency. Historians argue, however, that this framework unintentionally romanticized marriage under slavery.[3] The new *Roots* brings such issues to the forefront with an unapologetic dialogue about the custom's origins and its possible transmission into enslaved communities. Given the generational divisions that problematize this custom, the miniseries is speaking to a new, younger audience. The *Roots* remake follows a trend among Black youths who challenge this tradition's utility for a new generation. For many, jumping the broom's origins in slavery make the notion that it is an empowering ritual questionable.

## Conceptual Divisions in Popular Culture

The 2011 major motion picture *Jumping the Broom* explores class divisions between two Black American families. It also places the broomstick ritual within a broader discussion about the meaning of Blackness in the twenty-first century United States, in which one school of thought seeks to advance beyond the rhetoric that associates it with struggle and tradition, and the other believes that the key to preserving the uniqueness of Black identity is in retaining ancestral traditions. It is cultural tradition against cultural evolution, often positioned between generational and/or class divides. As depicted in the film, however, not all Black families view the custom favorably, which causes tension between the families' respective matriarchs, Pam Taylor, played by Loretta Devine, and Mrs. Watson, played by Angela Bassett.

During the rehearsal dinner, they argue about the relevance of jumping the broom in modern African American weddings. Viewers soon learn that each family's cultural affinities are directly tied to class. Taylor is a postal service employee from New York City, while Watson is a successful lawyer living on Martha's Vineyard. Holding the broomstick used at her own wedding, Taylor gives an emotionally charged explanation for why enslaved couples employed the ritual and its importance for those hoping to honor their ancestors. Watson arrogantly retorts that slavery had nothing to do with her own heritage, claiming that, in fact, her ancestors themselves "owned slaves."[4] The statement understandably meets with gasps from the predominantly Black wedding party. But it is not untrue. Scholars note that Black people, often mixed-race, did hold Black captives in many areas of the antebellum

South.[5] Black slaveowners were especially noticeable in locations influenced by French culture, specifically in Louisiana, where the biracial progeny of slaveowners were classified as "gens de colour" to distinguish them from "pure" African slaves.[6] Though not universal, it was not uncommon for this group to gain their freedom and inherit enslaved people. It is important to note, however, that free people of color were often themselves formerly enslaved or descended from people who held that status. Thus, Watson's retort is not completely factual, but predicated on the historical distinction her ancestors held from other people of African descent.

Though Watson's character is never completely developed, her mannerisms throughout the film give a few ties to this history. She speaks French, suggesting that she hails comes from a prominent family of free people of color from either a Haitian or Louisiana Creole background. Her husband, Mr. Watson, is a lighter-complexioned Black entrepreneur who also speaks French. The Watson's Francophone connection with slave ownership is likely a deliberate addition to the film's portrayals of class and status, as it suggests their money was accumulated and expanded across generations, possibly into the antebellum period. Though they are a Black family in the United States, the Watson's multigenerational wealth and prestige portray them as a distinct group from their potential in-laws. On the other end, Pam Taylor is a religious blue-collar worker and a single mother. References to her husband suggest he passed away when her son Jason was young and that he was raised within an extended kinship group that included blood relatives and family friends. Proud of her heritage and the resilience of her enslaved ancestors, she views jumping the broom as one way for African American couples to pay respect to the sacrifices of their forebears and always remember their roots. The issue, however, is that she appears disconnected from a new generation of affluent African Americans who see their future as what will define them, not the past. She is especially troubled that Jason appears to disassociate himself from his heritage as he enters a higher socioeconomic bracket.

Jason and his fiancée, Sabrina, provide only a few thoughts about the ceremony, asserting that jumping the broomstick did not belong in a "modern" wedding. The film spends most of its time tackling the question of identity and its association with class, race, heritage, and upward mobility. One of the film's climactic moments comes toward the end, when Jason and Sabrina must decide if they will jump the broom. Eventually, the broomstick wins out. Sabrina interrupts the ceremony to procure the broom and the camera focuses on their feet as they leap over it. No explanation is given for why the couple decided to include it, though it appears the jump was a way for both families to harmonize at the film's end, not due to any cultural awakening from Sabrina and Jason. It reflected a symbol through which both families joined together and placed their social divisions asunder. Though triumphant in this case, the movie's plot suggests that the broomstick wedding's centrality in Black weddings might be living on borrowed time.

The film's larger question asks how African Americans entering an upper-middle and upper class (predominantly white) society maintain their "Blackness." As sociologist Nicole Rousseau argues, *Jumping the Broom* represents class as a major source of the interfamilial divisions and simultaneously "idealizes and critiques a highly Eurocentric model" of respectability and Black family relations.[7] T. D. Jakes, the movie's producer and a megachurch pastor, hoped the film would portray the broomstick wedding as a positive aspect of Black American culture, as he emphasized its "African" roots in one interview about the movie. Similarly, various cast members and directors agreed that the ceremony was a key aspect of Black matrimonial traditions and reflected on its importance for remembering one's ancestors and initiating new beginnings.[8] Though the film does ultimately portray the custom in the same light, its deeper message about it is decidedly more complex. In one example, Jason has a confrontation with his cousin over why they never see each other, and after a brief argument, it is revealed that his cousin is uncomfortable around the white people who comprise a large percentage of Jason's new friends. Thus, Jason must defend his identity as he elevates himself economically, in a way that reveals a change in one's social and economic status can also alter one's racial self-conception. The broomstick custom in African American marriage brings out this issue. For if it is a "Black thing" to jump the broom, at least in the United States, should African Americans feel obliged to do it to gain a sense of racial or cultural authentication?[9] Jason and Sabrina's initial hesitation to include the custom in their "modern" wedding ceremony suggests that like those of the postbellum period who viewed the custom as a relic of a past they preferred to forget, younger African Americans appear to be moving beyond the revived tradition.

Though its matrimonial importance is now challenged, it is unlikely that jumping the broom will fully disappear from African American culture. It continues to enjoy references and features in television outlets and other forms of media.[10] The custom has been visually connected to Black matrimony throughout the twenty-first century on shows such as *Grey's Anatomy*, *Basketball Wives LA*, *Braxton Family Values*, *The Game*, *Growing Up Hip Hop*, and *This Is Us*.[11] It is represented as both a compelling event for Black Americans and a topic of intense discussion prior to a couple's nuptials. Additionally, the ceremony is linked primarily with African American culture in the vast majority of weddings shows, including multiple seasons of The Learning Channel's *Four Weddings*.[12] As Sociologist Michael Eric Dyson notes, the descendants of enslaved people must recognize that broomstick weddings provided a way for enslaved people to affirm to one another that they were in a committed relationship; it was, in part, the "fabric of their own moral existence."[13] Even those who reject it recognize that it is one of the oldest traditions found in African American history, and few question its importance for understanding ancestral history. Consequently, popular media encourages viewers to associate the custom with Black Americans, as they have few references to pagan traditions or the histories of specific Euro-American communities that historically used it.

## Cultural Appropriation, Appreciation, or Amalgamation?

Though the custom's roots among people in Europe are now thoroughly documented and many scholarly works are publicly available, one still finds disagreements regarding cultural ownership. Results from *Jet* magazine's online poll, "Can White Couples Jump the Broom?" indicate that, as of June 2020, nearly half of its respondents said "no," while about 31 percent did not see a problem with it.[14] The remaining 19 percent were undecided. In another example, an online journalist for hellobeautiful.com who presumed it has African origins castigated white people for jumping the broom, even after she learned about its European roots. The first version of the article rehashed the myth of Ghanaian origins and claimed that jumping the broom had a rich history that did not "involve anyone with less melanin than me."[15] Upon discovering the custom stems from groups in the British Isles, the author doubled down on the African origins thesis, arguing that since enslaved people were forced to use brooms and "clean up after their masters," elite whites "wouldn't dare put their privileged hands on a broom." Outside the problematic dismissal of the custom's European connections, the quotation reveals a presumption that all white people were slaveowners and held economic privileges, when, in reality, white Americans who owned Black people were a numerical minority and many white southerners were impoverished by the system. Historian Keri Leigh Merritt notes that on the eve of secession, slaveowners accounted for "about a quarter of the South's enumerated white population," and individuals had been falling out of this category for decades prior.[16]

Despite such evidence, however, the author from hellobeautiful.com maintained her original stance. She is not alone in this belief, since it is repeated in similar forums.[17]

A couple's motivation for using the ritual can be bound up in questions of cultural appropriation, which occurs when a dominant group assumes the "intellectual property" or cultural practices of a subordinated group and expresses the trait for its own social, political, or economic gain.[18] Accusations of appropriation become most apparent when the cultural form in question was once despised or criticized by the dominant group, but now is transformed into a trendy and desirable trait in its repackaged societal framework. The appropriated product is soon disassociated from its original culture, or, at the very least, the appropriators believe they have improved on it. One finds an especially stark divide in popular representations of music when white entertainers enter genres largely dominated by Black artists. Sociologist Jason Rodriquez argues that appropriation can be especially pernicious in the post–civil rights era when U.S. race relations are popularly guessed under the term "colorblind," the idea that white Americans claim to treat everyone equally irrespective of race. In speaking of hip-hop, Rodriquez argues that the "color-blind ideology allows individuals to appropriate cultural forms by providing the discursive resources to take the racially coded meanings out of hip-hop, and replace them with color-blind ones."[19] Given the consequences of a dominant group's appropriation of a cultural form, marginalized practitioners are typically suspicious that the new participants are not genuine. Dominant groups ignore that their participation is an expression of a societal privilege that allows them to enjoy the benefits of the cultural trait, while dodging the ridicule it might elicit against its marginalized innovators. Additional problems arise when cultural appropriation becomes synonymous with cultural theft. To escape accusations of cultural theft, a group or individual must accredit the originators of the cultural form and strive to use it in accordance with the way the original group did.

Some theorists reject the suffocating parameters of determining who can access a cultural trait not linked to their ancestry, warning that such "cultural insiderism" derails the advantages humans have gained in forming progressive, cosmopolitan societies.[20] But jumping the broom presents further challenges to the cultural appropriation argument. In considering its folkloric history and attachment to a diverse array of communities, it is difficult to conceptualize how it can be appropriated in the traditional sense. If an accusation of cultural appropriation relies upon a custom's unique and exclusive attachment to a specific cultural group that is then taken by an outsider who claims it for themselves, jumping the broom presents a challenge to this framework since it is impossible to know who first used it and for what purpose. Though we know it was first used amongst populations throughout Britain, the initial reasons for its adoption, let alone which population first developed it, remain an open question. Thus, its cultural origins are not entirely clear and the fluid nature under which it was transferred suggests that many groups can simultaneously contend it is uniquely imbedded within their cultural experience. Additionally, even if the first practitioners of jumping the broom are found in the British Isles, its modern cultural identity shifted by the 1990s, and it is, consequently, now primarily viewed as an African American custom. Thus, one can argue that its historically fluid transferal between groups precludes anyone from claiming exclusive rights to its practice. Equally problematic are the ideas surrounding the generalities under which people speak of culture and its attachment to one's ethnic or racial identity. Claiming that jumping the broom is an exclusively "Black," "Romani," or "Celtic" custom presumes that one's race or ethnic identity necessitates their performance of a certain set of cultural traits, but this book shows it was never universally embraced by any of the populations who practiced it. Some people rejected it, while others either claimed no knowledge of the custom or contended the ritual died with previous generations. Setting aside racial or ethnic exclusivity, an inherent problem in visualizing jumping the broom as a "cultural product" specific to one group is that it does not fit neatly into the accepted parameters that define cultural appropriation.

Jumping the broom is more accurately classified as originating and evolving among subaltern populations, placing it more comfortably in the transatlantic context that defines its diverse expressions. Different classes hold a variety of subcultures within them, even when inhabiting the same country, region, or town. The subcultures of marginalized groups helped to build and maintain their sense of community and provide a response "to the problems posed for them by their material and social class position and experience."[21] As an item defined by these many distinct cultural associations, the broomstick wedding is no less a "Black" cultural form even if its origins lie outside of Africa. Enslaved people did not need to create the ritual independently for them to lay claim to it. They followed earlier groups who also adapted it to their own cultural needs and engrained it into their communal identities. Those who practiced the custom were not concerned if other people acquired it. Enslaved people simply knew that couples on their own plantations did, and that was enough for them. Consequently, the descendants of enslaved people who wish to follow the ritual do not need a myth of African origins to validate their decision. Dismissing it as a "slave custom" unworthy of attention or reclamation misses the broader point of how cultural products are reshaped and reimagined when harnessing social solidarity. Similarly, neopagans and practitioners of European descent should be cautious in proclaiming it holds a pure cultural genealogy within their own communities, as it was never universally appealing to all European ethnic or pre-Christian religious groups, and nor is there much evidence that it was consistently practiced past the 1950s.

Modern enactments in the United States, the British Isles, and other parts of the Anglophonic world are typically performed in homage to the ancestors who used the matrimonial broomstick when few other options were available. Though jumping the broom is itself a simple action, this book shows the history of jumping the broom is complex and has links to various groups residing in locations separated by the Atlantic Ocean. One's familiarity with the custom largely depends on their place of origin and / or cultural identity. In the British Isles, nomadic groups and those who lived on society's margins found use for the ritual, while in the United States, it was, and is, linked mainly with enslaved African Americans and their descendants. This cultural diversity is where the broomstick wedding's historical record becomes complicated. Due to their histories of marginalization, some of these groups hope to protect their unique cultural identities by securing exclusive claims to the tradition. Anyone outside the group caught using the custom is condemned as a cultural appropriator.

Deciding who "owns" the custom is at the heart of this divide, and it seems likely that the debate will persist if the practice remains culturally relevant. Despite each group practicing the custom, it was not a universal practice for any of them. For instance, there were many Romani migrants who never used the broomstick traditions, just as many African Americans claimed it never existed upon their antebellum plantation.[22] The operations of history and memory in the modern era presume that one's current culture, or at least newer renditions of it, can easily transfer into the experiences of their ancestors. This partially explains why some people believe certain groups hold exclusive claim to the tradition and those outside the community hoping to use it should request prior permission. These divisions, however, are often reproduced by writings that are not heavily invested in the available primary sources, but written through the vantage point of a preconceived worldview informed by modern popular culture. For instance, despite knowledge of its European origins, many Americans still believe its origins lie in West Africa due to its nearly exclusive association with Black people in the United States.

Similarly, modern Europeans and white Americans who practice the custom assert they have the oldest ties to it and misunderstand its deep, intergenerational connections within the Black community in the United States. One could argue, in fact, that Black Americans hold the most prolific claims to the ceremony since they hold the largest collection of testimonials detailing its contours.

African Americans' collective respect for cultural heritage and revival of tradition deserves special recognition for salvaging and popularizing the custom. It is important to note that, apart from a few exceptions, each group generally stopped using the ritual by the mid-twentieth century. However, African Americans revived the custom in full force by the 1990s, and their efforts rapidly propelled it into the spotlight of American popular culture. Though people might disagree about its cultural origins, there is no doubt that modern practitioners of the broomstick wedding, whether in Europe or the United States, are indebted to the efforts of Black scholars, creators, and entrepreneurs in reviving a largely discarded custom. Without the cultural turn in slave studies, the rise of Black pride, or the release of Alex Haley's *Roots*, far fewer people, white or Black, would be jumping the broom. In this case, one's cultural identity does not necessarily require ties to a specific continent, and a multicultural tradition preserved through oral histories and folklore cannot be solely bound to any single group.

## A Royal Wedding

On May 19, 2018, Britain's Prince Harry, Duke of Sussex, married Meghan Markle, a biracial actress from Los Angeles, California. The wedding was a groundbreaking occasion for various reasons. One is that although Americans have married into the royal family, the practice is not common, and this was the first such union to occur in several decades. Markle is also a divorcee, a status that traditionally disqualified anyone from marrying a British royal, but it is her biracial ancestry that consumed media outlets and commentators. Descended from a Black woman and a white man, Markle is a departure from the wholly white, European bloodlines that secured the identities of British royalty for centuries. She embodies the possibilities for social and cultural change in a Western Europe that has rapidly diversified since the mid-twentieth century. A few opinion columns deemed this shift the "Blackening of Windsor," denoting an entry point for racial intermixture that reaches the highest levels of British social class. Black guests from elite circles filled the church to attend the ceremony, and Black American traditions were integrated into a traditionally posh British ceremony. Attica Locke, a writer for the acclaimed *Empire* series, exclaimed that the televised event ranked as one of the most important moments in African American history, placing it alongside the March on Washington, Barack Obama's first inauguration, and Halle Berry winning an Oscar.[23] Though some might disagree with the assessment, Locke is certainly correct that this union is unprecedented and that Markle's Black Americanness was a central feature.

Many spectators on both sides of the Atlantic recognize Markle as a woman of African descent, though she typically identifies as biracial. Her decision to use this category reflects a generational shift among younger Americans who are dissatisfied with singular categories, often feeling they are never truly accepted by either racial group.[24] In an autobiographical essay published in 2015, Markle reveals the difficulties she experienced coming of age in a world that fixated on racially homogenous families. Despite the acclaimed diversity of Southern California and the social liberalism of Hollywood, conceptions of race and ethnic identities remained parochial. As she noted of her entry into acting, "I wasn't black enough for the black roles and I wasn't white enough for the white ones, leaving me somewhere in the middle as the ethnic chameleon who couldn't book a job."[25] Markle's essay is eloquently written, exposing the uneasy juxtaposition that society places upon the identities of mixed-race people, especially those of European and African descent, and how it lingers in the psychology of people forced to navigate the Black/white binary. However, a closer look at Markle's experiences with racism unpacks the broader problems affecting those who hope to escape society's conformist racial standards.

Throughout the essay she notes various moments of racism permeating her life as a child and young adult, and *all* of them revolved around her Black identity. She reflects on her father's homogenously white town in Pennsylvania and his controversial decision to court and marry a Black woman; the moment her mother was called a "n——" for not exiting a parking space quickly enough; racist comments proliferating in social media at the revelation that her *Suits* character, Rachel Zane, had a Black father; and how the standard for Hollywood beauty was, until very recently, white, blonde, and blue-eyed. She does not divulge any severe discrimination against her white ancestry, which is not surprising for a city, state, and country that historically prizes whiteness over other identities. Though her "curly hair . . . freckled face . . . pale skin" has precluded her from acceptance as fully Black, she can never be white by American standards.[26] Though some African Americans might question her authentic Blackness due to the privileges allotted to lighter-complexioned people of color, the historical American standards of identity define her as a Black woman.[27] Consequently, the infatuation with Markle's Black American identity provided the most captivating media commentary on the couple's transatlantic cultural differences and how they could shape the royal ceremony.

As the racial label was firmly placed, many wondered how, or whether, African American traditions would influence the ceremony. Eventually, media outlets discovered that many distinguished Black celebrities and sports figures would be at the ceremony, attendees would be serenaded by a Black gospel choir, and Michael Curry, the first Black bishop of the American Episcopal Church, agreed to officiate the wedding. Although these additions already sent a clear message that this royal wedding broke with previous traditions, some wondered if jumping the broom, often viewed as the quintessential African American marriage tradition, would be included. A few eager observers initiated petitions to persuade the royal couple to literally "jump over the broom" to commemorate and affirm the perseverance of the "hundreds of thousands of unfreed people" who married despite the illegality of their unions.[28] Others suggested that the wedding's unexpected inclusion of Black traditions and guests might prompt the couple to include the ritual. Author and film producer Attica Locke became so overwhelmed with the Black aspects of the ceremony that she wondered, with a hint of levity, if Prince Harry and Meghan Markle would jump a broom "ribboned in kente cloth."[29] Given the custom's origins among communities in the British Isles, the focus on its Black American connection is important for understanding how popular culture attaches it to specific groups.

Confusion surrounding the ritual was vividly exposed in a PBS episode discussing preparations for the royal wedding. Hosted by Meredith Vieira, an American journalist and television personality, and Matt Baker, a British television host, the *Royal Wedding Watch* provided viewers an exclusive glimpse into the preparations for the ceremony. Episode 1, "A Wedding is Announced," gathered different panelists who provided perspective on the pending nuptials. After discussing various subjects, Vieira shifted the conversation to the couple's cultural differences and their ability to integrate different customs. Her exchange with June Sarpong, a British woman of Ghanaian descent, illustrates the misunderstandings many hold surrounding the broomstick's multicultural history and impact.

Toward the episode's end Vieira inquired how the royal couple might implement one another's cultural traditions, specifically asking for those considered exclusive to British citizens. Sarpong opined on the matter by first describing certain customs unique to America that are largely unknown in British nuptials. Paradoxically, among the first traditions mentioned was jumping the broom, as she stated, "Well, you in America . . . 'jump the broom,' we don't do that here." Following this single line, it became evident that none of the panelists knew of the practice, including Vieira, the American. When asked by her co-host how and why Americans jump the broom at weddings, Vieira laughingly stated, "I have never jumped a broom," and appeared genuinely confused by the question. Taken aback, Sarpong noted that she had seen many Americans jump over brooms at weddings she attended. Upon further reflection, however, she realized the ceremonies that featured the custom were those of a specific ethnic group: "Well, maybe they're sort of more African American weddings. Yeah, African American weddings, they jump the broom."[30] The conversation then shifted toward some rather perplexed discussion on the broomstick's meaning to those who use it and whether it is used after the ceremony and thus revealed that none of the panelists held any real understanding of the tradition's historical complexity.

In this case, the intersections of race, class, culture, and nationality, especially in a transatlantic context, became particularly convoluted. The panel's discussion on culturally specific traits collapsed both Harry and Markle's identities into a nationalist framework and assumed that "different subcultures based on class, race, or ethnic identity do not exist among "Americans" or the "British."[31] Markle's identity as a biracial woman from Southern California is quite distinct. Just as Vieira's question presumed that bride and groom were each bound to a specific set of undefined national traditions, Sarpong responded by using the first-person plural to represent the British position: "We don't do that." From a cultural standpoint, it is interesting to view a British woman of African descent claim that the custom does not exist in the land of its origin and suggest it is culturally specific to an oppressed group of African-descended people who acquired it from Anglophone oppressors. For Sarpong, the couple's nationality, to some extent, eclipsed their race until she considered that African Americans hold a unique culture within their nation state.[32]

American racial and ethnic groups, especially African Americans, have unique cultural traits that do not resonate with the entire national population. It is interesting to note that in her self-correction Sarpong does not say that "Black" people jump the broom, but specifies its use among "African Americans." This correctly denotes that national identity is a poor indicator for ascertaining one's cultural proclivities. From its inception, the broomstick wedding attracted subaltern populations seeking to validate their unions internally. Calling it a "British" or "American" custom is problematic, as it was only used by the type of people that British or American elites would sooner reject than embrace. It never captured the interest of the entire nation, nor has it ever been promoted as representative of the nation's cultural heritage. Recognizing the initial error, Sarpong notes this is an isolated ritual performed mainly by a specific group of Black people in a specific location: the descendants of enslaved people in the United States. The entire exchange reveals the difficulty in presuming that cultural customs can be generalized by all-encompassing categories such as nationality, race, or class. The historical context of the broomstick wedding proves that it is never completely embraced by every member of a specific ethnic or racial group, and that such folk customs were often maligned by many people within the very nations that housed such groups.

Theoretically, one could assert that Prince Harry, a British man, could engage the broomstick custom with his wife, who also hails from a group that historically used it. But there are problems in suggesting it was appropriate for this occasion. Though petitioners seemed to believe it would provide some symbolic justice to historically oppressed peoples, it is worth contextualizing the unique circumstances of this wedding. For her part, Markle made no public indication that she was interested in the custom and the degree to which she identifies as culturally Black American is difficult to calibrate from her early public statements. She tends to identify as biracial, and her cultural identity is more regional (Southern Californian), than racial. Regarding Prince Harry, he descends from the aristocratic class that mocked the ceremony and the groups who used it. One could imagine the royal family might suppress any attempt to engage a ritual that's single consistent trait is its use among subaltern populations on both sides of the Atlantic. Thus, while Harry hails from Britain, it is unlikely he holds any ancestral attachments to the custom. If one contextualizes the broomstick wedding from the vantage points of class and genealogy, Harry's participation in the ritual could be correctly criticized as appropriative. Still, the media's attention to the ritual and perceptions surrounding its purported nearly exclusive links to Black America reveal that it remains a relevant topic.

Despite the broomstick's multicultural and transatlantic history, it is Markle's Blackness that dominates any discussions surrounding the couple possibly jumping the broom. Commentators like the aforementioned Attica Locke asserted that including the broomstick ritual in the royal nuptials would be an empowering tribute to Black American culture, especially when conducted with an unapologetically Afrocentric flair. No reference to its practice in the British Isles was even hinted at, and in the one exchange noted above, it was actively denied that anyone in Great Britain practiced it. Though many European and Euro-American practitioners have revived the tradition to celebrate their own cultural heritages, its connection to Black American marital traditions unveils their important efforts in reviving and reinventing their ancestral customs, alongside their global influence in the realm of popular culture.

Regardless of whether a couple decides to jump the broom, it remains a fundamental component of cultural expression among populations seeking to find their roots, reject conformity, or participate in the cultural rituals of an increasingly multicultural and globalized society. For centuries, the broomstick wedding symbolized commitment for subaltern couples. A seemingly modest ceremony, its symbolic importance both continued and changed as it was adopted by different communities. The practice reveals a mystifying history of cooperation and cultural exchange between groups that felt isolated from elite society, and its influence transcended ethnic and racial boundaries on both sides of the Atlantic. Oral histories and written documents reveal that British Romani, Celts, the English, Louisiana Cajuns, African Americans, white Appalachians, and even isolated communities in the American West practiced some form of matrimonial broom-jumping.

The broomstick wedding's history is remarkably complex, as it intertwines the experiences of various peoples on both sides of the Atlantic Ocean. Consequently, its multicultural history has instigated some contention regarding its origins and who can claim it. Does any group "own" the broomstick wedding? The historical record suggests that this might be the wrong question. Instead of arguing that one group holds a monopoly over the custom, we should consider that jumping the broom embodies the essence of cultural transmission, change, and adaptation. Created and innovated by marginalized groups in Europe and the United States, jumping the broom exemplifies how oppressed peoples from Europe and Africa contributed to the unique cultural developments that permeate the Americas. Given its ubiquitous practice amongst populations who were impoverished, marginalized, and often illiterate, it is difficult to imagine how such a ritual *could* be appropriated by any of its associated communities, since no documents show any group has an exclusive claim to the custom. The adoption, rejection, and reintegration of the ceremony among many peoples reflect the notion that cultural identities are never fixed, but are productions that "undergo constant transformation."[33] Each group also altered it to fit its own needs and preferences. These traditions exemplify how groups can create dynamic cultural expressions that thwart the institutional forces that tried to eliminate their self-worth and creativity. In its past and present forms, jumping the broom has acquired many meanings. It is a celebration of heritage, a meaningful cultural ritual, a term of derision, and even a powerful political statement. Instead of castigating different communities for using the ritual or praising them for drawing from its symbolic strength, we should celebrate the resiliency of those historical figures who used it to affirm their love and commitment while surviving institutional and societal pressure, and relish the reality that modern practitioners seek to honor that memory.

# Notes

## Introduction

1. Hyatt, *Folklore from Adams County*, 465.

2. Thornton, *Africa and Africans*; Gomez, *Exchanging Our Country Marks*; Sweet, *Recreating Africa*; Young, *Rituals of Resistance*; Brown, *African-Atlantic Cultures*.

3. Rawick, *The American Slave*, supplement series 1, vol. 7, *Mississippi Narratives*, part 2, 87. Hereafter, citations to this work will use "ss" for "supplement series."

4. Puckett, *Folk Beliefs of the Southern Negroes*, 319.

5. Thompson, *Flash of the Spirit*, 109. See also Stuckey, *Slave Culture*, 13–14.

6. Desch-Obi, *Fighting for Honor*.

7. Davis, "A Review of the Conflicting Theories of the Slave Family"; Wetherell, "Slave Kinship"; Cody, "Naming, Kinship, and Estate Dispersal"; Joyner, *Down by the Riverside*; Burton, *In My Father's House*; Cody, "There Was No Absalom on the Ball Plantations"; Jones, *Born a Child of Freedom*, 37–63; Malone, *Sweet Chariot*; Stevenson, *Life in Black and White*, 226–257; Hudson, *To Have and to Hold*; Dunaway, *The African American Family*; West, *Chains of Love*, 43–79; Pargas, *The Quarters and the Fields*.

8. One of the few exceptions to this rule was Ophelia Settle Egypt's work, "Raggedy Thorns," which entitled an entire chapter "Jumping de Broomstick." However, Egypt's manuscript was rejected by many presses and remains unpublished. Versions of her manuscript can be found in the Ophelia Egypt Collection, Series E, Boxes 140-12, 140-13, Folder 2.

9. Exceptions to this general rule include O'Neil, "Bosses and Broomsticks"; Parry, "Married in Slavery Time"; Hunter, *Bound in Wedlock*, 46–48.

10. Sobel, *The World They Made Together*; Joyner, *Shared Traditions*.

11. Lamanna, Riedmann, and Stewart, *Marriages & Families*, 180.

12. The exceptions to this rule are those who affiliate themselves with neopagan communities in both the British Isles and the United States and who employ the custom in homage to a pre-Christian Celtic ancestry. See Dunwich, *Wicca Craft*, 59–60; Griffyn, *Wiccan Wisdomkeepers*, 17; Dunwich, *Witch's Halloween*, 155.

13. For recent journalistic treatments, see Shamsian, "Here's the Tangled History"; Eric Eddings, host, "Jumping the Broom," *The Nod* (podcast).

14. Quoted in Zhmud, *Pythagoras and the Early Pythagoreans*, 178.

15. Goodwin, *Plutarch's Essays and Miscellanies*, 263.

16. Goodwin, 263.

17. Roheim, "The Significance of Stepping Over," 13.

18. Biedermann, *Dictionary of Symbolism*, 50.

19. Addy, *Household Tales*, 102.

20. "A Polish Witch in Detroit," 1.

21. Roscoe, *The Baganda*, 17.

22. Some contend that Australia had a broom-jumping tradition, but most references are found in secondary sources or novels and are often not substantiated by primary sources. See Ihde, "'So Gross a Violation of Decency'"; Grieves, "The McClymonts of Nabiac"; Roberts, *The Broomstick Wedding*. One primary source does refer to it, but mainly as a children's game: "Letters on Australia," *Alta California*, November 16, 1852, 2.

23. Although this remains a neglected field, certain works have connected a few of these various groups to each other. See, for example, Williams, *Black Skin, Blue Books*, on transatlantic friendships between the Welsh and African Americans in the nineteenth and twentieth centuries. For other multicultural comparative analyses, see Brandon, "The Socio-Cultural Traits of the French Folksong"; Joyner, *Shared Traditions*.

24. Turner, *I Heard It through the Grapevine*, 40.

25. Camp, *Closer to Freedom*, 2.

26. Young, *Rituals of Resistance*, 12.

27. Dundes, "'Jumping the Broom'"; Sullivan "'Jumping the Broom.'" The exceptions to this general trend are articulated more fully in chapter 1, where I analyze the scholarly debates surrounding "irregular marriages" in the British Isles in the nineteenth century.

28. Probert has been arguing these and similar points in a series of articles for many years. For her newest findings, see Probert, *Marriage Law and Practice in the Long Eighteenth Century*. Chapter 1 addresses her many publications more fully.

29. Quisenberry, "Slavery in Kentucky," 1; Cade, "Out of the Mouths of Ex-Slaves," 302–303; Coleman, Jr., *Slavery Times in Kentucky*, 57–58; Morgan, "The Ex-Slave Narrative," 50; Owens, *This Species of Property*, 192; Sobel, *Trabelin' On*, 176–177; Brown, "Sexuality and the Slave Community," 3; Malone, *Sweet Chariot*, 224; Parent, Jr. and Wallace, "Childhood and Sexual Identity Under Slavery," 379–380; Hudson, *To Have and to Hold*, 159; Burton, *In My Father's House are Many Mansions*, 150; Reiss, *Blacks in Colonial America*, 53; Lucas, *A History of Blacks in Kentucky*, 19; Douglas, *Sexuality and the Black Church*, 66; Franke, "Becoming a Citizen," 252, 272; Moneyhon, "The Slave Family in Arkansas," 31–32; Nolen, *African American Southerners*, 22, 40; Schwartz, *Born in Bondage*, 204–205; Dunaway, *The African American Family*, 117–118; Jewett and Allen, *Slavery in the South*, 72, 108; West, *Chains of Love*, 33; Jackson II, *Scripting the Black Masculine Body*, 19; Byron, "'A Catechism for their Special Use,'" 137; Goring, "The History of Slave Marriage in the United States," 309–310; Foster, *'Til Death or Distance Do Us Part*, 91–93; Burke, *On Slavery's Border*, 204; Berry, "Swing the Sickle for the Harvest Is Ripe," 58; and Stevenson, *Life in Black and White*, 228–229. One work Stevenson inspired was Hine and Thompson, *A Shining Thread of Hope*, 80.

30. Many pivotal works in slave studies prior to the 1960s do not mention the custom. This may be due to a combination of unavailability of the narratives housed in the Library of Congress, as well as the fact that slave studies did not fully blossom until after the 1960s. See Philips, *American Negro Slavery*; Herskovits, *The Myth of the Negro Past*; Stampp, *The Peculiar Institution*; Elkins, *Slavery*. A few exceptions to this general trend are by scholars who either used the WPA narratives housed in the Library of Congress or relied on other oral histories that preceded the WPA project. See Cade, "Out of the Mouths of Ex-Slaves"; Coleman, Jr., *Slavery Times in Kentucky*; Taylor, "'Jumping the Broomstick.'"

31. Dawson, "Slave Culture," 467.

32. Reiss, *Blacks in Colonial America*, 53; Lucas, *A History of Blacks in Kentucky*, 19; Coleman, *Slavery Times in Kentucky*, 57–58; West, *Chains of Love*, 33; Foster, *'Til Death or Dis-*

*tance Do Us Part,* 91–93; White and White, *Stylin',* 32; Dunaway, *The African American Family,* 117–118; Douglas, *Sexuality and the Black Church,* 66; Berry, *Swing the Sickle,* 58.

33. Ophelia Egypt Collection, Series E, Box 140-12, Folder 1.

34. Genovese, *Roll, Jordan, Roll,* 480; Joyner, *Shared Traditions,* 52.

35. *American Slave,* vol. 1, *From Sundown to Sunup,* 86.

36. Brewer, "Afro-American Folklore." For the importance of ghostlore as a way to regulate social conduct see Gorn, "Black Spirits," 558–560.

37. Moody-Turner, *Black Folklore,* 7.

38. Morgan and Greene, "Introduction," 8. For other essays in Atlantic history that articulate the debates and controversies within the field see Bailyn, "The Idea of Atlantic History"; Games, "Atlantic History"; Games, *Migration and the English Atlantic World*; Coclanis, "Atlantic World or Atlantic/World?"; Canizares-Esguerra, *Puritan Conquistadors,* 215–233.

39. This book expands on my earlier study that used a smaller sample, but came to the same conclusion regarding how often it was used; see Parry, "Married in Slavery Time," esp. 291–293.

40. For works that argue it was the "main" custom used by slaves, see Raboteau, *Slave Religion,* 228; Hunter, *Bound in Wedlock,* 46, where it is referred to as the "most common" custom.

## Chapter One

1. Jones, "'Besom Wedding,'" 154.

2. Jones, 154

3. Jones, 156.

4. Jones, 153.

5. Jones, 155.

6. Parker, *Informal Marriage,* 67; Howell, *The Rural Poor,* 147; Day and Hook, "A Short History of Divorce"; Menefee, *Wives for Sale*; Outhwaite, *Clandestine Marriage in England,* 140.

7. Probert, "Chinese Whispers and Welsh Weddings"; Probert, *Marriage Law and Practice,* esp. 84–93. It should be noted that Probert does not completely deny that people could have jumped over a broomstick to marry prior to 1850, but her general conclusions speak to the notion that folklore collected in the early twentieth century that recalled early nineteenth-century broomstick weddings was largely due to the faulty memories of the populations that folklorists interviewed. While Probert does refer to African American slaves employing the ritual, she relegates this information to a single footnote and cites only one document, written from a white American's perspective, and Alan Dundes's brief article as authoritative texts; see *Marriage Law and Practice,* 92, fn. 119.

8. The quotation comes in the form of a reference from George Steevens in his commentary on playwright John Poole's parody of Shakespeare's *Hamlet* produced after the Restoration. See Poole, *Hamlet Travestie: In Three Acts with Annotations,* 82.

9. Malone's entry is not found in the original 1810 edition, but was included in later editions of Poole's burlesque rendition of *Hamlet.* See Poole, *Hamlet Travestie: in Three Acts. With Burlesque Annotations,* 94 (emphasis in original).

10. McKelvie, "Proverbial Elements in the Oral Tradition," 253; Myers, "The Black Poor of London," 19.

11. Jones, *Welsh Folklore*," 185. Some publications did suggest its connections to "irregular ceremonies." See, for example, "Beggars' Tricks," *Lancaster Intelligencer*, January 20, 1880, 1.

12. Jones, *Welsh Folklore*, 185.

13. Jones and Jones, *The Mabinogion*, 63; It is important to note that most later translations say "virgin," which validates Gantz, *The Mabinogion*, 106; Davies, *The Mabinogion*, 54.

14. Jones and Jones, *The Mabinogion*, 63.

15. Sullivan, "'Jumping the Broom,'" 20.

16. Probert, *Marriage Law*, 99; Probert, "Chinese Whispers," 211–228.

17. Probert, *Marriage Law*, 91.

18. For literature arguing for the extent of irregular unions, see Leneman and Mitchison, "Clandestine Marriage in the Scottish Cities"; Schellekens, "Courtship, the Clandestine Marriage Act, and Illegitimate Fertility"; Lemmings, "Marriage and the Law"; Bannet, "The Marriage Act of 1753."

19. Probert, "The Impact of the Marriage Act of 1753," 248.

20. Probert, *Marriage Law and Practice*, 92. For a focused study of the broomstick wedding, see Probert, "Chinese Whispers," 211–228. Probert does note that African Americans apparently used the ritual, but relegates the statement to a footnote and does not pursue the reasons they did so.

21. Owen, *Old Stone Crosses of the Vale*, 62–63.

22. Jones, "'Besom Wedding,'" 152, 155.

23. Jones, 159.

24. Maccoitir, *Irish Trees*, 20.

25. Pughe, *A Dictionary of the Welsh Language*, 153.

26. Jarman and Jarman, *The Welsh Gypsies*, 22.

27. Thompson, "The Ceremonial Customs of British Gypsies," 337–338; Jones, "'Besom Wedding,'" 164; Dundes, "Jumping the Broom"; Sullivan, "'Jumping the Broom': A Further Consideration"; Sullivan, "'Jumping the Broom': Possible Welsh Origins."

28. Sampson, *The Dialect of the Gypsies of Wales*, 355.

29. Lyster, "Marriage over the Broomstick," 199.

30. Lyster, 200–201.

31. Lyster, 201.

32. "Odd Customs of British Gypsies," *Breckenridge News*, June 19, 191, 2.

33. Davies, *A History of Wales*, 455.

34. Ashton, *Florizel's Folly*, 91–92.

35. Webb, *Gypsies: The Secret People*, 9.

36. Patten, *England as Seen by an American Banker*, 18.

37. Moorwood, *Our Gypsies*, 141–142.

38. Mayall, *Gypsy Travellers*, 92.

39. Quoted in Levinson and Silk, *Dreams of the Road*, 68.

40. "Odd Customs of British Gypsies." This article was also printed by several other newspapers throughout the month of June: "Odd Customs of the British Gypsies," *Chicago Defender*, June 1, 1912, 8; "Odd Customs of the British Gypsies," *Caldwell Watchman*, June 7, 1912, 4.

41. For descriptions of ceremonies that do not reference jumping the broom, see Simson, *A History of the Gipsies*, 179–180, 252–281.

42. "Gypsy People May Be Lost Tribe of Israel, Evangelist 'Gypsy' Smith Asserts," *The Lexington Herald*, November 21, 1920, 12.

43. "Leap Over Broomstick Is a Wedding Ceremony," *Ludington Daily News*, December 29, 1926.

44. Cooke, "Notes on Irish Folklore from Connaught," 299.

45. Burke, *Tinkers*, 2. See also Helleiner, *Irish Travellers*.

46. MacRitchie, "Irish Tinkers and Their Language," 351.

47. Hayes, "Irish Travellers and Images of Counterculturality," 63. On the same page another correspondent recalls that it might have been rendered "bucket" and claimed that couples jumped over a bucket for marriage.

48. The broomstick wedding's connections to Travellers are reflected in other literature. See Vesey-Fitzgerald, *Gypsies of Britain*, 65; Gardner, *The Meaning of Witchcraft*, 154.

49. Mooney, "The Funeral Customs of Ireland," 279.

50. Mooney, 280.

51. Trumbull, *The Threshold Covenant*, 142–143.

52. Curtin, *Myths and Folklore of Ireland*, 97.

53. As noted in in chapter 2, my data revealed that fifteen formerly enslaved people recalled the joining of hands being a component of the ceremony.

54. Flom, "Sun-Symbols of the Tomb-Sculptures"; O'Flaherty, "A Sketch of the History and Antiquities of the Southern Islands of Aran."

55. Trumbull, *The Threshold Covenant*, 143.

56. MacLeod, "'Jumping Over.'"

57. "Broomstick Marriages," *Journal of the Gypsy Lore Society* 5, no. 3 (1912): 235–236.

58. Dundes, "Jumping the Broom," 327; Roheim, "The Significance of Stepping Over," 16.

59. For an example, see "Is Marriage a Failure?"

60. Mayhew, *London Labour and the London Poor*, 336.

61. Stevenson, *Life in Black and White*, 228; Coleman, *Slavery Times*, 40; Day and Hook, "A Short History of Divorce."

62. St. Romwold, "The Blasphemer's Warning."

63. Dickens, "Narrative of Law and Crime," 40.

64. Dickens, *Great Expectations*, 336.

65. See, for instance, Beggs, *An Inquiry*, 29. More sources are cited below.

66. "New Way of Getting a Husband," *Boston Cultivator*, 10–11.

67. Heckethorn, *The Secret Societies*, 44–45.

68. "New Way of Getting a Husband," *Boston Evening Transcript*, 4; "Leap Year and its Observances," 4.

69. "Scotch Egyptians of the 19th Century," 179.

70. For more references see, Religious Tract Society, *The Sunday Home Family Magazine*, 75; Farmer, ed., *Slang and Its Analogues*, 335; "The Post Captain: or, Wooden Walls Well Manned."

71. See figure A.5: Image 1 "Marrying over the Broomstick." Though this image is now widely available throughout the internet, one of the earliest copies of the document is found at the British Library. It is the third woodcut in the collection *The New Marriage Act*, 7th ed. (London: British Library, 1822), General Reference Collection 1875.d.8 (102).

72. Hindley, *The History of the Catnach Press*.

73. Bell, *Ritual Theory*, 197.

74. Winterbottom, *An Account of the Native Africans*, 144.

75. Parry, "Love and Marriage," chap. 1.

76. For a sweeping history of marriage and its use among elite populations, see Coontz, *Marriage, a History*.

77. Webb, *Gypsies*, 120.

78. Webb, 120.

79. Levinson and Silk, *Dreams of the Road*, 68.

80. Lyster, "Marriage over the Broomstick," 199.

81. Sullivan, "Jumping the Broom: A Further Consideration," 204; Sullivan, "Jumping the Broom: Possible Welsh Origins," 22–23.

82. Knowles "Immigrant Trajectories," 246–266.

83. Lewis, *Welsh Americans*," 17.

84. Knowles, "Immigrant Trajectories," 247.

85. Dodd, *The Character of Early Welsh Emigration*; Fogleman, "Migrations to the Thirteen Colonies," 708–709; Henderson and Olasiji, *Migrants, Immigrants, and Slaves*, 54–55; Johnson, "The Welsh in the Carolinas."

86. Owen, *Welsh Folk Customs*, 142–186; Howells, *Cambrian Traditions*, 167–168; Crooke, "The Lifting of the Bride," 231–232.

87. Dickason, *Mr. Penrose*, 145.

88. The novel was never released during Williams's lifetime, but received its first posthumous publication in 1815, albeit significantly edited. See Williams, *The Journal of Llewellin Penrose*; Eagles, ed., *The Journal of Llewellin Penrose*, 140–141.

89. Dickason, *William Williams*, 20. Scholars studying maritime practices and colonial relations have been apt to view Penrose's account as an autobiographical representation of Williams. See Bolster, *Black Jacks*, 16.

90. The historiographical debate concerning the "African origins" and "creolization" of slaves is extensive. For the seminal works, see Herskovitz, *The Myth*; Mintz and Price, *The Birth of African-American Culture*. For some useful historiographical analyses of slave culture in African American and African Diaspora literature see Dawson, "Slave Culture"; Childs, "Slave Culture."

91. Stevenson, *Life in Black and White*, 228–229; Cott, *Public Vows*, 34–35; Cherlin, *The Marriage-Go-Round*, 45–46.

## Chapter Two

1. "Brooklyn City Court."

2. "Brooklyn City Court."

3. Cade, "Out of the Mouths," 303.

4. Morris, *Southern Slavery and the Law*, 437–438.

5. Brown, *Narrative of William Wells Brown*, 88.

6. Brown, *Clotel*, 57–58.

7. Chakkalakal, *Novel Bondage*, 16.

8. *American Slave*, vol. 18, *Fisk University Narratives*, 195; Lewis Whitmore, *Louisiana Series*, John B. Cade Collection: Opinions Regarding Slavery (digitized) hereafter Cade Digital Collection: ORS.

9. *American Slave*, vol. 15, *North Carolina Narratives*, 195.

10. *American Slave*, vol. 6, *Alabama*, 428. See also *American Slave*, vol. 12, *Georgia*, part 2, 69; *American Slave*, vol. 13, *Georgia*, part 4, 22; *American Slave*, ss 2, vol. 6, *Texas*, 2023; and *American Slave*, ss 2, vol. 8, *Texas*, 3209.

11. Parry, "Married in Slavery Time."

12. *American Slave*, ss 1, vol. 3, *Georgia Narratives*, 251; Hadden, *Slave Patrols*, 59; Hunter, *Bound in Wedlock*, 29–30.

13. Brown, *My Southern Home*, 46.

14. *National Anti-Slavery Standard*, April 8, 1847, 3.

15. Waugh, "Canadian Folklore from Ontario," 29.

16. Carleton, *The Suppressed Book about Slavery*, 215.

17. *American Slave*, vol. 7, *Oklahoma Narratives*, 348.

18. Scholarly literature has not deeply explored this ritual, nor determined its extent throughout the colonial period or the early American Republic. In the modern era news outlets often portray it as a custom practiced by various indigenous groups throughout the United States and Canada. See Marionneaux, "Tradition Woven through Indian Blankets," V4; Tepper, George, and Joseph, *Salish Blankets*, 66–70; Brand, "Hundreds Attend Ma-Chis Pow Wow," 1; Capo, *Wedding Traditions*, 172–174.

19. Perdue, Barden, and Phillips, *Weevils in the Wheat*, 245.

20. Hunter, *Bound in Wedlock*.

21. *American Slave*, vol. 14, *North Carolina Narratives*, part 1, 69; *American Slave*, vol. 6, *Indiana Narratives*, 63.

22. Forret, *Race Relations at the Margins*; McDonnell, "Money Knows No Master." For cross-racial fraternization among Southern whites and free people of color see Mills, "Shades of Ambiguity."

23. Morgan, "The Significance of Kin," 333; Wright, *African Americans in the Colonial Era*, 141.

24. Reiss, *Blacks in Colonial America*, 53.

25. Handler, "*The Old Plantation*," painting, 6. Scholars who have made this mistake include Melville Herskovitz (cited by Handler on p. 6), as well as Young, "Brooms," 83, and Isaac, *The Transformation of Virginia*, 420. This idea was even reported in a newspaper: Harris, "Africans in America," 01B.

26. Lawal, "Reclaiming the Past."

27. For a further explanation of this absence, see Wood, *Slavery in Colonial America*, 43–44.

28. Brickell, *The Natural History of North Carolina*, 274.

29. Bancroft, *Slave Trading in the Old South*; Johnson, *Soul by Soul*; Deyle, *Carry Me Back*.

30. Tadman, *Speculators and Slave*; Baptist, *The Half Has Never Been Told*.

31. Michel Martin, interview with Tera Hunter, *NPR New Discoveries in Black History* (podcast), February 11, 2010, https://www.npr.org/templates/story/story.php?storyId=123608207.

32. Curry, "The Narrative of James Curry."

33. *American Slave*, vol. 4, *Texas Narratives*, part 1, 28.

34. *American Slave*, vol. 3, *South Carolina Narratives*, 9.

35. Johnson, *Soul by Soul*, 215.

36. The collections used in this research sample include John B. Cade Slave Narratives collection, currently available online through Southern University at http://star.lib.subr

.edu/starweb/l.skca-catalog/servlet.starweb, as well as those obtained by employees of the Works Progress Administration found in *The American Slave* series edited by George P. Rawick, alongside edited collections from Virginia (Perdue, Barden, and Phillips, *Weevils in the Wheat*) and Louisiana (Clayton, *Mother Wit*). For an overview of the sample found in the WPA and edited collections see Parry, "Married in Slavery Time."

37. O'Neil, "Tying the Knots," 216. The total is complicated by the fact that some interviews are now lost and only exist as citations from their original authors. This is especially true of the interviews collected by John B. Cade, who initiated one of the earliest efforts to document slave life and culture among formerly enslaved people still alive.

38. O'Neil, "Tying the Knots," 216. Patrick O'Neal Suggests the phrases such as "had them jump" reveal coercion. See "Tying the Knots," 346, and O'Neil, "Bosses and Broomsticks," 43–44, fn. 21.

39. *American Slave*, vol. 2, *South Carolina Narratives*, part 1, 323. Patrick O'Neil suggests that the phrase "had them jump," alongside similar references, reveals coercion. See O'Neil, "Tying the Knots," 346, and O'Neil, "Bosses and Broomsticks," 43–44, fn. 21.

40. That "jack-leg" means "bogus" was discovered through research in black communities throughout Chicago by anthropologist John Langston Gwaltney; see his *Drylongso*, xvi.

41. *American Slave*, vol. 6, *Alabama Narratives*, 428. O'Neil, "Tying the Knots," 346, contends that the words "told" or "tell" suggest coercion.

42. For a full list of these narratives see O'Neil, "Tying the Knots," 343–347. In one example, George Taylor of Mobile, Alabama, stated "De way us married would be to go to de big house, an' ol' Marster had us to jump over a broom stick, and den us was considered married" (*American Slave*, vol. 6, *Alabama Narratives*, 372). In Jeff Calhoun's narrative the master performs the ceremony, but slaves could call off the wedding if they were unsure they wanted to marry. This action suggests that slaves could, in certain instances, make decisions within the ceremony, without worrying about wasting the master's time; see *American Slave* vol. 4, *Texas Narratives*, part 1, 189. The testimony of Lula Washington is also rather brief and does not express much coercion (*American Slave*, vol. 13, *Georgia Narratives*, part 4, 135). See also *American Slave*, vol. 12, *Georgia Narratives*, part 2, 261; *American Slave*, vol. 16, *Kentucky Narratives*, 33.

43. Schwartz, *Born in Bondage*, 204; "Raggedy Thorns," unpublished manuscript, Ophelia Egypt Collection, Series E, Box 140-13, Folder 2.

44. *American Slave*, vol. 17, *Florida Narratives*, 128.

45. The following narratives include coercive language in which slaves were "made," "commanded," or "told." I have also included references to narratives that display language that is particularly degrading, as well as situations in which the master appeared to forcibly insert himself into the ceremony. While I contend that problems arise in detailing coercive language within folk memory, these references are provided for the reader's further perusal. *The American Slave*, vol. 4, *Texas Narratives*, part 1, 152; *The American Slave*, vol. 8, *Arkansas Narratives*, part 2, 246; *American Slave*, vol. 9, *Arkansas Narratives*, part 3, 39; *American Slave*, vol. 11, *Arkansas Narratives*, 110, 198; *American Slave*, 12, *Georgia Narratives*, part 1, 307, and part 2, 276; *American Slave*, vol. 13, *Georgia Narratives*, part 3, 77, and part 4, 189–190; *American Slave*, vol. 15, *North Carolina Narratives*, 434–435; *American Slave*, vol. 16, *Virginia Narratives*, 13; *American Slave*, ss 1, vol. 6, *Mississippi Narratives*, 104, 154; *American Slave*, ss 1, vol. 7, *Mississippi Narratives*, 595; *American Slave*, ss 1, vol. 9, *Mississippi Narratives*, 1399–1400;

*American Slave,* ss 2, vol. 2, *Texas Narratives,* 281; *American Slave,* ss 2, vol. 7, *Texas Narratives,* 2587. See also Clayton, ed., *Mother Wit,* 108.

46. *American Slave,* vol. 13, *Georgia Narratives,* part 3, 16.

47. *American Slave,* vol. 12, *Georgia Narratives,* 207. See also Coleman, *Slavery Times,* 57.

48. *American Slave,* ss 2, vol. 3, *Texas Narratives,* part 2, 776.

49. For an early catalogue and explanation of this data, see Parry, "Married in Slavery Time," 306, fn. 2. My calculations include references to the master actually officiating the ceremony or giving some type of instruction, as well as moments when enslaved people claimed a white preacher performed the service, which I contend was most likely at the behest of the master.

50. *American Slave,* vol. 4, *Texas Narratives,* part 1, 46.

51. *American Slave,* vol. 8, *Arkansas Narratives,* part 1, 69. See also *American Slave,* vol. 13, *Georgia Narratives,* part 3, 77.

52. *American Slave,* vol. 4, *Texas Narratives,* part 1, 218.

53. *American Slave,* vol. 11, *Arkansas Narratives,* part 7, 198.

54. This quote stems from an essay published on the Library of Congress website, which gives a substantial overview of the WPA collections. The quote is found in the subsection "The Limitations of the Slave Narrative Collection," within the larger essay "An Introduction to the WPA Slave Narratives," accessed 25 May, 2020, https://www.loc.gov /collections/slave-narratives-from-the-federal-writers-project-1936-to-1938/articles-and -essays/introduction-to-the-wpa-slave-narratives/limitations-of-the-slave-narrative -collection/.

55. *American Slave,* vol. 6, *Mississippi Narratives,* 179.

56. *American Slave,* ss 1, vol. 5:5, *Indiana and Ohio Narratives,* 13.

57. Quoted in Brown, *Foul Bodies,* 351.

58. *American Slave,* vol. 7, *Mississippi Narratives,* part 2, 36.

59. Fett, *Working Cures;* Schwartz, *Birthing a Slave;* Dawson, *Undercurrents of Power;* Glave, *Rooted in the Earth.*

60. Douglass, *Narrative of the Life of Frederick Douglass,* 74.

61. *American Slave,* vol. 7, *Oklahoma Narratives,* 103.

62. Reference to the "sage broom" appears in *American Slave,* vol. 8, *Arkansas Narratives,* part 2, 242.

63. *American Slave,* vol. 9, *Arkansas Narratives,* part 4, 229.

64. Henery Hickmon, Missouri Narratives, Cade Digital Collection, ORS.

65. *American Slave,* ss 1, vol. 1, *Alabama Narratives,* 425.

66. Young, "Brooms," 81; *American Slave,* vol. 4, *Texas Narratives,* part 2, 223; *American Slave,* vol. 7, *Mississippi Narratives,* part 2, 36.

67. *American Slave,* vol. 9, *Arkansas Narratives,* part 4, 229.

68. *American Slave,* vol. 13, *Georgia Narratives,* part 4, 84–85.; "L. J. Evans," quoted in Cade, "Out of the Mouths of Ex-Slaves," 303.

69. *American Slave,* vol. 10, *Arkansas Narratives,* part 6, 125.

70. *American Slave,* vol. 9, *Arkansas Narratives,* part 4, 229.

71. *American Slave,* vol. 11, *Arkansas Narratives,* part 7, 177.

72. *American Slave,* vol. 8, *Arkansas Narratives,* part 2, 242.

73. Young, "Brooms," 81.

74. A more recent explanation of dirt floor installation comes from Gelles, "Down and Dirty," F1.

75. Pargas, *Slavery and Forced Migration*, 181–182; Dunaway, *The African American Family*, 89–90.

76. Young, "Brooms," 82.

77. *American Slave*, vol. 7, *Oklahoma Narratives*, 359. See also *American Slave*, vol. 11, *Arkansas Narratives*, part 7, 177; *American Slave*, vol. 7, *Mississippi Narratives*, part 2, 36.

78. Baquaqua, *Biography of Mahommah G. Baquaqua*, 50.

79. *American Slave*, vol. 7, *Oklahoma Narratives*, 161.

80. Green, *Ferry Hill Plantation Journal*, xx.

81. Baptist, *The Half Has Never Been Told*.

82. *American Slave*, vol. 6, *Alabama Narratives*, 317.

83. *American Slave*, vol. 7, *Mississippi Narratives*, part 2, 86.

84. Genie Gordon, Mississippi Series, Cade Digital Collection, ORS.

85. *American Slave*, vol. 8, *Arkansas Narratives*, part 2, 76.

86. Ellis and Ginsburg, "Introduction," 5.

87. *American Slave*, vol. 13, *Georgia Narratives*, part 3, 206.

88. *American Slave*, ss 1, vol. 1, *Alabama Narratives*, 425.

89. *American Slave*, vol. 13, *Georgia Narratives*, part 3, 74. See also *American Slave*, vol. 8, *Arkansas Narratives*, part 2, 246.

90. Kaye, *Joining Places*; Blassingame, *The Slave Community*; Genovese, *Roll, Jordan, Roll*.

91. *American Slave*, vol. 7, *Oklahoma Narratives*, 207.

92. *American Slave*, vol. 18, *Unwritten History of Slavery*, 78.

93. Fisher, *The Master's Slave*, 5.

94. Salam, *Till Talaq Do Us Part*.

95. Parry, "Married in Slavery Time," 292–294.

96. Robinson, *From Log Cabin to the Pulpit*, 152.

97. Parry, "White Southern Memories."

98. Burton, *Memories of Childhood's Slavery Days*, 5.

99. *American Slave*, vol. 12, *Georgia Narratives*, part 2, 175–176.

100. *American Slave*, vol. 13, *Georgia Narratives*, part 4, 189–190.

101. *American Slave*, vol. 12, *Georgia Narratives*, part 1, 67, 101, 307; *American Slave*, vol. 13, *Georgia Narratives*, part 3, 16.

102. Steiner, "Superstitions and Beliefs from Central Georgia," 263.

103. *American Slave*, vol. 4, *Texas Narratives*, part 1, 293.

104. "Is over a Century and a Quarter Old," 11.

105. *American Slave*, vol. 12, *Georgia Narratives*, part 1, 207.

106. Twenty-eight slaves out of the 145 respondents claimed that this was the way the ritual was performed. The number is significant, given that many of the responses do not give much detail about the ritual performance.

107. *American Slave*, ss 1, vol. 8, *Mississippi Narratives*, part 3, 1307.

108. Perdue, Barden, and Phillips, *Weevils in the Wheat*, 129.

109. Gaspar and Hine, *More than Chattel*; Morgan, *Laboring Women*; Glymph, *Out of the House of Bondage*.

110. *American Slave*, ss 2, vol. 6, *Texas Narratives*, part 5, 2048.

111. *American Slave*, ss 2, vol. 10, *Texas Narratives*, part 9, 4106.

112. Steiner, "Superstitions," 261.

113. Perdue, Barden, and Phillips, *Weevils in the Wheat*, 129.

114. Perdue, Barden, and Phillips, 134.

115. *American Slave*, vol. 2, *South Carolina Narratives*, part 1, 323.

116. *American Slave*, vol. 14, *North Carolina Narratives*, part 1, 287.

117. For more on the position of elders in slave communities see Close, *Elderly Slaves of the Plantation South*.

118. Livermore, *The Story of My Life*, 255.

119. Livermore, 255–256.

120. Livermore, 256.

121. *American Slave*, vol. 4, *Texas Narratives*, part 2, 23.

122. *American Slave*, vol. 12, *Georgia Narratives*, part 2, 175.

123. *American Slave*, ss 1, vol. 7, *Mississippi Narratives*, part 2, 87.

124. Puckett, *Folk Beliefs*, 156.

125. Puckett, 156.

126. Cora Armstrong quoted in *American Slave* vol. 8, *Arkansas Narratives*, part 1, 75. Betty Chessier quoted in *American Slave*, vol. 7, *Oklahoma and Mississippi Narratives*, 32.

127. *American Slave*, vol. 3, *South Carolina Narratives*, part 4, 147.

128. *American Slave*, vol. 3, *South Carolina Narratives*, part 4, 148.

129. Brown, *The Escape*, 26. See also Brown, *My Southern Home*, 42–46.

130. Pearson [Pocahontas, pseud.], *Cousin Franck's Household*, 170.

131. *American Slave*, vol. 12, *Georgia Narratives*, part 1, 101.

132. Livermore, *The Story of My Life*, 256.

133. *American Slave*, vol. 6, *Alabama Narratives*, 257.

134. *American Slave*, vol. 6, *Alabama Narratives*, 372.

135. *American Slave*, vol. 11, *Arkansas Narratives*, part 7, 198.

136. Perdue, Barden, and Phillips, *Weevils in the Wheat*, 122.

137. Berlin, *The Making of African American*, intro.

138. Summers-Effler, "Ritual Theory," 134.

139. See chapter 3 of this book for further explanation of this methodological issue.

*Chapter Three*

1. Black Federal Writer's Program, Collection No. 547, Respondent: Mary Harris.

2. *American Slave*, vol. 13, *Georgia Narratives*, part 4, 84.

3. *American Slave*, vol. 13, *Georgia Narratives*, part 4, 84–85.

4. *American Slave*, vol. 2, *South Carolina Narratives*, part 1, 185.

5. "The Freedmen's Bureau Issues Marriage Orders," 61.

6. See Blackmon, *Slavery by Another Name*, 13–38.

7. *American Slave*, vol. 18, *Unwritten History of Slavery*, 124.

8. Randolph, *From Slave Cabin to Pulpit*, 89–91.

9. Williams, *Help Me to Find My People*.

10. Schwartzberg, "'Lots of Them Did That,'" 574.

11. Du Bois, *The Negro American Family*, 27.

12. Hunter, *Bound in Wedlock*, 269.

13. Driskell, *Schooling Jim Crow*, 50.

14. "Good Move."

15. "Parents May Object Due to Lucy's Youth," 6. Another couple with nearly identical names was also reported to have been married at the same time. It is likely that this is the same couple. See "Negro Married Same Woman Nearly Fifty Eight Years Ago," 1.

16. "A Broomstick Marriage," 2.

17. Baker, *Homeless, Friendless, and Penniless*, 186.

18. *American Slave*, vol. 13, *Georgia Narratives*, part 4, 268.

19. "A Happy Couple," 1.

20. "Scholarly Papers."

21. In one 1907 account a Richmond minister consented to perform the marriage ceremony for a black couple, "knowing what prestige would come to the couple by reason of having been married by a white minister." See "Just as He Was," 1211.

22. The testimony of Bongy Jackson is quoted in Saxon, Dreyer, and Tallant, *Gumbo Ya-Ya*, 239.

23. "Shanties on the Capital," 6.

24. *American Slave*, vol. 6, *Mississippi Narratives*, 154.

25. Lewis, "The Life of Mark Thrash," 396.

26. *The American Slave*, vol. 6, *Mississippi Narratives*, 104.

27. *American Slave*, ss 1, vol. 3, *Georgia Narratives*, 273. See also *American Slave*, ss 2, vol. 6, *Texas Narratives*, 2007; *American Slave*, ss 2, vol. 8, *Texas Narratives*, 3232; *American Slave*, vol. 6, *Alabama Narratives*, 307, 344; *American Slave*, vol. 10, *Arkansas Narratives*, part 6, 83; *The American Slave*, vol. 11, *Arkansas Narratives*, part 7, 157; Perdue, Barden, and Phillips, *Weevils in the Wheat*, 89.

28. *American Slave*, vol. 13, *Georgia Narratives*, part 4, 216, 268; *American Slave*, vol. 16, *Kentucky Narratives*, 104.

29. For analyses that detail African Americans dealings with the Freedmen's Bureau both during and after the Civil War see Finley, *From Slavery to Uncertain Freedom*; Farmer-Kaiser, *Freedwomen and the Freedmen's Bureau*; Berlin and Rowland, *Families and Freedom*.

30. *Morning Olympian*, October 7, 1915, 2.

31. *Aberdeen Daily American*, May 10, 1917, 4.

32. *American Slave*, vol. 18, *Unwritten History of Slavery*, 124.

33. "Grand National Celebration."

34. *American Slave*, vol. 13, *Georgia Narratives*, part 4, 22.

35. *American Slave*, vol. 6, *Alabama Narratives*, 428. For similar references of how marriage meant more to slaves than to African Americans in the early twentieth century, see *American Slave*, vol. 12, *Georgia Narratives*, part 2, 69; *American Slave*, vol. 13, *Georgia Narratives*, part 4, 22; *American Slave*, ss 2, vol. 6, *Texas Narratives*, part 5, 2023; *American Slave*, ss 2, vol. 8, *Texas Narratives*, part 7, 3209. British Romani reflected similar sentiments when interviewed in 1910. See Lyster, "Marriage over the Broomstick," 199.

36. "The Orator of the Day," 1.

37. *American Slave*, vol. 9, *Arkansas Narratives*, part 4, 102. See also *American Slave*, vol. 6, *Alabama Narratives*, 346; *American Slave*, vol. 7, *Oklahoma Narratives*, 231; *American Slave*, vol. 8, *Arkansas Narratives*, part 2, 128; *American Slave*, vol. 13, *Georgia Narratives*, part 3, 125.

Some interviewees like Columbus Williams of Arkansas had heard of it happening, but had never actually seen it. See *American Slave*, vol. 11, *Arkansas Narratives*, part 7, 157.

38. *American Slave*, vol. 15, *North Carolina Narratives*, part 2, 195.

39. *American Slave*, ss 2, vol. 8, *Texas Narratives*, part 7, 3232. See also *American Slave*, vol. 10, *Arkansas Narrative*, part 6, 83; *American Slave*, vol. 6, *Alabama Narratives*, 307.

40. For other instances of marriage and embarrassment associated with slavery and broom-jumping, see *American Slave*, vol. 7, *Oklahoma Narratives*, 231, 295.

41. King, "Antebellum Negress Makes Plea Against War," 26.

42. *American Slave*, vol. 7, *Oklahoma Narratives*, 231.

43. Dunbar, "Aunt Tempy's Triumph."

44. *American Slave*, ss 2, vol. 9, *Texas Narratives*, part 8, 3406.

45. *American Slave*, ss 1, vol. 4, *Georgia Narratives*, part 2, 548. See also *American Slave*, ss 2, vol. 6, *Texas Narratives*, part 5, 2007; *American Slave*, vol. 9, *Arkansas Narratives*, part 4, 26.

46. *American Slave*, vol. 7, *Arkansas Narrative*, part 7, 110.

47. For similar thoughts on this process, see "Raggedy Thorns," unpublished manuscript, Ophelia Egypt Collection, Series E, Box 140-13, Folder 2.

48. For scholarship that questions the authenticity of the custom, see Blassingame, *The Slave Community*, 167; King, *Stolen Childhood*, 63; Kaye, *Joining Places*, 253 fn. 81.

49. Quoted in Foster, *'Til Death or Distance Do Us Part*, 90.

50. Foster, 91.

51. "Raggedy Thorns."

52. Montell, "A Folk History," 323.

53. Montell, 326.

54. *American Slave*, vol. 13, *Georgia Narratives*, part 3, 204.

55. *American Slave*, ss 1, vol. 7, *Mississippi Narratives*, part 2, 784.

56. "Plot Thickens in NFL Camps," 2.

57. *American Slave*, vol. 3, *South Carolina Narratives*, part 3, 30.

58. *American Slave*, vol. 3, *South Carolina Narratives*, part 3, 30.

59. Wangdangdula, "Alvin Gaines and the Themes- Let's Jump the Broomstick," YouTube video.

60. Dunak, "Ceremony and Citizenship," 406.

61. Dunak, 404–406, 413.

*Chapter Four*

1. "American Republican Demonstration," 5.

2. "Who Is It?"

3. Powell, "What's Love Got to Do with It?," chap. 5; Guyatt, *Bind Us Apart*, 175–182.

4. West, *Chains of Love*, 33.

5. Parry, "White Southern Memories," 305–307.

6. A. Burwell to Fanny K. Burwell, August, 1830, Box 1, Folder 2, Burwell-Catlett Papers, 1794–1887.

7. Jolliffe, *Chattanooga*, 56.

8. Stuart, *Moriah's Mourning*, 79–84.

9. "Odd Marriages," *Michigan Farmer*, August 21, 1883, 14, 34.

10. "Grand National Celebration of the 27th Anniversary of the Emancipation Proclamation."

11. *Daily Globe,* May 12, 1878.

12. "Who Is It?"

13. "Evidently Somewhat Annoyed," 2. Another reference to it as a "southern ceremony" appears in "Jumped Broomstick—Married," 2.

14. Fitzhugh, *Sociology for the South,* 216.

15. Whittlesey, *Bertha the Beauty,* 105.

16. "Marriage and Divorce," 4.

17. "From Gypsy Lore," 5.

18. "Hobson's Choice," 635; "Ft. Scott News," 4.

19. Simpson, *Horrors of the Virginia Slave Trade,* 28.

20. Pearson, *Cousin Francks.*

21. Pearson, 169.

22. Glymph, *Out of the House of Bondage;* Forret, *Slave against Slave.*

23. Glymph, *Out of the House of Bondage;* Jones-Rogers, *They Were Her Property.*

24. Southern and Wright, *Images,* 161.

25. Livermore, *The Story of My Life,* 256.

26. Livermore, 256.

27. Livermore, 256.

28. Toll, *Blacking Up,* 93; Birdoff, *The World's Greatest Hit;* Toll, "From Folktype to Stereotype," 41.

29. *Pop Goes the Weasel Songster,* 12–13.

30. Meer, *Uncle Tom Mania,* 64; Frick, *Uncle Tom's Cabin,* 109.

31. Collins, *Legends,* 5.

32. Caroline Ann "Meta" Morris Grimball, *Journal of Meta Morris Grimball,* 95.

33. Grimball, 95.

34. "Simplifiers; Jumping; Ceremony," 5.

35. Greeley, *Recollections,* 581.

36. *Proceedings of the American Philosophical Society,* 280; Hart, "Toot Makes a Match," 68.

37. Cabell, *Jurgen,* 274.

38. Caruthers, *The Knights of the Horse-Shoe,* 208.

39. Merrick, *Old Times in Dixieland,* 95–96.

40. Merrick, 95

41. Merrick, 96, 97.

42. Sawyer, *A Local Habitation,* 290.

43. "Married in a Jest," 179.

44. "Married in a Jest," 179.

## Chapter Five

1. Foster, "Broomstick Wedding."

2. At times, both populations are mentioned, as in the entry by Lipson-Walker, "Weddings," 493. In other collections, however, one or the other is more typical: Tallman, *Dictionary of American Folklore,* 164–165; Cody, "Marriage," 437.

3. "Gathered News Fragments," 21, 17.

4. Hyatt, *Folklore from Adams County*, 371.

5. Hyatt, 516.

6. *American Slave*, vol. 5, *Texas Narratives*, part 3, 244. For a description of how one enslaved person viewed the broomstick in the supernatural realm, see: *American Slave*, vol. 8, *Arkansas Narratives*, part 2, 76.

7. Hyatt, *Folklore from Adams County*, 527.

8. Hall, "Witchlore and Ghostlore," 91–92.

9. "Douglas Society," 3.

10. "A Polish Witch in Detroit," 1.

11. *American Slave*, vol. 18, *Unwritten History of Slavery*, 234.

12. *American Slave*, vol. 19, *God Struck Me Dead*, 121.

13. Censer, *North Carolina Planters*, 66; Cecil-Fronsman, *Common Whites*, 141.

14. Fischer, *Albion's Seed*, 282.

15. Morgan, *Slave Counterpoint*, 531; Morgan, "The Significance of Kin," 333.

16. For a selection of important missionary writings in colonial South Carolina, see Klingberg, *An Appraisal of the Negro*; Klingberg, *The Carolina Chronicle of Dr. Francis Le Jau*; Klingberg, *Carolina Chronicle: The Papers of Commissary Gideon Johnston*; Hooker, *The Carolina Backcountry*.

17. "Hobson's Choice," 3.

18. Quotations in Hall, *Sayings from Old Smoky*, 45.

19. Cross, "Folk-Lore from the Southern States," 254.

20. See Brown, *My Southern Home*, 70–82. In *Recreating Africa* James Sweet has argued that in Brazil many whites both believed and feared enslaved divination and West-Central African folkloric patterns.

21. Gutman, *The Black Family*, 277.

22. "Marriage a la Mode Americaine," 789; "Is Marriage a Failure?"

23. Aunt Fanny, "Aunt Fanny's First Marriage," 30–31.

24. Aunt Fanny, 34.

25. "Our Young Folks," E 991.

26. Thompson, *Essays*, 91.

27. Thompson, 92. Also see Allison, "Folk Beliefs Collected in Southeastern Illinois," 316–317; Williamson, "Superstitions from Louisiana," 230; Price, "Kentucky Folk-Lore," 34; Roberts, "Louisiana Superstitions," 172–173; Wiltse, "Some Mountain Superstitions of the South," 132; Parker, "Folk-Lore of the North Carolina Mountaineers," 245.

28. Hall, "Witchlore and Ghostlore," 91–92

29. Price, "Kentucky Folk-Lore," 34; Parker, "Folk-Lore of the North Carolina Mountaineers," 245.

30. Yarnell, *The Southern Appalachians*, 9.

31. Stoll, *Ramp Hollow*, 4.

32. The references to broomstick weddings are often found in Kentucky folk speech, but the expression is found throughout the United States as well. For Kentucky references, see *Kentucky Alumnus* 7 (October 1915): 45; Stuart, "Jumping the Broom," 26–28, 44; Tidwell, "Comments on Word-Lists in *PADS*," 16. For the notion of Kentucky as a "pan-Appalachian" region, see Williams, *Appalachia*, 117.

33. "Divorces in Kentucky," *New York Evangelist*, March 9, 1848, 39.

34. "The Republican Saint's Broom-Jumping Kentucky Marriage," 2.

35. Kelly, *Kildares of Storm*, 213.

36. Thomas, *Devil's Ditties*, 8.

37. An important group of graduate student folklorists at Laval University were pivotal in gathering large amounts of data on Cajun traditions in the early to mid-twentieth century, inspired by the pioneering work of Fortier's *Louisiana Folk Tales: In French Dialect and English Translation*. See Saucier, "Historie et traditions"; Brandon, "Moeurs et langue."

38. Rush, *The Cajuns*, 21–58.

39. Debien, "The Acadians in Santo Domingo"; Lowe, "Massachusetts and the Acadians"; Hamer, "The Fate of the Exiled Acadians"; Hudnut and Baker-Crothers, "Acadian Transients in South Carolina."

40. Arsenault, *History of the Acadians*, 189.

41. Brasseaux, *The Founding of New Acadia*, 7; Hall, *Africans in Colonial Louisiana*, 277.

42. For further explanation see Brasseaux, *The Founding of New Acadia*.

43. Hannay, *The History of Acadia*, 297.

44. Hannay, 297.

45. For explorations of sexual contact and social order, see Spear, "'They Need Wives'"; Usner, *Indians, Settlers, and Slaves*.

46. Courlander, *Negro Folk Music*, 164.

47. Brasseuax, *From Acadian to Cajun*, 8–9.

48. I briefly argue this case in Parry, "An Irregular Union," 122–123.

49. Brasseaux, *From Acadian to Cajun*, 7.

50. Brandon, "The Socio-Cultural Traits of the French Folksong," 30.

51. Ballowe, *Creole Folk Tales*, 160.

52. Ballowe, 163.

53. Ballowe, 164.

54. Ballowe, 164.

55. Brasseaux, *French, Cajun, Creole, Houma*, 37–84.

56. The phrase enters French publications in the late eighteenth century, but Probert rejects that it was ever practiced in France; see *Marriage Law and Practice*, 91.

57. Botkin, *A Treasury of Southern Folklore*, 65; Kane, *The Bayous of Louisiana*, 304. Scholars suggest that after World War II either that these types of rituals were forced out of these communities or that greater acceptance into American culture caused them to be downplayed. See Post, *Cajun Sketches*, 146–151; Ancelet, Edwards, and Pitre, *Cajun Country*, 51–52; Collard, "The Cajun Family."

58. Ramsey, *Cajuns*, 35.

59. Ramsey, 52.

60. Ramsey, 52.

61. The statement reflects similar sentiments from British Romani and enslaved people. For references to the enslaved, see *American Slave*, vol. 6, *Alabama Narratives*, 428; *American Slave*, vol. 12, *Georgia Narratives*, part 2, 69; *American Slave*, vol. 13, *Georgia Narratives*, part 4, 22; *The American Slave*, ss 2, vol. 6, *Texas Narratives*, part 5, 2023; *American Slave*, ss 2, vol. 8, *Texas Narratives*, part 7, 3209.

62. Johnson, *Roaring Camp*, 57.

63. Flower, *The Eye of the Northwest*, 73.

64. Allison, "Folk Beliefs Collected in Southeastern Illinois," 317.

65. "Wedding Anniversary," 1.

66. "Judge Hastings the Nicest Lover in the World," 14.

67. "Gypsy Riot Follows Broomstick Wedding," 13.

68. "Gypsy Riot."

69. "Gypsies Quarrel Over Girl Queen," 7.

70. "Gypsies Fight Fierce Battle," 5.

71. "Old Time Divorce in Colorado," 3.

72. "Old Time Divorce," 3.

73. "Brother Turner."

74. Hand, "American Folklore after Seventy Years," 9.

75. "Missouri Notes," 6.

76. Arloa McCormick to Julia Bullard Phillips, January 19, 1862, in Denny, "Private Correspondents" 206.

77. While Lee's song was popular in the United States, "Let's Jump the Broomstick" reached number 12 in the UK charts, making its impact in Britain more potent than within the US. For information on this song and her career see, Brenda Lee and Oermann, *Little Miss Dynamite*, 37, 75, 164, 173, 246, 288.

78. Capote, *House of Flowers*, 24–27.

79. Quoted in Hall, *Sayings from Old Smoky*, 45.

80. Examples of obvious figurative use are found in the following: "Queer Tricks of Beggars"; "Inmates of Soldiers' Home Leave to Attend State Reunion at Tupelo," 1; "Missouri Notes," 6; "St. Mary's Cullings," 2; "Beevities," 3; "Jumping the Broomstick," 4.

81. Amelia Earhart, *Garden of Praise*, accessed February 10, 2012, http://gardenofpraise.com/ibdearha.htm.

## Chapter Six

1. Haley, *Roots*, 310.

2. Haley, 325.

3. Fairchild, Stockard, and Bowman, "Impact of Roots"; Tucker and Shah, "Race and the Transformation of Culture"; Ball-Rokeach, Grube, and Rokeach, "Roots: The Next Generation"; Protinsky and Wildman, "Roots: Reflections."

4. Cole, *Jumping the Broom*, 10; Otnes and Pleck, *Cinderella Dreams*, 248; Jackson, "Reclaiming Roots," 4E; Oswald, *Lesbian Rites*, 62; Anosike, "Africa and Afro-Americans," 435.

5. Interview with Miss Ruby Magee: A Native Mississippian, May 18, 1972, http://digilib.usm.edu/cdm/compoundobject/collection/coh/id/4847/rec/1.

6. The quotation is from Stampp, *The Peculiar Institution*, 340. Other works in the historiographical canon that became notorious for these associations include Philips, *American Negro Slavery*; Elkins, *Slavery*.

7. Holland, "A Black Woman's Soliloquy," 22.

8. Morgan, "On Black Image and Blackness," 26.

9. Morgan, "The Ex-Slave Narrative," 50.

10. Jones, "A Cultural Middle Passage"; Blassingame, *The Slave Community*.

11. Jackson, "Reincarnation." The poem was originally published in 1969 and reprinted by *Black World*.

12. Quoted in Van Deburg, *Slavery and Race in American Popular Culture*, 132.

13. For the exclusion of African Americans from "American" public history, see Horton and Horton, *Slavery and Public History*.

14. Majors, "Society World: Cocktail Chitchat."

15. Bennett, "The World of the Slave," 52.

16. Bennett, *Before the Mayflower*.

17. Brown, "The Black Press Remembers 'Before the Mayflower' Author."

18. "Weekly Almanac," 46.

19. The letter written by William C. Henderson was published in the "Letters to the Editor" section of *Ebony*, April, 1971, 16.

20. Bennett, "The Roots of Black Love" (reprinted in February 1996 [p. 53] and sections reappeared in the June 2003 issue entitled "7 Biggest Lies About Blacks & Love & Sex"). Criticisms of the black family in slavery and freedom have a long historiographical tradition. For some of the more notorious works, see Frazier, *The Negro Family in the United States*; Stampp, *The Peculiar Institution*; Elkins, *Slavery*; Moynihan, *The Negro Family*.

21. Hunter, "Charity Mae Wallace Turns 105," A3.

22. Quoted in Martin, "Slave Spirituals on the Mall." The article was attached as an appendix to Barron, "Singing for the Ancestors," 108.

23. Beuford, "A Conversation with Earnest J. Gaines," 16; O'Brien, *Interviews with Black Writers*, 82; Laney, "A Conversation with Earnest J. Gaines"; Ferris, "A Conversation with Ernest Gaines"; Van Deburg, *Slavery and Race*, 144.

24. Klotman, "'Oh Freedom,'" 142.

25. Walker, "Willing to Pay the Price," 121.

26. Whitlow, *Black American Literature*, 136.

27. Walker, "How I Wrote Jubilee," 51.

28. Walker, Journal 22, 6, Margaret Walker Personal Papers, Digital Archives Project at Jackson State University (hereafter cited as MWPP-JSU). Digitized photocopies of Walker's journal are available at http://margaretwalker.jsums.edu.

29. Walker, "How I Wrote Jubilee," 62.

30. Klotman, "Oh Freedom," 141.

31. For Walker's own words, see Egejuru and Fox, "An Interview with Margaret Walker," 29; Freibert and Walker, "Southern Song."

32. Walker, "How I Wrote Jubilee," 65.

33. Walker, 62.

34. Walker, *Jubilee*, 143.

35. Walker, 141.

36. For an illustration of this absence, see Carmichael, *Trumpeting a Fiery Sound*, esp. 62; Graham, *Fields Watered with Blood*, esp. 48; Graham, *Conversations with Margaret Walker*.

37. It should be noted that Walker listed the books she read about slavery in the Old South, and none of them mentions this form of slave marriage. The books are Phillips, *American Negro Slavery*; Dodd, *The Cotton Kingdom*; Eaton, *A History of the Old South*; Olmstead, *A Journey in the Seaboard Slave States*; Kemble, *Journal of a Residence*.

38. Walker, *Jubilee*, 141.

39. Haley, *Roots*, 325.

40. Haley, 328.

41. Haley, 505.

42. Haley, 506.

43. Haley, 508.

44. Haley, 546. In another section, Tom, great-grandson of Kunta Kinte, notes that he approves of Amos, the "young man who appeared to be, at last, his sister's choice to jump the broom with" (Haley, 604).

45. Haley, 599.

46. Haley, 769.

47. Drafts-Early White, Box 23, Folder 14, AHP-UTLK.

48. Haley, *Roots*, 769.

49. Drafts-Early White, Box 23, Folder 14, AHP-UTLK.

50. For archival resources containing brief notes on the marriages of Kunta Kinte, Chicken George, and Tom, see Revisions and Notes about Specific Pages, Box 28, Folder 7. AHP-UTKL.

51. "Best Seller List," *New York Times*, 254; "Best Seller List," *New York Times*; McFadden, "Alex Haley Denies Allegation," 4; Gerber, "Haley's *Roots* and Our Own," 87–88.

52. Gerber, "Haley's *Roots*," 89.

53. "Mormons Help African Americans Trace Their Roots." Margaret Walker and Alex Haley are listed together in one article discussing the values of oral history, though Haley's work dominates the text. See Shockley, "Oral History," 787.

54. "Columbus School, Berkeley, CA., Our Roots," Box 15, Folder 4, AHP-UTKL.

55. Rein and Elliot, "*Roots*," 664.

56. "Why *Roots* Hits Home," 42–46.

57. Tucker and Shah, "Race and the Transformation of Culture," 325.

58. Protinsky and Wildman, "Roots: Reflections from the Classroom," 177.

59. Wills, "Taking Historical Novels Seriously," 42.

60. Current, "'Roots'—The Saga of Most Black Families in America," 167–172.

61. Fairchild, Stockard, and Bowman, "Impact of Roots," 316.

62. Howard, Rothbart, and Sloan, "The Response to 'Roots'"; Hur, "Impact of 'Roots'"; Surlin, "'Roots' Research."

63. Poindexter and Stroman, "Blacks and Television." Many studies conducted before and after *Roots* confirmed that racial groups were prone to watch programming specific to their racial identities. See: Surlin and Cooper, "The Jeffersons' and their Racially Integrated Neighbors"; Surlin and Tate, "'All in the Family'"; Allen and Bielby, "Blacks' Attitudes and Behaviors";

64. Marvin Kittman, "Roots: It Can Make your Blood Boil," *Miami News*, January 29, 1977, 2, in Margaret Walker, Box 77, Folder 2, AHP-UTKL.

65. Ottaway, "Tangled Roots," 17, 22. See also Courlander, "Kunta Kinte's Struggle," 294; Morrissey, "Oral History," 41–42; Law, "Book Review: *Roots* by Alex Haley"; Wright, "Uprooting Kunta Kinte," 208; Nobile, "Alex Haley's 'Roots,'" 4; Mills and Mills, "Roots and the New 'Faction'"; Mills and Mills. "The Genealogist's Assessment."

66. *Facts on File, Yearbook 1977*, ca. 1978, Box 7, Folder 2. AHP-UTKL; West, "Black Historians Reflect on Criticisms of *Roots*," 17; "Viewer Raps Udell's Feature on *Roots*"; Shenker,

"Some Historians Dismiss," 29. See also Bauer, "'[He] Didn't Come Here on the *May-flower*,'" 382–383; Wilkinson, "The Black Family: Past and Present," 832.

67. Various critiques, analyses, and apologetics noted this event. For a selection, see Nobile, "Uncovering Roots"; Page, "Alex Haley," 37.

68. "Suit Against Alex Haley Is Dismissed," 49.

69. Shirley and Wagner, *Alex Haley*, 81–82, dismiss Walker's claim. In other works largely dismissive of *Roots*, the Walker case is overlooked because it is not a useful example for proving their point. For one example, see Crouch, "The Roots Hoax Lives On."

70. "Alex Haley Posthumously Beheaded," 28.

71. Jacqueline Trescott, "Respected Scholar Margaret Walker Has Intense Feelings on Black Writers' Spiritual Alliance," *Washington Post*, April 27, 1977, in Box 77, Folder 2, AHP-UTKL.

72. "Haley Defends *Roots* Against 'Snipers,'" 18.

73. Numerous journal entries divulge this information. See, for example, Journal 101, 18, MWPP-JSU.

74. Journal 106, 18, MWPP-JSU.

75. Journal 102, 37, MWPP-JSU.

76. Journal 101, 34, 35, MWPP-JSU.

77. Box 49, Folder 2: August 1977, AHP-UTKL.

78. "Walker vs. Haley Trial Transcript," Box 48, Folder 2: Preliminary Meeting, AHP-UTKL; Box 49, Folder 1: July 1977, AHP-UTKL. "Jumping the broom" was listed as "ITEM #35" in one list presented by the prosecution, see Box 49, Folder 6: December 1977, 12, AHP-UTKL.

79. "Walker vs. Haley Trial Transcript."

80. "Walker vs. Haley Trial Transcript," Box 48, Folder 6: December 16, 1977, AHP-UTKL. See also "Walker vs. Haley Transcript," Box 48, Folder 3: December 12, 1977, AHP-UTKL.

81. Box 49, Folder 7: January 1978, AHP-UTKL.

82. Christopher Dickey, "Roots Author Facing Accusations: Novelist's Suit Charges Haley's Book Is 'Largely Copied,'" *Washington Post*, April 28, 1977, in Box 77, Folder 2, AHP-UTKL.

83. "Haley Denies Allegations He Copied," *Greensboro Daily News*, April 24, 1977, in Box 77, Folder 2, AHP-UTKL.

84. Quoted in John Pryor, "Judge Rules for Haley," *City News*, September, 22, 1978, 2, in Box 49, Folder 13: September 1978, AHP-UTKL.

85. Parry, "The Politics of Plagiarism."

86. Kornick, *Recent American Opera*, 156–158. For reviews, see also Freis, "World Premiere"; Redmond, "A Stirring Concert," 32; Tipton, "'Jubilee' Marks Cultural Union," 5.

87. Moore, "Routes," 8.

88. Journal 101, 45, MWPP-JSU. See also Journal 102, 12, MWPP-JSU.

89. Journal 101, 25, MWPP-JSU. Walker also spoke of other incidents that occurred during her public lectures: "As usual I was attacked by *one* black man who wanted to know if I wasn't mad because I did not have a movie made from my book. I said I am not mad, whom the gods would destroy, they first make mad" (Journal 106, February 13, 1980, MWPP-JSU).

90. Arnez, "From His Story to Our Story," 367.

91. Adams, "Television as a Gathering Place," 119. See also Christopher, Fabes, and Wilson, "Family Television Viewing"; Hess and Grant, "Prime-Time Television"; Gruber and Thau, "Sexually Related Content on Television and Adolescents of Color."

92. Wills, "Taking Historical Novels Seriously," 42.

93. References to broomstick weddings became increasingly frequent in *Ebony* and *Jet* during the 1980s and 1990s. See, for example, "Latest Trends in Tying the Knot"; Sims, "What the Bride of the '90s Wants"; Kinnon, "Wedding Gowns"; Majors, "Society World 'African-Inspired Nuptials'"; Majors, "Society World: Afrocentric Ceremony."

94. Green, *Broom Jumping*, 29.

95. Heidish, *A Woman Called Moses*, 303–308.

96. Gipson, "A Woman Called Moses!"

97. O'Connor, "TV: 'A Woman Called Moses," C21; West, "A Woman Called Moses," B1.

98. Brown Jr., "Let's Uproot TV's Image of Blacks," D35.

99. Heidish, *A Woman Called Moses*, 48.

100. Heidish, 69.

101. Heidish, 76.

102. Heidish, 80–81.

103. Heidish, 80.

104. Isaacs, *The Transformation of Virginia*; Sobel, *The World They Made Together*.

105. Wendkos, *A Woman Called Moses*.

106. Majors, "Society World: Cocktail Chitchat," March 6, 1980.

107. Majors, "Society World: Cocktail Chitchat," March 19, 1981.

108. Moore, "$5 Million Lottery Winner."

109. Majors, "Society World: Cocktail Chitchat," July 6, 1987.

110. "Latest Trends in Tying the Knot."

111. "Photo Standalone 46," C5.

112. Lynn, "The Robert Jordans Wed," 1B.

113. "Newlywed Honeymoon," C1.

114. "Buddhist Ceremony," 12.

115. "Somerset Homecoming," 7.

116. "Newlywed Honeymoon in Greek Islands."

117. "Talbert/Jefferson Jump the Broom," C1.

118. Stokes, "'Jumping Over the Broom," 8.

119. Yerger, "Jumping the Broom," 4. Yerger's letter was responding to an article that Stokes wrote in 1980 in which she examined wedding preparations and cited her original 1978 piece. For the 1980 article, see Oliver, "Jumpin' the Broom without the Crazies," 113.

120. Tapley, "Is Love Undergoing Change in African Tradition?"

121. Haley, *Roots*, 325.

*Chapter Seven*

1. Renee Minus White, "Winter Wedding with African Touch," 15.

2. White, 15; "Display Ad 19," *Philadelphia Tribune*, 5A.

3. Cole, *Jumping the Broom*.

4. "African-American Wedding Planner," 5.

5. Kasper, "Book Celebrates African Marriage Rituals," 1D; Jones, "Blacks Seek Catharsis," 43.

6. *Philadelphia Tribune*, September 24, 1993, 1C; Carrillo, "Community Affairs Calendar," *Philadelphia Tribune*, 1D; Kelly, "Marriage of African, American Tradition," 5D; Leeming, "African Heritage Reflected," C2; Millner, "Newlyweds' Leap of Faith," 5; Millner, "Married to Black Tradition," 5.

7. Dicks, "Jumping the Broom to Success," 1D.

8. See, for example, Woodham, "Newlyweds; Romance on the River," 5; Steelman, "Honoring the Past," 7; Allen, "Weddings/Celebrations: Vows," sect. 9, 17; Watkins, "Weddings: Vows," sect. 9, 9; "Weddings/Celebrations," sect. 9, 19; Phelan, "Jumping the Broom"; "Celebrating Connections; Rituals Reflect Their Commitment," V5; Hansen, "Welcome to the World of Weddings," D1; Moody, "Slave Descendants Face Struggles," 15; Marr, "Black History Gets a Big Celebration, Quantico Style."

9. Cole, *Jumping the Broom*, 7.

10. Cole, 7.

11. MacLeod, "'Jumping Over.'"

12. Woodham, "Something Old, Something New," C1.

13. Jacobson, *Roots Too*.

14. Kelley, *Into the Fire*, 111.

15. Bay, "The Historical Origins of Afrocentrism," 502.

16. Asante, *Afrocentricity*; Asante, *The Afrocentric Idea*. Additionally, one of the more controversial, and largely mainstream, Afrocentric works came from Bernal's *Black Athena*.

17. Bay, "The Historical Origins," 503, 504.

18. Though an emphasis on Egypt as an African civilization predates Afrocentrism, Asante and others largely follow the Senegalese scholar Cheik Anta Diop, who argues for a cultural unity between Egypt and "black Africa" in *The Cultural Unity of Black Africa*.

19. Much of this work was engaged by "Africanists," who, while agreeing Africa was central to the narrative of the Black Diaspora, tried to avoid generalizing "African culture." See Thornton, *Africa and Africans*; Adeleke, *The Case against Afrocentrism*.

20. Bay, "The Historical Origins," 502.

21. Williams, "In a 90's Quest for Black Identity."

22. Hartman, *A War for the Soul of America*, 127.

23. Hartman, 128.

24. Gilroy, *The Black Atlantic*, 190. For noteworthy critiques of Afrocentrism, see Levine, "The Use and Abuse of *Black Athena*"; Walker, *We Can't Go Home Again*; Gates, *Loose Canons*; Appiah and Gutmann, *Color Conscious*; Taylor, *Multiculturalism*; Marable, *Beyond Black and White*; de Montellano, Haslip-Viera, and Barbour, "They Were *NOT* Here before Columbus," 199–234; Snowden, "Misconceptions about African Blacks," 28–50.

25. Hartman, *A War for the Soul*, 128.

26. For overviews of Afrocentrism see Hartman, *A War for the Soul*; Bay, "The Historical Origins"; Hine, "The Black Studies Movement"; Moses, *Afrotopia*; Howe, *Afrocentrism*.

27. Jarrett L. Carter, "HBCU Legacy at Risk: Alumnae Share Reservations about Promoting Black College Experience for Future Generations," *Huffington Post*, December 6, 2012, https://www.huffingtonpost.com/2012/12/06/hbcu-legacy-at-risk-alumn-share-reservations _n_2252949.html.

28. Tetty-Fio, "Historical and Contemporary Black-American Geographies," 159.

29. Jellison, *It's Our Day*, 45, 98.

30. Ingraham, *White Weddings*, 137–138.

31. Ingraham, chap. 2.

32. Engstrom and Semic, "Portrayal of Religion."

33. Ingraham, *White Weddings*, 137–138.

34. Bellan-Boyer, "Review," 429–434.

35. "1st SaFire Mid-Atlantic Women's Conference," 4.

36. Green quoted in Barnes, "Broom-Jumping Rite Recalls Black Tradition," B3.

37. Green, *Broom Jumping*, 3.

38. Green, 3.

39. "Business Bridal Show Has African Touch," A5; "Around the Southside," K2; "Getting Hitched," 24.

40. Dyson quoted in Jones, "Blacks Seek Catharsis."

41. Millner, "Married to Tradition."

42. Reynolds, "Jumping the Broom," B8.

43. Cullen, "Jumping the Broom," A6.

44. Dunham, "Sweep of History Helps Propel a Boom in Keepsake Brooms," 2.

45. Dunham, 2.

46. "Old and New Customs Mingle," C1; "Jumping the Broom Slave Custom," C1.

47. Padilioni, Jr., "The History and Significance of Kente Cloth."

48. Watson, "Jumping the Broom Began with Slaves," G4; Person-Lynn, "Why Do We Jump the Broom?" A7.

49. Engstrom and Semic, "Portrayal of Religion," 152, 154.

50. Sturgis, *The Nubian Wedding Book*, 88–94.

51. Fleetwood, *The Afrocentric Bride*, 168.

52. Anyiam, *Jumping the Broom in Style*, 1.

53. Freehling, "Jumping the Broom," G1.

54. Forret, *Slave against Slave*.

55. O'Meally and Fabre, Introduction, 7.

56. Mitchell, "Celebrating the Black Family's Survival," B7.

57. Mitchell, "Seven Lucky Steps to Jumping the Broom," F12.

58. Hinton, "Couples 'Jump the Broom,'" 1E. See also Bennett, "Jump the Broom," 5A.

59. Shaw, "Vows; Sabrina Diggs and Serigne N'Diaye"; Bisbee, "Into Africa," 80. For additional statements regarding slaves being "forbidden to marry" see Lowney, "They Give Traditional Weddings Old Meaning," B1.

60. Jones, "More Black Americans Explore Roots in Slavery," 32A; Thomas, "Slavery Inspires Wedding," 1; "Slaves Originated 'Jumping the Broom,'" C5; Johnson, "Weddings with Afrocentric Flair"; Thomas, "Bride's Wedding Inspired from Times of Slavery," 4; Joseph, "New Bridal Magazine Puts Women of Color, Black Traditions First," 1C.

61. Makete, "A Ceremony Steeped in Tradition," E1; Freeman, "Afrocentric Weddings Add Culture to Tradition," 21T.

62. Ogunleye, *The African Roots*, uses only a mention of the ceremony by the formerly enslaved author William Wells Brown's book *My Southern Home* (1880; 1968), to argue for the broomstick wedding's arrival and usage in North America. However, Brown's narrative

makes no reference to the custom's origins, nor suggests it was a particularly desirable practice for all enslaved people. See pages 41–46 of his narrative.

63. Long, *Something Old, Something New*, 27; Jones, *Happy Is the Bride*; Blumberg, *York's Adventures*, 12; Janes, *Encyclopedia of African American Society*, 2:876; Bird, "Jumping the Broom"; Baker, *The Washingtons of Wessyngton Plantation*, 93; Calkhoven, *Harriet Tubman*, 42; Trotter, *The African American Experience*; Nichols, *African Americans*, 14; Anyiam, *Jumping the Broom in Style*, 1; Randall, *Marriage*, 43; Pujols, "Film Review of Noah's Arc," 102; Alexander and Rucker, *Encyclopedia of African American History*, 1:158; Lamanna and Reidmann, *Marriages, Families, and Relationships*, 183.

64. "Jumping the Broom," http://archive.harvestbird.com/2005/12/22/jumping-the-broom/, accessed June 16, 2014.

65. Locke, "Young Entrepreneur marries African, European Traditions," 1D.

66. Strong, "Jumping the Broom," 37.

67. Gerri Majors, "Society World: Cocktail Party Chit-Chat," *Jet*, November 11, 1971, 39; Gerri Majors, "Society World," *Jet*, April 24, 2000, 31; Gerri Majors, "Society World," *Jet*, May 31, 1993, 31; Knowles, "Owners of 2 Cute Create Distinctive African Fashions," 26MB; Page, "Wedding Traditions," 8; Castle, "Union Rooted in Heritage," B1.

68. Wright, *Jumping the Broom*, unpag.

69. "Review of *Jumping the Broom*," https://www.publishersweekly.com/978-0-8234 -1042-2/.

70. Roback and Devereaux, "Children's Books," 81.

71. Hearne, "Jumping the Broom (Book Review)," 378.

72. Early, "'Jumping the Broom' and Now Let Me Fly,'" 22.

73. In a review of a children's work called *Christmas in the Big House, Christmas in the Quarters* Roger Sutton noted that "the illustrations, like those in Courtni Wright's *Jumping the Broom*, uncomfortably teeter into the picturesque" ("Review: Christmas in the Big house, Christmas in the Quarters," 57).

74. An example of one positive review is Barbara Osborne Williams's, who notes that the "collaboration of text and soft delicate watercolors paints perhaps the peace found in a strong spiritual connection for Africans who knew who they really were" ("Jumping the Broom," 115).

75. Helmso, *Jump the Broom*, 13.

76. Helmso, *Saltar la Escoba*. Information for Helmso's background comes from Tracy, "Local Self-Taught Children's Book Author Living Her Dream."

77. Close, *Elderly Slaves*.

78. Porter, *Addy's Wedding Quilt*, 21.

79. Porter, 32.

80. Black, *Jumping the Broom*, unpag.

81. Black, afterword.

82. Rochman, "Review: Jumping the Broom," 410.

83. Lyons, *Ellen's Broom*, unpag.

84. For reviews see Lukehart, "Review: Ellen's Broom"; "Ellen's Broom"; Naidoo, "Review: Ellen's Broom." For one exception that argues the emotions appear "subdued," see "Review: Ellen's Broom," 55.

85. Ulen, "For Children."

86. Odean, "Stories of Black History and Heroes," 8.

87. Todd, *Carolina Clay*, 226–227.

88. Cheng, *Etched in Clay*, 15.

89. Cheng, 48.

90. Cosson, *Harriet Tubman*, 14, 21. See also Benge and Benge, *Harriet Tubman*, 61. Even when not explicitly saying so, some authors have attempted to link the ceremony with Tubman's story. See, for example, McGowan and Kashatus, *Harriet Tubman*, 18. In one of the more careful analyses, Catherine Clinton, *Harriet Tubman*, notes the existence of the slave custom, but does not suggest that John and Harriet performed it.

91. Lyons, *Letters from a Slave Girl*, 136.

92. Lyons, 18. See Lyons, 142, for a paragraph describing the function of the broomstick wedding in the slave community.

93. Jacobs, *Incidents in the Life of a Slave Girl*.

94. Person-Lynn, "Why Do We Jump the Broom?"

95. Tapley, "Dr. Maulana Karenga: Father of Kwanzaa."

96. Millner, "Newlyweds Leap of Faith," 5.

97. "Jumping the Broom," *Fayetteville Observer*, November 5, 1995.

98. "Jumping the Broom."

99. Dundes, "Jumping the Broom," 328.

100. Sullivan, "Jumping the Broom: A Further Consideration"; Sullivan, "Jumping the Broom: Possible Welsh Origins.".

101. Johnson, "African American Quilts," 169.

102. "Local Judge Lets Couples Jump the Broom," http://www.judgemarable.net/Articles.htm.

103. Wilson, *The Piano Lesson*, 44.

104. Lemann, *The Promised Land*; Berlin, *The Making of African America*; Wilkerson, *The Warmth of Other Suns*.

105. Grissom, *The Kitchen House*, 46.

106. Kunka, "Intertextuality and the Historical Graphic Narrative," 182.

107. Baker, *Nat Turner*, 97–99.

108. In the United States the novel was published under the title *Someone Knows My Name*, due to the negative connotations that "Negro" carries in the country.

109. Virgo, *The Book of Negroes*, episode 2.

110. Parker, *The Birth of a Nation*.

111. Stuckey, *Slave Culture*; Thompson, *Ring Shout*.

112. Meyer, "Finding Words for Slavery," https://www.washingtonpost.com/archive/local/2001/02/22/finding-words-for-slavery/b48f18c2-981e-4a54-89ee-699cca0d6d78/?utm_term=.76cb64ef19b3.

113. Lynch, "Facing History Head-On," C8. See also Tyson and Dungey, "'Ask a Slave,'" 39.

114. The interview was featured in *Past and Present: The Colonial Williamsburg Podcast*, September 27, 2010, http://podcast.history.org/2010/09/27/jumpin-the-broom/.

115. Interview, *Past and Present*.

116. For some additional readings accessing the lasting impact of *Roots* in American culture both before and after Haley's death, see: Baye, "Alex Haley's Roots Revisited"; Moore,

"Alex Haley's *Roots*"; Peoples, "Revisiting Roots after 25 Years"; Ball and Jackson, *Reconsidering Roots.*

117. Leeds-Hurwitz, *Wedding as Text,* 5.

## Chapter Eight

1. Stephens, "What Child Is This?," 244.

2. Barksdale, "Why *Noah's Arc* Is Still Relevant to Queer Black Men 10 Years Later," https://www.huffingtonpost.com/entry/why-noahs-arc-is-still-relevant-to-black-queer -men-10-years-later_us_57e1a04ce4b05d3737be4fcc.

3. Barsotti, "Black, Sexual and Gay," 26.

4. Polk, *Noah's Arc.*

5. Similar ideas are espoused in the announcements of same-sex couples of color, in that jumping the broom is noteworthy for its connections to slavery. See, for example, "Wedding Announcement," 3.

6. See Levin, "Awaiting a Full Embrace of Same-Sex Weddings"; Neal, "Jumping the Broom to Equality," https://www.huffingtonpost.com/mark-anthony-neal/new-york-gay -marriage_b_913653.html; Morris, "Gay Marriage? How Straight."

7. Moyce, "Denial of Marriage Still Exists," 2.

8. Otnes, *Cinderella Dreams,* 231–237.

9. "Wiccan High Priestess Zsuzsanna Budapest," 278.

10. Lewin, *Recognizing Ourselves,* 23.

11. "The Well of Horniness," 12.

12. Sherman, ed., *Lesbian and Gay Marriage,* passim; Sullivan, *Virtually Normal*; Warner, *The Trouble with Normal*; Gioia, "*Normal Heart* Playwright Larry Kramer Discusses Same-Sex Marriage," http://www.playbill.com/article/normal-heart-playwright-larry-kramer-discusses -same-sex-marriage-com-189571.

13. On the one available recording of the production taken on February 20, 1993, viewers can see that gender diversity is well represented, but racial and ethnic diversity is greatly lacking. See "The Wedding Project: Jumping the Broom DVD," Carton 25, Theatre Rhinoceros Records, 1968–2009. A list of actors is also available in the production's program. Production Files: Jumping the Broom, Carton 3, Folder 2, Theatre Rhinoceros Records, 1968–2009. Hereafter cited as TRR, UC Berkeley.

14. "Production Files: Jumping the Broom," Carton 3, Folder 2, TRR, UC Berkeley.

15. "Production Files: Jumping the Broom," Carton 3, Folder 2.

16. The plays that mention the broomstick are entitled "The Plateauing of the Species" by Dean Backus in Carton 9, Folder 27, and "The Handfasting," Carton 9, Folder 24, both located in TRR, UC Berkeley.

17. Production Files: Jumping the Broom, Carton 3, Folder 2, TRR, UC Berkeley.

18. Text is available in "Morgan Speaks I, January 31, 1993," Carton 9, Folder 22, TRR, UC Berkeley.

19. Tom W. Kelly, "Jumping the Broom," in Production Files: Jumping the Broom, Carton 3, Folder 2, TRR, UC Berkeley.

20. "Jumping the Broom, Program," Production Files: Jumping the Broom, Carton 3, Folder 2, TRR, UC Berkeley.

21. Baxter, "Ar'nt We a Couple?," 161.

22. Phuong Ly, "3000 Gay Couples Wed in Washington Ceremony," *Edmonton Journal*, April 30, 2000, A8.

23. Donnelly, "Vows that Can't Be Voted Down," A19.

24. Donnelly, A19.

25. "Marriage should not just be for heterosexuals," 9.A.

26. Associated Press, "Gays Embrace Mayor for Officiating Ceremony," http://www.nbcnews.com/id/21886346/ns/us_news-life/t/gays-embrace-mayor-officiating-ceremony/#.WoGmMakna8o.

27. Segal, *And Then I Danced*, 199.

28. Lewin, *Recognizing Ourselves*, 136.

29. TwoBadTourists (@twobadtourists), "@huffpostgay @c_wong79 Jumping the broom at our 2010 wedding. Not legal in AZ but it didn't stop us! #OurQueerWedding," October 6, 2014, https://twitter.com/twobadtourists/status/519265864856924161.

30. "Two Bad Tourists."

31. For information on this couple and their primary goals, see https://www.twobadtourists.com/about-us/. Accessed May 30, 2020.

32. Isom, "Jumping the Broom," 43.

33. Hunter, *Bound in Wedlock*, chap. 3. For a recent examination of families and communities of free people of color see Dangerfield, "Hard Rows to Hoe."

34. Ayers and Brown, *The Essential Guide*, 117.

35. Brooks, "Black on Black Love," 37.

36. Ziyad, "For Black Queers," http://www.slate.com/blogs/outward/2017/06/29/is_lgbtq_visibility_politics_inherently_anti_black.html; Owens, "Now Is the Time to Start Talking about Racism in the LGBT Community," https://www.huffingtonpost.com/ernest-owens/now-is-the-time-to-start-_b_7261390.html; Phillip Henry, "Philadelphia Pride Flag Opposition."

37. Barajas, "Gurl, Am I Appropriating Black Women?"

38. Michael Arceneaux, "If You're Mad about the Black and Brown Stripes Added to the Rainbow Flag."

39. Ashley, "Gay Liberation," 29.

40. Bassichis and Spade, "Queer Politics and Anti-Blackness."

41. Morgan, *Laboring Women*.

42. Padilla, "Jumping the Broom: Finding Love in Prison." For literature on gender and men's same-sex relations in American prisons, see Sloan, *Masculinities*; Jenness and Fenstermaker, "Agnes Goes to Prison"; Sabo, Kupers, and London, *Prison Masculinities*; Propper, "Love, Marriage, and Father-Son Relationships."

43. Berger, "Mass Incarceration and Its Mystification"; Rael, "Demystifying the 13th Amendment"; Dennis R. Childs, "Slavery, the 13th Amendment, and Mass Incarceration: A Response to Patrick Rael"; Childs, *Slaves of the States*.

44. McQueeney, "The New Religious Rite," 51.

45. McQueeney, 62.

46. Wilson, *Jumpin' the Broom*.

47. For perspective on this divide, see Asanti, "Jumping the Broom," 30; Skerritt, "Race and Perception," 1E.

48. Equality Maryland Foundation and National Black Justice Coalition, *Jumping the Broom*, 5.

49. Riley, "Baltimore Anti-Marriage Flyers Target Race."

50. Moddie-Mills, *Jumping Beyond the Broom*, 1.

51. Rousseve and Mason, *Jumping the Broom*.

52. Rousseve's dance recently resurfaced for another performance in April 2018: Roy, "Archiving Black Dance." See also Rousseve's own website: https://www.davidrousseve.com /jumping-the-broom/.

53. Kiesling, "The Missing Colors of the Rainbow."

54. Crenshaw, "Mapping the Margins," 1242.

## Chapter Nine

1. Aleta, "Jumping the Broom."

2. Aleta.

3. Skousen, "Jumping the Broom."

4. Smith, "You Know You're West Indian If . . . ," 43.

5. Zuill, *Bermuda Journey*, 181. Also see Smith, *Slavery in Bermuda*, 46; Packwood, *Chained on the Rock*, 82.

6. *American Slave*, volume 12, *Georgia Narratives*, part 1, 207; *American Slave*, ss 2, vol. 5, *Texas Narratives*, part 4, 1662; Fisher, *The Master's Slave*, 5.

7. Jarvis, *In the Eye of All Trade*, 29.

8. Dawson, *Undercurrent of Power*.

9. Bernhard, *Slaves and Slaveholders*, 17.

10. For an examination the fatal nature of sugar cultivation, see Schwartz, *Tropical Babylons*.

11. Jarvis, *In the Eye of All Trade*, 102.

12. "The Report of Governor Popple," 49.

13. For the 1844 census, see Williams, *An Historical and Statistical Account of the Bermudas*, 342.

14. Tucker, *Thoughts and Expressions*, 35.

15. Dawson, *Undercurrents of Power*, 200, 216. Frey and Wood, *Come Shouting to Zion*.

16. Holsey, "Black Atlantic Traditions," 508.

17. Gilroy, *Ain't No Black in the Union Jack*; Gordon and Anderson, "The African Diaspora," 282–296; Thomas, *Modern Blackness*; Street, "Malcolm X"; Perry, "'Little Rock' in Britain," 155–177.

18. "Lesbians Jump the Broom in Ja," 2.

19. Dennis-Benn, "Jamaica's First Lesbian Wedding."

20. "A-List Romance: Jamaica."

21. Ellington, ". . . And the Groom Sang for his Bride."

22. "Our Family Wedding (2010)."

23. On the Black national anthem, see Perry, *May We Forever Stand*.

24. In at least one case I found a Black woman and Latino man jump the broom together, as she felt it an important piece of her heritage: Hopkins, "Apodaca Park Hosts Juneteenth Celebration," 1A.

25. For cultural loss see Elkins, *Slavery*. For cultural historians who challenged Elkins and the cultural loss thesis, see Genovese, *Roll, Jordan, Roll*; Blassingame, *The Slave Community*; Stuckey, *Slave Culture*.

26. Otnes, *Cinderella Dreams*, 247.

27. Lewin, *Recognizing Ourselves*, 136.

28. Lewin, 135.

29. Blake, "Ask Dr. Sherry."

30. Molly, "Jumping the Broom: Interracial Marriage."

31. Molly, "Jumping the Broom."

32. Shay, "Is It Wrong to 'Jump the Broom.'"

33. Karazin and Littlejohn, *Swirling*, 3.

34. Cole, *Jumping the Broom*, 14.

35. Anyiam, *Jumping the Broom in Style*, 7.

36. "A Very Special Wedding: Blending Two Cultures, One Love."

37. Grant, "Are You Planning (or Had) on 'Jumping the Broom' at Your Wedding?"

38. Shamsian, "Here's the Tangled History."

39. Luse and Eddings, "Jumping the Broom."

40. In 1979, the notion that one would "hop the broomstick" in Indiana was featured as an expression of rural folk in a dictionary. See Lewis, "A Dictionary of How Just Plain Folks Talk, C1. However, physical expressions of the custom among Southerners and Midwesterners are largely missing from the historical record.

41. Jacobson, *Roots Too*, 11–71.

42. Boyle, "Daily Apple Cuts Cavities."

43. Diamond, "Couple Gets Lavish Cajun Wedding."

44. Ellzey, "Jumping the Broom."

45. Rice, *Cajun Alphabet*, unpag.

46. For a review of chiravari in North America, see Palmer, "Discordant Music"; Gunn, "An Oregon Charivari"; Johnson, "Charivari/Shivaree."

47. Rice, *Cajun Alphabet*, unpaginated.

48. "Adrienne Young and Little Sadie, 'Jump the Broom,' 7/15/04 Grey Fox Bluegrass Festival," YouTube, https://www.youtube.com/watch?v=J2v5wZGfing.

49. Dykes, "Roaming Market Couple," 3.

50. Bowers, "Why Big Fat Gypsy Weddings Betray Us Real Romanies."

51. Moyce, "Denial of Marriage Still Exists," 2.

52. Angerberger, "Jumping the Broom May Be Jumping Cultures."

53. Kaldera and Schwartzstein, *Handfasting and Wedding Rituals*, 22, 89–90; Hovey, *Passages Handfasting*; Griffyn, *Wiccan Wisdomkeepers*, 17; Dunwich, *Witch's Halloween*, 155; Dunwich, *Wicca Craft*, 59–60.

54. Bradley, "Canadian Is Power behind Equal Rights for Witches," 5A.

55. Andrews, "Witching—Shaman Brings Faith out of Closet," 17; Gowen, "Witches Bring Their Craft out of the Broom Closet," E1.

56. "A Nice Day for a Witch Wedding," https://www.scotsman.com/news/nice-day-witch-wedding-2511612#gsc.tab=0

57. Houlihan, "Now, the Bride and Broom," 9.

58. Monaghan, "Now Pagans Can Raise a Toast to Bride and Broom," 8.

59. Carda, "Wiccan Marriage and American Marriage Law."

60. Houlihan, "Now, the Bride and Broom," 9.

61. Bradley, "Canadian Is Power behind Equal Rights," 5A; Andrews, "Witches Follow Ancient Traditions," 6C; McLaughlin and Thompson, "Bride and Broom," 13; "Ritual Is Based on Pagan Principles," 11; "Broomstick Leap Gets Couple Off to a Flying Start," 12.

62. Zuckerman, "'Jumping the Broom,'" D1.

63. Gillies, *The Originals*, season 2.

## Conclusion

1. Mario Van Peebles, *Roots*, episode 2.

2. Haley, *Roots*, 325.

3. Forret, *Slave against Slave*; Baptist, *The Half Has Never Been Told*.

4. Akil, *Jumping the Broom*.

5. Johnson and Roark, *Black Masters*; Koger, *Black Slaveowners*; Daudert, *Andrew Durnford*.

6. Allen, *Slaves, Freedmen and Indentured Laborers*, 89–97; Bryan, *The Haitian Revolution*, 8–9; Fick, *The Making of Haiti*, chap. 1; Hanger, *Bounded Lives, Bounded Places*, 70–79.

7. Rousseau, "Social Rhetoric," 465.

8. "Jumping the Broom—The Tradition."

9. Parry, "Jumping the Broom."

10. "Jumping the Broom" is referenced in two songs by rap duo OutKast: "Call the Law" (2006) and "International Player's Anthem (I Choose You)" (2007). It was also referenced by Hip Hop duo Run The Jewels in their 2013 song "Banana Clipper," as way to avoid obtaining "papers" for one's wedding.

11. On episode 10 of its ninth season, *Grey's Anatomy* portrayed characters Miranda Bailey and Ben Warner, both Black physicians, jumping over a broom at the conclusion of their nuptials. While the show does not comment upon the meaning of the custom, its appearance is a definitive statement that the show's creator, Shonda Rhimes, an African American woman, wanted to display the ceremony's important cultural symbolism. For *Braxton Family Values*, see Strong, "Jumping the Broom," 15. For a transcript of the broomstick wedding discussion on *Braxton Family Values*, see http://www.wetv.com/shows/braxton-family-values/blog/we-tells-all-braxton-family-values-wedding-daze (accessed September 21, 2018). For a clip that references jumping the broom on *Growing Up Hip Hop*, see https://www.youtube.com/watch?v=yRuRfowszRM (accessed October 12, 2018). In season 7, episode 9, of *The Game*, Kelly, a white woman, and Chardonnay, a black woman, discuss Chardonnay's upcoming wedding to her fiancé, Jason, also an African American. When Chardonnay reveals to Kelly that she and Jason are jumping the broom, Kelly responds with condescension and sarcasm. In season 2, episode 3 of *Basketball Wives LA* Jackie and Doug Christie jump the broom as an anniversary celebration, thereby both commemorating their heritage as African Americans and demonstrating support for same-sex marriage rights. On *This Is Us*, season 3, episode 16, two characters are shown jumping over the broom in a flashback of their wedding.

12. Though one can watch the past episodes of *Four Weddings* to gain an understanding of the custom's appearance, references to jumping the broom are included in the "Bride

Bios" page of the website https://www.tlc.com/tv-shows/four-weddings/, season 10 (accessed October 10, 2019).

13. Michael Eric Dyson (Interview Transcript), "All in with Chris Hayes" *NBC News*, April 24, 2014.

14. Thompson, "Can White Couples Jump the Broom?"

15. Young, "White Couple Jumps the Broom."

16. Merritt, *Masterless Men*, 345.

17. Young, "White Couple Jumps the Broom"; Shantell E. Jamison, "Dear White People: No, It Isn't OK to Jump the Broom," *Ebony*, September 18, 2017, https://www.ebony.com /life/white-people-jumping-the-broom-marriage.

18. Scafidi, *Who Owns Culture?*, 9.

19. Rodriquez, "Color-Blind Ideology," 647.

20. Gilroy, *The Black Atlantic*, esp. 31–35.

21. Clarke et al., "Subcultures, Cultures, and Class," 15.

22. "Among the Gypsies"; Levinson and Silk, *Dreams of the Road*, 62–68; Parry, "Married in Slavery Time."

23. Locke, "Meghan Markle."

24. Susan Saulny, "Black? White? Asian?" *New York Times*, A1; Masuoka, "Political Attitudes and Ideologies."

25. Markle, "I'm More than an Other."

26. Markle, "I'm More than an Other." For a useful analysis of the dizzying obsessions with judging her Blackness, see Lee, "Meghan Markle."

27. For extended attention to mixed-race identities see Hobbs, *A Chosen Exile*.

28. Lance Davis, "Prince Harry Needs to Jump over the Broom," Change.org, December 2017, https://www.change.org/p/meghan-markle-prince-harry-needs-to-jump-over-the -broom.

29. Locke, "Meghan Markle."

30. "A Wedding Is Announced."

31. For the difficulties in presuming certain cultural traits are connected to specific racial groups, see Baker, *Anthropology and the Racial Politics*, 3–5.

32. Laniyonu, "A Comparative Analysis of Black Racial Group Consciousness."

33. Hall, "Cultural Identity and Diaspora," 394.

# Bibliography

*Archives*

Baton Rouge, LA
    Southern University
        John B. Cade Collection: Opinions Regarding Slavery (digitized)
Berkeley, CA
    Bancroft Library, University of California, Berkeley
        Theatre Rhinoceros Records
Chapel Hill, NC
    Southern Historical Collection, University of North Carolina
        Thaddeus Ferree Papers
Hattiesburg, MS
    The University of Southern Mississippi Center for Oral History and Cultural Heritage
        Interview with Miss Ruby Magee: A Native Mississippian (digitized)
Jackson, MS
    Margaret Walker Center, Jackson State University
        Margaret Walker Personal Papers (digitized)
Knoxville, TN
    University of Tennessee Libraries, Knoxville, Special Collections
        Alex Haley Papers
Lexington, KY
    University of Kentucky, Special Collections
        John Winston Coleman Jr. collection on slavery in Kentucky, 1780–1940
New Orleans, LA
    Amistad Research Center, Tulane University
        Black Federal Writer's Program, Collection No. 547
Washington, DC
    Moorland-Spingarn Research Collection, Howard University
        Ophelia Egypt Collection
Williamsburg, VA
    Swem Library, College of William and Mary
        Burwell-Catlett Papers, 1794–1887

*Cinema, Television, and Media*

Akil, Salim, dir. *Jumping the Broom*. Culver City, CA: TriStar Pictures, 2011. DVD.
Foster, Lewis, dir. "Broomstick Wedding." *The Adventures of Jim Bowie*, season 1, episode 6, October 12, 1956. American Broadcasting Corporation. https://www.youtube.com /watch?v=bOpPb8dbHLU&t=11s.

Gillies, Daniel, dir. *The Originals*, season 2. Decatur, GA: Bonanza Productions, 2014. Netflix.

Neal, Stephen. "A Wedding Is Announced." *PBS Royal Wedding*, episode 1, May 14, 2018. Public Broadcasting Service.

Parker, Nate. *The Birth of a Nation*. Los Angeles, CA: BRON Studios, 2016. DVD.

Polk, Patrik-Ian. *Noah's Arc: Jumping the Broom*. New York: Logo TV, 2008. DVD.

Rousseve, David. *Jumping the Broom*. 2005, 2018. https://www.davidrousseve.com/jumping-the-broom.

Van Peebles, Mario. *Roots*, episode 2. New York: History Channel, 2016. DVD.

Virgo, Clement. *The Book of Negroes*, episode 2. Toronto, Canada: Conquering Lion Pictures, 2015. DVD.

Wilson, Debra A. *Jumpin' the Broom: The New Covenant*. Antwerp, Belgium: Moyo Entertainment, 2006. DVD.

Wendkos, Paul, dir. *A Woman Called Moses*. Beverly Hills, CA: National Broadcasting Corporation, 1978. DVD.


*Newspapers, Magazines, and Digital Content*

"1st SaFire Mid-Atlantic Women's Conference." *New Journal and Guide*. September 2, 1992, 4.

"A Broomstick Marriage." *University Missourian*. October 24, 1912, 2.

"A Happy Couple." *Sedalia Weekly Bazoo*. July 2, 1889, 1.

"A-List Romance: Jamaica." *Caribbean World*. August 6, 2014. https://caribbeanworld-magazine.com/home/magazine/a-list-romance/.

"A Nice Day for a Witch Wedding." *news.scotsman.com*. September 16, 2004. https://www.scotsman.com/news/nice-day-witch-wedding-2511612#gsc.tab=0.

"A Polish Witch in Detroit." *Pittsburgh Dispatch*. February 22, 1892, 1.

"A Very Special Wedding: Blending Two Cultures, One Love." *Bryan Times*. January 30, 2003.

"African-American Wedding Planner Gets Rave Reviews." *St. Louis Post-Dispatch*. May 16, 1993, 5.

Aleta. "Jumping the Broom: An Anarchist Perspective on Marriage." August 11, 2016. https://steempeak.com/@agirlandhernap/jumping-the-broom-an-anarchist-perspective-on-marriage.

"Alex Haley Posthumously Beheaded in the Village Voice." *New York Amsterdam News*. February 27, 1993, 28.

Allen, Jenny. "Weddings/Celebrations: Vows." *New York Times*. September, 22, 2002. Sect. 9, 17.

"American Republican Demonstration." *New-York Daily Tribune*. October, 18, 1856, 5.

"Among the Gypsies." *Harper's Bazaar*. March 20, 1880, 12–13.

Ancelet, Barry Jean, Jay D. Edwards, and Glen Pitre. *Cajun Country*. Jackson: University Press of Mississippi, 1991.

Andrews, Robert M. "Witches Follow Ancient Traditions that Honor the Earth." *St. Paul Pioneer Press*. April 15, 1990, 6C.

———. "Witching—Shaman Brings Faith out of Closet." *Richmond Times-Dispatch*. May 23, 1990, 17.

Angerberger, Tom. "Jumping the Broom May Be Jumping Cultures, Virginia Beach Wedding Shows." Roanoke.com. February 11, 2005. http://www.roanoke.com/business /wb/xp-18372.

Arceneaux, Michael. "If You're Mad about the Black and Brown Stripes Added to the Rainbow Flag, You're Probably White Nonsense." *TheRoot.com.* June 20, 17. https:// www.theroot.com/if-youre-mad-about-the-black-and-brown-stripes-added-to -1796226799.

"Around the Southside: College Park Couple Makes Clean Sweep at Black Family Event." *Atlanta Journal and Constitution.* June 10, 1993, K2.

Associated Press. "Gays Embrace Mayor for Officiating Ceremony." *NBCNEWS.com.* November 19, 2007. http://www.nbcnews.com/id/21886346/ns/us_news-life/t/gays -embrace-mayor-officiating-ceremony/#.WoGmMakna8o.

Aunt Fanny. "Aunt Fanny's First Marriage and Its Tragical Ending." In *Our Young Folks: An Illustrated Magazine for Boys and Girls,* edited by J. T. Trowbridge, Gail Hamilton, and Lucy Larcon, 30–31. Boston: Ticnor and Fields, 1867.

Barajas, Jaime. "Gurl, Am I Appropriating Black Women?" *Medium.com.* September 10, 2017. https://medium.com/tartmag/gurl-am-i-appropriating-black-women -859b679ff256.

Barksdale, Aaron. "Why *Noah's Arc* Is Still Relevant to Queer Black Men 10 Years Later." *Huffington Post.* September 21, 2016. https://www.huffingtonpost.com/entry/why-noahs -arc-is-still-relevant-to-black-queer-men-10-years-later_us_57e1a04ce4b05d3737be4fcc.

Barnes, Cynthia. "Broom-Jumping Rite Recalls Black Tradition." *Richmond Times-Dispatch.* March 1, 1992, B3.

Barron, Mary Jo Sanna. "Singing for the Ancestors." *Black Perspective in Music* 13, no. 1 (1985): 91–114.

Barsotti, Natasha. "Black, Sexual and Gay." *Xtra! West: Vancouver's Gay and Lesbian News.* July 2, 2009, 26.

Baye, B. W. "Alex Haley's *Roots* Revisited." *Essence* 22 (February 1992): 88–91.

"Beevities." *Idaho Avalanche.* November 17, 1877, 3.

Bennett, Adeyela. "Jump the Broom to Honor African Ancestors during your Marriage Ceremony." *Broward Times.* May 4, 2007, 5A.

Bennett, Lerone. Jr. "The Roots of Black Love: New Research Underscores Strong Bonds of Black Concern." *Ebony* 36, no. 10 (August 1981): 31–37.

———. "The World of the Slave." *Ebony* 26, no. 4 (February 1971): 52–56.

Berger, Dan. "Mass Incarceration and Its Mystification: A Review of the 13th." *Black Perspectives.* October 22, 2016. https://www.aaihs.org/mass-incarceration-and-its -mystification-a-review-of-the-13th/.

"Best Seller List." *New York Times.* May 8, 1977.

"Best Seller List." *New York Times.* October 22, 1976, 254.

Bisbee, Dana. "Into Africa; Ceremony Blends Cultures as Couple 'Jump the Broom.'" *Boston Herald.* December 6, 1998, 80.

Blake, Dr. Sherry. "Ask Dr. Sherry: My White Fiancé and I Want to Jump the Broom at Our Wedding, but My Family Is Against It." *Essence.* November 10, 2017. https://www .essence.com/amp/love/ask-dr-sherry-black-bride-want-jump-broom-white-fiance -wedding/.

Bowers, Jake. "Why Big Fat Gypsy Weddings Betray Us Real Romanies." *The Sun.* February 10, 2011. https://www.thesun.co.uk/archives/news/361932/why-big-fat-gypsy -weddings-betrays-us-real-romanies.

Boyle, Hal. "Daily Apple Cuts Cavities." *Tuscaloosa News.* February 27, 1960.

Bradley, Jeff. "Canadian Is Power behind Equal Rights for Witches." *Dallas Morning News.* May 8, 1988, 5A.

Brand, Carole. "Hundreds Attend Ma-Chis Pow Wow." *McClatchy-Tribune.* May 8, 2007, 1.

"Brooklyn City Court." *New York Times.* June 11, 1859.

"Broomstick Leap Gets Couple Off to a Flying Start." *Lincolnshire Echo.* September 12, 2006, 12.

"Brother Turner." *Adalk County News.* December 31, 1908.

Brown Jr., Roscoe C. "Let's Uproot TV's Image of Blacks." *New York Times.* February 18, 1979, D35.

Brown, Stacy M. "The Black Press Remembers 'Before the Mayflower' Author, Freedom Fighting Journalist Lerone Bennett Jr." *Black Press USA.* February 16, 2018. https://www .blackpressusa.com/the-black-press-remembers-before-the-mayflower-author-freedom -fighting-journalist-lerone-bennett-jr/.

"Buddhist Ceremony at Summer Wedding for Young Couple." *Afro-American.* July 16, 1983, 12.

"Business Bridal Show Has African Touch." *Atlanta Journal and Constitution.* May 13, 1993, A5.

Carrillo, Karen. "Community Affairs Calendar: June 17–23." *New York Amsterdam News.* June 19, 1993.

Carter, Jarrett L. "HBCU Legacy at Risk: Alumnae Share Reservations about Promoting Black College Experience for Future Generations." *Huffington Post.* December 6, 2012. https://www.huffingtonpost.com/2012/12/06/hbcu-legacy-at-risk-alumn-share -reservations_n_2252949.html.

Castle, Mona Lisa. "Union Rooted in Heritage: More Couples Adding Ethnic Touches to Their Weddings." *Florida Times-Union.* April 1, 1996, B1.

"Celebrating Connections; Rituals Reflect Their Commitment." *South Bend Tribune.* October 31, 2004, V5.

Childs, Dennis. "Slavery, the 13th Amendment, and Mass Incarceration: A Response to Patrick Rael." *Black Perspectives.* December 12, 2016. https://www.aaihs.org/slavery-the -13th-amendment-and-mass-incarceration-a-response-to-patrick-rael/.

Cole, Harriette. "Jump the Broom." *Essence* 23, no. 10 (1993).

Crouch, Stanley. "The Roots Hoax Lives On." *New York Daily News.* January 21, 2002.

Cullen, Maryanne Motter. "Jumping the Broom." *Intelligencer Journal.* February 11. 1999, A6.

Current, Gloster B. "'Roots'—The Saga of Most Black Families in America." *Crisis: A Record of the Darker Races* 84, no. 5 (1977): 167–172.

Davis, Lance. "Prince Harry Needs to Jump over the Broom." *Change.org.* December 2017. https://www.change.org/p/meghan-markle-prince-harry-needs-to-jump-over-the -broom.

Dennis-Benn, Nicole Y. "Jamaica's First Lesbian Wedding." *Equally Wed.* Accessed 20, 2018. https://equallywed.com/first-jamaica-lesbian-wedding/.

Diamond, Sara. "Couple Gets Lavish Cajun Wedding." *Tuscaloosa News.* June 4, 1989.

Dicks, Sherri H.R. "Jumping the Broom to Success while Empowering Her People." *Philadelphia Tribune.* October 12, 1993, 1D.

"Display Ad 19." *Philadelphia Tribune.* September 24, 1993, 5A.

"Divorces in Kentucky." *New York Evangelist.* March 9, 1848, 39.

Donnelly, Jennifer. "Vows that Can't Be Voted Down." *Washington Post.* November 7, 2008, A19.

"Douglas Society." *Bisbee Daily Review.* November 8, 1910, 3.

Dunbar, Paul Laurence. "Aunt Tempy's Triumph: Stories of Old Plantation Days." *Saturday Evening Post* 171, no. 36 (1899): 567.

Dunham, Kemba J. "Sweep of History Helps Propel a Boom in Keepsake Brooms—Some Blacks Incorporate Them into Marriage Ceremonies." *Wall Street Journal.* October 15, 1999, 2.

Dykes, Mervyn. "Roaming Market Couple Say I Do the Gypsy Way." *Evening Standard* (New Zealand). March 13, 2006, 3.

Early, Gerald. "'Jumping the Broom' and Now Let Me Fly' (Book Review)." *New York Times.* August 4, 1994, 22.

Eddings, Eric, host. "Jumping the Broom." *The Nod* (podcast). February 19, 2018. https://www.gimletmedia.com/the-nod/jumping-the-broom.

"Ellen's Broom." *Kirkus Reviews* 80, no. 1 (2012): 2461.

Ellington, Barbara. ". . . And the Groom Sang for his Bride." *Jamaica Gleaner.* August 20, 2006.

Ellzey, Bill. "Jumping the Broom." *Daily Comet.* October 21, 2001.

"Evidently Somewhat Annoyed." *Cleveland Gazette,* December 13, 1913, 2.

Freehling, Alison. "Jumping the Broom—Many African American Couples Are Remembering Their Past by Borrowing Wedding Customs from Their Ancestors." *Daily Press* (Newport News, VA). August 8, 1999, G1.

Freeman, Rasheim. "Afrocentric Weddings Add Culture to Tradition." *The Sun (Baltimore, Md).* June 4 2006, 21T.

Freis, Richard. "World Premiere: A Triumph for Opera." *Clarion-Ledger.* December 22, 1976.

"Gathered News Fragments, &c." *Maine Farmer.* April 21, 1853, 21, 17.

Gelles, David. "Down and Dirty." *New York Times.* February 8, 2007, F1.

"Getting Hitched: Jumping the Broom." *New York Amsterdam News.* October 23, 1993, 24.

Gioia, Michael. "*Normal Heart* Playwright Larry Kramer Discusses Same-Sex Marriage." *Playbill.* July 28, 2011. http://www.playbill.com/article/normal-heart-playwright-larry-kramer-discusses-same-sex-marriage-com-189571.

Gipson, Gertrude. "A Woman Called Moses!" *Los Angeles Sentinel.* November 3, 1977.

"Good Move." *Charleston News.* January 21, 1873.

Gowen, Anne. "Witches Bring Their Craft out of the Broom Closet." *Washington Times.* June 3, 1991, E1.

"Grand National Celebration of the 27th Anniversary of the Emancipation Proclamation." *The Bee* (Washington, DC). October 4, 1890.

Grant, Mellie. "Are You Planning (or Had) on 'Jumping the Broom' at Your Wedding?" *LipStickAlley.com.* November 12, 2017. https://www.lipstickalley.com/threads/are-you-planning-or-had-on-jumping-the-broom-at-your-wedding.1318361.

"Gypsies Fight Fierce Battle." *Los Angeles Herald.* September 5, 1906, 5.

"Gypsies Quarrel Over Girl Queen." *Los Angeles Herald.* September 3, 1906, 7.

"Gypsy Riot Follows Broomstick Wedding." *San Jose Mercury*. September 6, 1906, 13.

"Haley Defends *Roots* Against 'Snipers' and Gets Honorary Degree." *Jet*. May 12, 1977, 18.

Hansen, Darah. "Welcome to the World of Weddings." *Vancouver Sun*. March 1, 2008, D1.

Harris, Lyle V. "'Africans in America': New PBS Documentary Fills in the Gaps About Slavery That Are Too Often Present in Our Modern-Day History Lessons." *Atlanta Journal and Constitution*. October 19, 1998, 01B.

Hearne, Betsy. "Jumping the Broom (Book Review)." *Bulletin of the Center for Children's Books* 47 (July/August 1994): 378.

Henderson, William C. "Letters to the Editor." *Ebony*. April, 1971, 16.

Henry, Phillip. "Philadelphia Pride Flag Opposition Is a Sign of Racism in the LGBTQ Community." *TeenVogue.com*. June 21, 2017. https://www.teenvogue.com/story/philadelphia-pride-flag-opposition-racism-lgbtq-community.

Hinton, Carla. "Couples 'Jump the Broom'—Marriage-Play Examines Trials, Successes of Marriage in Black Community." *The Oklahoman*. March 17, 2009, 1E.

"Hobson's Choice," *New England Galaxy and United States Literary Advertiser*, December 11, 1829.

Holland, Mignon. "A Black Woman's Soliloquy: In the Face of Fire I Will Not Turn Back." *Negro Digest* 17, no. 10 (August 1968): 20–23.

Hopkins, T. S. "Apodaca Park Hosts Juneteenth Celebration." *Las Cruces Sun-News*. June 19, 2005, 1A.

Houlihan, Liam. "Now, the Bride and Broom." *Herald Sun*. September 16, 2005, 9.

Hunter, Dale R. "Charity Mae Wallace Turns 105." *Los Angeles Sentinel*. April 2, 1981, A3.

"Inmates of Soldiers' Home Leave to Attend State Reunion at Tupelo." *Daily Herald* (Mississippi). June 7, 1921, 1.

"Is Marriage a Failure?" *Judy: The London Serio-Comic Journal*. January 16, 1889, 32.

"Is over a Century and a Quarter Old." *St. Louis Republic*. December 1, 1897, 11.

Isom, Kevin. "Jumping the Broom." *Gay and Lesbian Times*. August 10, 2000, 43.

Jackson, Mae. "Reincarnation." *Black World* 19 (1970): 35.

Jackson, Nathan. "Reclaiming Roots: Black Americans 'Jump the Broom' in African Inspired Weddings." *Boca Raton News*. November 14, 1993, 4E.

Jamison, Shantell E. "Dear White People: No, It Isn't OK to Jump the Broom." *Ebony*. September 18, 2017. https://www.ebony.com/life/white-people-jumping-the-broom-marriage.

Johnson, Donchell. "Weddings with Afrocentric Flair." *Examiner (NJ)*. November 4, 2010.

Jones, Charisse. "Blacks Seek Catharsis by Bringing Slavery's Long Shadow to the Light." *New York Times*. April 2, 1995, 43.

——— "More Black Americans Explore Roots in Slavery." *Dallas Morning News*. April 16, 1995, 32A.

Joseph, Toni Y. "New Bridal Magazine Puts Women of Color, Black Traditions First." *Asbury Park Press*. August 26, 1992, 1C.

"Judge Hastings the Nicest Lover in the World." *The San Francisco Call*. November 21, 1896, 14.

"Jumped Broomstick—Married." *Kansas City Star*. October 18, 1913, 2.

"Jumping the Broom." *Fayetteville Observer*. November 5, 1995.

"Jumping the Broom—The Tradition," *Jumping the Broom Facebook Page*. Posted August 31, 2011. https://www.facebook.com/JumpingTheBroom/videos/1465029082127/.

"Jumping the Broom Slave Custom Mingles with Wedding Rituals of Old African Tribes in New American Traditions." *Pittsburgh Post-Gazette.* February 18, 1997, C1.

"Jumping the Broomstick." *Charlotte Daily Observer.* February 3, 1912, 4.

"Just as He Was." *Harper's Weekly.* August 17, 1907, 1211.

Kasper, Shirl. "Book Celebrates African Marriage Rituals." *Kansas City Star.* April 26, 1993, 1D.

Kelly, Katy. "Marriage of African, American Tradition." *USA Today.* May 26, 1993, 5D.

King, Sarah Singleton. "Antebellum Negress Makes Plea against War." *Southern Magazine* 4, no. 4 (1938): 26–27.

Knowles, Tiffani. "Owners of 2 Cute Create Distinctive African Fashions." *Miami Herald.* February 11, 2001, 26MB.

"Latest Trends in Tying the Knot." *Ebony* 43, no. 8 (June 1988), 31–34.

"Leap Year and its Observances." *Southern Argus.* February 4, 1892, 4.

Lee, Shannon. "Meghan Markle and the Problem with Policing the Identity of Mixed-Race People." *The Lily.* December 7, 2017. https://www.thelily.com/meghan-markle-and-the-problem-with-policing-the-identity-of-mixed-race-people/.

Leeming, David A. "African Heritage Reflected." *Vancouver Sun,* March 15, 1994, C2.

"Lesbians Jump the Broom in Ja." *Weekly Gleaner* (Jamaica). June 13, 2012, 2.

Levin, Dan. "Awaiting a Full Embrace of Same-Sex Weddings." *New York Times.* July 28, 2010.

Lewis, Joy Schlaben. "A Dictionary of How Just Plain Folks Talk: A Dictionary of Plain Folks' Talk." *New York Times.* September 5, 1979, C1.

"Local Judge Lets Couples Jump the Broom." *CPSA Courier.* October 1, 2006. http://www.judgemarable.net/Articles.htm.

Locke, Attica. "Meghan Markle, the 'Blackening of Windsor,' and Why that Matters." *Hollywood Reporter.* May 22, 2018. https://www.hollywoodreporter.com/news/royal-wedding-meghan-markle-blackening-windsor-why-matters-live-tv-guest-column-1114136.

Locke, Michelle. "Young Entrepreneur marries African, European Traditions." *Philadelphia Tribune.* December 5, 1995, 1-D.

Lowney, Pam. "They Give Traditional Weddings Old Meaning." *Virginian Pilot.* September 5, 1998, B1.

Lukehart, Wendy. "Review: Ellen's Broom." *School Library Journal* 58, no. 1 (2012): 81.

Luse, Brittany, and Eric Eddings. "Jumping the Broom." *Nod Podcast.* February 19, 2018.

Ly, Phuong. "3000 Gay Couples Wed in Washington Ceremony." *Edmonton Journal.* April 30, 2000, A8.

Lynch, Marilyn J. "Facing History Head-On." *Washington Post.* October 23, 1994, C8.

Lynn, Mary. "The Robert Jordans Wed in a Beautiful Ceremony." *Call and Post.* August 2, 1980, 1B.

Majors, Gerri. "Society World: Cocktail Chitchat." *Jet.* April 24, 2000, 31.

———. "Society World: Cocktail Chitchat." *Jet.* May 31, 1993, 31.

———. "Society World: Cocktail Chitchat." *Jet.* November 11, 1971, 39.

———. "Society World 'African-Inspired Nuptials.'" *Jet.* May 1, 1995, 29.

———. "Society World: Afrocentric Ceremony." *Jet.* May 10, 1999, 28.

———. "Society World: Cocktail Chitchat." *Jet.* March 6, 1980, 36.

———. "Society World: Cocktail Chitchat." *Jet.* March 19, 1981, 22.

———. "Society World: Cocktail Chitchat." *Jet*. July 6, 1987, 31.

Makete, Lebo. "A Ceremony Steeped in Tradition; Centuries-Old Customs Have Continued to Influence This Special Occasion." *The Star (South Africa)*. November 10, 2011, E1.

Marionneaux, Susan. "Tradition Woven through Indian Blankets." *Yakima Herald-Republic*. August 10, 2000, V4.

Markle, Meghan. "I'm More than an Other." *Elle*. December 22, 2015. https://www.elle.com/uk/life-and-culture/news/a26855/more-than-an-other/.

Marr, Ryan. "Black History Gets a Big Celebration, Quantico Style." *Free Lance-Star*. February 18, 2010.

"Marriage a la Mode Americaine." *Saturday Review of Politics, Literature, Science, and Art*. December 18, 1869, 789.

"Marriage and Divorce." *Columbus Enquirer-Sun* April 10, 1919, 4.

"Marriage should not just be for heterosexuals Series: Letters." *St. Petersburg Times*. April 2, 1996, 9.A.

Martin, Judith. "Slave Spirituals on the Mall." *Washington Post*. July 4, 1970.

Martin, Michel. Interview with Tera Hunter. *NPR New Discoveries in Black History*. Podcast audio. February 11, 2010. https://www.npr.org/templates/story/story.php?storyId=123608207.

McFadden, Robert D. "Alex Haley Denies Allegation that Parts of 'Roots' Were Copied from Novel Written by Mississippi Teacher." *New York Times*. April 24, 1977, 4.

McLaughlin, Pauline and Dawn Thompson. "Bride and Broom." *Daily Mail*. September 17, 2004, 13.

Meyer, Eugene L. "Finding Words for Slavery." *Washington Post*. February 22, 2001. https://www.washingtonpost.com/archive/local/2001/02/22/finding-words-for-slavery/b48f18c2-981e-4a54-89ee-699cca0d6d78/?utm_term=.76cb64ef19b3.

Millner, Denene. "Married to Black Tradition: Afrocentric Weddings Draw from a Diverse Heritage." *New York Daily News*. May 25, 1997, 5.

——— "Newlyweds' Leap of Faith: Jumping the Broom, a Ritual Rooted in Slavery, Rises in Popularity." *New York Daily News*. April 28, 1996, 5.

"Missouri Notes." *Kansas City Star*. May 28, 1907, 6.

Mitchell, Marsha. "Celebrating the Black Family's Survival of Many Trials and Tribulations." *Los Angeles Sentinel*. August 26, 1993, B7.

———. "Seven Lucky Steps to Jumping the Broom." *Los Angeles Sentinel*. July 22, 1993, F12.

Molly. "Jumping the Broom: Interracial Marriage." *WeddingWire.com*. March 9, 2011. https://www.weddingwire.com/wedding-forums/jumping-the-broom-interracial-marriage/08dea25df83bef4b.html.

Monaghan, Gabrielle. "Now Pagans Can Raise a Toast to Bride and Broom." *Sunday Times*. February 21, 2010, 8.

Moody, Sharon Tate. "Slave Descendants Face Struggles." *Tampa Tribune*. October 26, 2008, 15.

Moore, Trudi S. "$5 Million Lottery Winner Has $50,000 Wedding to Remember." *Jet*. July 18, 1983, 15–16.

Morgan, Kathryn L. "On Black Image and Blackness." *Black World/Negro Digest* 23, no. 2 (December 1973): 22–29, 84–85.

Morris, Bob. "Gay Marriage? How Straight." *The New York Times*. March 7, 2004.

Morrissey, Charles T. "Oral History and the Boundaries of Fiction." *Public Historian* 17, no. 2 (1985): 41–42.

Moyce, Delene. "Denial of Marriage Still Exists." *Experience*. April 7, 2000, 2.

Naidoo, Jamie Campbell. "Review: Ellen's Broom." *Library Media Connection*. August 1, 2012, 64.

Neal, Mark Anthony. "Jumping the Broom to Equality." *HuffPost* (blog). October 8, 2011, https://www.huffingtonpost.com/mark-anthony-neal/new-york-gay-marriage_b _913653.html.

"Negro Married Same Woman Nearly Fifty Eight Years Ago." *Bisbee Daily Review*. September 3, 1912, 1.

"New Way of Getting a Husband." *Boston Cultivator*. March 11, 1848, 10–11.

"New Way of Getting a Husband." *Boston Evening Transcript*. January 31, 1848, 4.

"Newlywed Honeymoon in Greek Islands." *Los Angeles Sentinel*. August 9, 1984, C1.

Nobile, Philip. "Alex Haley's 'Roots' Is Bad History." *Reading Eagle*. May 14, 1977, 4.

———. "Uncovering Roots." *Village Voice*. February 17, 1993.

O'Connor, John J. "TV: 'A Woman Called Moses' with Cicely Tyson." *New York Times*. December 11, 1978, C21.

Odean, Kathleen. "Stories of Black History and Heroes." *Providence Journal*. February 19, 2012, 8.

"Old and New Customs Mingle as Talbert-Clay Pledge Their Troth." *Los Angeles Sentinel*. September 2, 1993, C1.

"Old Time Divorce in Colorado." *Omaha Daily Bee*. October 2, 1874, 3.

Oliver, Stephanie Stokes. "Jumpin' the Broom without the Crazies: How to Plan your Wedding and Keep Everyone Happy." *Essence* 11, no. 2 (1980): 113.

Ottaway, Mark. "Tangled Roots." *Sunday Times* (London). April 10, 1977, 17, 22.

"Our Family Wedding (2010)." *The Numbers: Where Data and the Movie Business Meet*. Accessed June 11, 2019. https://www.the-numbers.com/movie/Our-Family -Wedding#tab=summary.

"Our Young Folks." *North American and United States Gazette*. December 28, 1866, E 991.

Owens, Earnest. "Now Is the Time to Start Talking about Racism in the LGBT Community." *HuffingtonPost.com*. May 13, 2016. https://www.huffingtonpost.com /ernest-owens/now-is-the-time-to-start-_b_7261390.html.

Padilioni Jr., James. "The History and Significance of Kente Cloth in the Black Diaspora." *Black Perspectives*. May 22, 2017. https://www.aaihs.org/the-history-and-significance-of -kente-cloth-in-the-black-diaspora/.

Padilla, Omar. "Jumping the Broom: Finding Love in Prison." *Washington Square News*. October 15, 2019. https://nyunews.com/2019/10/15/jumping-the-broom-finding-love -in-prison/.

Page, Clarence. "Alex Haley—His Facts and Truths." *Gadsden Times*. March 13, 1993, 37.

Page, Ron. "Wedding Traditions Play Major Role in Ceremonies." *Fuquay-Varina Independent*. March 19, 2006, 8.

"Parents May Object Due to Lucy's Youth." *Hartford Herald*. September 4, 1912, 6.

*Past and Present: The Colonial Williamsburg Podcast*. September 27, 2010. http://podcast .history.org/2010/09/27/jumpin-the-broom/.

Pennington, Patience. *A Woman Rice Planter.* New York: The MacMillan Company, 1914.

Person-Lynn, Kwaku. "Why Do We Jump the Broom?" *Los Angeles Sentinel.* November 29, 2001, A7.

Phelan, Christine. "Jumping the Broom; The Many Cultures of the Continent Come to Vivid Life in a Traditional African Wedding in Lowell." *Lowell Sun.* April 25, 2004.

"Photo Standalone 46." *Los Angeles Sentinel.* November 1, 1979, C5.

"Plot Thickens in NFL Camps." *Chicago Tribune.* August 18, 1987, 2.

"Queer Tricks of Beggars." *New York Times.* January 2, 1880.

Quisenberry, A. C. "Slavery in Kentucky." *Lexington Herald.* July 10, 1910, 1

Rael, Patrick. "Demystifying the 13th Amendment and Its Impact on Mass Incarceration." *Black Perspectives.* December 9, 2016. https://www.aaihs.org/demystifying-the-13th -amendment-and-its-impact-on-mass-incarceration.

"Review: Christmas in the Big house, Christmas in the Quarters." *Bulletin for the Center of Children's Books* 48 (1994): 57.

"Review: Ellen's Broom." *Publishers Weekly.* November 28, 2011, 55.

"Review of *Jumping the Broom.*" *Publisher's Weekly.* February 28, 1994. https://www .publishersweekly.com/978-0-8234-1042-2/.

Reynolds, Michele Miles. "Jumping the Broom—This Symbol of Starting a New Life Together Is Making a Comeback." *Cheboygan Daily Tribune.* March 27, 2012, B8.

Riley, John. "Baltimore Anti-Marriage Flyers Target Race." *Metroweekly.* October 11, 2012. https://www.metroweekly.com/2012/10/baltimore-anti-marriage-fliers/.

"Ritual Is Based on Pagan Principles." *Bristol Post.* November 4, 2010, 11.

Roback, Diane, and Elizabeth Devereaux. "Children's Books—Jumping the Broom by Courtni C. Wright and Illustrated by Gershom Griffith." *Publishers Weekly* 241, no. 1 (1994): 81.

Rochman, Hazel. "Review: Jumping the Broom and A Day with Daddy." *Booklist.* October 15, 2004, 410.

Roy, Molly. "Archiving Black Dance: Gesel Mason Preserves, and Dances, the Work of African American Choreographers." *sightlinesmag.org.* August 27, 2018. https:// sightlinesmag.org/archiving-black-dance-gesel-mason-preserves-and-dances-the-work -of-african-american-choreographers.

Saulny, Susan. "Black? White? Asian? More Young Americans Choose All of the Above." *New York Times.* January 30, 2011, A1

Shamsian, Jacob. "Here's the Tangled History behind Why Some Couples Jump over a Broom at Their Wedding." Insider.com. April 14, 2017. http://www.thisisinsider.com /jumping-the-broom-wedding-tradition-meaning-history-2017-4.

"Shanties on the Capital." *Colorado Springs Gazette.* September 2, 1918, 6.

Shaw, Dan. "Vows; Sabrina Diggs and Serigne N'Diaye." *New York Times.* March 19, 1995.

Shay. "Is It Wrong to 'Jump the Broom' at Your Wedding If You're Marrying a White Guy?" *yahoo.com.* March 2, 2009. https://answers.yahoo.com/question/index?qid =20090302121910AAMFudG&page=2.

Shenker, Israel. "Some Historians Dismiss Report of Factual Mistakes in *Roots.*" *New York Times.* April 10, 1977, 29.

"Simplifiers; Jumping; Ceremony." *Duluth News Tribune.* July 2, 1922, 5.

Sims, Muriel L. Whetstone. "What the Bride of the '90s Wants in Her Big Day, Her Man, and Her Love Life." *Ebony* 52, no. 8 (June 1997): 58.

Skerritt, Andrew J. "Race and Perception." *St. Petersburg Times.* January 2, 2004, 1E.

Skousen, Lesley. "Jumping the Broom: The Evolution of a Wedding Tradition." *Footnoting History Podcast.* April 19, 2014. https://www.footnotinghistory.com/home/jumping-the -broom-the-evolution-of-a-wedding-tradition.

"Slaves Originated 'Jumping the Broom.'" *Pittsburgh Post-Gazette.* February 18, 1997, C5.

"Somerset Homecoming to Reunite Slave Descendants Is a First in North Carolina." *Afro-American.* August 30, 1986, 7.

"St. Mary's Cullings." *Savannah Tribune.* October 28, 1899, 2.

Steelman, Ben. "Honoring the Past." *Sunday Star News.* February 4, 2001, 7.

Stokes, Stephanie J. "'Jumping Over the Broom' Is Better." *Essence* 8, no. 10 (1978): 8.

Stuart, Jesse. "Jumping the Broom: Love in the Mountains." *Collier's.* January 1, 1938, 26–28, 44.

"Suit Against Alex Haley Is Dismissed." *Montreal Gazette.* September 22, 1978, 49.

"Talbert/Jefferson Jump the Broom." *Los Angeles Sentinel.* March 2, 1989, C1.

Tapley, M. "Dr. Maulana Karenga: Father of Kwanzaa." *New York Amsterdam News.* December 24, 1994.

———. "Is Love Undergoing Change in African Tradition?" *New York Amsterdam News.* April 5, 1986.

"The Freedmen's Bureau Issues Marriage Orders." *Prologue: The Journal of the National Archives* 37 (Spring 2005): 61.

"The Orator of the Day." *Richmond Planet.* January 9, 1892, 1.

"The Republican Saint's Broom-Jumping Kentucky Marriage." *Gazette Fort Worth Texas.* September 30 1884, 2.

"The Well of Horniness." *Dykespeak.* November–December 1993, 12.

Thomas, Karen M. "Bride's Wedding Inspired from Times of Slavery." *Mobile Register.* August 25 1995, 4

———. "Slavery Inspires Wedding." *Columbia (Washington).* August 27, 1995, 1.

Thompson, L'Oreal. "Can White Couples Jump the Broom?" *Jet.* November 11, 2014. https://www.jetmag.com/jetlove/poll-can-white-couples-jump-the-broom/.

Tipton, Nancy. "'Jubilee' Marks Cultural Union." *Jackson Daily News.* November 22, 1976, 5.

Tracy, Kate. "Local Self-Taught Children's Book Author Living Her Dream." *Alaska Star.* March 30, 2006.

Ulen, Eisa Nefertari. "For Children: A Celebration of Black Married Life." *The Crisis* 119, no. 2 (2012): 39.

"Viewer Raps Udell's Feature on *Roots.*" *Indianapolis Recorder.* November 12, 1977.

Wangdangdula. "Alvin Gaines and the Themes- Let's Jump the Broomstick." YouTube video, 2:04. September 28, 2011. https://www.youtube.com/watch?v=s-LK0YL0O7A.

Watkins, Mel. "Weddings: Vows." *New York Times.* May 26, 2002, sect. 9, 9.

Watson, Pernell. "Jumping the Broom Began with Slaves." *Daily Press* (Newport News, Va.). May 7, 2000, G4.

"Wedding Anniversary." *St. John's Review.* February 14, 1913, 1.

"Wedding Announcement." *Women's Monthly* 9, no. 5 (2001): 3.

"Weddings/Celebrations." *New York Times*. September 29, 2002, sect. 9, 19.

"Weekly Almanac." *Jet*. May 22, 1975, 46.

West, Hollie I. "A Woman Called Moses." *Washington Post*. December 11, 1978, B1.

West, Malcolm R. "Black Historians Reflect on Criticisms of *Roots*." *Jet*. April 28, 1977, 17.

White, Renee Minus. "Winter Wedding with African Touch." *New York Amsterdam News*. December 26, 1992, 15.

Williams, Barbara Osborne. "Jumping the Broom: Book Review." *School Library Journal* 40 (April 1994): 115.

Williams, Lena. "In a 90's Quest for Black Identity, Intense Doubts and Disagreement." *New York Times*. November 30, 1991.

"Who Is It?" *Daily National Journal*. March 29, 1831.

Woodham, Martha. "Newlyweds: Romance on the River." *Atlanta Journal and Constitution*. September 8, 1996, 5.

———. "Something Old, Something New: 'Traditional' Wedding Ceremonies Vary Widely to Reflect Ancient Histories, Modern Heritages or Blended Customs." *Atlanta Journal and Constitution*. June 7, 1993, C1.

"Why *Roots* Hits Home." *Time*. February 14, 1977, 42–46.

Yerger, V. B. "Jumping the Broom." *Essence* 11, no. 5 (1980): 4.

Young, Adrienne, and Little Sadie. "'Jump the Broom,' 7/15/04 Grey Fox Bluegrass Festival." YouTube. https://www.youtube.com/watch?v=J2v5wZGfing.

Young, Danielle. "White Couple Jumps the Broom & We're Like, No You Can't Do That." November 11, 2014. https://hellobeautiful.com/2753548/history-of-jumping-the-broom/.

Ziyad, Hari. "For Black Queers, Invisibility Is Often the Best Liberation Strategy." *Slate.com*. June 29, 2017. http://www.slate.com/blogs/outward/2017/06/29/is_lgbtq_visibility_politics_inherently_anti_black.html.

Zuckerman, Faye B. "'Jumping the Broom'—The Wicca Way to get Married." *Providence Journal*. February 18, 2006, D1.

## Scholarly Articles and Book Chapters

Adams, Paul. "Television as a Gathering Place." *Annals of the Association of American Geographers* 82, no. 1 (1992): 117–135.

Allen, R. L., and W. T. Bielby. "Blacks' Attitudes and Behaviors toward Television." *Communication Research* 6, no. 4 (1979): 407–436.

Allison, Lelah. "Folk Beliefs Collected in Southeastern Illinois." *Journal of American Folklore* 63, no. 249 (1950): 317–346.

Anosike, Benji J. O. "Africa and Afro-Americans: The Bases for Greater Understanding and Solidarity." *Journal of Negro Education* 51 (Autumn 1982): 434–448.

Arnez, Nancy L. "From His Story to Our Story: A Review of *Roots—The Saga of an American Family* by Alex Haley." *Journal of Negro Education* 46, no. 3 (1977): 367–372.

Ashley, Colin P. "Gay Liberation: How a Once Radical Movement Got Married and Settled Down." *New Labor Forum* 24, no. 3 (2015): 28–32.

Bailyn, Bernard. "The Idea of Atlantic History." *Itinerario* 20, no. 1 (1996): 19–44.

Ball-Rokeach, Sandra J., Joel W. Grube, and Milton Rokeach. "Roots: The Next Generation—Who Watched and with What Effect?" *Public Opinion Quarterly* 45 (Spring 1981): 58–68.

Bannet, Eve Tavor. "The Marriage Act of 1753: 'A Most Cruel Law for the Fair Sex.'" *Eighteenth-Century Studies* 30, no. 3 (1997): 233–254.

Bassichis, Morgan, and Dean Spade. "Queer Politics and Anti-Blackness." In *Queer Necropolitics*, edited by Jin Haritaworn, Adi Kuntsman, and Silvia Posocco, 192–204. London: Routledge, 2014.

Bauer, Margaret D. "'[He] Didn't Come Here on the *Mayflower*': A Defense of Alex Haley's *Roots*." In *Crossroads: A Southern Culture Annual*, edited by Ted Olsen, 377–401. Macon, GA: Mercer University Press, 2005.

Baxter, Randolph W. "Ar'nt We a Couple? A Historical Comparison of Slave Marriages and Same-Sex Marriages." In *Defending Same-Sex Marriage*. Vol. 3. *The Freedom to Marry Movement. Education, Advocacy, Culture, and the Media*, edited by William A. Thompson and Martin Dupuis, 149–163. Westport, CT: Praeger, 2007.

Bay, Mia. "The Historical Origins of Afrocentrism." *Amerikastudien/American Studies* 45, no. 4 (2000): 501–512.

Beuford, Fred. "A Conversation with Earnest J. Gaines (1972)." *Conversations with Earnest Gaines*, edited by John Lowe, 16–24. Jackson, MS: University Press of Mississippi, 1995.

Bird, Stephanie Rose. "Jumping the Broom." In *The Greenwood Encyclopedia of African American Folklore*. Vol. 2. Edited by Anand Prahlad, 733–735. Westport, CT: Greenwood Press, 2006.

Brandon, Elizabeth. "Moeurs et langue de la paroisse Vermillon en Louisiane." PhD diss., Laval University, 1955.

———. "The Socio-Cultural Traits of the French Folksong in Louisiana." *Revue de Louisiane/Louisiana Review* 1 (1972): 19–52.

Brewer, J. Mason. "Afro-American Folklore." *Journal of American Folklore* 60, no. 238 (1947): 377–382.

Brooks, Siobhan. "Black on Black Love: Black Lesbian and Bisexual Women, Marriage, and Symbolic Meaning." *Black Scholar* 47, no. 4 (2017): 32–46.

Cade, John B. "Out of the Mouths of Ex-Slaves." *Journal of Negro History* 20, no. 3 (1935): 294–337.

Carda, Jeanelle Marie. "Wiccan Marriage and American Marriage Law: Interactions." MA thesis, Georgia State University, 2008.

Chesnutt, Charles W. "A Deep Sleeper." In *The Conjure Woman and Other Conjure Tales*, edited by Richard H. Brodhead, 136–145. Durham, NC: Duke University Press, 1993.

Childs, Matt D. "Slave Culture." In *The Routledge History of Slavery*, edited by Gad Heuman and Trevor Burnard, 170–186. New York: Routledge, 2011.

Christopher, F. Scott, Richard A Fabes, and Patricia M. Wilson. "Family Television Viewing: Implications for Family Life Education." *Family Relations* 38, no. 2 (1989): 210–214.

Clarke, John, Stuart Hall, Tony Jefferson, and Brian Roberts. "Subcultures, Cultures, and Class." In *Resistance through Rituals: Youth Subcultures in Post-War Britain*, edited by Stuart Hall and Tony Jefferson, 3–59. 1975; London: Routledge, 2006.

Coclanis, Peter A. "Atlantic World or Atlantic/World?" *William and Mary Quarterly* 63 (October 2006): 725–742.

Cody, Cheryll Ann. "Marriage." In *Dictionary of Afro-American Slavery*, edited by Randall M. Miller and John David Smith, 437. Westport, CT: Greenwood Press, 1988.

———. "Naming, Kinship, and Estate Dispersal: Notes on Slave Family Life on a South Carolina Plantation, 1786 to 1833." *William and Mary Quarterly* 39, no. 1 (1982): 192–211.

———. "There Was No Absalom on the Ball Plantations: Slave Naming Practices in the South Carolina Low Country, 1720–1865." *American Historical Review* 92, no. 3 (1987): 563–596.

Collard, Clyde V. "The Cajun Family: Adjustment to Modern Trends." In *The Culture of Acadiana: Tradition and Change in South Louisiana*, edited by Steven L. Del Sesto and Jon L. Gibson, 111–118. Lafayette: University of Southwestern Louisiana Press, 1975.

Cooke, J. "Notes on Irish Folklore from Connaught, Collected Chiefly in North Donegal." *Folklore* 7, no. 3 (1896): 299–301.

Courlander, Harold. "Kunta Kinte's Struggle to Be African." *Phylon* 47, no. 4 (1986): 294–302.

———. *Negro Folk Music, U.S.A.* New York: Columbia University Press, 1963.

Crenshaw, Kimberle. "Mapping the Margins: Intersectionality, Identity Politics, and Violence against Women of Color." *Stanford Law Review* 43, no. 6 (1991): 1241–1299.

Crooke, W. "The Lifting of the Bride." *Folk-Lore* 13, no. 3 (1902): 226–251.

Cross, Tom Peete. "Folk-Lore from the Southern States." *Journal of American Folklore* 22, no. 84 (1909): 251–255.

Curry, James. "The Narrative of James Curry." In *Slave Testimony: Two Centuries of Letters, Speeches, Interviews, and Autobiographies*, edited by John W. Blassingame, 139–140. Baton Rouge: Louisiana State University Press, 1977.

Dangerfield, David W. "Hard Rows to Hoe: Free Black Farmers in Antebellum South Carolina." PhD diss., University of South Carolina, 2014.

Davis, David Brion. "A Review of the Conflicting Theories of the Slave Family." *Journal of Blacks in Higher Education*, no. 16 (Summer 1997): 100–103.

Davis, John. "The Post Captain: or, Wooden Walls Well Manned." In *The Omnibus of Modern Romance*, edited by James Mowatt, 89–173. New York: James Mowatt, 1844.

Dawson, Kevin. "Slave Culture." In *The Oxford Handbook of Slavery in the Americas*, edited by Mark M. Smith and Robert Paquette, 465–488. Oxford: Oxford University Press, 2011.

Day, Randall D., and Daniel Hook. "A Short History of Divorce." *Journal of Divorce* 10, no. 3–4 (1987): 57–58.

Debien, Gabriel. "The Acadians in Santo Domingo: 1764–1789." In *The Cajuns: Essays on Their History and Culture*, edited by Glenn R. Conrad, 21–96. Lafayette: The Center for Louisiana Studies, 1978.

De Montellano, Bernard Ortiz, Gabriel Haslip-Viera, and Warren Barbour. "They Were NOT Here before Columbus: Afrocentric Hyperdiffusionism in the 1990s." *Ethnohistory* 44, no. 2 (1997): 199–234.

Denny, Edward W. "Private Correspondents: Civil War Era Letters from the Papers of Julia Anna Phillips." PhD diss., Arizona State University, 2009.

Dunak, Karen N. "Ceremony and Citizenship: African American Weddings, 1945–1960." *Gender and History* 21, no. 2 (2009): 402–424.

Dundes, Alan. "'Jumping the Broom': On the Origin and Meaning of an African American Wedding Tradition." *Journal of American Folklore* 109, no. 433 (1996): 324–329.

Egejuru, Phanuel, and Robert Elliot Fox. "An Interview with Margaret Walker." *Callaloo* 6 (May 1979): 29–35.

Ellis, Clifton, and Rebecca Ginsburg. Introduction. In *Cabin, Quarter, and Plantation: Architecture and Landscapes of North American Slavery*, edited by Clifton Ellis and Rebecca Ginsburg. New Haven, CT: Yale University Press, 2010.

Engstrom, Erika, and Beth Semic. "Portrayal of Religion in Reality TV Programming: Hegemony and the Contemporary American Wedding." *Journal of Media and Religion* 2, no. 3 (2009): 145–163.

Fairchild, Halford H., Russell Stockard, and Philip Bowman. "Impact of *Roots*: Evidence from the National Survey of Black Americans." *Journal of Black Studies* 16 (March 1986): 307–318.

Ferris, Bill. "A Conversation with Ernest Gaines." *Humanities* 19 (July/August 1998): 61–70.

Flom, George T. "Sun-Symbols of the Tomb-Sculptures at Loughcrew, Ireland, Illustrated by Similar Figures in Scandinavian Rock-Tracings." *American Anthropologist* 26, no. 2 (1924): 139–159.

Fogleman, Aaron. "Migrations to the Thirteen British North American Colonies, 1700–1775: New Estimates." *Journal of Interdisciplinary History* 22, no. 4 (1992): 691–709.

Freibert, Lucy M., and Margaret Walker. "Southern Song: An Interview with Margaret Walker." *Frontiers: A Journal of Women's Studies* 9, no. 3 (1987): 50–56.

Games, Alison. "Atlantic History: Definitions, Challenges, and Opportunities." *American Historical Review* 111 (June 2006): 741–757.

Gerber, David A. "Haley's *Roots* and Our Own: An Inquiry into the Nature of a Popular Phenomenon." *Journal of Ethnic Studies* 5, no. 3 (1977): 87–111.

Gordon, Edmund T., and Mark Anderson. "The African Diaspora: Toward an Ethnography of Diasporic Identification." *Journal of American Folklore* 112, no. 445 (1999): 282–296.

Gorn, Elliot J. "Black Spirits: The Ghostlore of Afro-American Slaves." *American Quarterly* 36, no. 4 (1984): 549–565.

Grieves, Vicki. "The McClymonts of Nabiac: Interracial Marriage, Inheritance and Dispossession in Nineteenth-Century New South Wales Colonial Society." In *Rethinking the Racial Moment: Essays on the Colonial Encounter*, edited by Barbara Brookes and Alison Holland, 125–156. Newcastle upon Tyne, UK: Cambridge Scholars Publishing, 2011.

Grimball, Caroline Ann "Meta" Morris. *Journal of Meta Morris Grimball: South Carolina, December 1860–February 1866*. Accessed 27, 2019. https://docsouth.unc.edu/fpn /grimball/grimball.html, 95.

Gruber, Enid, and Helaine Thau. "Sexually Related Content on Television and Adolescents of Color: Media Theory, Physiological Development, and Psychological Impact." *Journal of Negro Education* 72, no. 4 (2003): 438–456.

Gunn, Rex. "An Oregon Charivari." *Western Folklore* 13, no. 2/3 (1954): 206–207.

Hahn, Steven. "Class and State in Postemancipation Societies: Southern Planters in Comparative Perspective." *American Historical Review* 95, no. 1 (1990): 75–98.

Hall, Stuart. "Cultural Identity and Diaspora." In *Colonial Discourse and Post-Colonial Theory: A Reader*, edited by Patrick Williams and Laura Chrisman, 392–403. New York: Columbia University Press, 1994.

Hamer, Marguerite B. "The Fate of the Exiled Acadians in South Carolina." *Journal of Southern History* 4, no. 2 (1938): 199–208.

Hand, Wayland D. "American Folklore after Seventy Years: Survey and Prospect." *Journal of American Folklore* 73, no. 287 (1960): 1–11.

Handler, Jerome. "*The Old Plantation* Painting at Colonial Williamsburg: New Findings and Some Observations." *African Diaspora Archaeology Network Newsletter* 13, no. 4 (December 2010): 6.

Hart, Bessie G. "Toot Makes a Match." In *Werner's Readings and Recitations*, edited by Pauline Phelps, 68. New York: Edgar S. Werner & Company, 1899.

Hayes, Michael. "Irish Travellers and Images of Counterculturality." In *Counter-Hegemony and the Irish "Other,"* edited by Thomas Acton and Michael Hayes, 45–74. Newcastle upon Tyne, UK: Cambridge Scholars Press, 2006.

Hess, Donna J., and Geoffrey W. Grant. "Prime-Time Television and Gender-Role Behavior." *Teaching Sociology* 10, no. 3 (1983): 371–388.

Hine, Darlene Clark. "The Black Studies Movement: Afrocentric-Traditionalist-Feminist Paradigms for the Next Stage." *Black Scholar* 22, no. 3 (1992): 11–18.

Holsey, Bayo. "Black Atlantic Traditions: History, Race, and Transnationalism in Ghana." *Cultural Anthropology* 28, no. 3 (2013): 504–518.

Howard, J. G. Rothbart, and L. Sloan. "The Response to 'Roots': A National Survey." *Journal of Broadcasting* 22, no. 3 (1978): 279–287.

Hudnut, Allison, and Hayes Baker-Crothers. "Acadian Transients in South Carolina." *American Historical Review* 43, no. 3 (1938): 500–513.

Hur, K. K. "Impact of 'Roots' on Black and White Teenagers." *Journal of Broadcasting* 22, no. 3 (1978): 289–298.

Ihde, Erin. "'So Gross a Violation of Decency': A Note on Wife Sales in Colonial Australia." *Journal of the Royal Australian Historical Society* 84, no. 1 (1998): 26–38.

Jenness, Valerie, and Sarah Fenstermaker. "Agnes Goes to Prison: Gender Authenticity, Transgender Inmates in Prisons for Men, and Pursuit of 'The Real Deal.'" *Gender and Society* 28, no. 1 (2014): 5–31.

Johnson, Lloyd. "The Welsh in the Carolinas in the Eighteenth Century." *North American Journal of Welsh Studies* 4, no. 1 (2004): 12–19.

Johnson, Loretta T. "Charivari/Shivaree: A European Folk Ritual on American Plains." *Journal of Interdisciplinary History* 20, no. 3 (1990): 371–387.

Johnson, Pearlie Mae. "African American Quilts: An Examination of Feminism, Identity, and Empowerment in the Fabric Arts of Kansas City Quilters." PhD diss., University of Missouri–Kansas City, 2008.

Jones, Bobby Frank. "A Cultural Middle Passage: Slave Marriage and Family in the Ante-Bellum South." PhD diss., University of North Carolina–Chapel Hill, 1965.

Jones, W. Rhys [Gwenith Gwynn]. "'Besom Wedding' in the Ceiriog Valley." *Folklore* 39, no. 2 (1928): 149–166.

Kiesling, Elena. "The Missing Colors of the Rainbow: Black Queer Resistance." *European Journal of American Studies* 11, no. 3 (2017). https://journals.openedition.org/ejas/11830.

Klotman, Phyllis Rauch. "'Oh Freedom'—Women and History in Margaret Walker's *Jubilee*." *Black American Literature Forum* 11, no. 4 (1977): 139–145.

Knowles, Anne Kelly. "Immigrant Trajectories through the Rural-Industrial Transition in Wales and the United States, 1795–1850." *Annals of the Association of American Geographers* 85, no. 2 (1995): 246–266.

Kunka, Andrew J. "Intertextuality and the Historical Graphic Narrative: Kyle Baker's *Nat Turner* and the Styron Controversy." *College Literature* 38, no. 3 (Summer 2011): 168–193.

Laney, Ruth. "A Conversation with Earnest J. Gaines." *Southern Review* 10 (January 1974): 3, 13–14.

Laniyonu, Ayobami. "A Comparative Analysis of Black Racial Group Consciousness in the United States and Britain." *Journal of Race, Ethnicity, and Politics* 4, no. 1 (2019): 117–147.

Law, Robin. "Book Review: *Roots* by Alex Haley." *Oral History* 6, no. 1 (Spring 1978): 128–134.

Lawal, Babatunde. "Reclaiming the Past: Yoruba Elements in African American Arts." In *The Yoruba Diaspora in the Atlantic World*, edited by Toyin Falola and Matt Childs, 291–324. Bloomington: Indiana University Press, 2004.

Lemmings, David. "Marriage and the Law in the Eighteenth Century: Hardwicke's Marriage Act of 1753." *Historical Journal* 39, no. 2 (1996): 339–360.

Leneman, Leah, and Rosalind Mitchison. "Clandestine Marriage in the Scottish Cities, 1660–1780." *Journal of Social History* 26, no. 4 (1993): 845–861.

Levine, Molly Myerowitz. "The Use and Abuse of *Black Athena*." *American Historical Review* 97, no. 2 (1992): 440–460.

Lewis, Roscoe E. "The Life of Mark Thrash." *Phylon Quarterly* 20 (1959): 389–403.

Lipson-Walker, Carolyn. "Weddings." In *The Encyclopedia of Southern Culture*, edited by Charles R. Wilson and William Ferris, 493. Chapel Hill: University of North Carolina Press, 1989.

Lowe, Richard G. "Massachusetts and the Acadians." *William and Mary Quarterly* 25, no. 2 (1968): 212–229.

Lyster, M. Eileen. "Marriage over the Broomstick." *Journal of the Gypsy Lore Society* 5, no. 1 (1911–1912): 199–201.

MacLeod, W. C. "'Jumping Over' from West Africa to South America." *American Anthropologist* 30, no. 1 (1928): 107–111.

MacRitchie, David. "Irish Tinkers and Their Language." *Journal of the Gypsy Lore Society* 1, no. 6 (1889): 350–357.

"Married in a Jest: or the Tables Turned on a Practical Joker." In *The Rural Repository, Devoted to Polite Literature: Containing Moral and Sentimental Tales, Original Communications, Biographies, Traveling Sketches, Amusing Miscellany, Humorous and Historical Anecdotes, Poetry, &c, &c*. Hudson, NY: William B. Stoddard, 1847–1848.

Masuoka, Natalie. "Political Attitudes and Ideologies of Multiracial Americans: The Implications of Mixed Race in the United States." *Political Research Quarterly* 61, no. 2 (2008): 253–267.

McDonnell, Lawrence T. "Money Knows No Master: Market Relations and the American Slave Community." In *Developing Dixie: Modernization in a Traditional Society*, edited by Winfred B. Moore Jr., Joseph F. Tripp, and Lyon G. Tyler Jr., 31–44. Westport, CT: Greenwood Press, 1988.

McKelvie, Donald. "Proverbial Elements in the Oral Tradition of an English Urban Industrial Region." *Journal of the Folklore Institute* 2, no. 3 (1965): 244–261.

McQueeney, Krista B. "The New Religious Rite: A Symbolic Interactionist Case Study of Lesbian Commitment Rituals." *Journal of Lesbian Studies* 7, no. 2 (2003): 49–70.

Mills, Gary B. "Shades of Ambiguity: Comparing Antebellum Free People of Color in 'Anglo' Alabama and 'Latin' Louisiana." In *Plain Folk of the South Revisited*, edited by Samuel C. Hyde, Jr., 161–186. Baton Rouge: Louisiana State University Press, 1997.

Mills, Gary B., and Elizabeth Shown Mills. "The Genealogist's Assessment of Alex Haley's *Roots*." *National Genealogical Society Quarterly* 72 (March 1984): 35–49.

———. "*Roots* and the New 'Faction': A Legitimate Tool for CLIO?" *Virginia Magazine of History and Biography* 89 (January 1981): 3–26.

Montell, William Lynwood. "A Folk History of the Coe Ridge Negro Colony." 2 Vols. PhD diss., Indiana University, 1964.

Mooney, James. "The Funeral Customs of Ireland." *Proceedings of the American Philosophical Society* 25, no. 128 (1888): 243–296.

Moore, David Chioni. "Routes: Alex Haley's *Roots* and the Rhetoric of Genealogy." *Transition* 64 (1994): 4–21.

Moore, Jesse T. "Alex Haley's *Roots*: Ten Years Later." *Western Journal of Black Studies* 18 (Summer 1994): 70–76.

Morgan, Kathryn L. "The Ex-Slave Narrative as a Source for Folk History." PhD diss., University of Pennsylvania, 1970.

Morgan, Philip D. "The Significance of Kin." In *The Slavery Reader*. Vol. 1. Edited by Gad J. Heuman and James Walvin, 322–354. New York: Routledge, 2003.

Morgan, Philip D., and Jack P. Greene. "Introduction: The Present State of Atlantic History." In *Atlantic History: A Critical Appraisal*, edited by Jack P. Greene and Philip D. Morgan, 3–34. Oxford: Oxford University Press, 2009.

"Mormons Help African Americans Trace Their Roots." *Journal of Blacks in Higher Education*, no. 31 (Spring 2001): 70–71.

Myers, Norma. "The Black Poor of London: Initiatives of Eastern Seamen in the Eighteenth and Nineteenth Centuries." In *Ethnic Labour and British Imperial Trade: A History of Ethnic Seafarers in the UK*, edited by Diane Frost, 7–21. London: Frank Cass and Company, 1995.

O'Flaherty, John T. "A Sketch of the History and Antiquities of the Southern Islands of Aran, Lying Off the West Coast of Ireland; with Observations on the Religion of the Celtic Nations, Pagan Monuments of the Early Irish, Druidic Rites, &c." *Transactions of the Royal Irish Academy* 14 (1825): 99–110.

O'Neil, Patrick. "Bosses and Broomsticks: Ritual and Authority in Antebellum Slave Weddings." *Journal of Southern History* 75, no. 1 (2009): 29–48.

Palmer, Bryan D. "Discordant Music: Charivaris and Whitecapping in Nineteenth-Century North America." In *Crime and Deviance in Canada: Historical Perspectives*, edited by Chris McCormick and Len Green, 48–66. Toronto: Canadian Scholar's Press, 2005.

Parker, Haywood. "Folk-Lore of the North Carolina Mountaineers." *Journal of American Folklore* 20, no. 79 (1907): 241–250.

Parry, Tyler D. "Jumping the Broom: A Black Thing or Nah." *Griots Republic*, June 2017. http://www.griotsrepublic.com/jumping-broom/.

———. "Love and Marriage: Domestic Relations and Matrimonial Strategies among the Enslaved in the Atlantic World." PhD diss., University of South Carolina, 2014.

———. "Married in Slavery Time: Jumping the Broom in Atlantic Perspective." *Journal of Southern History* 81, no. 2 (2015): 273–312.

———. "The Politics of Plagiarism: *Roots*, Margaret Walker, and Alex Haley." In *Reconsidering Roots: Race, Politics, and Memory*, edited by Erica L. Ball and Kellie Carter Jackson, 47–62. Athens: University of Georgia Press, 2017.

———. "White Southern Memories and the Legacy of 'Slave Marriage' in the United States." *Journal of Global Slavery* 1, nos. 2–3 (2016): 296–324.

Peoples, Betsy. "Revisiting *Roots* after 25 Years." *New Crisis* 109, no. 1 (2002): 10–11.

Perry, Kennetta Hammond. "'Little Rock' in Britain: Jim Crow's Transatlantic Topographies." *Journal of British Studies* 51, no. 1 (2012): 155–177.

Poindexter, P. M., and C. A. Stroman. "Blacks and Television: A Review of the Research Literature." *Journal of Broadcasting* 25, no. 2 (1981): 103–122.

Powell, Carolyn J. "What's Love Got to Do with It?: The Dynamics of Desire, Race, and Murder in the Slave South." PhD diss., University of Massachusetts, Amherst, 2002.

Price, Sadie F. "Kentucky Folk-Lore." *Journal of American Folklore* 14, no. 52 (1901): 30–38.

Probert, Rebecca. "Chinese Whispers and Welsh Weddings." *Continuity and Change* 20, no. 2 (2005): 211–228.

———. "The Impact of the Marriage Act of 1753: Was It Really 'A Most Cruel Law for the Fair Sex'?" *Eighteenth-Century Studies* 38, no. 2 (2005): 247–262.

Propper, Alice M. "Love, Marriage, and Father-Son Relationships among Male Prisoners." *Prison Journal* 69, no. 2 (1989): 57–63.

Protinsky, Ruth A., and Terry M. Wildman. "Roots: Reflections from the Classroom." *Journal of Negro Education* 48 (Spring 1979): 171–181.

Pujols, Alexis J. "Film Review of Noah's Arc: Jumping the Broom." *Journal of GLBT Family Studies* 6, no. 1 (2010): 102.

Redmond, Michael. "A Stirring Concert Honors U.S. Composer." *Newark Star-Ledger*. June 12, 1989, 32.

Rein, Martin, and Jeffrey M. Elliot. "*Roots*: A New Approach to Teaching Black History." *Negro History Bulletin* 40, no. 1 (1977): 664–667.

Roberts, Hilda. "Louisiana Superstitions." *Journal of American Folklore* 40, no. 156 (1927): 144–208.

Rodriquez, Jason. "Color-Blind Ideology and the Cultural Appropriation of Hip-Hop." *Journal of Contemporary Ethnography* 35, no. 6 (2006): 645–668.

Roheim, Geza. "The Significance of Stepping Over." In *Fire in the Dragon and Other Psychoanalytic Essays on Folklore*, edited by Alan Dundes, 12–18. Princeton, NJ: Princeton University Press, 1992.

Rousseau, Nicole. "Social Rhetoric and the Construction of Black Motherhood." *Journal of Black Studies* 44, no. 5 (2013): 451–471.

Saucier, Corinne. "Historie et traditions de la paroisse des Avoyelles en Louisiana." PhD diss., University of Laval, 1949.

"Scholarly Papers." *Journal of Blacks in Higher Education* 44 (Summer 2004): 158.

Schellekens, Jona. "Courtship, the Clandestine Marriage Act, and Illegitimate Fertility in England." *Journal of Interdisciplinary History* 25, no. 3 (1995): 433–444.

Schwartzberg, Beverly. "'Lots of Them Did That': Desertion, Bigamy, and Marital Fluidity in Late-Nineteenth-Century America." *Journal of Social History* 37, no. 3 (2004): 573–600.

Shockley, Ann Allen. "Oral History: A Research Tool for Black History." *Negro History Bulletin* 41, no. 1 (1978): 787–789.

"Scotch Egyptians of the 19th Century." *Journal of the Gypsy Lore Society* 1, no. 1 (1888): 179.

Smith, Faith. "'You Know You're West Indian If . . .': Codes of Authenticity in Colin Channer's *Waiting in Vain*." *Small Axe* 5, no. 2 (2001): 41–59.

Snowden, Frank M., Jr. "Misconceptions about African Blacks in the Ancient Mediterranean World: Specialists and Afrocentrists." *Arion: A Journal of Humanities and the Classics* 4, no. 3 (1997): 28–50.

Spear, Jennifer M. "'They Need Wives': Metissage and the Regulation of Sexuality in French Louisiana, 1699–1730." In *Sex, Love, Race: Crossing Boundaries in North American History*, edited by Martha Hodes, 35–59. New York: New York University Press, 1999.

St. Romwold. "The Blasphemer's Warning." In *The Ingoldsby Legends*, edited by Richard Harris Barham, 51. London: Richard Bentley and Son, 1882.

Steiner, Roland. "Superstitions and Beliefs from Central Georgia." *Journal of American Folklore* 12, no. 47 (1899): 261–271.

Stephens, Vincent. "What Child Is This?: Closely Reading Collectivity and Queer Childrearing in 'Lackawanna Blues' and 'Noah's Arc.'" *African American Review* 44, no. 1/2 (2011): 235–253.

Street, Joe. "Malcolm X, Smethwick, and the Influence of the African American Freedom Struggle on British Race Relations in the 1960s." *Journal of Black Studies* 38, no. 6 (2008): 932–950.

Strong, Imani. "Jumping the Broom: Myth, Memory, and Neo-Traditionalism in African-American Weddings." MA thesis, University of Oxford, 2014.

Sullivan, Andrew. *Virtually Normal: An Argument about Homosexuality*. 1995; New York: Alfred A. Knopf, 1996.

Sullivan, C. W., III. "'Jumping the Broom': A Further Consideration of the Origins of an African American Wedding Custom." *Journal of American Folklore* 110 (Spring 1997): 203–204.

———. "'Jumping the Broom': Possible Welsh Origins of an African-American Custom." *Southern Folklore* 55, no. 1 (1998): 15–23.

Summers-Effler, Erika. "Ritual Theory." In *Handbook of the Sociology of Emotions*, edited by Jan E. Stets and Jonathan H. Turner, 135–154. New York: Springer, 2006.

Surlin, S. H. "'Roots' Research: A Summary of the Findings." *Journal of Broadcasting* 22, no. 3 (1978): 309–320.

Surlin, S. H. and C. F. Cooper. "The Jeffersons' and Their Racially Integrated Neighbors: Who Watches and Who is Offended?" Presented to the Southern Speech Communication Association, San Antonio, Texas, 1976.

Surlin, S. H., and E. D. Tate. "'All in the Family': Is Archie Funny?" *Journal of Communication* 26, no. 4 (1976): 61–68.

Tadman, Michael. "The Demographic Cost of Sugar: Debates on Slave Societies and Natural Increase in the Americas." *American Historical Review* 105, no. 5 (2000): 1534–1575.

Taylor, Orville. "'Jumping the Broomstick': Slave Marriage and Morality in Arkansas." *Arkansas Historical Quarterly* 17, no. 3 (1958): 217–231.

Tetty-Fio, E. L. "Historical and Contemporary Black-American Geographies." In *Race, Ethnicity and Place in a Changing America*, 3rd ed., edited by John W. Frazier, Eugene L. Tettey-Fio, and Norah F. Henry, 153–168. Albany, NY: State University Press of New York, 2016.

"The Report of Governor Popple, May 2, 1749." *Bermuda Historical Quarterly* 25, no. 2 (1968): 35–61.

Thompson, T. W. "The Ceremonial Customs of British Gypsies." *Folklore* 24, no. 3 (1913): 314–356.

Tidwell, James Nathan. "Comments on Word-Lists in PADS." *Publication of the American Dialect Society* 13, no. 1 (1950): 16–21.

Toll, Robert C. "From Folktype to Stereotype: Images of Slaves in Antebellum Minstrelsy." *Journal of the Folklore Institute* 8, no. 1 (1971): 38–47.

Tucker, Lauren R., and Hemant Shah. "Race and the Transformation of Culture: The Making of the Television Miniseries *Roots*." *Critical Studies in Mass Communication* 9 (December 1992): 325–336.

Tyson, Amy M., and Azie Mira Dungey. "'Ask a Slave' and Interpreting Race on Public History's Front Line, Interview with Azie Mira Dungey." *Public Historian* 36, no. 1 (2014): 36–60.

Walker, Margaret. "How I Wrote Jubilee." In *How I Wrote Jubilee and Other Essays on Life and Literature*, edited by Maryemma Graham, 50–68. 1972; New York: The Feminist Press at the City University of New York, 1990.

———. "Willing to Pay the Price." In *Many Shades of Black*, edited by Stanton L. Wormley and Lewis H. Fenderson, 119–130. New York: William Morrow and Company, 1969.

Waugh, F. W. "Canadian Folklore from Ontario." *Journal of American Folklore* 31, no. 119 (1918): 63–72.

Wetherell, Charles. "Slave Kinship: A Case Study of the South Carolina Good Hope Plantation, 1835–1856." *Journal of Family History* 6, no. 3 (1981): 294–308.

"Wiccan High Priestess Zsuzsanna Budapest." In *Lesbian and Gay Marriage: Private Commitments and Public Ceremonies*, edited by Suzanne Sherman. Philadelphia: Temple University Press, 1992.

Wilkinson, Doris. "The Black Family: Past and Present: A Review Essay." *Journal of Marriage and Family* 40, no. 4 (1978): 829–835.

Williamson, George. "Superstitions from Louisiana." *Journal of American Folklore* 18, no. 70 (1905): 229–230.

Wills, John E., Jr. "Taking Historical Novels Seriously." *Public Historian* 6, no. 1 (1984): 39–46.

Wiltse, H. M. "Some Mountain Superstitions of the South." *Journal of American Folklore* 12, no. 45 (1899): 131–135.

Wright, Donald R. "Uprooting Kunta Kinte: On the Perils of Relying on Encyclopedic Informants." *History in Africa* 8 (1981): 205–217. This is all the information available about date of publication.

Yep, Gust A., and John P. Elia. "Racialized Masculinities and the New Homonormativity in LOGO's *Noah's Arc*." *Journal of Homosexuality* 59, no. 7 (2012): 890–911.

Young, Stacy L. "Brooms." In *World of a Slave*. Vol. 2. Edited by Martha B. Katz-Hyman and Kym Rice, 83. Santa Barbara, CA: Greenwood, 2011.

## Books

Addy, Sidney Odall. *Household Tales and Traditional Remains*. London: Sheffield, Pawson and Brailsford, 1895.

Adeleke, Tunde. *The Case against Afrocentrism*. Jackson: University Press of Mississippi, 2009.

Alexander, Leslie M., and Walter C. Rucker, eds. *Encyclopedia of African American History*, vol. 1. Santa Barbara, CA: ABC-CLIO, 2010.

Allen, Richard B. *Slaves, Freedmen and Indentured Laborers in Colonial Mauritius*. New York: Cambridge University Press, 1999.

Anyiam, Thony C. *Jumping the Broom in Style: A Collection of Styles and Information for the Entire Wedding Party*. Bloomington, IN: AuthorHouse, 2007.

Appiah, Kwame Anthony, and Amy Gutmann. *Color Conscious: The Political Morality of Race*. Princeton, NJ: Princeton University Press, 1996.

Arsenault, Bona. *History of the Acadians*. Montreal: Lemeac, 1978.

Asante, Molefi Kete. *The Afrocentric Idea*. Philadelphia: Temple University Press, 1987.

———. *Afrocentricity: The Theory of Social Change*. 1980; Trenton, NJ: African World Press, 1988.

Ashton, John. *Florizel's Folly*. London: Chatto and Windus, 1899.

Ayers, Tess, and Paul Brown, *The Essential Guide to Gay and Lesbian Weddings*. New York: The Experiment, 2012.

Baker, John. *The Washingtons of Wessyngton Plantation: Stories of My Family's Journey to Freedom*. New York: Atria Publishing, 2009.

Baker, Kyle. *Nat Turner*. New York: Abrams Comicarts, 2008.

Baker, Lee D. *Anthropology and the Racial Politics of Culture*. Durham, NC: Duke University Press, 2010.

Baker, Ronald L., ed. *Homeless, Friendless, and Penniless: The WPA Interviews with Former Slaves Living in Indiana*. Bloomington: Indiana University Press, 2000.

Ball, Erica, and Kellie Carter Jackson, eds. *Reconsidering Roots: Race, Politics, and Memory*. Athens, GA: University of Georgia Press, 2017.

Ballowe, Hewitt L. *Creole Folk Tales: Stories of the Louisiana Marsh Country*. Baton Rouge: Louisiana State University Press, 1948.

Bancroft, Frederic. *Slave Trading in the Old South*. Columbia: University of South Carolina Press, 1931.

Baptist, Edward E. *The Half Has Never Been Told: Slavery and the Making of American Capitalism*. New York: Basic Books, 2016.

Baquaqua, Mahommah Gardo. *Biography of Mahommah G. Baquaqua*. Detroit: Geo. Pomeroy and Co., 1854.

Beggs, Thomas. *An Inquiry into the Extent and Causes of Juvenile Depravity*. London: Charles Gilpin, 1849.

Bell, Catherine. *Ritual Theory, Ritual Practice*. New York: Oxford University Press, 1992.

Bellan-Boyer, Lisa. "Review." *Journal of Religion and Health* 44, no. 4 (2005): 429–434.

Benge, Janet, and George Benge. *Harriet Tubman: Freedombound*. Lynnwood, WA: Emerald Books, 2002.

Bennett, Lerone, Jr. *Before the Mayflower: A History of Black America, 1619–1962*. New York: Johnson Publishing, 1962.

Berlin, Ira. *The Making of African American: The Four Great Migrations.* New York: Viking Press, 2010.

Berlin, Ira, and Leslie S. Rowland, eds. *Families and Freedom: A Documentary History of African-American Kinship in the Civil War Era.* New York: The New Press, 1997.

Bernal, Martin. *Black Athena: The Afroasiatic Roots of Classical Civilization.* Vol. 1. New Brunswick, NJ: Rutgers University Press, 1987.

Bernhard, Virginia. *Slaves and Slaveholders in Bermuda, 1616–1782.* Columbia: University of Missouri Press, 1999.

Berry, Daina Ramey. *Swing the Sickle for the Harvest Is Ripe: Gender and Slavery in Antebellum Georgia.* Urbana: University of Illinois Press, 2007.

Biedermann, Hans. *Dictionary of Symbolism.* New York: Facts on File, 1992.

Birdoff, Harry. *The World's Greatest Hit: Uncle Tom's Cabin.* New York: S. F. Vanni, 1947.

Black, Sonia W. *Jumping the Broom.* Broadway, NY: Scholastic, 2004.

Blackmon, Douglas. *Slavery by Another Name: The Re-Enslavement of Black People in America from the Civil War to World War II.* New York: Doubleday, 2008.

Blassingame, John W. *The Slave Community: Plantation Life in the Antebellum South.* 1972; Oxford: Oxford University Press, 1979.

Blumberg, Rhoda. *York's Adventures with Lewis and Clark: An African American's Part in the Great Expedition.* New York: Harper Collins, 2004.

Bolster, W. Jeffrey. *Black Jacks: African American Seamen in the Age of Sail.* Cambridge, MA: Harvard University Press, 1998.

Botkin, B. A. *A Treasury of Southern Folklore: Stories, Ballads, Traditions, and Folkways of the People of the South.* New York: Crown Publishers, 1949.

Brasseaux, Carl A. *The Founding of New Acadia: The Beginnings of Acadian Life in Louisiana, 1765–1803.* Baton Rouge: Louisiana State University Press, 1988.

———. *French, Cajun, Creole, Houma: A Primer on Francophone Louisiana.* Baton Rouge: Louisiana State University Press, 2005.

———. *From Acadian to Cajun: Transformation of a People, 1803–1877.* Jackson: University Press of Mississippi, 1992.

Brickell, John. *The Natural History of North Carolina. With an Account of the Trade, Manners, and Customs of the Christian and Indian Inhabitants.* 1737; Murfreesboro, NC: Johnson Publishing Company, 1968.

Brown, Kathleen. *Foul Bodies: Cleanliness in Early America.* New Haven, CT: Yale University Press, 2009.

Brown, Ras Michael. *African-Atlantic Cultures and the South Carolina Lowcountry.* Cambridge: Cambridge University Press, 2014.

Brown, William Wells. *Clotel; Or, The President's Daughter: A Narrative of Slave Life in the United States.* London: Partridge and Oakey, 1853.

———. *The Escape; or, A Leap for Freedom. A Drama in Five Acts.* Edited by John Ernest. Knoxville: University of Tennessee Press, 2001.

———. *My Southern Home; Or, The South and Its People.* Boston: A. G. Brown and Co., 1880.

———. *Narrative of William Wells Brown, a Fugitive Slave, Written by Himself.* Boston: Anti-Slavery Office, 1847.

Burton, Annie L. *Memories of Childhood's Slavery Days.* Boston: Ross Publishing Company, 1909.

Bryan, Patrick E. *The Haitian Revolution and Its Effects*. Oxford: Heinemann Educational Publishers, 1984.

Burke, Mary. *Tinkers: Synge and the Cultural History of the Irish Traveller*. Oxford: Oxford University Press, 2009.

Burton, Orville Burton. *In My Father's House Are Many Mansions: Family and Community in Edgefield, South Carolina*. Chapel Hill: University of North Carolina Press, 1985.

Cabell, James Branch. *Jurgen: A Comedy of Justice*. New York: Robert McBride and Company, 1919.

Calkhoven, Laurie. *Harriet Tubman: Leading the Way to Freedom*. New York: Sterling Publishing, 2008.

Camp, Stephanie M. H. *Closer to Freedom: Enslaved Women and Everyday Resistance in the Plantation South*. Chapel Hill: University of North Carolina Press, 2004.

Canizares-Esguerra, Jorge. *Puritan Conquistadors: Iberianizing the Atlantic, 1550–1700*. Stanford, CA: Stanford University Press, 2006.

Capo, Ava Laboy. *Wedding Traditions from Around the World*. Bloomington, IN: AuthorHouse, 2013.

Capote, Truman. *House of Flowers: Vocal Selections from the Off-Broadway Musical*. New York: Edwin H. Morris and Company, 1968.

Carleton, George W. *The Suppressed Book about Slavery*. New York: G. W. Carleton and Co., 1864.

Carmichael, Jacqueline Miller. *Trumpeting a Fiery Sound: History and Folklore in Margaret Walker's Jubilee*. Athens: University of Georgia Press, 1998.

Caruthers, William Alexander. *The Knights of the Horse-Shoe; A Traditionary Tale of the Cocked Hat Gentry of Old Dominion*. Wetumpka, AL: Charles Yancy, 1845.

Cecil-Fronsman, Bill. *Common Whites: Class and Culture in Antebellum North Carolina*. Lexington: University Press of Kentucky, 1992.

Censer, Jane Turner. *North Carolina Planters and Their Children, 1800–1860*. Baton Rouge: Louisiana State University Press, 1984.

Chakkalakal, Tess. *Novel Bondage: Slavery, Marriage, and Freedom in Nineteenth-Century America*. Urbana-Champaign: University of Illinois Press, 2011.

Cheng, Andrea. *Etched in Clay: The Life of Dave, Enslaved Potter and Poet*. New York: Lee & Low Books, 2013.

Cherlin, Andrew. *The Marriage-Go-Round: The State of Marriage and the Family in America Today*. New York: Vintage, 2009.

Childs, Dennis. *Slaves of the States: Black Incarceration from the Chain Gang to the Penitentiary*. Minneapolis: University of Minnesota Press, 2015.

Clayton, Ronnie W., ed. *Mother Wit: The Ex-Slave Narratives of the Louisiana Writer's Project*. New York: P. Lang, 1990.

Clinton, Catherine. *Harriet Tubman: The Road to Freedom*. New York: Little Brown, 2004.

Close, Stacey K. *Elderly Slaves of the Plantation South*. 1997; New York: Routledge, 2014.

Cole, Harriette. *Jumping the Broom: The African American Wedding Planner*. New York: Henry Holt and Company, 1993.

Coleman, J. Winston, Jr. *Slavery Times in Kentucky*. Chapel Hill: University of North Carolina Press, 1940.

Collins, Earl A. *Legends and Lore of Missouri.* San Antonio, TX: The Naylor Company, 1951.

Coontz, Stephanie. *Marriage, a History: From Obedience to Intimacy, or How Love Conquered Marriage.* New York: Viking, 2005.

Cosson, M. J. *Harriet Tubman.* Edina, MN: ABDO Publishing Company, 2008.

Cott, Nancy. *Public Vows: A History of Marriage and the Nation.* Cambridge, MA: Harvard University Press, 2000.

Curtin, Jeremiah. *Myths and Folklore of Ireland.* 1890; Charleston, SC: Forgotten Books, 2007.

Daudert, Charles J. *Andrew Durnford: Portrait of a Black Slave Owner.* Kalamazoo, MI: Hansa-Hewlett Publishing, 1999.

Davies, John. *A History of Wales.* 1990; New York: Penguin, 2007.

Davies, Sioned, ed. and trans. *The Mabinogion.* Oxford: Oxford University Press, 2008.

Dawson, Kevin. *Undercurrents of Power: Aquatic Culture in the African Diaspora.* Philadelphia: University of Pennsylvania Press, 2018.

Desch-Obi, T. J. *Fighting for Honor: The History of African Martial Art Traditions in the Atlantic World.* Columbia: University of South Carolina Press, 2008.

Deyle, Steven. *Carry Me Back: The Domestic Slave Trade in American Life.* Oxford: Oxford University Press, 2005.

Dickason, David H., ed. *Mr. : The Journal of a Seaman, by William Williams.* Bloomington: University of Indiana Press, 1969.

Dickason, David Howard. *William Williams: Novelist and Painter of Colonial America, 1727–1791.* Bloomington: University of Indiana Press, 1970.

Dickens, Charles. *Great Expectations.* 1861; Ware Wordsworth Editions, 1992.

———. "Narrative of Law and Crime." *The Household Narrative of Current Events.* London: Bradbury & Evans, 1850.

Diop, Cheik Anta. *The Cultural Unity of Black Africa.* 1963; London: Karnak House, 1989.

Dodd, Arthur Herbert. *The Character of Early Welsh Emigration to the United States.* Cardiff: University of Wales Press, 1957.

Dodd, William E. *The Cotton Kingdom: A Chronicle of the Old South.* New Haven, CT: Yale University Press, 1919.Douglas, Kelly Brown. *Sexuality and the Black Church: A Womanist Perspective.* Maryknoll, NY: Orbis Books, 1999.

Douglass, Frederick. *Narrative of the Life of Frederick Douglass, an American Slave. Written by Himself.* Boston: Anti-Slavery Office, 1845.

Driskell, Jay Winston, Jr. *Schooling Jim Crow: The Fight for Atlanta's Booker T. Washington High School and the Roots of Black Protest Politics.* Charlottesville: University of Virginia Press, 2014.

Du Bois, W. E. B. *The Negro American Family.* Atlanta, GA: Atlanta University Press, 1908.

Dunaway, Wilma A. *The African American Family in Slavery and Emancipation.* Cambridge: Cambridge University Press, 2003.

Dunwich, Gerina. *Wicca Craft: The Modern Witch's Book of Herbs, Magick and Dreams.* New York: Citadel Press, 1991.

———. *Witch's Halloween: A Complete Guide to the Magick, Incantations, Recipes, Spells, and Lore.* Avon: The Provenance Press, 2007.

Eagles, John, ed. *The Journal of Llewellin, a Seaman.* London: Taylor and Hessey, 1825.

Eaton, Clement. *A History of the Old South: The Emergence of a Reluctant Nation*. London: Macmillan, 1952.

Elkins, Stanley. *Slavery: A Problem in American Institutional and Intellectual Life*. Chicago: University of Chicago Press, 1959.

Equality Maryland Foundation and National Black Justice Coalition. *Jumping the Broom: A Black Perspective on Same-Gender Marriage*. Self-published, 2005.

Farmer, John S., ed. *Slang and Its Analogues, Past and Present: A Dictionary, Historical and Comparative, of the Heterodox Speech of All Classes of Society for More than Three Hundred Years*. Vol. 1. London: Poulter, 1890.

Farmer-Kaiser, Mary. *Freedwomen and the Freedmen's Bureau: Race, Gender, & Public Policy in the Age of Emancipation*. New York: Fordham University Press, 2010.

Fett, Sharla. *Working Cures: Healing, Health, and Power on Southern Slave Plantations*. Chapel Hill: University of North Carolina Press, 2002.

Fick, Carolyn E. *The Making of Haiti: The Saint Domingue Revolution from Below*. Knoxville: University of Tennessee Press, 1990.

Finley, Randy. *From Slavery to Uncertain Freedom: The Freedmen's Bureau in Arkansas, 1865–1869*. Fayetteville: University of Arkansas Press, 1996.

Fischer, David Hackett. *Albion's Seed: Four British Folkways in America*. Oxford: Oxford University Press, 1989.

Fisher, Miles Mark. *The Master's Slave: Elijah John Fisher, a Biography*. Philadelphia, PA: The Judson Press, 1922.

Fitzhugh, George. *Sociology for the South, or the Failure of Free Society*. Richmond, VA: A. Morris, 1854.

Fleetwood, Therez. *The Afrocentric Bride: A Style Guide*. New York: Amber Books, 2003.

Flower, Frank A. *The Eye of the Northwest. First Annual Report of the Statistician of Superior, Wisconsin*. Milwaukee: King, Fowle & Co., 1890.

Forret, Jeff. *Race Relations at the Margins: Slaves and Poor Whites in the Antebellum Southern Countryside*. Baton Rouge: Louisiana State University Press, 2006.

———. *Slave against Slave: Plantation Violence in the Old South*. Baton Rouge: Louisiana State University Press, 2016.

Fortier, Alcee. *Louisiana Folk Tales: In French Dialect and English Translation*. Boston: Houghton, Mifflin, and Company, 1894.

Foster, Francis Smith. *'Til Death or Distance Do Us Part: Love and Marriage in African America*. Oxford: Oxford University Press, 2010.

Frazier, E. Franklin. *The Negro Family in the United States*. Chicago: University of Chicago Press, 1940.

Frey, Sylvia, and Betty Wood. *Come Shouting to Zion: African American Protestantism in the American South and the British Caribbean to 1830*. Chapel Hill: University of North Carolina Press, 1998.

Frick, John W. *Uncle Tom's Cabin on the American Stage and Screen*. New York: Palgrave MacMillan, 2012.

Games, Alison. *Migration and the Origins of the English Atlantic World*. Cambridge, MA: Harvard University Press, 1999.

Gantz, Jeffrey, ed. and trans. *The Mabinogion*. New York: Penguin Classics, 1976.

Gardner, Gerald Brosseau. *The Meaning of Witchcraft*. Boston: Red Wheel/Weiser Books, 2004.

Gaspar, David Barry, and Darlene Clark Hine, eds. *More than Chattel: Black Women and Slavery in the Americas*. Bloomington: University of Indiana Press, 1996.

Gates, Henry Louis, Jr. *Loose Canons: Notes on the Culture Wars*. London: Oxford University Press, 1992.

Genovese, Eugene D. *Roll, Jordan, Roll: The World the Slaves Made*. New York: Random House, 1972.

Gillis, John R. *For Better, for Worse: British Marriages, 1600 to the Present*. Oxford: Oxford University Press, 1985.

Gilroy, Paul. *Ain't No Black in the Union Jack: The Cultural Politics of Race and Nation*. 1987; New York: Routledge, 2002.

———. *The Black Atlantic: Modernity and Double Consciousness*. London: Verso, 1993.

Glave, Dianne D. *Rooted in the Earth: Reclaiming the African American Environmental Heritage*. Chicago: Lawrence Hill Books, 2010.

Glymph, Thavolia. *Out of the House of Bondage: The Transformation of the Plantation Household*. Cambridge: Cambridge University Press, 2008.

Gomez, Michael. *Exchanging Our Country Marks: The Transformation of African Identities in the Colonial and Antebellum South*. Chapel Hill: University of North Carolina Press, 1998.

Goodwin, William W., ed. *Plutarch's Essays and Miscellanies: Comprising All His Works Collected under the Title of "Morals," Translated from the Greek by Several Hands*. Boston: Little, Brown, and Company, 1906.

Graham, Maryemma, ed. *Conversations with Margaret Walker*. Jackson: University of Mississippi Press, 2002.

———. *Fields Watered with Blood: Critical Essays on Margaret Walker*. Athens: University of Georgia Press, 2001.

Greeley, Horace. *Recollections of a Busy Life*. New York: J. B. Ford and Co., 1868.

Green, Danita Rountree. *Broom Jumping: A Celebration of Love. A Complete Guide to Keeping Traditions Alive in our Family*. Richmond, VA: Entertaining Ideas, 1992.

Green, Fletcher M., ed. *Ferry Hill Plantation Journal, January 4, 1838–January 15, 1839*. Chapel Hill: University of North Carolina Press, 1961.

Griffyn, Sally. *Wiccan Wisdomkeepers: Modern-Day Witches Speak on Environmentalism, Feminism, Motherhood, Wiccan Lore, and More*. Boston: Red Wheel, 2002.

Grissom, Kathleen. *The Kitchen House*. New York: Simon and Schuster, 2010.

Guyatt, Nicholas. *Bind Us Apart: How Enlightened Americans Invented Racial Segregation*. New York: Basic Books, 2016.

Gwaltney, John Langston. *Drylongso: A Self-Portrait of Black America*. New York: Random House, 1980.

Hadden, Sally. *Slave Patrols: Law and Violence in Virginia and the Carolinas*. Cambridge, MA: Harvard University Press, 2001.

Haley, Alex. *Roots: The Saga of an American Family*. Garden City, NY: Doubleday, 1976.

Hall, Gwendolyn Midlo. *Africans in Colonial Louisiana: The Development of Afro-Creole Culture in the Eighteenth Century*. Baton Rouge: Louisiana State University Press, 1992.

Hall, Joseph S., ed. *Sayings from Old Smoky: Some Traditional Phrases, Expressions, and Sentences*. Asheville, NC: The Cataloochee Press, 1972.

Hanger, Kimberly S. *Bounded Lives, Bounded Places: Free Black Society in Colonial New Orleans, 1769–1803*. Durham, NC: Duke University Press, 1997.

Hannay, James. *The History of Acadia: From Its Discovery to Its Surrender to England by the Treaty of Paris*. St. John, New Brunswick, Canada: J. & A. McMillan, 1879.

Hartman, Andrew. *A War for the Soul of America: A History of the Culture Wars*. Chicago: University of Chicago Press, 2015.

Heckethorn, Charles William. *The Secret Societies of All Ages and Countries*. London: Richard Bentley and Son, 1875.

Heidish, Marcy. *A Woman Called Moses: A Novel Based on the Life of Harriet Tubman*. Boston: Houghton Mifflin Company, 1976.

Helleiner, Jane. *Irish Travellers: Racism and the Politics of Culture*. Toronto: University of Toronto Press, 2000.

Helmso, Candy Grant. *Jump the Broom*. Katonah, NY: Richard C. Owen Publishers, 1997.

———. *Saltar la Escoba*. Katonah: Richard C. Owen Publishers, 1998.

Henderson, George, and Thompson Olasiji. *Migrants, Immigrants, and Slaves: Racial and Ethnic Groups in America*. New York: University Press of America, 1995.

Herskovits, Melville J. *The Myth of the Negro Past*. Boston: Beacon Press, 1941.

Hill, Lawrence. *Someone Knows My Name*. New York: W. W. Norton, 2008.

Hindley, Charles. *The History of the Catnach Press at Berwick-Upon-Tweed, Alnwick and Newcastle-Upon-Tyne, in Northumberland, and Seven Dials, London*. London: Booksellers' Row, 1886.

Hine, Darlene Clark, and Kathleen Thompson. *A Shining Thread of Hope: The History of Black Women in America*. New York: Broadway Books, 1998.

Hobbs, Allyson. *A Chosen Exile: A History of Racial Passing in American Life*. Cambridge, MA: Harvard University Press, 2014.

Hooker, Richard J., ed. *The Carolina Backcountry on the Eve of the Revolution: The Journal and Other Writings of Charles Woodmason, Anglican Itinerant*. Chapel Hill: University of North Carolina Press, 1953.

Horton, James Oliver, and Lois E. Horton. *Slavery and Public History: The Tough Stuff of American Memory*. Chapel Hill: University of North Carolina Press, 2006.

Hovey, Kendra Vaughan. *Passages Handfasting: A Pagan Guide to Commitment Rituals*. Avon, MA: Provenance Press, 2008.

Howe, Stephen. *Afrocentrism: Mythical Pasts and Imagined Homes*. New York: Verso, 1998.

Howell, D. *The Rural Poor in Eighteenth-Century Wales*. Cardiff: University of Wales Press, 2000.

Howells, W. *Cambrian Traditions, Comprising Ghosts, Omens, Witchcraft, Traditions, &c. To which are Added A Concise View of the Manners and Customs of the Principality and Some Fugitive Pieces*. 1831; London: Norwood Editions, 1972.

Hudson, Larry. *To Have and to Hold: Slave Work and Family Life in Antebellum South Carolina*. Athens: University of Georgia Press, 1997.

Hunter, Tera. *Bound in Wedlock: Slave and Free Black Marriage in the Nineteenth Century*. Cambridge, MA: Belknap Press, 2017.

Hyatt, Harry Middleton. *Folklore from Adams County, Illinois*, 2nd ed. New York: Alma Egan Hyatt Foundation, 1965.

Ingraham, Chrys. *White Weddings: Romancing Heterosexuality in Popular Culture*. 1999; New York: Routledge, 2008.

Isaacs, Rhys. *The Transformation of Virginia, 1740–1790*. Chapel Hill: University of North Carolina Press, 1982.

Jacobs, Harriet. *Incidents in the Life of a Slave Girl, Written by Herself*. Boston: Published for the Author, 1861.

Jacobson, Mathew Frye. *Roots Too: White Ethnic Revival in Post-Civil Rights America*. Cambridge, MA: Harvard University Press, 2006.

Janes, Gerald David, ed. *Encyclopedia of African American Society*. Vol. 2. Newbury Park, CA: Sage Publications Inc., 2005.

Jarman, Eldra, and A. O. H. Jarman. *The Welsh Gypsies: Children of Abram Wood*. Cardiff: University of Wales Press, 1991.

Jarvis, Michael. *In the Eye of All Trade: Bermuda, Bermudians, and the Maritime Atlantic World, 1680–1783*. Chapel Hill: University of North Carolina Press, 2010.

Jellison, Kathleen. *It's Our Day: America's Love Affair with the White Wedding, 1945–2005*. Lawrence: University Press of Kansas, 2008.

Johnson, Michael P., and James L. Roark. *Black Masters: A Free Family of Color in the Old South*. New York: W. W. Norton, 1986.

Johnson, Susan Lee. *Roaring Camp: The Social World of the California Gold Rush*. New York: W. W. Norton, 2000.

Johnson, Walter. *Soul by Soul: Life inside the Antebellum Slave Market*. Cambridge, MA: Harvard University Press, 1999.

Jolliffe, John. *Chattanooga*. Cincinnati: Wrightson and Co., 1858.

Jones, Gwyn, and Thomas Jones, eds. and trans. *The Mabinogion*. 1949; London: J. M. Dent, 1974.

Jones, Leslie. *Happy Is the Bride the Sun Shines On*. New York: McGraw-Hill, 2003.

Jones, Norrece T. *Born a Child of Freedom, and yet a Slave: Mechanisms of Control and Strategies of Resistance in Antebellum South Carolina*. Hanover, NH: University Press of New England, 1990.

Jones, T. Gwynn. *Welsh Folklore and Folk-Custom*. 1930; Totowa, NJ: Rowman and Littlefield, 1979.

Jones-Rogers, Stephanie E. *They Were Her Property: White Women as Slave Owners in the American South*. New Haven, CT: Yale University Press, 2018.

Joyner, Charles. *Down by the Riverside: A South Carolina Slave Community*. Urbana: University of Illinois Press, 1984.

———. *Shared Traditions: Southern History and Folk Culture*. Champaign: University of Illinois Press, 1999.

Kaldera, Raven, and Tannin Schwartzstein. *Handfasting and Wedding Rituals: Inviting Hera's Blessing*. St. Paul, MN: Llewellyn Publications, 2003.

Kamma, Anne. *If You Lived When There Was Slavery in America*. New York: Scholastic, 2004.

Kane, Harnett T. *The Bayous of Louisiana*. New York: William Morrow & Company, 1943.

Karazin, Christelyn D., and Janice Rhoshalle Littlejohn. *Swirling: How to Date, Mate, and Relate Mixing Race, Culture, and Creed*. New York: Atria, 2012.

Kaye, Anthony. *Joining Places: Slave Neighborhoods in the Old South*. Chapel Hill: University of North Carolina Press, 2007.

Kelley, Robin D. G. *Into the Fire: African Americans since 1970*. New York: Oxford University Press, 1996.

Kelly, Eleanor Mercein. *Kildares of Storm*. New York: The Century Company, 1916.

Kemble, Francis Ann. *Journal of a Residence on a Georgian Plantation*. New York: Harper and Brothers Publishers, 1983.

King, Wilma. *Stolen Childhood: Slave Youth in Nineteenth-Century America*. Bloomington: Indiana University Press, 1995.

Klingberg, Frank J., ed. *An Appraisal of the Negro in Colonial South Carolina: A Study in Americanization*. Washington, DC: Associated Publishers, 1941.

———, ed. *The Carolina Chronicle of Dr. Francis Le Jau, 1706–1717*. Berkeley: University of California Press, 1956.

———, ed. *The Carolina Chronicle: The Papers of Commissary Gideon Johnston, 1707–1716*. Berkeley: University of California Press, 1946.

Koger, Larry. *Black Slaveowners: Free Black Slave Masters in South Carolina, 1790–1860*. Jefferson, NC: McFarland and Company, 1985.

Kornick, Rebecca Hodell. *Recent American Opera: A Production Guide*. New York: Columbia University Press, 1991.

Lamanna, Mary Ann, Agnes Riedmann, and Susan Stewart. *Marriages & Families: Making Choices in a Diverse Society*. Boston, MA: Cengage Learning Inc., 2014.

Lee, Brenda, and Robert K. Oermann. *Little Miss Dynamite: The Life and Times of Brenda Lee*. New York: Hyperion Books, 2002.

Leeds-Hurwitz, Wendy. *Wedding as Text: Communicating Cultural Identities through Ritual*. Mahwah, NJ: Lawrence Erlbaum Associates, 2002.

Lemann, Nicholas. *The Promised Land: The Great Black Migration and How It Changed America*. New York: Alfred A. Knopf, 1991.

Levinson, Martin, and Avril Silk. *Dreams of the Road: Gypsy Life in the West Country*. Edinburgh: Birlinn, 2007.

Lewin, Ellen. *Recognizing Ourselves: Ceremonies of Lesbian and Gay Commitment*. New York: Columbia University Press, 1998.

Lewis, Ronald L. *Welsh Americans: A History of Assimilation in the Coalfields*. Chapel Hill: University of North Carolina Press, 2008.

Livermore, Mary A. *The Story of My Life; Or, the Sunshine and Sorrow of Seventy Years*. Hartford, CT: A. D. Worthington & Co., 1899.

Long, Becky. *Something Old, Something New: 701 Creative Ways to Personalize Our Wedding*. Minnetonka, MN: Meadowbrook Press, 1998.

Lucas, Marion B. *A History of Blacks in Kentucky: From Slavery to Segregation, 1760–1891*. Frankfort: Kentucky Historical Society, 1992.

Lyons, Kelly Starling. *Ellen's Broom*. New York: G. P. Putnam's Sons, 2012.

Lyons, Mary E. *Letters from a Slave Girl: The Story of Harriet Jacobs*. New York: Charles Scribner's Sons, 1992.

Maccoitir, Niall. *Irish Trees: Myths, Legends and Folklore*. Cork, Ireland: Collins Press, 2003.

Mackillop, James. *A Dictionary of Celtic Mythology.* Oxford: Oxford University Press, 1998.

Malone, Ann Patton. *Sweet Chariot: Slave Family and Household Structure in Nineteenth-Century Louisiana.* Chapel Hill: University of North Carolina Press, 1992.

Marable, Manning. *Beyond Black and White: Transforming African American Politics.* New York: Verso, 1995.

Mayall, David. *Gypsy Travellers in Nineteenth-Century Society.* Cambridge: Cambridge University Press, 1988.

Mayhew, Henry. *London Labour and the London Poor.* Vol. 1. London: W. Clowes and Sons, 1865.

McGowan, James A., and William C. Kashatus. *Harriet Tubman: A Biography.* Santa Barbara, CA: ABC-CLIO, 2011.

Meer, Sarah. *Uncle Tom Mania: Slavery, Minstrelsy, and Transatlantic Culture in the 1850s.* Athens: University of Georgia Press, 2005.

Menefee, Samuel. *Wives for Sale: An Ethnographic Study of British Popular Divorce.* New York: St. Martin's Press, 1981.

Merrick, Caroline E. *Old Times in Dixieland: A Southern Matron's Memories.* New York: The Grafton Press, 1901.

Merritt, Keri Leigh. *Masterless Men: Poor Whites and Slavery in the Antebellum South.* New York: Cambridge University Press, 2017.

Mintz, Sidney, and Richard Price. *The Birth of African-American Culture: An Anthropological Perspective.* Boston: Beacon Press, 1976.Moddie-Mills, Aisha C. *Jumping beyond the Broom: Why Black Gay and Transgender Americans Need More than Marriage Equality.* Washington, DC: Center for American Progress, 2012. https://www .americanprogress.org/wp-content/uploads/issues/2012/01/pdf/black_lgbt.pdf.

Moody-Turner, Shirley. *Black Folklore and the Politics of Racial Representation.* Jackson: University Press of Mississippi, 2013.

Moorwood, V. S. *Our Gypsies in City, Tent, and Van.* London: Williams Clowes and Sons, 1885.

Morgan, Jennifer L. *Laboring Women: Reproduction and Gender in New World Slavery.* Philadelphia: University of Pennsylvania Press, 2011.

Morgan, Philip D. *Slave Counterpoint: Black Culture in the Eighteenth-Century Chesapeake and Lowcountry.* Chapel Hill: University of North Carolina Press, 1998.

Moses, Wilson. *Afrotopia: The Roots of African American Popular History.* New York: Cambridge University Press, 1998.

Moynihan, Daniel P. *The Negro Family, the Case for National Action.* Washington, DC: Department of Labor, 1965.

Morris, Thomas D. *Southern Slavery and the Law 1619–1860.* Chapel Hill: University of North Carolina Press, 1996.

Neasham, Mary. *The Spirit of the Green Man.* Somerset, UK: Green Magic, 2004.

Nichols, Brenda Dabney. *African Americans of Henrico County.* Charleston, SC: Arcadia Publishing, 2010.

O'Brien, John, ed. *Interviews with Black Writers.* New York: Liveright, 1973.

O'Meally, Robert, and Genevieve Fabre, eds. *History and Memory in African American Culture.* New York: Oxford University Press, 1994.

Ogunleye, Tolagbe. *The African Roots of Jumping the Broom.* Philadelphia: Cowrie Publishing, 2004.

Olmstead, Frederick Law. *A Journey in the Seaboard Slave States, with Remarks on their Economy*. London: Sampson Low, Son & Co., 1856.

Olson, Ted, and Anthony P. Cavender, eds. *A Tennessee Folklore Sampler*. Knoxville: University of Tennessee Press, 2009.

Oswald, Ramona Faith. *Lesbian Rites: Symbolic Acts and the Power of Community*. New York: Harrington Park Press, 2003.

Otnes, Cele. *Cinderella Dreams: The Allure of the Lavish Wedding*. Berkeley: University of California Press, 2003.

Outhwaite, R. B. *Clandestine Marriage in England, 1500–1850*. London: Palgrave Macmillan, 2003.

Owen, Elias. *Old Stone Crosses of the Vale of Clwyd and Neighbouring Parishes: Together with Some Account of the Ancient Manners and Customs and Legendary Lore Connected with the Parishes*. London: B. Quaritch, 1886.

Owen, Trefor M. *Welsh Folk Customs*. 1959; Cardiff: William Lewis, 1974.

Packwood, Cyril Outerbridge. *Chained on the Rock: Slavery in Bermuda*. New York: E. Torres, 1975.

Pargas, Damian. *The Quarters and the Fields: Slave Families in the Non-Cotton South*. Gainesville: University Press of Florida, 2010.

———. *Slavery and Forced Migration in the Antebellum South*. Cambridge: Cambridge University Press, 2015.

Parker, Stephen. *Informal Marriage, Cohabitation and the Law, 1750–1989*. London: Palgrave MacMillan, 1990.

Paston, George. *Social Caricature in the Eighteenth Century*. 1905; New York: Benjamin Blom, 1968.

Patten, Claudius Buchanan. *England as Seen by an American Banker: Notes of a Pedestrian Tour*. Boston: D. Lithrop and Company, 1936.

Pearson, Emily Clemens [Pocahontas, pseud.]. *Cousin Franck's Household: Or, Scenes in the Old Dominion*. Boston: Upham, Ford and Olmstead, 1853.

Perdue, Charles L., Thomas E. Barden, and Robert K. Phillips, eds. *Weevils in the Wheat: Interviews with Virginia Ex-Slaves*. 1976; Charlottesville: University of Virginia Press, 1992.

Perry, Imani. *May We Forever Stand: A History of the Black National Anthem*. Chapel Hill: University of North Carolina Press, 2018.

Phillips, Ulrich B. *American Negro Slavery: A Survey of the Supply, Employment and Control of Negro Labor as Determined by the Plantation Regime*. New York: D. Appleton and Co., 1918.

Poole, John. *Hamlet Travestie: In Three Acts with Annotations*. London: J. M. Richardson, 1810.

———. *Hamlet Travestie: in Three Acts. With Burlesque Annotations, after the Manner of Dr. Johnson and Geo. Steevens, Esq. and the Various Commentators*. London: Sherwood, Neely, and Jones, 1817.

*Pop Goes the Weasel Songster*. 1853; Philadelphia: Fisher and Brother, 1938.

Porter, Connie. *Addy's Wedding Quilt*. Middleton, WI: Pleasant Company Publications, 2001.

Post, Lauren C. *Cajun Sketches from the Prairies of Southwest Louisiana*. Baton Rouge: Louisiana State University Press, 1962.

Probert, Rebecca. *Marriage Law and Practice in the Long Eighteenth Century: A Reassessment.* Cambridge: Cambridge University Press, 2009.

*Proceedings of the American Philosophical Society Held at Philadelphia for Promoting Useful Knowledge.* Philadelphia: McCalla & Company, 1888.

Puckett, Newell Niles. *Folk Beliefs of the Southern Negroes.* Chapel Hill: University of North Carolina Press, 1928.

Pughe, William Owen. *A Dictionary of the Welsh Language, Explained in English; with Various Illustrations, from the Literary Remains and from the Living Speech of the Cymmry.* London: Thomas Gee, 1832.

Raboteau, Albert. *Slave Religion: The 'Invisible Institution' in the Antebellum South.* 1978; New York: Oxford University Press, 2004.

Ramsey, Carolyn. *Cajuns on the Bayous.* New York: Hastings House Publishers, 1957.

Randall, Ronne. *Marriage.* New York: Rosen Publishing Group, 2009.

Randolph, Peter. *From Slave Cabin to the Pulpit: The Autobiography of Peter Randolph.* Boston: James H. Earle, 1893.

Rawick, George P., ed. *The American Slave: A Composite Autobiography,* 19 vols. Westport, CT: Greenwood Press, 1972.

———, ed. *The American Slave: A Composite Autobiography,* Supplement Series 1, 12 Vols. Westport, CT: Greenwood Press, 1977.

———, ed. *The American Slave: A Composite Autobiography,* Supplement Series 2, 10 Vols. Westport, CT: Greenwood Press, 1979.

Reiss, Oscar. *Blacks in Colonial America.* Jefferson, NC: McFarland and Company, 1997.

Religious Tract Society. *The Sunday Home Family Magazine for Sabbath Reading.* London: William Clowes and Sons, 1879.

Rice, James. *Cajun Alphabet, Full Color Edition.* Gretna, LA: Pelican Publishing Company, 2003.

Roberts, Beth. *The Broomstick Wedding.* El Cajon, CA: Rainbow Bay Books, 2000.

Robinson, William H. *From Log Cabin to the Pulpit, or, Fifteen Years in Slavery.* Eau Claire, WI: James H. Tifft, 1913.

Roscoe, John. *The Baganda: An Account of Their Native Beliefs and Customs.* London: MacMillan and Company, 1911.

Rush, William Faulkner. *The Cajuns: From Acadia to Louisiana.* New York: Farrar, Straus and Giroux, 1979.

Sabo, Don, Terry A. Kupers, and Willie London, eds. *Prison Masculinities.* Philadelphia: Temple University Press, 2001.

Salam, Ziya Us. *Till Talaq Do Us Part: Understanding Talaq, Triple Talaq, and Khula.* New York: Penguin Random House, 2018.

Sampson, John. *The Dialect of the Gypsies of Wales.* Oxford: Clarendon Press, 1926.

Saucier, Corinne. "Historie et traditions de la paroisse des Avoyelles en Louisiana." PhD diss., Laval University, 1949.

Sawyer, Walter Leon. *A Local Habitation.* Boston: Small, Maynard & Company, 1899.

Saxon, Lyle, Edward Dreyer, and Robert Tallant, eds. *Gumbo Ya-Ya: A Collection of Louisiana Folk Tales.* Boston: Houghton Mifflin, 1945.

Scafidi, Susan. *Who Owns Culture?: Appropriation and Authenticity in American Law.* New Brunswick, NJ: Rutgers University Press, 2005.

Schwartz, Marie Jenkins. *Birthing a Slave: Motherhood and Medicine in the Antebellum South*. Cambridge, MA: Harvard University Press, 2006.

———. *Born in Bondage: Growing Up Enslaved in the Antebellum South*. Cambridge: President and Fellows of Harvard College, 2000.

Schwartz, Stuart B., ed. *Tropical Babylons: Sugar and the Making of the Atlantic World, 1450–1680*. Chapel Hill: University of North Carolina Press, 2004.

Segal, Mark. *And Then I Danced: Traveling the Road to LGBT Equality*. New York: Akashic Books, 2015.

Shirley, David, and Heather Lehr Wagner. *Alex Haley*. New York: Chelsea House Publishers, 2005.

Simpson, John Hawkins. *Horrors of the Virginia Slave Trade and of the Slave-Rearing Plantations*. London: A. W. Bennett, 1863.

Simson, Walter. *A History of the Gipsies: With Specimens of the Gipsy Language*. London: Sampson Low, Son, and Marston, 1865.

Sloan, Jennifer Anne. *Masculinities and the Adult Male Prison Experience*. London: Palgrave MacMillan, 2016.

Smith, James Earnest. *Slavery in Bermuda*. New York: Vantage Press, 1976.

Sobel, Mechal. *The World They Made Together: Black and White Values in Eighteenth-Century Virginia*. Princeton, NJ: Princeton University Press, 1987.

Southern, Eilenn, and Josephine Wright. *Images: Iconography of Music in African-American Culture, 1770s–1920s*. New York: Garland, 2000.

Stampp, Kenneth B. *The Peculiar Institution: Slavery in the Ante-Bellum South*. New York: Alfred A. Knopf, 1956.

Stevenson, Brenda E. *Life in Black and White: Family and Community in the Slave South*. Oxford: Oxford University Press, 1996.

Stoll, Steven. *Ramp Hollow: The Ordeal of Appalachia*. New York: Hill and Wang, 2017.

Stuart, Ruth McEnery. *Moriah's Mourning*. New York: Harper and Brothers Publishers, 1898.

Stuckey, Sterling. *Slave Culture: Nationalist Theory and the Foundations of Black America*. Oxford: Oxford University Press, 1987.

Sturgis, Ingrid. *The Nubian Wedding Book*. New York: Crown Publishers, 1997.

Sweet, James H. *Recreating Africa: Culture, Kinship, and Religion in the African-Portuguese World, 1441–1770*. Chapel Hill: University of North Carolina Press, 2003.

Tadman, Michael. *Speculators and Slave: Masters, Traders, and Slaves in the Old South*. Madison: University of Wisconsin Press, 1989.

Tallman, Marjorie. *Dictionary of American Folklore*. New York: Philosophical Library, 1959.

Taylor, Charles. *Multiculturalism: Examining the Politics of Recognition*. Princeton, NJ: Princeton University Press, 1994.

Tepper, Leslie H., Janice George, and Willard Joseph. *Salish Blankets: Robes of Protection and Transformation, Symbols of Wealth*. Lincoln: University of Nebraska Press, 2007.

Thomas, Deborah. *Modern Blackness: Nationalism, Globalization, and the Politics of Culture in Jamaica*. Durham, NC: Duke University Press, 2004.

Thomas, Jeanette. *Devil's Ditties: Being Stories of the Kentucky Mountain People*. Chicago: W. Wilbur Hatfield, 1931.

Thompson, Katrina Dyonne. *Ring Shout, Wheel About: The Racial Politics of Music and Dance in North American Slavery*. Urbana: University of Illinois Press, 2014.

Thompson, Lawrence S. *Essays on the Folklore of Kentucky and the Ohio Valley*. Lexington, KY: Erasmus Press, 1971.

Thompson, Robert Farris. *Flash of the Spirit: African and Afro-American Art and Philosophy*. New York: Vintage, 1984.

Thornton, John. *Africa and Africans in the Making of the Atlantic World, 1400–1800*. Cambridge: Cambridge University Press, 1998.

Todd, Leonard. *Carolina Clay: The Life and Legend of Slave Potter Dave*. New York: W. W. Norton, 2008.

Toll, Robert C. *Blacking Up: The Minstrel Show in Nineteenth-Century America*. Oxford: Oxford University Press, 1977.

Trotter, Joe William. *The African American Experience*. Boston: Houghton Mifflin, 2001.

Trumbull, Henry Clay. *The Threshold Covenant: or, the Beginning of Religious Rites*. New York: Charles Scribner's Sons, 1896.

Tucker, Joy Wilson. *Thoughts and Expressions*. Bermuda: Self-published, 1983.

Turner, Patricia A. *I Heard It through the Grapevine: Rumor in African American Culture*. Berkeley: University of California Press, 1993.

Usner, Daniel H. *Indians, Settlers, and Slaves in a Frontier Exchange Economy: The Lower Mississippi Valley Before 1783*. Chapel Hill: University of North Carolina Press, 1992.

Van Deburg, William L. *Slavery and Race in American Popular Culture*. Madison: University of Wisconsin Press, 1984.

Vesey-Fitzgerald, Brian. *Gypsies of Britain: An Introduction to their History*. 1944; Exeter, Great Britain: David and Charles, 1973.

Walker, Clarence E. *We Can't Go Home Again: An Argument about Afrocentrism*. Oxford: Oxford University Press, 2001.

Walker, Margaret. *Jubilee*. Cambridge, MA: The Riverside Press, 1966.

Warner, Michael. *The Trouble with Normal: Sex, Politics, and the Ethics of Queer Life*. New York: The Free Press, 1999.

Webb, G. E. C. *Gypsies: The Secret People*. London: Herbert Jankins, 1960.

West, Emily. *Chains of Love: Slave Couples in Antebellum South Carolina*. Chicago: University of Illinois Press, 2004.

White, Shane, and Graham J. White. *Stylin': African American Expressive Culture from Its Beginnings to the Zoot Suit*. Ithaca, NY: Cornell University Press, 1998.

Whitlow, Roger. *Black American Literature: A Critical History*. New York: Rowman & Littlefield, 1974.

Whittlesey, Sarah J. C. *Bertha the Beauty: A Story of the Southern Revolution*. Philadelphia: Claxton, Remsen and Haffelfinger, 1872.

Wilkerson, Isabel. *The Warmth of Other Suns: The Epic Story of America's Great Migration*. New York: Random House, 2010.

Williams, Daniel G. *Black Skin, Blue Books: African Americans and Wales, 1845–1945*. Cardiff: University of Wales Press, 2012.

Williams, Heather Andrea. *Help Me to Find My People: The African American Search for Family Lost in Slavery*. Chapel Hill: University of North Carolina Press, 2012.

Williams, John Alexander. *Appalachia: A History*. Chapel Hill: University of North Carolina Press, 2002.

Williams, William. *The Journal of Llewellin Penrose, a Seaman*. 4 Vols. London: John Murray, 1815.

Williams, William Frith. *An Historical and Statistical Account of the Bermudas: From Their Discovery to the Present Time*. London: T. C. Newby, 1848.

Wilson, August. *The Piano Lesson*. New York: Plume, 1990.

Winterbottom, Thomas. *An Account of the Native Africans in the Neighbourhood of Sierra Leone; to Which Is Added, An Account of the Present State of Medicine among Them*, vol. 1. London: C. Whittingham, 1803.

Wood, Betty. *Slavery in Colonial America, 1619–1776*. New York: Rowman & Littlefield, 2005.

Wright, Courtni C. *Jumping the Broom*. New York: Holiday House, 1994.

Wright, Donald R. *African Americans in the Colonial Era: From African Origins through the American Revolution*. Wheeling, IL: Harlan Davidson, 2010.

Yarnell, Susan Y. *The Southern Appalachians: A History of the Landscape*. Asheville, NC: U.S. Department of Agriculture, 1998.

Young, Jason R. *Rituals of Resistance: African Atlantic Religion in Kongo and the Lowcountry South in the Era of Slavery*. Baton Rouge: Louisiana State University Press, 2007.

Zhmud, Leonid. *Pythagoras and the Early Pythagoreans*. 1994; Oxford: Oxford University Press, 2012.

Zuill, William. *Bermuda Journey: A Leisurely Guidebook*. New York: Coward-McCann, Inc., 1946.

# Index

Page numbers that are in italics indicate a figure.

Dave the Potter, 162–63

Dawson, Kevin, 189

*Diary of Llewelyn Penrose* (also *The Journal of Penrose*), 34, 41; as an autobiographical character, 34–35

Dickens, Charles, 28

dirt floors, 52–53

divorce, 19, 49, 55, 90, 98, 144; and marriage under slavery, 37, 62–63; and the Romani, 23; and rural white communities, 117; in Wales, 14–15, 62

domestic slave trade, 43–44, 60, 65

Du Bois, W. E. B., 72–73, 137, 146

Dundes, Alan, 8, 21, 27; criticizes "African origins" of broomstick wedding, 165–66

Dyson, Michael Eric, 150, 183, 211

Earhart, Amelia, 119

*Ebony*, 85, 122, 125–26, 136; features on "jumping the broom," 139–40

Eddings, Eric, 197

Egypt, Ophelia Settle, "Raggedy Thorns," 9, 223n8

*Ellen's Broom*, 159–60

emancipation, 70–72, 74, 78, 86, 89; post-, 81, 158

English, 9, 12, 16, 27–28, 30–32, 34, 98, 109, 111, 220; associated with jumping the broom, 106; laborers, 4; language, 147; mocking the broomstick wedding, 89; navvies, 28; sailors, 6

enslaved people: culture and, 8–9, 95–97, 120–22, 123–24, 126, 134, 139, 146, 207; and marriage, 3, 40–42, 64, 66, 69, 71, 79, 81, 94, 105, 122, 125–26, 131, 161, 170, 173–74, 185; scholarship on, 53, 82, 122, 124, 171, 215, 224n30; status distinctions, 61–62

*Essence*, 141–42, 144

*Essential Guide to Gay and Lesbian Weddings, The*, 180

family, 21, 61, 107, 130, 136, 138, 145; African American structure of, 72, 73, 125–26, 183; class differences between families,

208–10; cultural differences between families, 192–98; during Jim Crow, 72–75; Romani, 201; royal, 215–16, 219; separation of enslaved, 43, 74, 121–22, 156, 162, 184; social class and white southerners, 105–7; and *The Piano Lesson*, 166–67

Fitzhugh, George, 90

folk customs and rituals, 7, 34–35, 40, 46, 76, 78, 106–7, 127, 131, 137, 201, 219; and ancestors, 198; and mythical origins, 152; and racism, 87; ridiculed, 121

folklore: across cultures, 215; African American, 10, 57, 59, 62, 127, 145, 151–52, 156; and Alex Haley's *Roots*, 133; in Appalachia, 110; and brooms, 50–51, 58; Cajun, 114; European, 5–6, 166; and folkways, 10, 106; Irish, 24–27; and Margaret Walker's *Jubilee*, 129; and oral traditions, 7, 15–16, 128, 137, 220; Romani, 21–22; Welsh, 17, 19, 30; white southerners, 104–5, 107

folklorists, and jumping the broom, 21, 109, 123–24

folk speech, 83–84, 118–19, 237n32

Freedmen's Bureau, 71–72

freedom. *See* emancipation

French-Canadian, 111

Gaines, Earnest, 127

Gambia, 136

gender: and broomstick weddings, 14, 161, 180, 182; and power, 31, 38, 135, 181; and slavery, 58–63

genealogy, 126

Genovese, Eugene, 9, 138

Ghana, and "African Origins" thesis, 149–50, 152, 211

Gillis, John R., 15

Gillray, James, "Scotch Wedding," 29

Glymph, Thavolia, 92

Great Migration, 167

Green, Danita Rountree, 137, 165; and origins of jumping the broom, 149–50, 152; as a wedding officiant, 149, 154

and interracial marriage, 192–97; into
spouse's arms, 23, 28; into the bed, 49,
55; as a "joke," 101; jump over three
times, 55, 157, 189; jump separately, 22, 23,
24, 62, 107; and Kentucky, 110, 197, 200;
and a large gathering, 58, 102, 139,
140–41, 169; largely ignored in histories,
3; and legality, 24, 104, 217; and
legitimacy, 24, 75, 100; in Louisiana,
100–101, 203; modern myths surrounding, 152–55; as a multicultural custom,
204; multiple jumps, 1–2, 55, 157, 189; as
negative, 58, 60–61, 123–24, 201; as a new
"trend," 140; in the North, 107–9; as a
"northern" custom, 89; not embraced
by all enslaved people, 66; as an old
custom, 91; only completed by woman,
62; only form of marriage, 47, 140;
origins unknown, 9, 41–42, 111–12,
212–13, 215; placed in the doorway, 58, 59,
91, 104, 109; popularity of, 12, 221; and
the problem of national history, 218–19;
reality challenged, 77; rejected by some
enslaved and formerly enslaved people,
78–81; reversed jump, 1, 57; as a "Scotch
Wedding," 28–30; as a secret event, 47,
55, 168, 184; slaveholders views of, 87–88,
90, 129; slaveowners attended, 56; as a
"southern" ceremony, 89; speculation on
colonial period, 41–42; as a superior
form of marriage, 24; and television, 124;
and those enslaved in the house, 55;
touching broom as disqualification, 161,
167; with two brooms, 21, 49, 194;
viewed as symbol of mockery, 28, 89–91,
91–96, 100–101, 108; visual depictions,
29, 32; White ministers at slave wedding,
46, 55; and "white people," 198–204
*Jumping the Broom* (Courtni Wright),
155–56; criticisms of, 156
*Jumping the Broom* (film): class divisions
explored, 208–9; conceptions of slavery
within, 209; controversy about jumping
the Broom, 208, 209–10
*Jumping the Broom* (Sonia Black), 159

*Jumping the Broom: The African American
Wedding Planner*, 144–46, 150
*Jumpin' The Broom: The New Covenant*, 183
"Jump the Broom" (bluegrass song),
199–200
justice of the peace, 45, 71, 78
juvenile literature, 161–64

Kalunga line, 2
Karazin, Christelyn D., 195
Karenga, Maulena, 164–65
kente cloth: broomstick wrapped in, 217;
worn during wedding, 148, 151
kissing the horseshoe, 40
*Kitchen House*, 167
Kunta Kinte: and the broomstick wedding,
120–21, 130–31, 155, 205–8; differences in
remake vs. original *Roots*, 207; differences in *Roots'* novel vs. television
adaptation, 142–43; as symbolic
ancestor, 120

Le Grand Derangment. *See* Treaty of Paris
"Let's Jump the Broomstick": Alvin Gaines
and the Themes, 84–85; as sung by
Brenda Lee, 118–19
Lewin, Ellen, 194
Lewis, Lennox, 192
LGBTQ, 172–73; colorblindness and,
178–79, 180, 185; generally viewed as
white, 177–78; racial divisions within,
180, 184–85
Livermore, Mary Ashton Rice, 94–95
*Los Angeles Sentinel*, 140, 153
Louisiana. *See* Cajuns
Lyons, Kelly Starling, 159
Lyster, M. Eileen, 22

*Mabinogi*, 16, 21, 24; and the "chastity test," 17
marriage: definitions of a "real," 14, 76, 79;
and ethnocentrism, 31; and legality, 40,
43, 71, 185; registration of (after slavery),
75–76; and reproduction, 91; and slavery,
14, 38–44, 56, 78; as social control, 32;
and social divisions, 75, 79

MIX
Paper from
responsible sources
FSC® C008955
FSC
www.fsc.org